Simon John DeVries

Shining White Knight

A Spiritual Memoir

Vista Visions

Copyright © 2002
Simon J. De Vries
ALL RIGHTS RESERVED

All photographs reproduced in this volume, including those on the front and back covers, were made by or for the author, or by family members and friends. B/W bitmap images reproduce actual photographs, all of which are by the author except photos made by the armed forces and the stock photo on p. 315.

Printed in the U.S.A. by Morris Publishing, 3212 E. Hwy 30, Kearney, NE 68847, tel. (800) 650-7888

Copies of this work may be obtained from selected bookstores or directly from the author at 2013 N. Cross Creek Dr., SE, Grand Rapids MI 49508, tel (616) 241-5610, e-mail «simonjdv@wmis.net» , website http://www.VistaVisions.net

ISBN 0-9724364-0-5
Library of Congress Catalogue Control Number: 2002093985

Price $21.95

To all young persons
of the twenty-first century
seeking to know
to whom their life belongs

*Best regards from
Simon J. DeVries*

Contents

PREFACE xi

1 A LIFE NOT MY OWN 1

2 THE NINETEEN TWENTIES -- WHEN I BECOME "ME" 11
I am born and receive my name 13
My father 14
My mother 17
The Tammingas and the DeVrieses 20
Family, church and school in my early childhood 21
Early discoveries 24
Finding out about Santa Claus 25
Two time I run away and am punished 25
Three times cars almost kill me 27
Neighborhood boys try to poison me 27
Painting up like a clown 28
My parents forget my birthday 28
I swallow our ice-cream money 29
Death comes too soon for some schoolmates 29
Feeling depressed over an injured cat 30
Things I remember doing in the 1920's 31

3 THE NINETEEN THIRTIES -- WHEN I BEGIN A SEARCH FOR MY TRUE CALLING 33
Things I remember doing in the 1930's 35
Going fishing with Hank and Dad 36
Being beaten on by an older boy 36
Miss Te Sla puts the fear of God in me 37
Boarding with Aunt Jen 38
Music 39
Mrs. Riggle pulls Mom's hair 40
A temporary move to Littleton 41
New challenges in Littleton Grade School 42
Surviving in our cold farmhouse during the winter of 1932 43
Our great migration to California 44
Picking up the pieces 46
Encountering a crazy lady 47
Meeting Jackie Stansbury 48
Brother Bob breaks both arms 48
I am saved from a pedophile 49
Living among Frisian dairymen 49
Another town, a new school, and new things to do 50
Fun with Leo Edwards 51

vi Contents

Being mistaken for Okies on the way back to Colorado	52
Ninth grade in Denver Christian School	53
Arvin Roos and I make confession of faith (Confirmation)	54
A good life at 5280 South University Boulevard	55
A marvelous Bible	57
Jobs	57
Milking an injured cow	58
Littleton High School	59
Staining the bedroom window screen	60
Breaking into a house	60
Sneaking off to the movies	61
My eviction from Mr. Jump's bookbinding class	62
Unsupervised weight-lifting	63
Vernon Pinckney, a talented friend	63
A perilous climb up Turk's Head	64
A grandiose and unrealizable scheme	66
Back to California, where we come close to being orphans	67
Two wasted weeks in transition back to Denver	70
Twelfth grade at South High School in Denver	71
A severe sickness	72
An experiment with eating undercooked beans	73
I get headed toward the ministry	74
A summer job at a mountain mink ranch	76
I arrive at my apparent destiny	78
A family all together for the last time	78
4 THE NINETEEN FORTIES -- WHEN I BECOME A MAN	**81**
New experiences and influences	83
My life with Grandma De Vries	86
Financing my studies	92
Visiting my friend Arvin Roos at college	94
My first date	95
I become active in the Mission Society	95
Social groups at Calvin College	96
My work on a construction job and my first kiss	97
Participating on Calvin's debate team	98
I test my wings as a fledgling missionary	100
My failure as a Bible salesman	101
Hitchhiking back to college	103
My first date with Betty Schouten, my future wife	104
Betty and I almost break up	105
What I learn while off the road in a rainstorm	106
Bad luck with cars	108

Despondency over my romantic attachment	108
How we became engaged	110
Betty puts my grandmother in her place	111
Being beaten on by Oakdale Park Christians	112
Betty becomes a victim of a squeeze-play	113
My summer job at Pando	114
I am called to war	116
My senior studies at Calvin College	118
Senior physical education	120
My arrival at Parris Island	121
Feeling low in boot camp	124
Learning to shoot straight	127
Cutting through military bluster	129
My arrival at Quantico	131
Officer Candidate School	133
My most momentous week	137
I receive my gold bars	139
Our wedding night.	140
Our so-called honeymoon	142
Platoon Leader School	145
Our arrival in Columbus, Georgia	148
Learning Army communications at the Infantry School	150
Still together at Harvard	154
Hanging on in Greenville, North Carolina	157
Betty walks like a zombie	160
"Temporary training" on Midway	161
The birds of Midway	166
Innocent and not so innocent fun	166
Waiting out our time until rotation	168
R. and R. on the big island	170
My war draws to a close	173
Hitchhiking home on a destroyer escort	174
Three Marine brothers return home from their wars	177
Trying to make ends meet as a civilian	180
Getting off on the wrong foot with my brother-in-law to be	182
The arrival of our first child	182
Betty's non-part in her sister's wedding	184
A snug apartment for "Baby and We"	184
My new academic venue	186
My interview with the Home Missions Board	187
Moving to better quarters	189
A "new" car	190
Social life at Calvin Seminary	191

Professor Hendriksen censors conditional election	192
Practical training in Calvin Seminary	193
Stuck in the mud on a preaching engagement	196
A seminary choir tour to California	197
Casting my line free to another vessel of theological learning	199
Rough passage to Shanks Village	207
A new home and a new school	211
A summer semester at Union Theological Seminary	214
Dr. Muilenburg tells me I am "honest"	216
Standing at the turning-point of my career	218

5 THE NINETEEN FIFTIES -- WHEN I BECOME A "MAN OF GOD"   219

Mid-century: a hinge in my budding career	221
My initial literary effort	221
An impromptu interview with a disillusioned Christian Reformed scholar	222
Paramus Chapel and the Jackson Whites	224
I am attacked by a Paramus rooster	225
Church-extension work in Harlem	226
My S.T.M. thesis on "the fear of God"	227
Nursing Minnie	230
1950, a summer of transition	231
Examinations, calls, and the birth of a little son	231
We arrive as a family in Prairie City	235
A stupid mishap in the parsonage kitchen	237
Support for the pastor	238
Chicken chasing	239
Mud cars	240
Golf	241
The untimely death of Gerrit Schouten	242
Pastoral duties	244
Pheasant hunting	247
A doubly perilous flight to Philadelpha	248
My week in the Des Moines Veterans Hospital	250
A roundabout route to Synod in Grand Rapids	251
Frustration and disillusionment on a synodical committee	253
Deciding which call is from the Lord	255
A difficult move to Passaic	258
Ministering in an urban environment	259
Harsh treatment for one of Christ's humble followers	262
Social life for the pastor	263
Pine Street Christian School	265

Progress toward a Union doctorate	266
A rough trip home from an interview at Calvin College	269
Preparing for a study year in the Netherlands	271
A "Southern Cross" crossing	273
A meeting of world-known scholars in Strasbourg	276
Orientation in Noordwijk aan Zee	278
Life in a Dutch fishing town	280
Churches in Katwijk	282
Our living quarters	284
Making do in the local schools	286
Visiting relatives	286
My work at the University of Leiden	288
Getting around in Holland	291
Thanksgiving Day in Leiden	292
Eating Dutch pancakes	293
Lecturing to Dutch high-school teachers	294
Officiating at the funeral of Henry Zylstra	295
Discovering skeletons in my closet	297
Working with the "Kuenen gezelschap"	300
A baby with a "waterhead"	303
Visiting scenes of World War II	304
My big chance: an appointment at Drew Theological School	305
Disillusionment with Drew	307
We make the decision to leave Drew	309
I defend my dissertation and receive my doctoral degree	312
My provisional return to the Christian Reformed pastorate	317
A camping trip to Michigan by way of California	319
My father berates me for deviation from strict orthodoxy, I	322
Our life and work in Holland, Michigan	324
New adjustments for our children	327
Standing between the past and the future	328
Canoeing in Algonquin Park	329
The unstable situation in the Christian Reformed Church at the close of the decade	332
My manifesto	333

6 THE NINETEEN SIXTIES AND BEYOND -- WHEN I BECOME GOD'S MAN BY BEING "MY OWN MAN" 339

The prospect of an appointment at New Brunswick Theological Seminary	341
Welcoming Dutch relatives as immigrants	343
A peremptory interview with the Calvin Seminary faculty	344
Enigmatic treatment by the New Brunswick president and board	348

x   Contents

Tattlers on the Calvin board receive a tick on their fingers	350
A Reformation Day sermon that backfired	351
James Muilenburg promotes me as Union's hot prospect	354
The Christian Reformed Synod demonstrates zeal for dogmatic purity and scorn for its Church Order	360
Averting the inquisition the synod intended for me	363
My father berates me for deviation from strict orthodoxy, II	366
I move my camp to Hope and Western	367
Our Waukazoo Woods intermezzo	368
Feelers from two Methodist seminaries	370
Dean Dunn visits Grand Rapids in a snowstorm	372
I find my niche at the Methodist Theological School in Ohio	374
A place of beauty and comfort to call our home	376
At last a living wage	378
Favorable omens	380
Participating in the program of Ohio's new Methodist seminary	381
The work of training future ministers in Old Testament interpretation	387
My changing relationship to James Muilenburg in the late sixties and early seventies	393
A devil in my paradise	398

7 A COMMISSION FULFILLED 405

I reach the true goal of my quest: being scientifically as well as theologically honest about Holy Scripture	407
My mature self-understanding	411
APPENDIX: Some fruits of my biblical interpretation	415

Preface

EVERYTHING I tell in this history is true. It is not fiction. Of course there are many things that have happened to me that are not included. That is why I call it a memoir and not an autobiography. I have told the things that have mattered, that have shaped my life, that have given it significance, that have exemplified the theme of divine commission and divine leading. I have told the things I want to pass on to others, things that may help other persons recognize and submit to God's presence in their lives as I have in mine.

I have tried to be as accurate as possible in reporting what happened to me and how I reacted to it. I request the reader to do justice to my intent in paying heed to the distinction between the narrative stance of the sections in italic script and that of the sections in roman script. The former express how I saw things at the time I was experiencing them, while the latter express how I think about them now, in mature reflection. True, each type may contain elements of subjectivism, even my present mature reflections. I will gladly stand by how I think and what I say, but when I present myself as speaking as a young child or juvenile, the reader should expect me to say how I experienced them at the moment and how I interpreted them in terms of my particular stage of intellectual and moral development.

I tell about some bad things that happened to me, but always within the perspective of the abounding good life that has prevailed over all evil. "Lead us not into temptation, but deliver us from evil." This is a prayer that God has always answered; if I was not spared temptation, I was at the end of all evil delivered.

Others who have helped me shape this story, or have stimulated my memory when it was vague and corrected it when confused, have been my brother Henry W. De Vries, my sister Angela Ruth Posthuma, my wife Betty M. De Vries, my son Garry P. De Vries, and my daughter Judith K. Kammeraad, together with dear friends and fellow-pilgrims old and new -- Robert J. Dever, Rev. Arvin Roos, Dr. George Stob, and Dr. J. Harold Ellens. Though I have not tried to tell their individual stories, they have helped me say mine, as they have helped me live the fruitful and adventuresome life that God has given me.

1
A Life Not My Own

THE BATTERED OLD WARRIOR APPEARS IN TARNISHED armor as he kneels at the gateway of Elysium. For long, he has cast off the purple cloak of superpiety given him at his grandmother's house and in the Mission Society at college. But the marks of combat are on him. Here on his back is the mark of the deprivations he endured in his pre-college years. Here is the large scar left by the War he has been in -- the big War! Here is a deep dent made by his miseducation at seminary, only imperfectly repaired at graduate school. Here is a deep crease made at his first teaching job. Here is an actual hole through the metal, made when his pursuers aimed a blow at him on his escape from the denomination he had been loyally and unrewardingly serving. Along with these, there are little scars and dents, many and of various kinds. Nonetheless he will stand ready for further battle, if that be necessary. His armor is still intact and his weapons sharper than ever.

In the spring of 1962 I arrived at the crowning moment of my career, my appointment as Associate Professor at the theological seminary where I would remain for the next thirty years. Although the juvenile image of a *shining white knight* did not occupy my imagination to the extent that it did in my youthful years, I continued to consider myself in God's loyal service. I most definitely intended to discern God's will to the extent that this was possible, but my self-image was now refocused in terms of the more mundane metaphor of the professional ladder. I saw myself standing just at the bottom of that ladder -- or possibly one step up -- with a long way to climb to the top. Even from the next-to-bottom rung, I could glimpse wide new vistas; a whole new world was opening up for me. The only thing that remained applicable from the shining white knight image was the certainty that there would still be war, and that dutiful service would still be required of me. There would now be fighting Methodist style, seminary style, academia style. I could not yet glimpse this coming struggle, nor did I wish to acknowledge it when I was in it, for I preferred to imagine that I had now been transported into a perfect realm of light and brotherliness. Only reluctantly and gradually, I came to realize that I still had to be on my guard against any who might attack me and the things I stood for.

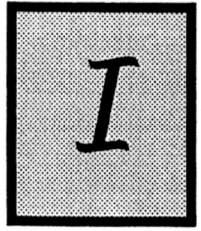 have written this book because I want to tell how I had arrived at this moment and what happened as a consequence. It is a story with the potential of instructing and inspiring others. In telling it I hope to show that there has been something quite unusual about my life and career. Early on, I felt that my life was not simply my own to live, but one commissioned and guided by one higher and more powerful than myself. I was not stiff or robotic in my sense of service to God. Instead, I aspired after an openness to transcendental leading; a willingness to retain God always in my focus and to consider his will and purpose before all else; a deep concern for humanity as fellow bearers of God's image; a love for the truth above all manner of ecclesiastical and scientific dogmatisms; a special instinct and firm hand for identifying clues to the solution of scriptural conundrums, which has become my professional specialty as a scholar and seminary teacher.

1. My narrative in the past and in the present. The arrangement of my narrative into successive sections of italic and roman scripting is an attempt to bring to expression my own personal and professional notion of *time*. It is a subject about which I have done special research without claiming to understand every aspect of it.

In my own published analyses of the Old Testament concept of time I have shown that a great deal is to be learned from studying the ways in which the ancient Hebrews spoke about historical events.[1] They did not do this abstractly or theoretically, but rather assumed a special understanding of time in the terminology they used in speaking of events in time.[2] This has suggested to me, first of all, that there is something schematic and artificial about our western way of thinking about time. We who are heirs of the classical tradition tend to think of time in terms of a sequence from past events to present events to future events. In the Old Testament, on the con-

---

[1] See extensive studies on the biblical concept of time in my books, *Yesterday, Today and Tomorrow* (Grand Rapids and London, 1975) and *From Old Revelation to New* (Grand Rapids, 1995).
[2] See my book, *The Achievements of Biblical Religion* (Lanham, MD, 1983), pp. 293ff.

trary, one finds oneself in an ever-ongoing and continually renewed and replenished present, from which one may gain one's bearing on the past and the future. As a consequence of this understanding, the everywhere present parenesis that urges responsible action in the present moment occupies a central position, standing between a remembered past and an eschatological future. This corresponds perfectly to our own normal psychological experience of time, in which we continually find ourselves not in a past or in a future, but in an onmoving, ever-renewed present.

I think that this notion may be applied quite legitimately to the cosmological question, but, leaving that aside, the main thing for most of us to do is to view the events of one's past existence as still present -- not only as recalled and imagined, but as a facet of one's previous experience that continues to have significance and bearing on what is happening at the present moment in each individual's life. For me, this intends to say that the same little boy that I was when only four is the same boy -- though now long grown and well on the way to decay and decrepitude -- who has become a man, myself. Much the same pertains with regard to our anticipated future life, and it is far better to allow our experienced past and our imagined future to shed light on our existential present moment than to turn this around and follow the way of secular existentialism, treating the present as the position from which we are to understand our past and our future.

That is just as wrong as it can be! The biblical way by comparison is healthy-minded because it integrates all the aspects of one's experience, bringing past and future together in their relation to a present moment of responsible choice. The secular way, on the contrary, is essentially schizophrenic. It repudiates the present as irrelevant except as a point from which one may flee in order to take refuge in the past, and in which future events are like a desert storm, blowing past while one hides one's head in the sand.

In consequence of this line of analysis I have adopted for this spiritual memoir a literary format by which the past is retained in a perpetual present. Although I have actually reconstructed these reminiscences almost entirely from unrecorded memories, they are presented here as fragments from a diary. I do this, however, for philosophical rather than literary reasons. Certain remembered past events in my life -- the ones in italics -- are cast in the form of ongoing present events, told in the first person. These past-made present reminiscences invite the reader to participate directly in the experiences I am describing, which is a superior way of empathizing with someone else. It is an intimate sharing in the events of another person's life by being there in one's concern and imagination. Nevertheless, I also move freely and frequently back in the roman font to the customary prose form of past-tense narration with appropriate exposition. I do this in order to draw in the perspective of a particular event's causes and results, thereby enabling the reader to assume the broader view of an entire chain of unique moments in which the quasi-present events, given in italics, are but links. The reader will find himself or herself especially relishing the first-personal anecdotal accounts, but my reflective expositions upon them are useful and necessary because the events which I shall be describing require the interpretive context of my own total life and history, recounted as accurately as I am able to recall as I experienced them.

2. The special quality of my life and career. I have always felt that I was different, special, unique -- and that in spite of the leveling effect of being just one of three De Vries boys born soon after one another, three peas in a pod; or of living under the leveling impact of Depression-era poverty; or of knocking about from one shabby house to another, from one mediocre school to another. It is not that I felt that I was somehow superior to my two brothers; I may have been, but I didn't allow myself to think it. Still, I seemed to realize that I was special or unique in that I was able in every new situation in which I found myself to rationalize causes, circumstances, and outcome, and thereby to get some idea of where life was taking me.

I did this in response to the shattering effect of the nomadic kind of existence into which we as children were thrust as a consequence of our father's itchiness and sense of adventure. I tried not to allow myself to be threatened by changes in circumstances but rose up instead to face them, whatever they might be. As a family, we did not become like gypsies; we were more like a band of knights, on the march to position ourselves to deal with one giant after another with a view to coming out on top at the end. My older brother Henry had much the same imagination as I did with regard to handling new situations, but eventually was challenged much less severely; my younger brother Robert, on the other hand, was possessed by a far wilder and undisciplined imagination, of a kind that avoids rather than copes with reality.

Otherwise than my brothers or my sister, I was very much like my father. What I am saying is that Dad never stopped imagining new ways to live his life, and neither did I. Coming out of a first-generation immigrant family, he neither complained about nor settled for what had been handed him, but reached out instead in new directions to overcome his handicaps and improve the quality of his life. Perhaps this came about because he had so little on his one sister and his two (later three) brothers. Never in all the years that I was able to observe him did I see a smile, a handshake, a kiss, pass between them. It was evident that his siblings bored him to death and that his parents took advantage of him. They made him the workhorse and the butt of all complaints. The others could goof-off and malinger; he had to produce. He had to be on the ball, helping his father mix paint, hauling the potatoes from the cellar, harnessing the horse to the wagon, fighting the bullies at school who were picking on his sister. That is the way it was also with me -- at least partially so -- for my older brother could often get by with bluff and my younger brother could get by with avoiding responsibility and remaining unattached, whereas I had to be there in the thick of everything, standing up to Hank on the one end and sheltering Bob on the other end.

Through the years I have received evidence that I possess an above-average all-around intellect. This has not come entirely through education, of which I have had far more than the others -- twenty-six years of formal education, to be precise. Education may make one more intelligent, but one needs to be bright in the first place in order to benefit from education. What I mean is that I possessed certain native gifts and was gradually coming to recognize them. Other persons also came to recognize them, not only kind uncles and appreciative teachers. They saw also that I had integrity and the ability to make and keep commitments. They knew that I stood with those who devote themselves to the good, the true, and the beautiful, rather than with those who spoil and tear down.

3. My strong sense of obligation. Along with a certain sense of specialness or uniqueness went a growing sense of obligation. At home I always tried to perform every assigned chore willingly, promptly, and intelligently. Naturally, our parents gave our eldest brother, Henry, the heavy end to carry, and he was willing and intelligent in doing so. From infancy my younger brother, Bob, learned shirking and never seemed to accept responsibility in anything. It was my lot to stand between the two. But when I mention my own special sense of obligation, I am thinking chiefly of my sense of what I felt God wanted me to do.

When God, working through human persons in positions of influence in order to help and guide me, led me to become enrolled as a freshman at a Christian college I never expected to get to attend, I felt that I had surely come there by his calling, and must accordingly be always obedient to his call and sensitive to the directions in which he might lead me. I am very glad indeed that I did not at the time have too monolithic a conception of God's rule for my life, but was able to adapt myself and develop an ever clearer concept of what I should be doing in my ministry on his behalf. If God was creating the design for my life and career, he was also allowing me to participate in the execution of its details. But I have always tried to remember who the Boss was -- not necessarily the president of Synod, nor the chairman of the home-missions committee, nor a professor at the seminary. Imagine, I have even had to face down my own father at times when he chose to stand in the way of my burgeoning self-awareness as a professional teacher and scholar! I did so with the comforting thought that Dad had himself stood up to his own father and mother when they attempted to stand in the way of his own self-development.

4. My inclination toward loyal relationships. My life has been marked as well by a capacity for intimacy and immediateness with certain others who were willing to enter into a close relationship with me. I mention God above all. I was motivated in my precocious piety by the desire to have a very private and personal acquaintance with God. Of little concern to me were rules, and dogmas did not interest me. I only cared for persons, for God as a divine Person above all.

This trait enabled me long ago to form a warm friendship with my boyhood friend, Arvin Roos, who shared a similar sense of devotion to God's plan for our lives. I was able to perceive Arvin's special gifts and be thankful for them. That is how I reacted to God. I reacted in the same way to Arvin. Arv helped me know God better, as I helped him know God better.

That is also how it was when I discovered my life companion,

Betty Schouten. From the day I met her I loved her. She has loved me from the identical moment, and to the same degree. Furthermore, the love we have for each other enables us to love God more perfectly. Betty never stands in the way of my spiritual development, nor I in hers, but we help each other grow into a fuller man/womanhood and a greater closeness with God.

What I mean to say is that when I make friends, I tend to keep them. Similarly my friends -- my true friends -- have remained faithful to me. One friend in particular has been a light upon my pathway and the guide of my life -- Professor James Muilenburg, my *Vater Doctor* and the mentor of my early career. Early on I was able to acquiesce in the recognition that God was leading and shaping my life through this man's good ministrations. Far more clearly than I did myself, he knew what I should become and where I should go to fulfill my calling and my destiny. By having so profound a trust in me, Dr. Muilenburg enabled me to believe more fully in myself, well enough to assume the heavy load of teaching putative ministers. As I look back over the many years of my preaching and teaching career, I stand amazed at the trust in me that never allowed him to waver in his approval and support. Representing in this respect God's own devotion, he remained my faithful guide and counsellor to the end of his life.

Early on I had Arvin. Soon I had Betty, who outshone Arvin as the sun outshines the moon. Then I had James Muilenburg, who became my confidant and true spiritual father. There were others; I mention in particular among my fellow ministers Dr. George Stob and Dr. J. Harold Ellens, who have done good and generous things to help me, and who have cheered me whenever I have talked with them. In addition to these, among mentors and colleagues in the professorate I have been particularly blessed over the years by Samuel Terrien, Pieter de Boer, Van Bogard Dunn, and Peter Ackroyd.

These very special friends and helpers have been like Christs to me, bringing me closer to the God whom I seek to serve. Perhaps they stand out in my special gratitude and awareness because, apart from them, my life would have been a very lonely life. Since I am a public man, it is hard for those who know me well to remain altogether passive and indifferent towards me, or I towards them. I have inherited from my mother and her family a strong desire for warm social contact with as many as will allow it; yet there are those

10 Shining white knight

whose envy puts me on a pedestal where I think I do not belong, and others whose lack of sympathy and understanding puts me in the dirt beneath their feet, where I most certainly do not belong. If a genie offered me one wish, it would be for everyone to like me, but since that cannot be -- for there is no such thing as universal admiration -- I shall wish at least to be acknowledged for my integrity in the service of God and my fellow human beings, and for my passion for truth, justice, and beauty.

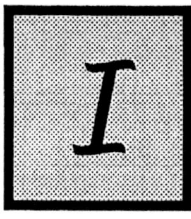
n what follows I shall tell my story in periods to show my personal development and the stages in my career as minister, seminary professor, and Old Testament scholar. Each of the central chapters of this book will cover a decade or more of my life:

- The nineteen twenties -- when I become "me"
- The nineteen thirties -- when I begin a search for my true calling
- The nineteen forties -- when I become a man
- The nineteen fifties -- when I become a "man of God"
- The nineteen sixties and beyond -- when I truly become God's man by being "my own man"

2
The Nineteen Twenties --
When I Become "Me"

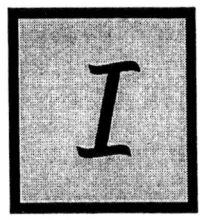**am born and receive my name.** My older brother Henry, or Hank, was named after our grandfather Hendrik de Vries. This was appropriate because our Hank was the first male grandchild of our father's own family. It was expected that I should be named after our maternal grandfather, Simon (Symon) Tamminga, even though there were older male cousins on our mother's side, the sons of our Uncle Sid (Sikke); if either of them had been named Simon, that would not have prevented me from being named Simon as well, but they weren't. The first was called Ed, after a dear uncle who died of tuberculosis as a teenager. The second was named Samuel to placate Grandpa Tamminga, but he said that that was not close enough, there had to be a real Simon. In spite of this pressure, my father firmly decreed, as my birth drew near, that Simon was a tease-name in America and therefore he would refuse to allow a son of his -- if a son it was to be -- to be stuck with a name that would subject him to teasing and derision. That is why I was to be called John, after my paternal great-grandfather, Johannes Bijlsma, as were two of my father's brothers, Joe (Johannes) and John (Jan).

I am born at home on December 20th, 1921. A day of so afterward my mother's mother, still in her fifties, suffers a severe stroke that leaves her paralyzed and speechless. As soon as my mother is able to take me outside into the winter weather, she bundles me up and brings me on the streetcar to her mother's house to show me. One can only imagine the tender scene that takes place in the bedroom where sorely stricken Engeltje lies! When it becomes time for my mother to leave, Grandma nods her head toward the dresser drawer, where my mother finds an envelope inscribed in Dutch, "For Baby Simon." Grandma and Grandpa are not well off; in fact, they have lived in poverty both in the Netherlands and in the United States. This fact makes the more astounding what Mother finds in the envelope, twenty-five dollars, which she of course will have no trouble spending on my care.

14   The 1920's: I am born and receive my name

When my mother shows this to my dad, he has to give in and allow me to be named Simon. He does so with the proviso that I am always to be called by my middle name, John. I never get to know these grandparents. Grandma dies of her stroke within a week, and Grandpa dies within a year or two. He continues to live in the name he has bequeathed to me.

My father. When I was born, my father, Peter H. De Vries (1895-1990), was 26 years old and had already seen a lot of life. His parents were Hendrik de Vries (1866-1932) and Elisabeth Bijlsma de Vries (1867-1949). He was born in a Dutch immigrant enclave at Prospect Park, NJ, a suburb of Paterson. He attended a Christian (i. e., Calvinist) parochial school there. He was accustomed to helping his parents with the family duties, and had particular charge over the family horse and wagon. As his father's painting business flourished, the family moved to a more rural setting at Midland Park, NJ, where his father and mother eventually went into the grocery business. Dad got no further in school than the ninth grade. He did desire more schooling, but when he asked his father's permission, the reply was, "Jonge, wil je Dominee worden?"[1] That settled the matter because that was not his aspiration. I think that in the following years he often regretted not having been able to go to high school. He had a keen and curious mind. He was inventive, industrious, and hard working.

In that time house painters would mix large quantities of white lead by hand, using linseed oil as a liquifying agent. Dad had to help in this chore. He and his father mixed the white lead the evening before using it, and his father would add the pigment as he began the job. When he was finished for the day, he would carefully wash all the oil and paint from his hands before sitting down for supper. Nonetheless, some lead always did leach through Grandpa's skin and entered his bloodstream. Gradually Grandpa developed all the bad symptoms of lead poisoning and had to quit the painting business entirely. He took up the grocery business as a substitute. Not long after that the family moved to Denver. That was in 1911, before any of the children were grown, and the youngest was only three.

My Dad helped in a grocery store that his father bought on South Emerson Street in Denver. He began thinking about getting away

---

[1]"Do you intend to become a minister, Boy?"

from the tight parental control to which he was subjected. He found work away from home, but this did not satisfy him because he was still living in the parental home, and so long as this continued he was obligated to contribute his wages to the family budget. He would in fact hand over his entire pay to his mother at the end of each week. She would leave him with nothing more than streetcar fare for the following week, plus a nickel to spend on himself.

Dad was now a teenager and he saw clearly that there was little prospect of getting ahead financially so long as he remained with his parents. He borrowed fifty dollars from a family friend with the promise to repay it after six months, and set off to Grand Rapids, MI, as the old adventure stories say, "to seek his fortune." He found a lodging place on Cherry Ave., SE in the home of an invalid lady who fell in love with him, and he remained there in a somewhat compromising situation until thrown out one day by the jealous husband, a perpetual wanderer who returned home from time to time from his drunken binges. It was just as well that this arrangement ended when it did, for who knows how much trouble might have lain ahead for this lonely and adventurous lad under such circumstances? Dad was understandably reticent about saying much about it.

Dad's daily work went better than his social life. He told of getting a job selling a hundred pairs of 1890's ladies' and men's dress shoes, the kind with the pointed toes, all with long rows of buttons. This took place in a store rented by the owner of the shoes. Dad sold them all in an astonishingly brief period of time. He then found a better, more steady job with a Mr. Sterling, operator of an electrical-goods store on Eastern Ave. That is where Dad acquired the practical understanding of electricity that later led him to electrical construction work as a vocation. All this while, Dad lived on little more than bread in order to be able to repay the fifty dollars on time.

Dad never did say whether he returned to Denver during that period. While what was called "the Great War" (usually referred to as World War I) was being fought in Europe, and after America entered the fray on the side of the Allies in April of 1917, Dad immediately enlisted in the Army and was sent to train at Corpus Christi, TX. There were old pictures of him sitting on a horse, but he went into the Engineers, not the Cavalry. The Army Engineers used numerous strong horses in order to haul the things they worked on in the camps and on the battlefields, such as pontoons for bridges, trenching materials, and barbed wire for no-man's land. This could be as

16   The 1920's: My father

perilous as standing in the trenches and fighting with rifles and bayonets, perhaps more so because the Engineers often had to perform their duties under fire.

Dad was in charge of one of the horses. His unit went to France with Gen. J. J. Pershing in 1918 to become part of the American First Army, stationed on the far right (east) of the battle line. In September of that year this army seized the St. Mihiel salient, which had been in German hands since 1914. Dad never said whether he was directly involved in hostilities around St. Mihiel; probably not, since this was a very fast operation not requiring trenches or pontoon
bridges. In a brilliant move, Col. George C. Marshall (destined to become Army Chief of Staff in World War II) wheeled Pershing's army about within a few weeks and prepared them to attack the Germans on the Meuse-Argonne front. This army suffered a large number of casualties, but succeeded in all but pushing the Germans out of France during the weeks just prior to November 11, Armistice Day. We used to hear Dad tell of this operation, although it is unlikely that he would have come under direct fire. There were certainly situations in the Meuse-Argonne which might have brought him within range of the German guns. He definitely did stand in harm's way. One way or another, he was our hero. He had plenty of ribbons and souvenirs to show us.

After the armistice Pershing's army followed the Germans out of France and went on to occupy major cities on the Rhine. Dad finally came home in 1919, following President Woodrow Wilson's participation in the drafting of the Treaty of Versailles. The speech that this famous man gave the troops on board the ship deeply impressed his mind. All in all, Dad was no different from most American veterans of that war in that his mind was vastly expanded by having participated in a momentous event of history.

When Dad returned to the United States, he also came home to

Denver, where he obtained an excellent job with the Sturgeon Electric Co., a major contractor. He realized, when visiting the Tamminga home, that he was in love with a daughter of the family whom he had previously known for many years. This was the lovely Kate, the eldest of two surviving daughters. The wedding took place on November 19, 1919, and a first child was born the following September. Within the ensuing four years, three more babies were born.

My dad had one special trait that would continue to affect our family history and our individual development: a drive to get ahead financially. Besides putting in full working weeks at his job, Dad would do as his father had done before him, buying up dilapidated houses and moving us into them, then repairing and redecorating them in order to resell them at a good profit. I can remember perhaps a dozen such houses. So long as we were grade-schoolers, this gypsy-like existence had little negative effect on us children's social development because we continued to attend the same church and school. Besides, Dad's family and Mother's family all lived in south Denver and we saw them as often as we wished.

My mother. At the time of my birth my mother, Catherine Tamminga De Vries (1896-1976), was 25 years old. Her baptized name was Cornelia, but she preferred the name Catherine and was called Kate. Her parents were Simon Tamminga (1856-1923) and Engeltje Beintema Tamminga (1862-1922). Prior to her marriage to my Dad she worked as a practical nurse and almost died from overwork during the flu epidemic of 1918. Previously she had been a maid in the private estate of the Singer family out on Long Island, her boss being the inventor of the famous sewing machine. Since this was long in the past when she became our mother, she did not in my memory tell us much about this time of poverty and servitude. Nevertheless I have some remembrance of her speaking guardedly of this as an essentially humiliating position, yet one that made an important contribution to the needs of the Tamminga family. In the early 1910's the galloping tuberculosis epidemic killed three of her siblings, infecting Mother also, though she managed to survive without requiring hospitalization. She gave us children some hints of the bitter sorrow that had come upon her family. Occasionally I would still hear the aunts and uncles speak of it. No doubt this experience explains why she had such a tender heart for new families arriving in Denver in hopes of being cured of this dreadful infection.

The 1920's: My mother

A new phase in the history of the Tamminga family began with a railroad trip to Denver. The Christian Reformed congregation in West Sayville, to which the family belonged, took up a large love-offering to pay for their railroad fares. Once they established their roots in the south Denver enclave, most of the family found gainful employment. Uncle Will or Bill (Wiebe) organized a construction company in partnership with Edsko Hekman, who later moved to Grand Rapids and became wealthy in the furniture business.

Grandpa Tamminga, after whom I am named, had little schooling and never did anything but menial labor. All the same, he was intelligent as well as devout. I have a poem of his that he composed in 1899, "Een oude visscher (An Old Fisherman)," written in a beautiful formal cursive and marked by good rhythm and rime. Neither he nor my grandmother reached seventy. Grandma Tamminga's brother also lived in West Sayville. His name was John Beintema and he owned a flourishing dairy. I shall have something interesting to tell about him later. Like her brother, Grandma Tamminga had been brought up on a Frisian dairy farm.

The earliest strong memories I have of my mother are associated with the birth of our only sister, Angela Ruth. This happened in 1925, when I was not yet four. I remember the novel sight of my mother's breast, exposed to nourish our new sister. Little Ruthie -- or Annie Ruth as we called her -- was praised and fondled. We did everything possible to spoil her.

Our poor mother did not seem to be very strong. Sometimes we would find her weeping without any apparent cause. My Dad and the relatives said that she was suffering from a "nervous breakdown." This happened on two separate occasions during my early childhood. Mother had to go to a hospital for a while each time, and when she came home she needed a lot of rest. Without her to take care of us, we first had a substitute live-in mother, a Mrs. Venema, who was very kind to us. The second time, we children had to be farmed out to relatives. Hank and I stayed with our favorite relative, Aunt Jen Tamminga.

Part of Mother's problem was that she had her uturus and overaries removed following the birth of Ruth, and nothing was done by the doctors to replace her lost hormones. They did not yet know about estrogen replacement thereapy. In addition, my mother was suffering from a form of major depression, which from all accounts afflicted some of her brothers and her sister as well. Mom was to be hospitalized with severe depression four separate times during her life. She mainly had to get better through rest, but this still left her shaky and nervous. Mother's condition was heredity and all four of her children have shown mild or severe symptoms of the same affliction. Dad constantly refused to recognize and admit this fact. He kept saying that it all came from Mother's having had to work herself into exhaustion during the terrible flu epidemic of 1918.

Living with Dad was not easy for Mother because of his susceptibility to tantrums and morose sullenness, which would always be hard for her to deal with. I think that Dad may have been suffering from his own brand of chronic depression. In addition, he was much like his own father, Grandpa De Vries. Maybe he had a touch of lead poisoning like Grandpa: who knows?

There were three behavioral peculiarities of my mother that are best explained as the results of the humiliating experiences of her childhood. For one thing, she was an absolute fanatic about sound nutrition, for the simple reason that she herself had so often suffered from an inadequate diet while growing up. Often her father simply did not earn enough to keep his large family well fed. In his job as a gatherer, he was at the mercy of nature and the market. When nature would be generous, the market price would be low from an excess of supply; when nature would be stingy, prices would be high but there would not be enough supply to give the gatherer much benefit from them. In other words, the market for oysters was poor when the harvest was abundant, good when the harvest was poor. Thus when Mother's own family came along she would do everything short of force-feeding us. It was "Eat that egg; I would have loved to have had one to eat when I was a child." Or, "If you don't eat your vegetables I'll just bring them over to the Buschbach family, and they will be glad to eat them."

A second characteristic of my mother was that she had absolutely no restraint about begging. She would beg the doctor to let her not pay his bill. For emergencies she would take us to the Denver General Hospital, where she could get medical care for nothing, or virtually nothing. She would take us to a dental clinic where we could get our cavities filled free. Needless to say, we three boys always wore hand-me-downs, either from one another or from relatives. I think Mother had only one dress, the one I would see her wear on Sundays, and Dad had only the one suit.

As far as Mother is concerned, this undoubtedly reflected the habits and practices of her early years. In my opinion there is nothing enobling about being poor, but only in the struggle to overcome it. The best thing that was to come out of this bitter experience was that Mother was pretrained to cope with the Great Depression when it came along.

A third aspect of Mother's behavior was her extreme gregariousness and affability. Almost all the Tammingas were like this. They loved to be together, having a good time, because their closeness and great concern for one another was what brought them through past calamities. Getting along with people was what they learned from dealing with those who were in a position to help them. I was willing to learn a lot from my mother, but I would hate to beg or to take a back seat. I had a deep suspicion about her admonition always to be humble, wondering whether it was just an expression of her lifelong habit of getting into favor with those able to give her some benefit.

In spite of their shortcomings, it was clear that Dad and Mother always continued to love each other and their children. They provided good role models for us in shaping our own individual lives.

The Tammingas and the DeVrieses. These two families were day-to-night opposites. My mother, Kate or Catherine, the oldest surviving Tamminga daughter, loved to socialize with her family. She had a sister, Angelina, whom we called Aunt Lena, but who preferred to be called Aunt Angie. Both she and our sister Ruth were named for Grandma Tamminga, Engeltje, which means "Little angel." The uncles we knew were Will (Wiebe), Sid (Sikke), John and Gerrit, four of them. I heard them talking at times of their deceased brother Eddie and sister Lucy, but there were others as well who died young. There had been a sister Gitsche, who died in infancy. In spite of losing these siblings so young, as well as their parents -- or perhaps because of it -- the Tammingas generally enjoyed life and loved to get together. We especially enjoyed the gala Christmas celebration each year. However, my mother did not need a special day to enjoy her family. She often went out for morning coffee with one of them, or invited them into her home. She especially enjoyed the wives of her brothers, Aunt Jen of Uncle Will, Aunt Sue and later Aunt Rick of Uncle Sid, and Aunt Alice of Uncle John, along with adult children such as Johanna and Jean, the eldest daughters of Uncle Sid. Other members of Mother's happy club were Uncle Sid's sister, Jen Ockers, and Dad's mother, Grandma De Vries. The three eldest brothers were involved in the construction business. Uncle Gerrit was a Presbyterian minister.

My father Peter had one sister, Trina, who married another painter-decorator by the name of Joe Martens. The one child born to them, Betty, was named after Grandmother Elisabeth De Vries. After Trina, Dad was the oldest, and he was followed by three brothers, two of whom (Joe and John) were close to him in age, and the baby of the family, Jake or Jack (baptismal name: Joppe), who was born a decade or so later. There were others, including a Douwe, who were still born or died in infancy. There was not the same spirit of devotion to one another in this family as there was among the Tammingas. My experience of Trina is that she was domineering and hypercritical. What I observed about Joe was that he was intellectually torpid as well as hypochondriacal, and about John that he hardly ever spoke, shunning company. Jake or Jack, on the other hand, was affable and well adjusted. That is because he was the baby and received special affection growing up.

Another thing that I observed about this family was that whenever the children spoke to one of their parents, they were required to address them in the third person, not the second. For instance, if one of the children wished to say, "Ma, what do you want me to wear?," he had to say instead, "Ma, what does Ma want me to wear?" My dad told the story of helping his father with carpenter work. Every time he would hand his father a nail, he would say, "If you please, Pa." This formula was repeated again and again until Grandpa got exasperated and told him to stop. Dad told also that his father continued to suffer much from the effects of his lead poisoning. He would find him underneath the house, crying piteously, evidently not wishing Grandma to know about it. Furthermore, I don't think that Grandpa's own home in the Netherlands was a happy one.

Family, church and school in my early childhood. In our traditional way, our family faithfully practised its daily devotions consisting of Bible reading following each meal and prayers both before and after meals. Usually it was Dad who said the prayers, but sometimes it would be Mother. She was usually brief, but Dad could be fairly long. Always, to test whether we children were listening, we were required to say, when the parental prayer was concluded, "Amen," but this did not prove much because it was automatic for us, and we would be able to say it half asleep. In inculcating this routine, Dad and Mom did not worry about making us too pious. Our family prayers and Bible reading did not make church and Christian school superfluous.

Our family was living according to the mores of a typical ethnic and religious enclave in one of America's new cities, Denver, CO. When I was born, Denver was growing out of its pioneer past. It was destined to develop one day into a metropolis, but I did not see it. It was small by comparison with major cities like New York, Chicago and Los Angeles. My father, more than my mother, had become well acclimated to American culture. As a veteran of the Great War, Dad had joined the American Legion. His job as journeyman electrician offered him the opportunity as well to become a part of the nation's unionized labor movement. Although he never became active in either organization, these did have some influence on his ideologies and encouraged a somewhat independent attitude toward church and school, as well as the kind of family life he and our mother created for us. Without Dad's broadness of sympathy, our own life might have been far more narrow and legalistic.

I do not know why my Dad's parents decided to move to Denver; it was not because of tuberculosis. My mother's parents came there because Denver had a dry climate and was recommended by physicians for their tuberculosis patients. Another reason was that that was where the sister denominations, the Reformed Church in America (RCA) and the Christian Reformed Church (CRC), had joined hands to build a sanitorium for the cure of tuberculosis under the inspired leadership of the veteran minister, Idzerd Van Dellen, who had earlier brought a group of tuberculosis sufferers to Maxwell, NM, but the town he tried to build there could not succeed economically because it was in a remote area, hence he brought them to Denver. It was his church, the First Christian Reformed in Denver, where both families became members and became acquainted with each other. Grandpa De Vries bought a neighborhood grocery store, while Grandpa Tamminga found custodial work in the Denver park department.

As I have said, Grandpa De Vries continually suffered with the nervousness and depression that resulted from lead poisoning. That may be the reason why he had an emotional falling out with Rev. Van Dellen while serving as elder. At the time of my baptism, our De Vries grandparents had become members of the newly formed First Reformed Church (RCA). My parents made the same move out of honor for their father and mother, as did the family of Uncle Joe. Dad and Mother planned to have us attend the Denver Christian School, which enrolled a significant number of pupils from the First Reformed, along with those from the First Christian Reformed. In those early years there was generally a warm spirit of camaraderie among the members of these two south Denver churches.

Somewhat later, Grandpa De Vries made up with Rev. Van Dellen and rejoined the First CRC, dutifully followed by Uncle Joe and his family, but my father and mother refused to make this empty gesture of family solidarity and remained loyal members of the First RCA church. Dad was highly respected and well liked there. It was only in the late 1930's that my parents finally withdrew from First Reformed in order to join the newly established Second CRC -- a fateful move for me because it was to result in my later association with the CRC rather than the RCA in my pastoral ministry.

My own worship experience in the First Reformed Church was much like what it would have been in the First Christian Reformed Church. While I was quite little, both churches had a Dutch language service each Sunday, but this was eventually dropped by both, though first in First Reformed. Dad served as deacon in this church for some years. There was less spirit there of legalism and separatism, and more interest in other evangelical churches and inter-church organizations, than there was generally in the CRC. Another difference was the lack of weekly sermons on the Heidelberg Catechism, which was mandated for the CRC. All the same, I generally found church services and Sunday School quite boring since First Reformed made the mistake of calling a pastor with very little talent for preaching. We children hated Sunday School, which we were forced to sit through after first sitting through the boring morning service. This consisted mainly of reciting memory verses from Scripture and listening to extremely dull explanations of the lessons. Add to this discomfort the fact that we were also forced to attend a youth program called Christian Endeavor on late Sunday afternoon, prior to the regular evening church service, which we were likewise obliged to attend.

Because my birthday was in December, I was still four when I started school; i.e., kindergarten. I had a generally interesting kindergarten experience at McKinley school on South Logan St., three blocks from where we lived. We did not learn reading or arithmetic, only coloring and cutting things out. I walked back and forth

24   The 1920's: Family, church and school

to kindergarten and passed a candy store on the way, stopping in whenever I had a penny to spend.

My first grade through fifth grade were spent in the Christian School, where the curriculum was probably much like that in the public schools except in having no sport or physical training. Instead it had prayers, hymn singing, and daily Bible lessons. My teachers rated from poor to mediocre, with two exceptions: (1) one who was kind, good, and interesting, my fifth-grade teacher, Miss Veenstra, and (2) the one I especially hated, Miss Te Sla.

Among the students attending Christian School, there was little difference to notice so far as church affiliation is concerned, but the CRC ministers did manage to assert discrimination by dismissing the RCA children when they arrived on Wednesday afternoons to teach catechism to the CRC children. Although we Reformed were certainly glad not to be kept longer in our seats, we thought we were able to detect a look of malicious self-vaunting in the eyes of those who we thought considered themselves the spiritually elite as they watched us go out the door. What disturbed me most was the question why these two churches had to be separate when they had so much in common, but I refused to believe that the CRC children were any better in the Lord's eyes than we were.

Early discoveries

Whenever I find out how to do things I become very happy and proud of myself. I wanted to wink like grownups, but never could. One day I am playing in a coal bin and get a bit of coal in my right eye. I keep closing and opening that eye to wash the coal out with tears, and then I discover that I can do it whenever I want to. I can wink just like Dad and Mom and Hank!

I wanted to skip like the other children, but never could. Then one day I am actually skipping without knowing it. I find out that it is between walking and running. It is fun and I am proud of myself for finding out how to do it.

I tried to tie my shoelaces in bows, like my brother Hank. I never could, and that made me sad. Then one day I succeed! I can tie my shoelaces in bows, just like the older kids.

These are all things I couldn't do and wanted to do very much. Something else I suddenly learn is that I am really alive and am a person all by myself. I was alive before, and I was a real person before, but I didn't ever think about it like now. Now I am thinking about it, and all of a sudden I feel scared and awfully funny. Here I am in the middle of a great big world, all by myself. I run to my dad and say, "Daddy, I just found out that I am really me, and I am here and am alive. I am scared thinking about it." "Yes, Johnny," Dad replies, "being a real person is a scary thought, but it also wonderful. You are you, and not somebody else. You can think your own thoughts and perform your own deeds. But this doesn't mean you are really alone, because we love you and will always take care of you. Besides, God is always with you. He knows you and loves you, and he will always hold your hand when you are afraid, just as Mom and I do."

Finding out about Santa Claus

I always thought that Santa Claus wasn't real because I would see other Santa Clauses when I went to other stores, and besides, they had different voices, and some were fat and others skinny. So one day I ask my Dad if Santa Claus is real, and he says, "No, Santa Claus is not a real person here on earth. Think of him as existing in heaven, just as God does." But I'm not sure that this is a good reason. Does Santa Claus live up in heaven with God?

Two times I run away and am punished. Even my early childhood years were filled with adventure -- but not always of the kind one would wish. In the first place, I was growing up in a quite charming Denver, still in its blooming youth, not entirely grown up out of its frontier past. One should imagine my being able to look outside the window each morning to see the magnificent Front Range of the Rockies spread out before my eyes! I loved the mountains -- loved them both with reverence and with passion. I told my dad about this on one occasion, but he could not understand my feelings for the mountains. Then I asked him why he did not love the mountains, and I could scarcely comprehend the reason that he gave: "Well, son, I grew up back in New Jersey, where looking at mountains was not part of my daily experience. I actually hated it when my parents made us move here. The mountains were there for us to look at, but we didn't feel that we would wish to climb up into them."

As a curious and fearless four-year old, I am allowed to play wherever I wish in the neighborhood, but of course I am warned about crossing busy streets like South Broadway, just a block away. I have a special friend who is also called Johnny. One morning when the Rockies are summoning us, he and I start walking west from Lincoln Street, crossing Broadway, and continue on in the same direction a long ways until we reach the banks of the South Platte River. This is as close as we can get to the mountains. We stay for a long while on the banks of the river, jumping on the rocks and playing games. When we get very tired and realize how hungry we are, we think of going home; but along the way we are picked up by police, who tell us that we are very naughty and have caused our parents to worry. It is almost supper time when we arrive home. After a scolding and some tearful hugs, I am warned that if I ever "run away" from home again, I will be tied up with a rope.

But I still cannot remember as well as I should. Not intending to disobey our parents, Johnny and I do go wandering soon again, but this time we go no farther than the yard of the Gates Rubber factory, just across Broadway, where we play and jump as before until my father drives up in his car and takes us home, really scolding us harshly this time.

Dad is as good as his word. Tying me with a long rope to the clothes pole in the back yard, and with knots I can't untie, he uses this as my leash. Only my mother and my sister, "Anny Ruth," go to church this morning while Dad and my brothers stay home to watch me. They leave me alone all morning in the yard, all tied up like this, with nothing to do but cry. I can hear my brothers playing and having a good time. I guess I have learned my lesson this time. I won't run away anymore.

Three times cars almost kill me

The first time a car almost kills me, it is someone else's car. We live at 1228 South Lincoln here in Denver. I am playing at Peggy and Phyllis's house across the street. It is pitch black outside and someone is calling me to come home. I yell that I am coming and run out into the street. I will always remember that the street has gravel instead of pavement because it doesn't hurt me very much when I fall down, which is what happens when headlights suddenly appear and blind me. The car screeches to a halt. The driver gets out and picks me off the gravel, and I am taken crying but unhurt into our house, where I am told, "I hope you have learned your lesson not to run into the street without looking." But I did look! The car just came out of nowhere.

The second time I am in danger of getting killed is when I am in a car. Maybe it is Uncle Gerrit's car because it is strange to me. The bad thing about this car is that the doors have their hinges at the rear and the latch in front, so that the air movement tends to push them open. I can't imagine a car with this flaw ever being allowed! Anyway, it is not our car. I know it is Uncle Gerrit's car because we have just come out of a vocal recital and are on our way home. Uncle Gerrit has been inviting Mother to them, but I don't know why I have to go to them too. I hate them because the screechy sopranos hurt my ears. Something unexpected happens when I pull on the door handle. The door flies open just as we are turning left and I fall out into the street where other cars are coming. This too is a gravel street. I am not hurt, however, just scratched and scared.

The third time I am almost in a fatal accident involving cars is when I am enjoying riding my sled down a snowy street near our house. There aren't supposed to be any cars on this street because it has been closed off, but all of a sudden there is one coming up the hill right at me, and I can't stop my sled! Luckily, the car does stop, but I can't help banging into its bumper. Anyway, I am not hurt, that's what counts. The driver takes me and my sled right home and tells my mother and father what has happened. They are not mad or upset at me. They hug and kiss me and tell me not to slide anymore where there are cars. I guess I now understand the reason why not. Cars are very dangerous!

Neighborhood boys try to poison me

I am only four and we are still living on South Lincoln Street. On

28   The 1920's: Neigborhood boys try to poison me

my way to McKinley School I am often threatened by two brothers who live two houses away from our house. They show me the blades of their pocket knives and tell me they are going to cut my ears off. That is why I am amazed and delighted one day when, instead of speaking mean to me, they ask me if I would like to see the swell tent they have in their back yard. Once I am inside, they tell me to sit down on a campstool, and then they ask me if I am thirsty. When I say yes they hand me a glass of clear liquid that looks like water, but is actually gasoline. From that moment onward I don't know what happened. I am home and I feel very sick. I keep vomiting and retching, and I feel just awful. I must have actually drunk some of that liquid! That's what my mother says happened. Our house is full of people, policemen and firemen among them. Somebody says those boys will be arrested and be taken to jail. I hope I never see them again!

Painting up like clowns
I am about five now and manage to get into a lot of trouble. One day a neighbor boy (not Johnny from Lincoln Street) and I are looking for something to do, and what we get into is some paint -- house paint, that is. "Hey, let's be clowns and paint our faces," says my friend. So we find a brush and get to work on each other's face, covering everything but the mouth and eyes. We really do look funny! We are disappointed, though, when other kids refuse to look at us, and before long we begin to wish we hadn't done it. The paint smells bad and makes my face itch and burn. I want to get it off real bad, but don't know how. I decide to go home and ask my Dad to get it off for me. To my great relief, he is more sorry for me than angry. First he blots the paint with towels and rags, but it is already too dry and not much comes off. So he has to scrub it with awful, smelly, burning turpentine! He has to scrub and scrub. It hurts a lot, but I just have to endure the pain. My face is left fiery red and burning, but Dad has some salve that helps. If this is what clowns have to endure, I don't want to become one!

My parents forget my birthday. What was not very nice about having my birthday on December 20 was that my parents were likely to slight it in the rush to prepare for Christmas. One year they forgot it completely and I complained to my mother about it. She said that this was too bad, they were sorry, but they would make up for it by combining my birthday celebration with Christmas, giving me an extra large Christmas present. I had to be content with that, but I thought that a child should never be forgotten on his birthday. It made it seem as if his parents did not truly love him and were not glad he had been born, even though this could not possibly be true because my parents often showed that each child was special and precious to them.

Trying to console me with the promise that I will get a bigger present does not make me happy, I still feel neglected. Why did I have to be born so close to Christmas?

I swallow our ice-cream money
Our family is enjoying an outing in a city park. There are swings, teeter-totters, slides, and other toys to play on. Dad wishes to purchase ice-cream cones for us children. He puts a quarter in my hand and says, "Johnny, take this quarter and get ice-cream cones for the four of you, and then bring me the change." This sounds like a big transaction, but the cones are a nickel apiece, and Dad will get a nickel back. I take off for the ice-cream stand, but a just-vacated swing tempts me to pause and take a swing or two. "I'll need both hands on the chains, so how will I hold Dad's quarter?" I put it in my mouth and start to swing higher and higher. Involuntarily I gulp and swallow the quarter. It hurts as it slides down my throat. I try to gag and cough it up, but to no avail. Panicky and crestfallen, I run to Dad to tell him what has happened. He consoles me and gives me another quarter, cautioning me to be more careful this time. Mom says, "You had better enjoy your cone because we have to get your quarter back. You will have to use the potty so we can find it!" And that is what happens.

Death comes too soon for some schoolmates
Carl Toeset, who is in Hank's class at school, catches a steel ball used for lawn bowling on his temple and is in a coma for a while, but recovers. This is when I learn the meaning of the words, "coma" and "temple," but, more importantly, I learn how close to injury and even death we all are, even as children.

One of my own classmates, a bright girl named Jean Afman, actually did die while I was a student at Denver Christian School.

Like Carl, she was injured on the school grounds because of inadequate supervision. She was high-jumping over a slender wooden bar and broke it when she knocked it down and fell on it. A sharp fragment penetrated her thigh and she died of blood poisoning.

Two classmates who died after I left this school were Jim Lont, still a young boy when he drowned in a gravel pit, and Kenny Van Wyk, who went down with his ship when it was struck by a Kamikaze near Okinawa in 1945. One other juvenile who died of an injury while I was in this school was Arthur Frens. He got run over by a train.

Our family knows the Frens family very well because they are members with us of the First Reformed Church. They live near a railroad. Art is in the practice of jumping aboard the train while it is moving slowly in order to get a ride home. One time the train is moving faster than he thinks and he slips. His leg is caught under a wheel and is completely severed. I think he is taken to a hospital, but he stays alive for a few hours, receiving numerous transfusions of blood. Our Dad is one who gives blood, but this is all in vain because Art dies during the night. He is only twelve years old! This is when I learn what it means to grieve. We were going to have a prayer service in church for him, but instead we will be going to his funeral!

Feeling depressed over an injured cat

There is a cat caught in a trap or something between two garages a short distance from this house into which we have recently moved. One day I hear it yowling piteously as I walk home from school. I tell my mother, but she replies, "Well, I'm sure the people who live there will know about it, and will do something." But they don't do anything about it. The cat doesn't stop yowling and nobody seems to care. I would have gone to that house and told the people living there, but I am too shy. We have just moved here ourselves and I don't know anybody. I don't know which cat it is or who it belongs to. When I hear it screaming and crying I know it is in agony. I feel helpless to do anything and at the same time guilty because I haven't done anything. I want to rescue the cat but I can't. When I simply cannot stand it anymore, I tell my Dad, but he doesn't seem to know what to do, either. After another day the yowling stops. I don't know whether the cat has died or somebody has rescued it. It is a long time before I am over my bad feelings.

Things I remember doing in the 1920's
   Fetching the Sunday funnies on Saturday night
   Spending time in Uncle Will's mountain cabin
   Having picnics in the Denver mountain parks
   Shooting marbles, playing with jack-knifes
   Visiting the Museum of Natural History
   Getting books from Platte library

   Swimming in Washington Park lake
   Playing on swings, teeter-totters, slides and monkey-bars
   Playing party games: spin the bottle, postoffice, ghost stories
   Fourth of July: firecrackers and fireworks
   Halloween: soaping windows, throwing garbage, pulling trolley cables
   Sledding, ice-skating and snowball fighting
   Squeezing through the Knothole to root for the Denver University football team
   Celebrating with the Tamminga relatives on Christmas Eve
   Taking rides at Elitch's Garden or Lakeside

3
The Nineteen Thirties--
When I Begin a Search for my True Calling

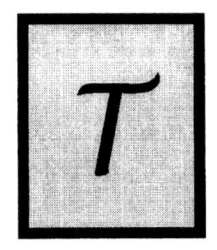

The decade of the nineteen thirties was for us DeVrieses, as for many Americans, a time of estrangement, desperation and, towards the end, opportunity. It changed me as a socially adjusted and generally content young boy into a confused and troubled teen-ager. I wanted to amount to something in the world but now saw no way to do it. My schooling was disconnected and mediocre, I no longer had the familiar friends of the 1920's, and I had no sense of belonging anywhere. Almost by reaction, I greeted the gorgeous horizon of forests and peaks as the place of my destiny, but it too was elusive and inaccessible. A great war -- greater than the one my father had been in -- was looming on the horizon. When all assurances were gone and my prospects for a good future had been reduced to almost zero, One greater than myself intervened and took me to places I never knew or dreamed of.

Things I remember doing in the 1930's
In Denver and vicinity, 1930-33, 1935-38, 1938-1939
    Summer jobs: yardwork, farmwork, selling
        magazines
    Ice-skating at Cherry Hills, sledding
    Riding and repairing bicycles
    Using guns: BB and .22 cal.
    Raising rabbits and chickens
    Feeding and milking a cow
    Learning how to drive cars
    Helping with remodeling: cement work, roofs
    Camping, climbing, hiking
    Schoolyard football in Littleton
    Schools: Denver Christian, Littleton Grade, Littleton High,
        Golden High, South Denver High

In California, 1933-35, summer of 1938
    Boy scouting: troop meetings, working for ranks and merit
        badges, jamborees
    Shop lifting, smoking corn silk
    Swimming in salt water at Long Beach Lagoon and Pike pier
    Fireworks at Halloween
    Schools: Washington Grade, Clearwater Junior High

The 1930's: Going fishing with Hank and Dad

Going fishing with Hank and Dad

We are in the Colorado mountains on our way to Gunnison, where we are going to stay in a tent and go trout fishing. Hank and I don't actually have fishing gear, but maybe if the fishing is good Dad will buy some for us. Dad is borrowing his own equipment from Mom's brother, Uncle Will. He has rod and reel, waders, net, and wicker basket for carrying his catch if he catches anything. Dad loves fishing as well as hunting, but seldom indulges in them because he is constantly working. Once Dad actually went bear hunting with some electrician friends of his and brought some bear meat home for us to eat. It was very good!

All evening it rains hard. Likewise most of the night. We eat a meal in our tent that has been prepared by Dad. There is not much to do and we soon become bored. It is raining too hard to be outside. Dad entertains us with some stories. He reads a passage from the Bible and prays. We sing some hymns together. Dad puts out the kerosene lantern and we drop off to sleep, hoping for good weather tomorrow. I do very much hope that it won't rain tomorrow because Dad says that the fish won't bite while it is raining.

It rains all day tomorrow. Late in the afternoon, we pack our gear and fold up our soggy tent. Dad says he has had enough. He can't go through another night of rain, and we may as well go home where we can be dry and comfortable. Hank and I feel the same way. We are deeply disappointed that we have failed even to get our fishline wet. All the same, it has been fun to go camping with our dad.

Being beaten on by an older boy. The only fist-fight I ever had while a child was something I could not avoid because to challenge my tormentor was the only way to stop him. This happened while we were living at 1786 South Logan St. in the early thirties -- our last stop in the Denver enclave before the bad decade to come exposed us to a harsh and cruel world outside.

For some time I have been pushed around and ridiculed by a boy in the grade above me -- actually the grade Hank is in. I don't think Hank knows this is going on. I am angry and resentful at this boy. His name is Richard and he also lives, I think, on South Logan, somewhat south of where we live. Maybe what he is doing to me, seen objectively, is not meant so badly, but I am always in a state of mind to resist being bullied by older boys because that is how stand-

ing up to my older brother has trained me. Anyhow, Richie will not quit and I threaten to fight him. He can't lose face by backing down, so as soon as school is out that day, he and his supporters walk a block to the area behind the First Reformed Church. I and Hank, practically without any supporters to cheer us on, follow. Richie and I square off at each other. I ferociously attack him and give him a cut on his lip. He pounds back at me and gives me a black eye. That accomplished, we break off and hurry home. Hank praises me for being so brave and so "tuff." My Dad nods his head with approval when he arrives home.

That boy and I were to see little of each other in the future, mainly because he and I attended different churches though attending the same school. It was good that my dad and older brother supported and approved my direct way of resolving an intolerable situation. If I had not received this support, I would have been shamed and humiliated.

Miss Te Sla puts the fear of God in me
It is June, 1931, and I am about to complete fourth grade in Denver Christian School. Our teacher has the reputation of being the meanest in the school, and I find out why when I cross her at a class picnic. Miss Te Sla (who wouldn't be mean with a name like that!) has taken her class to City Park to see the exhibits in the Museum of Natural History. We have been instructed to take a lunch from home. At her invitation we gather about her to eat our lunch. She sharply instructs us, "Do not throw anything on the ground!" Either I am not listening very well, or I make my own interpretation, which is, "She does not want us to throw paper wrappers on the ground, but she doesn't say anything about breadcrusts. They should be all right to throw away because the birds and squirrels will come to get them." So I slyly throw some breadcrusts behind me. As we stand up to go, Miss Te Sla espies my crusts. My name is not on them, but somehow she knows they are mine (mainly because they are near where I am sitting). She glares at me and asks in a voice as cold as ice, "Johnny De Vries, are those your breadcrusts?" I want to lie, but it looks as if she has the goods on me, so I murmur, "Y-yes, Miss Te Sla, I'm sorry." "Well, we shall see how sorry you are when we all get back to school on Monday!"

38   The 1930's: Miss Te Sla puts the fear of God in me

If she were a professional torturer in the castle of a wicked king, Miss Te Sla couldn't have made the rest of my outing and, in fact, my entire weekend, more miserable for me. "Why doesn't she just slap me or spank me, and get it over with?" Next Monday morning, the first thing after prayer and hymn-singing, she calls me up to the blackboard in front of all the children and makes me write a hundred times, "I will not throw refuse on the ground."

That event taught me two important lessons: (1) that I shouldn't always be second-guessing what older people tell me, particularly those who are in authority; and (2) that not all women are sweet and kind. It is too bad that cross and twisted persons like Miss Te Sla get into the profession of teaching children. I don't know anything about her except what she taught me on this occasion: that some grownups are to be feared, if not truly respected.

Boarding with Aunt Jen. We didn't see Uncle Will very often, but Aunt Jen was always there. She was very sweet and cheerful. We children loved her, and it was clear that she loved us too. Probably this was because she had no children of her own. She grew up in West Sayville, NY, where her father, Capt. Jacob Kwaak, skippered an oysterboat. That is where Aunt Jen knew the Tamminga's and of course Uncle Will. Beyond this bit of information, there was a vast chasm in my store of knowledge. All I knew was that, once in Denver, Uncle Will got into contracting and established his own business. He and Aunt Jen were well off, but generous to their relatives, especially their sister Kate, our mother, and us her family.

I was glad both times I got to board with Aunt Jen for a while. The first time it was Bob and I who were there, the second time it was Hank and I. It was always a treat to dine at Aunt Jen's table because she was a wonderful cook. I guess that is why she was so heavy; she evidently ate lots of her own cooking. My favorite delicacy was her cherry jelly. Wonderful!

Bob and I are at Aunt Jen's house because Mom is sick and in the hospital. Hank went to stay at Uncle Joe De Vries's, but Dad made him come home and stay with him when he reported that he had to take a bath with Little Henry in the same bathwater, and Little Henry did a poop in the water. Gross, gross!

Hank and I are together at Aunt Jen's this time while Dad and Mom go to Grand Rapids to attend Grandpa De Vries's funeral. He wasn't very old, just 65. He died of coronary thrombosis, which means a clot in his heart. Grandma will now be a widow and will have only Uncle Jake with her. I'm not sure, but I think he is attending Calvin College and intends to study to be a doctor.

Music. There was no music in the life of my childhood family except what we got in church and Christian school. Neither Dad nor Mother had enjoyed the opportunity to acquire a taste for music in their own parental homes since whatever singing they actually did as they grew up was that of the Dutch psalms. Upon moving their membership to the First Reformed Church of Denver, they had learned to sing hymns as well, but these were heavy on the sentimental and evangelistic side. Probably the one thing that we children actually enjoyed about attending church and Sunday School was the opportunity to join lustily in congregational singing. In addition, we learned to sing hymns in the Christian school. To me, singing was fun, as well as uplifting and inspiring.

We boys had virtually no chance to become acquainted with musical instruments. However, I was allowed to take harmonica lessons from a local musician named Mr. Smith at fifty cents per lesson and was invited to join his harmonica band in giving concerts. I would have enjoyed this very much but something awful happened to ruin it.

As the band arrives at Bethesda Sanatorium one Sunday afternoon to give the patients a harmonica concert, Mr. Smith heedlessly slams my finger in his car door. It bleeds profusely and I cry from the pain. Then he bawls me out for crying, so I suffer from two kinds of agony simultaneously, physical and psychological. I plot revenge by thinking, "I won't take lessons from him anymore! I don't care if I don't get to play in his old concert!"

What enjoyment of music was there to be in my future? A year or two after the episode recounted, during my brief attendance at Washington School in Bellflower, CA, I was to have my only course ever in primary or secondary school music. That would be where I was to spend the final months of my sixth grade, and though this school would not have much to offer, it would give me the opportunity to learn about musical instruments and symphonies. We would be taught how to sing parts. Then later, while living at 5280 South University Blvd. south of Denver, our family would acquire a used piano, but Ruthie would be the only one allowed to take lessons for it. We boys would tinkle on the keys a bit, but otherwise would have no opportunity to learn the mysteries of how music is produced. Once each Saturday, however, we were to be privileged, as were numerous grateful Americans, to listen to the Texaco opera broadcasts on the radio. That would be when we would begin to learn the glories of beautiful music.

Mrs. Riggle pulls Mom's hair. This also happened while we were living at 1878 South Logan St. in Denver, our last stop before moving to a farmhouse outside Littleton in 1932. We had a big fracas in our back yard that resulted in serious injury because of a prayer I said.

Two bad things happen. First, Hank gets into a fight with the boy who lives across the alley from us, Arthur Riggle. This boy goes crying into his house once Hank is through with him. A moment later his mother comes screaming and fuming into our back yard saying she is going to beat Hank up. She calls for Mother to come out and talk to her. When Mother does so, this crazy Riggle woman grabs Mother by the hair and threatens to beat her if she ever lets Hank lay a hand on her Arthur again. Mom is of course in an awful dither and begins to cry. This is the kind of trouble nobody can manage and nobody wants. In all the hubbub, Hank gets by without a reprimand. We all assume that Art Riggle must be pretty bad, to judge from this awful mother of his.

That is the first bad thing that happens. When I say my prayers that same night I ask God to punish this boy and his mother, but I soon have reason to regret saying this prayer. Arthur is at a farm and falls off a haystack, then splits his skull open when he hits a mower blade on the ground. So God does listen to my prayer! Maybe I had better watch out what I pray for! I begin to feel very guilty, thinking that my prayer has actually caused this dreadful accident. To make things right, I pray that God will make Art better, and he does that too! Art is soon back to normal, all healed.

This did not make us friends. I didn't tell Arthur that I prayed for him to get hurt and then prayed for him to get healed. From this time on we saw very little of him and nothing at all of his wierd mother, mostly because we ourselves soon moved away from the neighborhood.

A temporary move to Littleton. In the summer of 1932 our family was forced to move to Littleton, a town of about 2000, a few miles south of Englewood. This was caused by our Dad's declining income. The Depression had hit the building trades very hard, and there was very little work left for anyone. Once again, drastic adjustments were required of us all.

Our parents were now feeling the full effects of the Great Depression. One day I heard my dad tell my mother that his pay had been cut to $18 per week. They decided that they could not live on this with four children and would have to move out of the house in which we had been living and move to an old farmhouse just outside Littleton,[1] which could be rented for very little. Dad purchased an old model T Ford and moved us lock, stock, and barrel to the old farmhouse, from which he would drive to wherever his job might be.

During my ten or so years we had moved over and over again, but this was the first time we moved outside our south Denver community. All was brand new to us: a new church, a new school, a new town to shop in.

It will be hard to make the drastic adjustment with which we are now faced, but the worst to adjust to will be this drab and shabby house. It promises to offer us poor shelter when winter comes, I can see that myself. Also, it is very small, too small. Mom and Dad have one of the bedrooms. We three boys share a second bedroom and even have to sleep in the same bed. Ruthie sleeps on the sofa in the living room.

Dad has had to buy a better car because he now has to drive to work in Denver, but the car he buys is old and only slightly better than the one we had before. It is a Model T Ford that has to be cranked by hand. Dad says he feels comfortable buying this old car because he is very well acquainted with maintaining and even repairing the Model T. This is true: Dad drove all the way from Denver to California and back in one of these in 1921. Be that as it

---

[1] The very same place where the notorious Columbine shootings were to occur in the 1990's. When we lived there, there was not much to the town itself, which was surrounded on all sides by open land and farmsteads. Littleton was named after a nineteenth-century militiaman and Indian fighter.

may, this car may prove to be more of a problem, and at a time that may be inconvenient and cause serious trouble..

During the summer we children enjoy exploring the town and its surroundings. We have chickens and rabbits. Our favorite rabbit is a beautiful white angora named Eleanor. We take note of the fact that, once winter starts, we will have wonderful hills to sled on.

New challenges in Littleton Grade School

All four of us go to school in the town of Littleton. I wind up in the sixth-grade class in Littleton Grade School -- my first return to the public school system since kindergarten. I am proud to be enrolled in grade 6-A rather than in 6-B because the teacher sees that the work I have been having in Denver Christian is far advanced over that of 6-B. He has trouble pronouncing my family name, "De Vries." It's a good thing that he doesn't know my real first name, "Simon," or the kids would poke fun at me for sure. I am very shy, and blush when nobody can pronounce my name. I am also self-conscious about having come from a "Christian" school. But my teacher is a swell guy and expresses admiration when I show that my schooling is advanced over what the public school children are receiving.

When the first day ends, I take off for home, which is maybe five or six blocks away. Just outside the school premises there is a gang of boys who don't like my name, are resentful about my being a top student, and intend to haze me. They howl at me and show their fists. I can't expect to fight off so many, so I take off and run as fast as possible for home. That ends the matter as far as they are concerned because I have shown them that I am superior in at least one physical accomplishment, running like a deer! All in all, this is an unsettling experience, entirely unlike anything that used to happen in the more sheltered environment of the Dutch enclave in south Denver.

In this class I learn about heroic figures from Greek mythology, such as Zeus and Ulysses -- taboo in Denver Christian. I will also have new experiences in how American society works under stress. School children from poor families get to enroll in a government lunch program, and it is there that I have my first taste of chili, which takes some getting used to, but does fill one's tummy.

Generally I am well accepted at this school. I enjoy playing real tackle football (without equipment, of course) in the schoolyard. That too is something we never got to do in Denver.

Not so good is my first exposure to pornography in the form of some very dirty artwork featuring well-known cartoon characters. Some kids got hold of it from a man who was passing it around.

More worth remembering was the glimpse I caught of the future president, Franklin D. Roosevelt. I was standing in a crowd of people at the railroad station while a train passed by with the presidential candidate on the rear platform, waving. People were saying that he had a plan to save our country from the Depression, and that we should vote for him. I wished that I could vote for him, but I was far too young.

Surviving in our cold farmhouse during the winter of 1932. The winter of 1932 turned out to be a bitter one, with much snow and very low prevailing temperatures. We had a very hard time keeping warm in our battered farmhouse, which had to be heated entirely by a wood stove standing in the kitchen. The house was uninsulated and drafty. To make matters worse, we all came down with the flu and had to take turns nursing one another.

Dad had a dreadful time keeping the car running. There was no garage, so it stood outside at night and Dad had to scrape the snow and chop the ice off it in the morning before he could go to work. The possibility of starting it when the temperatures dropped below zero depended on his strategy of draining the crankcase oil when he would come home from work and keep the oil warm beside the stove during the night. Before pouring the warm oil back in, Dad brought hot coals from the stove and placed them directly under the engine. But one bitterly cold morning this did not do the trick, so he placed firewood on the coals, which caught fire, and then set the engine ablaze, so that Dad had to shovel sand on it to extinguish it. What a bust!

Mom tries to prepare nutritious food for us, but we get less and less meat. Dad butchers the chickens one by one, then the bunnies Eleanor has borne. Finally it is Eleanor's turn. She gets into Mom's dutch oven, but when her remains are handed out for us to eat, we all burst out crying and refuse to eat. What an atrocity, what a grief! This is when I realize how dreadful our situation has become. I begin to think of the possibility of our actually starving. Mom says though that we still have it better than her family did when her father could not bring home any pay from the oyster business. In her case it is sore upon sore, callous upon callous!

Eventually my parents found a house in south Denver to rent as a temporary substitute. There was no comparison between it and the wretched shack we had been living in. Unfortunately we could no longer pay the rent there, either, so we did not get to live there long.

I now enter the sixth-grade class in Denver Christian where, for a short time, Arvin Roos's mother, Alida Decker Roos, is my teacher. If only I could have had her as my teacher throughout my years in grade school! She is sweet, encouraging, patient, but absolutely demanding of the best in her students.

Our great migration to California. Since 1929 the economy had become steadily worse. Denver had only 125,000 inhabitants and there was very little industry. The building trades had been especially susceptible. Each week Dad would tell of still another worker who had been laid off. His own pay became smaller and smaller until there was no more work even for him as Mr. Sturgeon's prime craftsman. Because there would be no more work, there would be no more pay and no money for buying food or paying rent. This was when we found out that our dad was no quitter. He decided to look for work somewhere else, and that somewhere else was in southern California, which had recently suffered a devastating earthquake. "Many buildings there have been destroyed and must be rebuilt," Dad said, "Surely there will be work there for me!"

We were now forced to leave the rented house in south Denver in which we had rescued ourselves from the Littleton farmhouse. We had to dispose of all our furniture, all our excess clothing, and virtually every personal possession.

We children must give away all our toys. I have a wonderful set of books with the title, "Heroes of the Cross," which is about missionaries in far-away countries. Reading them almost makes one want to be a missionary himself. But this set has to be left in the house because nobody wants it. I feel as if I have abandoned a dear friend.

Dad got rid of the ancient Ford and bought a second-hand Maxwell, which needed some work if it were to carry the six of us to California. This was to be a real migration, a trek like that of the forty-niners except in that it would require days and not months. When all was ready, we piled in the Maxwell and headed south toward the New Mexico line. There was a good road from Denver to Santa Fe, then beyond it the famous Highway 66 all the way to Los Angeles. The first night out, we reached Walsenburg, CO, where we stayed the night for $2 in our very first "cottage camp" cabin. All four of us kids slept on the floor. On we went for five more days, staying overnight in whatever lodgings we could find. We saw the pueblo Indians in Acoma. We saw a drunken Navaho threatening to hit us head-on before rolling over when his car went off the pavement. We stopped briefly at the CRC mission station at Rehoboth, NM. We passed through the magical Painted Desert and the Petrified Forest. We passed by towering, snow-peaked San Francisco Mountain near Flagstaff, then we passed through Kingman in Arizona, then Needles and the awesome Mohave Desert in California. Outside the town of Barstow the car blew a gasket. While we kids played games in the desert, Dad helped a mechanic install a new one.

Dad can take this all in stride because he made an even more strenuous trip in 1921, when the road from Salt Lake City to Los Angeles was gravel, or just dirt. We have had nothing as rough as that on this trip. Broke as we are, and bleak as our prospects seem, we are strangly elated about the whole affair. It is a bully good adventure! We are seeing things of strange and unimaginable beauty, God's world unspoiled. Yes, God is here too, and God is with us. Besides, we have a dad who always seems able to figure out what to do.

Once the gasket was replaced, we were on our way again. We climbed the long grade to Victorville and then coasted into San Bernardino. In Riverside we stopped at a roadside stand where beautiful, juicy oranges were for sale, fifteen cents for a whole lug! We spent the fifteen cents and we all enjoyed as much of this delicious fruit as we wished. I ate so many oranges that I broke out with hives the following day.

We arrived at last in the little town of Hynes, south of Los Angeles. Here we were the guests of Uncle Joe Martens, Aunt Trina, and their daughter Betty. They were very good to us and helped us find an empty house to rent in Bellflower, the next town east.

Picking up the pieces. Before the earthquake, Camping's Bakery had stood prominently on the Bellflower main street, but it was now lying as rubble scattered over the pavement in front of it. This meant that Betty Martens was out of a job because she had been Mr. Camping's sales clerk. Mr. Camping had in fact moved the oven and what machinery he had salvaged to a shed behind his own house, where he resumed baking Dutch-style bread, cakes and cookies.

I discover that it is not just any kind of baked goods that Mr. Camping is making, but real Dutch pastry in the highest tradition. We have never tasted anything like it before, but we now become acquainted with it because our mom is doing some ironing for Mrs. Camping and she receives her pay in the form of these wonderul Dutch baked goodies. For a while, that is the only income we have. There is no work for Dad.

Soon we had to move to an even smaller house because Dad had been unable to find work in spite of his confident expectations. His reasoning had been: everything is demolished, it will be rebuilt as soon as possible, I will get work. What he had not foreseen was that nobody would have the money to rebuild anything. Southern California had been as hard hit by the Depression as any region in the country, maybe even worse because so many refugees like us were coming there to try their luck.

We were now living on our parents' last savings. A PWA[2] project that had just begun in Bellflower seemed to be Dad's last chance, laying a storm-sewer. The one they were building was to run directly in front of our house. It was interesting to watch the gang of laborers with their shovels, throwing up the dirt and laying the tiles. Dad would have taken this work if he had had to; he was not too proud! Instead he hung up a sign saying, "Electrical Appliances Repaired Here." When the neighbors saw this sign, many whose toasters, fans, and radios were broken brought them to Dad to repair because they could not afford to buy new. We lived on what they were willing to pay.

[2] "Public Works Administration," an early New Deal program, mainly for make-work projects

As usual, we all do our best to adjust to our new circumstances. My sixth-grade schooling has now been interrupted three times, and I am enrolled in the sixth grade at Washington School in Bellflower. There is not in fact any such school -- that is to say, no school building. It is all rubble lying on the ground. It has been almost totally demolished in the earthquake. Classes are now being held in improvised structures of various kinds. When the family soon moves to still another dwelling in Bellflower, one even smaller, I remain in Washington School while Hank, Bob and Ruth go off to other schools.

It is while living here in a tiny, run-down house on Artesia Boulevard that the depth of our poverty comes home to me. Somehow we are getting enough to eat. This is because food is so cheap. We never have money to buy new clothes. We kids are utter paupers. I never own a single dime of my own! We boys are forced to wear harsh, ill-fitting denim (called "overall slacks"). I am always uncomfortable in denim and will hate it until I die. Another way our family saves money is by "allowing" us boys to go around barefoot. I even go to Washington School barefoot. But the majority of the students do the same.

Encountering a crazy lady

Here in Bellflower I am in the habit of cutting through people's yards to save extra steps, but what just happened has scared me into thinking I had better quit. As I have done a few times before, I walk right across this lady's property and this time she is outside waiting for me. She has a very strange look on her face and her eyes seem to glow. "Well then, young man," she says, "since you are here on my property, perhaps you would like to see the inside of my house. Come on in and I'll give you some milk and cookies." She is holding her screendoor open and is pointing inside. I don't know whether to run or stay, so I stay, which is easier. I do not want to aggravate her more than I already have. Inside her kitchen she shows me a chair and then gives me cookies and a glass of milk, talking real fast the whole time in a crazy way. I drink the milk carefully, thinking of the time those boys gave me gasoline to drink and tried to poison me. The milk is okay, and so are the cookies. When the crazy lady pauses to catch her breath, I jump up and step towards the door. "Thanks a lot, ma'am," I say, "I have to hurry home. My mother is expecting me." I don't think she really is, but the ruse succeeds. The crazy lady remains glued to her chair and can do nothing to stop me. As I run towards home, I look back to see her waving. I don't wave back.

Meeting Jackie Stansbury

I am on recess with some sixth-grade boys. We are playing in the sand outside Washington school. There are little bugs that we are watching. When we cover one of them with sand, we look to see where it will come out. A little crater begins to form, and a few seconds later there it is, outside the sand in the crater! One of the boys who are watching tells us his name is Jackie Stansbury. He has a sort of wild look in his eye, not like that of the crazy lady, but tough and hard. "Do you know me?" he asks. "I'm like one of those bugs trying to get out. I just came to school for the first time yesterday because I have been away at Reform School and just got out. That's not actually a school, but a prison for bad kids like me who have committed a serious crime." "What crime did you commit?" someone asks. "It was easy," says Jackie. "I noticed that the front door to this lady's house was open and I could see that she was outside, working in her garden. So I just snuck in and looked around. In her bedroom, on her bed, lay her purse. I opened it and took all the money out. Too bad I didn't get to spend it because somebody saw me, and before long the police took me to jail. I'll be smarter next time!"

Brother Bob breaks both arms

This sounds pretty stupid, but it really happens. My younger brother Bob and I are attending summer vacation Bible school a mile or so from where we live. We always have to walk both ways and are eager to accept rides when they are offered. On this particular day, no one offers, but I see that a flatbed truck from a store near our home has unloaded its freight and is about to depart. It must be going toward our house! Sizing up the situation, I say, "Come on, Bob, let's catch a ride home!" We both hop on. I say, "We'll have to jump off when he slows down for the red light," but as he appoaches it, the driver speeds up instead of slowing down. I manage to jump off safely, but Bob remains on the truck. It speeds onward until it is almost out of sight. I am thinking, "It will soon be at the Pacific Electric Railway crossing and will have to slow down and stop if there is a train coming. I hope so!" A train does come by, I can see it in the distance. Minutes pass as I walk slowly in the direction in *which Bob has gone. Soon I am able to discern a small group of boys riding this way on bicycles, and before long I can see that they are carrying someone who is sitting on the top bar of one of the bicycles. "I do believe it is Bob." It is Bob. He is crying in pain. The boy who is carrying him on his bike says, "When the truck came up to the railroad, it speeded up to get across before the train came. He tried to jump off, but fell on his arms instead, and now I think they are broken." These kind boys take me on another of their bikes and bring us both home. We find that Bob's arms are broken, all right. The doctor puts both arms in casts, and for the next two months we have to feed him by hand, and even help him go to the toilet. I feel very guilty and responsible that this bad thing has happened because we did what boys should never do: steal rides on trucks.*

I am saved from a pedophile

Fearless me, I dare hitchhike without a companion, this time on a major road near Bellflower. Rather than walk home all the way, I hold out my thumb. A car slows down and stops. I run to catch up and am welcomed into the car by the driver, who chats gaily with me for a few minutes before saying, "Let's see what you've got there." I don't know what he means but soon find out. While holding the steering wheel with his left hand, he pokes his right hand under my belt and reaches for my genitals underneath my underwear, massaging them gently and remarking, "A pretty good set of tools you've got there!" I am paralyzed with fear at the thought of what he might do next, but manage to say, "Please, mister, right up ahead is where I've got to get out." It isn't, but I will gladly walk if I can just get away from this frightening man. Fortunately for me, he is willing to stop and let me out. A reason might be that I am twelve years old, and maybe pedophiles like him prefer younger victims, say those under ten.

I am not sure whether I will tell my parents. Probably not, because I am afraid to get scolded by them. But I don't think I will hitchhike anymore. One thing I know for sure, God has been protecting me today from something very, very bad.

Living among Frisian dairymen. The little house we were living in was on Artesia Blvd. in Bellflower, running eastward toward the town of Artesia. Right here was probably the country's largest concentration of Frisian-American dairymen. You could tell you were near the dairies of Bellflower from the smell, and it wasn't the smell of flowers! These good folk had gathered here to produce milk for the Los Angeles metropolis. Both Mom and Dad understood some Frisian because their individual parents had spoken it at home along with Dutch.[3] Mom was familiar with Frisian dairymen since her own uncle John Beintema in West Sayville was one of them.

Our tiny house on Artesia Boulevard was just one block from a large dairy. The owner was glad to have us bring our glass jugs and buy his rich milk, fresh from the cooling machine, for twenty cents per gallon. It was up to us boys to go there every day to get more fresh milk, which we all enjoyed and benefitted from. This milk was wholesome in spite of its not being pasteurized. It was the prompt and thorough cooling that assured this, and that is what gave Dad his idea for a better job.

After doing some exploring, Dad purchased the tools and equipment he would need in order to service the numerous cooling machines belonging to the dairymen. It helped that Dad could speak some Frisian with them. He came to be highly regarded for his superior work, and the dairymen, whose products remained always in demand, were able to pay him well for his services. Thus we as a family began to prosper once again.

Our church life was markedly influenced by our parents' sense of ethnic solidarity since they chose to attend the First CRC in Bellflower, which many of the dairymen attended. In the services and activities at the church there was no Frisian, but they did have an afternoon service in Dutch.

We children understand very little of the Dutch language, but snicker because it sounds so funny when the minister, reading the Decalogue, intones, "Nog zijnen os, nog zijnen ezel, nog iets wat uws naasten is."[4]

Another town, a new school, and new things to do. After a while we found a more adequate dwelling in the nearby town of Hynes, and this required still another change of schools.

Hank and I go together to nearby Clearwater Junior High School. From its curriculum I profit most from the program in physical edu-

---

[3].Frisian is an entirely separate language belonging to the Germanic language group. It is more similar to English than are either Dutch (Netherlandic) or German.
[4]."Neither his ox nor his ass, nor anything belonging to thy neighbor."

cation and from various shop courses: metal-working, tin-smithing, wood-working. How proud Hank and I are to bring home a fresh new aluminum frying-pan that we have ourselves forged from old scraps!

It was a new world to us, one that demanded adjustments. We grew more daring and adventuresome. One program that Hank and I profited from immensely was the Boy Scouts of America. Without the Boy Scouts I, just reaching puberty, might have got into serious trouble. With never a dime to call our own, we went so far as to steal little items such as wallets and jack-knives from the counters of the five and dime store. When we began to realize that this was dangerous as well as sinful, we quit.

I think Dad got the idea of allowing us to join the Scouts because Mother's brother-in-law, Andrew Groenink, is a Scout commissioner up north in Alameda and highly recommends this program. In actual fact, the Boy Scouts do much to turn us in the right direction and draw the best from us. Hank and I are both proud to be able to earn numerous merit badges through our hard work!

We both came close to achieving the highest rank, that of Eagle Scout, before we were forced to abandon it when moving back to our old home in Denver. Another casualty of our unrootedness!

Fun with Leo Edwards. The Edwards family lived just behind us in Hynes, CA, where we lived for almost two years. To me Leo Edwards was someone special. First, I had never heard of, let alone met, anyone with the name "Leo." Next, I had never met anyone with a family name made from a given name, "Edward" in this case. Something else that was unusual about Leo and his family was that they had a goat which they milked. The family drank all the milk. Leo let me taste some, and I found it very rich and pleasant to drink. Finally, this family was novel to me because instead of chickens, they raised geese and ducks. Once, Mother used one of their duck eggs to bake a cake.

We had lots of fun playing with Leo. One interesting thing he taught us was to use rotten wood from a fallen tree as punk. We would carve out a 3″ to 4″ long piece of this and then punch a hole in one end, through which we would push the fuse of a firecracker. We would light the other end of the punk with a match, place punk and firecracker in front of somebody's front door, and wait for the explosion. We would of course be hiding nearby out of sight when Bang! it would go off and the owner would come dashing out to find out what had happened. We did this a lot and never got caught.

I am with Leo and my brother Hank on the edge of a runoff pond from a nearby dairy. It is green looking and it stinks because it catches the water used in cleaning out the stalls. We shouldn't even be playing near or in it, but this is all we have and we need some water to sail our boat in. Yes, we have a boat, one that we made ourselves. It is big enough to hold one person. We made its frame out of wood and then stretched oilcloth around the frame, sealing the seams with wax and tar. Leo knew how to do this. He knows a lot.

Leo is going to ride in the boat. He has a two-bladed paddle. Hank and I hold the boat steady as Leo steps in. With his weight the boat immediately sinks down in the water. The seams begin to leak and Leo sees that all is in vain. We will never be able to ride around in that boat!

That is enough for Leo, but my brother Hank makes a raft and gets me to help carry it to a pond, a different one this time, more out of sight. Hank steps out onto the raft. It sways and begins to tip. Hank loses his balance and falls Kerplunk! into the filthy water. He manages to sneak home and take a bath without our mother finding out what happened. It's a wonder he didn't get some awful disease!

Being mistaken for Okies on the way back to Colorado. In the summer of 1935 Dad received a cordial invitation from Mr. Sturgeon to come back and work for him. Things are much better now, he said. Roosevelt's New Deal had done a lot of good in getting men back to work. I had heard about the dust bowl that had driven thousands of farm families from their homes in Oklahoma and eastern Colorado. We had observed quite a lot of dust and tumble weeds driven by the wind near Denver, where we previously lived. Mr. Neal Roos, Arvin's father, had often complained of the damage done by drought and dust to his crops and fields. I had also heard that those dust-bowl refugees had been coming here to California in search of work. John Steinbeck tells about them in his book, *The Grapes of Wrath*. Some remained close to Los Angeles, but most went up into the San Joaquin Valley where there were abundant crops needing to be harvested. But I never saw an "Okie" or any other kind of migrant worker. That is why I was so astonished at what a rude cop in Fresno said to us, calling us Okies and ordering us to get out of his city park.

We have closed everything up in the Bellflower-Hynes area and are on our way back to Denver. I am not unhappy about this. In fact, I am glad to go back to my beloved mountains. Oh sure, there are mountains in California, but the ones I can see outside L.A. are not very high in comparison with the magnificent Rockies, and they almost never have snow on them.

Dad and Mom have talked over Mr. Sturgeon's invitation and have decided that we would be better off in Denver, so here we are on our way to Colorado, driving north to avoid the Mohave Desert during the late summer. We will travel through northern Nevada, Utah, Wyoming, and northern Colorado. We have entered this town of Fresno just at supper time and have found a pretty park with picnic benches where we may sit to eat our sandwiches. We are halfway through our meal when a police cruiser drives up and parks. The ugliest, meanest-looking cop you ever saw ambles up, scowling. "All right, you good for nothing Okies," he says, "we don't allow drifters and no-goods in this city. You had better be out of here in the next ten minutes or I'm coming after you and I will throw you out!" This really gets Dad's dander up. He retorts, "What do you mean, calling us drifters and no-goods? I want you to know we are not from Oklahoma, but we are hard-working California citizens on our way to Colorado. We have a perfect right to use your precious city park. We've paid our taxes all right, just like every other citizen." This stops the swaggering cop in his tracks. He swings his arms menacingly, as if to show that he would still like to intimidate us. As he climbs back in his car and drives off, Dad says, "The sooner we are out of this state, the better, if this is the way they treat upstanding people like us! And if they treat us like this, think of how badly they must treat people who are really destitute!"

Ninth grade in Denver Christian School. Back for ninth grade in the same building in which I was once a first-grader, I would have had nothing to inspire me, were it not for two wonderful male teachers, Mr. Forrest "Bub" Decker and Mr. Gerrit Pothoven. I was especially attracted to Mr. Decker because he was the brother of

Arvin Roos's wonderful mother Alida, my sometime sixth-grade teacher. He was also the son of Rev. Frederick Dekker, a well-known RCA minister.

Arv is in this class too. I have been his close friend since kindergarten at McKinley School. We both belong to the same church, First Reformed, and whenever I have attended Christian School in Denver we have been classmates.
 Mr. Pothoven teaches Bible and Mr. Decker teaches English. I like Bible a lot the way Mr. Pothoven brings it alive, but English with Mr. Decker is the best course I have ever had. He is in fact the eighth-grade teacher, but we have him for English in the ninth grade because he is so good. I just devour books like Sir Walter Scott's Ivanhoe. *Mr. Decker makes it extremely interesting by helping us see the characters as real, living people. An assignment that I find especially helpful is to write down every word I do not know and then write out next to it the definition given in the dictionary. The importance of this exercise is that it teaches me to look for the specific meaning of every word as used in particular passages. "Anyone who uses words incorrectly may have to use many words to say what he means, but he who uses them correctly needs only a few." That's what Mr. Decker teaches me, and he's right!*
 Mr. Pothoven, who is also the principal, says that I am his very best student, and accordingly he appoints me to serve as crossing guard at the corner of Florida Ave. and Washington St. It is nice to be recognized, but I observe that responsibilities seem to go along with praise and distinction.

Arvin Roos and I make confession of faith (Confirmation). The Reformed Church where we attended was more than a little marked with a tinge of pietism. They didn't very much like the idea of children just being confirmed, or formally acknowledged to be what they already were; i.e., Christians by virtue of their baptism. That is the mode of the Roman Catholics, Lutherans, and Anglicans. On the other hand, they were not like the Anabaptists and German Pietists, who acknowledged a person to be a Christian only upon his mature and responsibly made affirmation that he had come to true saving faith in Christ, and by virtue of this now took his rightful place in God's covenant. Much influenced by the example of God's old covenant with Israel, of which infant circumcision was the operative symbol, they were nevertheless not content, as the CRC people were, in placing all emphasis on the covenant status of their children in the light of their baptism as infants and on the basis of their parents' Christian confession. The RCA people with whom I grew up still expected a great deal of their young people when they appeared before the consistory asking permission to make their public confession of faith. More than the CRC people, they were looking for a positive and even dramatic experience.

The public ceremony in which my friend Arvin and I make confession of our faith takes place in the First Reformed Church of Denver, CO. It is an event of moving emotion and high spiritual joy for both of us, especially for the fact that we do so while we are only 14. I am moved by the well-chosen hymn, "O happy day, O happy day, when Jesus took my sins away!" Yet I am not sure that I am now any different than I was before doing this. I have now confessed publicly what I have always believed and never doubted: that Jesus has taken my sins away. The experience that has brought us to the Consistory meeting with this confession was in fact a series of dramatic lectures that we recently attended together in a local Baptist church, the point of which being that the world is nearing an end and that Christ will soon appear. I am not at all sure whether to believe this. Yet this is what has brought us to a sufficient intensity of self-awareness as to bring us to confess that Jesus Christ is our personal Savior.

How strange that it was dispensationalistic preaching in the Baptist church that led us to affirm Christ, but still, we did this in a Reformed rather than pietistic manner! Interestingly, my own father told me once that it was the preaching of the popular evangelist, Billy Sunday, that inspired him to make his own confession of faith, which took place in the First CRC of Denver. Spiritually speaking, we may need the spice of emotion to stimulate our religious self-consciousness, but we also need the meat and potatoes of solid biblical teaching to nourish our faith.

A good life at 5280 South University Boulevard. It was very easy to remember our new house number, which is the total number of feet in a mile. Also, 5280 feet is how high Denver lies above sea-level. Furthermore, this was not a real boulevard, just a gravel road. (It was an extension of a real boulevard inside the Denver city limits.) Anyway, this was where we settled down within a year of returning from southern California. Our home was another ex-farmhouse, but one far superior to the shack we lived in near Littleton back in 1932. It had two and a half acres of land, which we sharecropped with a farmer who came to put in the seeds. It also had a chicken house and a pen where we raised chickens for their meat and eggs. In addition, there was a shed where we could keep a cow for her milk. To make the tally complete, there was also a large garage.

The house was well built and had good architectural lines, with two dormers on the front roof. It had wood siding painted white and a shake roof painted green. The arrangement inside the house was open and commodious. We all had bedrooms upstairs. Downstairs there was a kitchen, a living room, a dining room, a bathroom, and a sleeping porch. From the former owners we inherited a large and decorative cookstove, fired by wood, where Mom prepared wonderful meals. There was also a coal furnace in an unfinished cellar beneath the kitchen.

This house becomes the center of our life for the next couple of years. Dad drives to work in Denver. Hank goes to Englewood High School. I go to Littleton High School. Bob and Ruth attend a country school nearby. We all return to Mom's supper at the day's end in this cheery house. There is lots of room in the vicinity, and we take advantage of it. There is a small creek to play in and the Highline flume, an irrigation ditch where we swim. During winter we ice-skate on a frozen pond that in summer serves as a hazard on the famous Cherry Hills Country Club.

We become friends with the Wolf family next door north, as well as with the Pinckney family a few houses distant to the south. The Wolf boys prove to be a bad influence because they drink a lot and get into accidents.

Dad likes this house so well that he does not hesitate to carry out major renovations: a new furnace and poured cement walls and floors in the basement, new plastering in the living room and dining room. Hank and I are required to help extensively in all these projects. What we get out of it is valuable experience in various aspects of the building profession, including our first involvement in painting.

I shall never forget how, when applying green paint to the roof, Hank and I had a duel in which we actually threw paint at each other from the pails we were using. Fortunately for us, Dad never found out about this. He also began to allow us to use the family car for occasions of special interest for young people. This place really meant "home" and stability to us, and we hoped devoutly that we would not be forced to leave it again.

A marvelous Bible
Somehow we have acquired a wonderful Bible with all kinds of notes. I love to sit in one of the dormer windows upstairs and read from it. I am especially intrigued with the explanations it gives for the strange visions in the book of Daniel. All the marching back and forth that is predicted in chapters 10 and 11 actually came to pass, just as Daniel says. How wonderful that God would predict everything in such detail long before it actually happened!

Jobs
My first paid job is for a few weeks of yard work during the summer of 1936, between finishing ninth grade at the Denver Christian School and starting high school in Littleton. My parents have lined up work for me at the upscale residence of a Mr. Burgess, an executive at the Bell Telephone Co. in Denver. Three days per week I go to his house and work for three hours. He does not tell me what work to do. He just says, "Find what needs to be done and do it." I work outside in all sorts of weather trying to look busy, sometimes actually working. Mr. Burgess has a mean Irish terrier who doesn't like me, and I don't like him. Nor do I like Mr. Burgess very much, and I never see his wife. Maybe he doesn't have one, and that may be why he has no kids, either. My pay is 15 cents per hour, bringing in the royal wage of $1.35 by the end of the week. The first time I bring this pittance to my mother, she sighs, "Oh John, is that all?" Which doesn't do my already deflated ego any good. But Mom keeps it because she really needs it.

Another time Mr. Neal Roos, Arvy's father, hires me for just one day to do some discing on his field with the use of his two horses. He promises to pay me $2 at the end of the day for this work. Again I am given a job I do not know how to do. He says, "Tell the horses 'gee' for right turn and 'haw' for left turn. Drive them straight down the field in parallel lines, turning at the ends. Make sure all the soil is *touched by the discs." This is a day that seems never to end. I am weary as a dog when I am through and hope never to be asked again. Probably I won't!*

I hardly became acquainted with money. There were still plenty of jobs for me to do, to be sure, but I did not get any money for doing them. These were the chores I was assigned in and around the house. Dad grew up helping his parents, so too my mother. I needed not to be sorry to be expected to work. I think that it is bad for a teenager to be allowed to believe that he is of no use to his parents, and that there is no worthwhile contribution for him to make to the prosperity and wellbeing of his family.

Milking an injured cow. To help keep expenses down, our family raised chickens for eggs and meat, but my father saw an opportunity to save even more by making the purchase of a heifer that was due to begin producing milk. We boys had to drive along the surrounding country roads in our Chevy coupe in order to cut stands of wild alfalfa and bring it home for our young cow to eat. Dad was the one who would do the milking, which would be in the morning before he went to his job and in the late afternoon when he came home. It took several weeks before there was much of a flow, and the best the cow ever yielded was about two quarts. Once Dad got the hang of it, he said I would have to take the afternoon shift because he was often delayed on the job. First he had me watch him massage the teats to get milk. Then he watched me, and we were in business. Two extra quarts of milk per day was a welcome supplement to our family larder.

Dad tries to make the cow get along on the alfalfa we bring in, but pretty soon we cannot find much anymore and the cow is not getting

enough. This leads her to do something real bad. She is allowed to roam the entire two and a half acres that belong to us. One day she notices some alfalfa a yard or two outside the fence and tries to get it. She pokes her head through the parallel strands of barbed wire but cannot reach it that way. Next she tries to jump over the wire and gets hung up on the top strand. Thrashing around to get free, she manages to catch one teat on a barb and rips a two-inch gash in the length of it. She comes home bawling in pain and still hungry. Then I have a real problem, "How am I supposed to milk her that way, with a long tear on one of her teats? She can hardly stand me touching it, let alone squeezing it to get the milk out!" Anyhow I try. I milk the three good teats. When Dad comes home he puts some healing salve on the wound. But neither he nor I can milk the injured teat, and before long the milk becomes clogged in it. Dad speaks to the farmer from whom he bought the heifer, and the farmer buys her back for half the price Dad gave him for her. We are all disappointed, and more than a little shocked, to see how quickly our enterprise can turn to nothing. It is a rare day when Dad gets skunked on a business deal like this!

Littleton High School. When our family moved to our house at 5280 S. University Blvd., Hank enrolled at Englewood High School while I enrolled at the High School in Littleton. Being in a tuition-paying district, we could choose which we wanted to attend. Its effect was that I had returned to the scene of our 1932 farmhouse fiasco, but with far more pleasant results.

The first thing one should note is that I must travel three miles each way to school. The choice is mine whether to walk, hitchhike, or ride a bicycle. Having acquired a new coaster-brake model from Sears Roebuck, I gladly choose the third option. This works pretty well except in hail, rain and snow. Once in a while my dad takes pity on me and drives me to school. The possession of a bike is a great liberating factor for me since I am now free to join my friend, Arvin Roos, on one or another foray into the great outdoors. One should imagine how the overpowering proximity of the Front Range of the Rocky Mountains has affected my imagination. The air is absolutely clear, allowing one to see the farthest great peak within the circle of the western horizon. From our position one can see Pike's Peak fifty miles to the south or Long's Peak fifty miles to the north -- in other words, one can see geographical points lying at least a hundred miles apart. Even more overpowering is the view directly west, a whole range of high and semi-high peaks dominated by magnificent Mount Evans. Furthermore, most of the land in the vicinity of Littleton is open range land or in farms. The sparkling clear South Platte River runs nearby, inviting me to explore along it and beyond it, as it did when I was a mere lad of four.

I have mentioned that my brief attendance at the grade school in Littleton was mainly positive -- the earliest tangible alternative to attending the Christian School in the south Denver Dutch enclave. Having experienced the entirely different setting of southern California, I now enroll in Littleton High School, which has between two hundred and three hundred students. Imagine how socially isolated I now find myself! This small high school has no official athletic program that amounts to anything. If there are plays or dances for the students, I don't know about them. By default emphasis has to be on academics. As in schools in general, Littleton High School has some poor teachers, many mediocre teachers, and a precious few good or excellent teachers. My favorite teacher is Mr. Samuelson, who is also school principal. His excellent course in Advanced Geography alerts me to the world crisis that is just at this time unfolding in Europe and the Far East.

Staining the bedroom window screen. Some questionable things we did while living at 5280 fall into the category of more or less innocent childhood mischief, but others were the product of our burgeoning adolescence. Some negative things happened simply because we lacked adequate supervision or through the arbitrariness of our elders.

Hank says it's okay, so all three of us boys do it. Instead of going downstairs at night to use the bathroom, we pee through the window screen. It isn't long before the screen begins to stink. Mom notices a strange stain on the screen and asks us directly, "Did you do this?" As much as we wish we could avoid detection, we have to say yes. Mom sets us to work with strong soap and a srubbing brush. She wishes she could scrub out our minds as easily.

Breaking into a house. This is just a figure of speech. Actually we did not break anything. All we were doing was entering a little vacation house by climbing up onto its flat roof, lifting off the hatch cover, and letting ourselves very carefully inside. In spite of appearances, we intended only to have a look to satisfy our curiosity. We would not have thought of taking or damaging anything.

Someone has built a small adobe structure on the creek behind our property at 5280 S. University. We don't know whom it belongs to, and have never even seen the owner. Nevertheless, it is so decorative and well kept inside that we know someone has spent a lot of money and effort to make it nice. The furniture and decorations follow a Mexican motif, but that does not mean that the owners are Mexicans or have actually lived in Mexico.

Climbing back out through the roof hatch isn't easy. We are not willing to stand on a chair or other piece of furniture, the reason being that we do not want the owner to be aware of our entry. We have enough sense to realize that if he should do so, he would almost certainly call the sheriff, and then there would be an investigation in which we might be implicated. We are adventurous and curious kids, not juvenile offenders.

The way we do it is to grasp the rim of the opening with our fingers turned inside toward our body and then swing our feet all the way up through the hatch and make an L, with our legs horizontal to our upper torso and head, which we then draw completely up through the hatch.

There! Hank and I are safely on the ground. We should better not do this again if we wish to stay out of trouble!

Sneaking off to the movies

We four De Vries kids, Hank, John, Bob and Ruth, are about to perpetrate a deception on our parents. Dad has lent us the family car, with Hank driving, so that we may attend a free operetta, "The Chocolate Soldier," in the Cheesman Park Pavilion. But at Hank's suggestion we are going off instead to see the movie, "Green Pastures," in an Englewood movie house. This is the first time that we have done anything like this, and our consciences suffer as a result. People are saying that this is such a wonderful movie, a true classic, and that everyone ought to see it. But there is no use in asking our parents' permission to go to it because they wouldn't allow it.

62   The 1930's: Sneaking off to the movies

As a matter of fact, Dad and Mother have been taking us to an occasional movie until quite recently, but they were so shocked at what they thought were a row of bare bosoms in "Flying Down to Rio," with Ginger Rogers and Fred Astaire, that they recanted and have declared all movies off limits. That is why it is such a pity that they won't be taking us to see "Green Pastures" or seeing it themselves. It is about the idea that Negro people have of heaven. "De Lawd" is a genial Negro grandfather type, surrounded by little Negro kids as angels and holding a fish fry for all his friends in heaven. I have misgivings about the appropriateness of depicting God is this earthy way. Isn't he supposed to be more like a magnificent king, ruling and judging the world?

I did not know how to deal with parody and artistic exaggeration. All the same, I was glad I saw this movie, even if we had to lie to our parents and as a consequence went around with a guilty conscience. It made a powerful impression on me by showing how people different from ourselves think about the Bible.

My eviction from Mr. Jump's bookbinding class. My secondary school did not neglect practical subjects. In Clearwater Junior High School in California I had had woodworking shop, tin-smithing shop, and metal-working shop. Here in Littleton High School I had a course in mechanical drawing, and later enrolled in Mr. Jump's bookbinding class, which I found interesting and educational. In each classroom session we would take a new step in manufacturing our own book cover. Mine came along very beautifully, and I expected a good grade such as A. I even embossed my book's title and author in gold letters on the front and on the spine. Nevertheless, as the course was about to end, I got into serious trouble with Mr. Jump and was thrown out of the class, an unexpected and undeserved turn of affairs.

Let me explain what happens. There is an older and larger boy in the class who takes perverse pleasure in deriding and taunting me, but never in such a way as to draw the teacher's attention. Mr. Jump is an adjunct and part-time teacher, his main job being that of funeral director. Perhaps not enough people have been dying in Littleton. Whatever the reason, he is in a grumpy mood this morning and shows that he will tolerate no monkey-business. He has us all standing next to our workbenches as he makes an important announcement. As I look at him and listen carefully to what he is saying, I notice my tormentor just beyond with his tongue out and his thumbs in his ears while wiggling his fingers. Forgetting momentarily where I am, I raise my hand and thumb my nose at him. Oops! Mr. Jump thinks that I am thumbing my nose at him! Instantly he shouts, "Get out of here! I don't want you in my class. I am going to give you an F for the course!"

Stunned by Mr. Jump's vehemence and angry that this wretched student has got me thrown out, I make my way directly to Mr. Samuelson's office to tell him what has happened. This is when I find out just how highly he regards me. He believes what I tell him and assures me that I will get full credit for the course, no matter what Mr. Jump says. Once he explains to Mr. Jump the actual state of affairs, he will no longer be angry. I hope not! Just the same, I have learned an important lesson in academic etiquette that I won't soon forget.

Unsupervised weight-lifting
I have always thought of my big brother Hank as muscular and athletic. He has what they call the "Tamminga build," being stockier and broader of shoulders than I. It's not that I am weak or slow, but I am pretty skinny and lanky. In fact, I tend to slouch. Dad is often reminding me to straighten up.

One day Hank finds out that Dr. George Parker, who is married to our cousin Ann, is teaching our cousin Billy and some other boys how to develop their muscles by lifting barbells. Hank says he wants to do it too, and asks me to come along to Dr. Parker's garage, where the weight-lifting class is being held. Although I have little confidence in my own ability, I go along. When we arrive, there are some boys lifting weights, but no Dr. Parker. Billy isn't there either. Hank tries lifting some weights. Then I try. We have no idea how much weight we should lift, or how to do it. I am puzzled and chagrined. Hank is too. After an hour, no one is there except us. We leave feeling foolish and frustrated. That is the end of weight-lifting for us! I will ever have a chance to become a real athlete!

Vernon Pinckney, a talented friend. My younger brother Bob and I enjoyed the company of Vernon Pinckney. I mentioned him before. Vernon lived a few hundred yards south on our so-called boulevard.

64   The 1930's: Vernon Pinckney, a talented friend

Two things were special about Vernon. First, he claimed that his ancestor was one of the signers of the Declaration of Independence. Second, he had loads of artistic talent and got Bob and me interested in drawing and painting.

We make male and female persons out of stiff paper and then design clothing for them, copying this from the magazine pictures. We cut out the paper figures with a scissors and make "paper dolls," whom we then clothe in these dresses and suits. This sounds girlish and sissy, but we don't worry about it. Another thing Vernon teaches us is how to create cartoons with characters and dialogue. We design and draw a real cartoon strip with our characters having things to say. We actually succeed in creating one complete sequence of framed events like the ones seen in the Sunday funnies.

This was fun for a while, but we quit when we got tired of it. Our friendship with Vernon was brought to an end when we sold our house and moved to California in 1938 for a second time. I wondered what was to happen with Vernon. With his talent, he seemed destined to become a professional artist or clothing designer. Bob later met Vernon in New York City, where he was working as an artist.

A perilous climb up Turk's Head. The Neal Roos family were living on a farm in Douglas County, near the right bank of the South Platte River, from where it was possible to get a good view to the south of a prominent crag in the Front Range of the Rockies. Arvin and I knew its name from reading maps: "Turk's Head." I did not think that it looked like a Turk's head, to me it looked more like a bent hairpin. We knew also that it was on the left, or western, bank of the South Platte. We also knew that there was a narrow-gauge railroad, mostly abandoned, following its course below it. We knew this because our Christian School picnic one Labor Day was held at a mountain park that we reached by riding up this same narrow-guage railroad.[5] Our plan was to cross the river where there was a bridge and then follow the railway bed until we reached the vicinity of Turk's Head, then climb up to it, returning by the same route. Arvin and I had no realization of how perilous it was going to be to make this climb or what the terrain would actually be like.

---

[5] Present-day Colorado Trail passes through this gap into the mountain interior.

We ride our bikes as far as we are able and then continue hiking up the railroad to where we are just below the craggy peak. However, once we leave the railroad and begin climbing, things begin to go wrong. It is far more difficult than we imagined to climb through the thick mesquite bushes growing on the slopes. We find that it is necessary to step over them because they are massed together, but one time I step high over a bush and my foot comes down on the other side squarely on top of something squishy. Simultaneously I am startled by a loud rattle. I have actually stepped on a large rattlesnake coiled asleep on the rock my foot came down on! I spring away in fright and get away as far as possible, thanking God that I have not been bitten. Fortunately, the snake seems as frightened as I am and slinks away.

This experience makes us very wary of the presence of rattlesnakes. Twice again on this hike we come close enough to rattlesnakes to hear them give their warning rattle, and make a wide berth. Our hostility towards them is thereby greatly aroused, leading us to actually kill a fourth rattler on the return, cutting off his rattle as a souvenir.

On the summit we find ourselves in pine woods and are able to make our way through relatively open ground to the craggy summit. With a brownie camera I have been given, I take a shot of the scrary look down. After *enjoying the magnificent view for a while, we head back down, but in a direction somewhat more southerly, hoping to reach the river and the railroad farther upstream and thereby save ourselves as much mesquite-hopping as possible. Where we do reach the river, however, the railroad is lying on the opposite or easterly bank. Thus to follow the river and railroad downstream involves us in struggling over very difficult terrain, with no path or track to help us. Before long we are fully exhausted and try to think whether there might be a better way. Our decision is to cross the swiftly flowing river right where we are. This turns out to be as perilous as stepping on coiled rattlesnakes because the water is very cold, very swift, and very deep -- up to our shoulders, in fact. Anyway, I try it first. I take all my clothes off, including my shoes, tie them tightly in a bundle, and throw them with a mighty heave across to the railroad bed. Then I cautiously wade in, struggling to keep my footing, and reach the opposite side in safety. Then Arv does the same. We are quite aware of the fact that, if we are swept under by the swift water, we will have to swim to avoid drowning.*

The rest of the story is anticlimax. We eventually found where the railway had crossed from the left bank of the river to the right bank. We also found our bridge, recovered our bikes, and pedaled home to the Roos farmhouse, altogether exhausted. We had a very interesting story to tell our parents and our brothers and sisters, leaving out some of the most scary details lest we be prohibited from making a trip similar to it in the future. We were fully cognizant that one or both of us might have been killed on this seemingly hazardless little hike into the mountains.

A grandiose and unrealizable scheme

It is a Sunday afternoon in the spring of 1938. Arv and I have been waiting outside the new farmhouse near Littleton, CO to which the Roos family has moved, while inside his parents and mine discuss what to do about the grandiose scheme we have proposed, which is to live the life of woodsmen-evangelists somewhere up in British Columbia and other remote parts of Canada. We want to go off on our own and live on beans and bear meat. We will travel all over, hiking or by canoe. We have in fact mapped out complete canoe routes extending from the western parts of Canada to the eastern parts. Two important elements are, however, missing from this scheme: (1) what we intend to use for money, and (2) whom we are going to evangelize and how. We have no clear idea at all about these two matters, but trust that we will be able to improvise as we go along.

We had been talking up this idea for almost two years and had now come to the point of seeking for a practical way of bringing it to reality. On a Friday in April, we agreed to put it before our respective parents that very weekend, and we both did so. That decision, at least, was practical, but what we proposed was incapable of being brought to realization. We had no money whatever. Our parents certainly wouldn't give us any, for they hadn't much themselves. But if anything were to come of our scheme, we would need to get their cooperation, and prior to that, their permission. We were not rebels, just dreamers!

After a while we are summoned inside the house to hear what our parents have to say. They cannot see how this scheme can possibly be carried out, and furthermore can find no practical value in it. Yet they recognize with great joy that we are high-minded and committed young men who deeply aspire to do God's work, even in a novel and unrealistic way such as this. What they want us to do is finish high school and then go on to college. After that we may train as missionaries, if that is what we desire, by studying at a seminary. Since I and my parents have recently shifted membership to the CRC, this will be Calvin College and Seminary for me, while Arv goes to Hope or Central, and then to Western or New Brunswick Seminary.

In spite of the element of fantasy in our scheming, we had taken an important step toward the realization of the destiny that God had in store for us.

Back to California, where we come close to being orphans. Our family expected to live at 5280 South University indefinitely, but had to give it up when Dad got the seven-year itch again! He had been hankering for California,[6] but waited to pull us up by the roots until our respective school-years ended. Finding a good buyer for the

---

[6.]Things were not going very well in the construction trade because this was 1938, the year of the so-called "Roosevelt recession."

68 The 1930's: We come close to being orphans

property, he moved us temporarily to a housekeeping unit at an Englewood motel. When the June of 1938 arrived, we departed. No one of us had any idea of the frightful experience that lurked ahead. It was destined to be a very bad time for Dad, but it was to be hard on Mother and us children as well.

This time the trip to southern California took three days rather than the six days of 1933. The day after our arrival we found a house to rent in Bellflower and moved in. Dad immediately began to scout around for the points of contact he needed in order to get started once again in the business of selling and servicing cooling machines for the dairymen, but he was not feeling well. He began to suffer with an infected right ear. It was in fact the mastoid bone behind his ear that was infected. How he got this infection, nobody could tell, but none of the familiar home remedies seemed to help. He started to run a fever, and within another day the pain had become unbearable. The only thing for him to do was check into a Veterans Hospital some miles from where we lived. Contrary to every hope and expectation, he remained there day after day and week after week, without any sign of improvement. He actually became mentally deranged from the constant and terrible pain. Without improvement, he seemed doomed to die soon. It would be only a matter of time.

We had the Martens family and some members of the Dutch community to help us, but essentially we were on our own. Mother tried to be courageous and optimistic. She had been through sickness and dying before. Every day she took a bus trip to visit Dad, but otherwise was too distraught to do much around the house. She wouldn't say it, but this time she was preparing herself for the eventuality of caring and providing for our family without Dad.

Mother tells us two older boys, Hank and me, that we must go out and look for jobs. Jobs during the Depression? "Take what you can get. We must eat, we must pay the rent." Hank finds a job at the Richfield refinery at Signal Hill, outside Long Beach, selling ice-cream, candy and tobacco from a bicycle equipped with a cold box, but soon, when he finds a better job helping Uncle Joe Martens in his house painting, I take over with the bicycle cart. It is very heavy and hard to pedal, and I have all I can do to pump it from place to place on my route. Fortunately, the refinery workers are kindly and generous. I actually find myself looking forward each day to going to work. It is helpful to me to be among friendly people during this trying time.

One day an older worker orders a box of snuff, handing over a piece of paper money. Assuming that it is a dollar bill, I fail to give it careful scrutiny and begin to count out a few coins as his change, but he says, "That's not enough change. Look at the bill I gave you!" It is a $100 bill with Benjamin Franklin's portrait on it. I am so nonplussed that I cannot think of a thing to say, but it doesn't matter because all the men break out with laughter and begin to pat me on the back because I'm a good sport about the joke they have pulled on me. I hand the $100 bill back to its owner and take a one-dollar bill from him in exchange.

It was a good thing to be able to laugh a little. I firmly expected that disaster was about to overtake our family and that I would spend the rest of my life at this kind of paltry job, trying to help support our family. Those were dark days. I feared for my dad's life. I feared for myself. I feared for our family.

In those trying circumstances, a closer bond was developing between Hank and me, based on the awesome fear of losing our father and provider.[7] It has been in adversity and trial, rather than at happy or uneventful times, that we have felt most like true brothers.

This awful stress and deprivation goes on for three months. One day Mother comes home from the hospital with good news: Dad is getting better! How we rejoice to hear it! The doctors are at last having success with the so-called wonder drug, sulfanilamide, which has recently been discovered. It is driving out the infection and Dad is beginning to be his old self again.

Finally Dad was discharged, but this sickness had been so shocking an experience for him -- as well as for us -- that he realized that he and we needed some stability, as well as a brand new start, in our more familiar surroundings in Denver. Without delay we started on the trip back to Colorado.

[7.]Many years later in 1990, at Dad's funeral, Hank and I met each other in the foyer of the funeral home prior to the service. Although we had not been accustomed to showing each other a great deal of affection, we spontaneously threw our arms around each other and began to sob. "Hank," I said, "I feel like an orphan, and now we finally are alone without our dad!" I was astonished at how strong my feelings of bereavement were. We were for the moment back in 1938 -- only now Dad was gone for good.

70   The 1930's: We come close to being orphans

Our dad is recovered, but all in all this has been a very scary experience. I have been close to becoming an orphan, and still worse, an immature orphan with the heavy responsibility of helping our entire family survive. No doubt such an experience toughens those who manage to live through it, but I am tired of the wounds and the callouses that go with such toughening!

Two wasted weeks in transition back to Denver. Dad's almost miraculous recovery from the severe mastoid infection that almost killed him in California brought us back to Colorado, but since we had no house to return to, we spent the first two weeks of September, 1938, living in Uncle Gerrit's manse in Golden while Dad and Mom looked for a suitable house in Denver. Mr. Sturgeon was glad to give Dad his old job back since he thought very highly of his work.

Our parents would have done better to have given us children freedom to run around loose rather than make us enroll in schools that would be only temporary, for in my case at least, the experience is confusing and dispiriting. For Bob and Ruth, this means a brick two-story school on the hill; for Hank and me, it means Golden High School. We enroll and start to take classes, but find it excessively hard to adjust quickly to an entirely new academic environment. Besides, the students are, and remain, utter strangers to us. One activity that I do enjoy at Golden High School is Glee Club, which offers Hank and me the opportunity to make use of our singing voices in harmony with others.

After school in Golden we find new things to explore. We go through the campus of the Colorado School of Mines, just west of Golden. We also visit the Coors Brewery on Clear Creek, east of the city. We all four together find a way to get into the junior high school where Bob and Ruth attend: climbing up a stainless-steel tube that functions as a fire escape. All we do is look, and we quickly leave for fear of getting caught. Even though we are not tempted to steal or vandalize, it is simple to see why young people like us, even when intending no wrong, get into criminal behavior through boredom and lack of supervision.

One other kind of undesirable behavior that we boys get into while lodging at Uncle Gerrit's manse is skinny-dipping in the ice-cold water of a very deep gravel pit outside the city. We do this only once. We know that such cold water can cause cramps, which may lead to death.

Twelfth grade at South High School in Denver.

Twelfth grade at South High School in Denver. Dad and Mom at last found a suitable house for us on South Washington Street in Denver. It was just adjacent to the Christian School, from which I had graduated three years previously. Once again I had to enroll in a brand new -- and this time very large -- school, South High, about half a mile away from our new residence. I was bewildered and intimidated, and my brother Hank just dropped out and looked for a job, a decision he later regretted.

I cannot exaggerate the difficulties that our family's migrant ways had come to place in the way of my academic progress. Things had gone well enough during my two years at Littleton because there was some stability and some excellent teachers, also because I had a wonderful friend and confidant in Arvy Roos. But starting out at South High after my two meaningless weeks in Golden was difficult and demoralizing.

When I enrolled at this strange and baffling new school, I was not a happy boy. I would say that I was depressed. Mom made it a humiliating experience by pushing me into applying for free textbooks on the claim of family poverty.

Do I have to wear "Poverty" as a badge? Poverty indeed! Will I ever escape it? I go through enrolment procedures, but have few choices because the classes have already been meeting for two weeks. Laconically I allow the staff to choose for me. A good selection is Art, which I find wonderfully expanding. Since I have already started Spanish in Littleton, I sign up for Spanish II and find the vivacious teacher entertaining, as well as very easy on the eyes. I take a second year of Chemistry with Mr. Collier and find it intriguing as well as educational. One course, Economics, is a real disaster. It is all about corporations and equities, which have no tangible reality for me. I am, furthermore, unable to make up the two lost weeks and end up getting an E for the course.

During the second semester I am more on the ball and sign up for courses I really want, such as Astronomy and Geology. The teacher I shall never forget is Mr. St. John. Can you imagine so wonderful a name as that? Mr. St. John takes me through the intriguing mysteries of Plane and Solid Geometry. As I prepare to graduate, I take pride in knowing that I have done rather well, considering the disruptions. Though I have no prospect whatever of being able to afford college, I do take satisfaction at having completed the necessary courses for entering college, except possibly Latin.

72   The 1930's: Twelfth grade at South High School

With all the jumping around of the past five years, I am tending to become reclusive and antisocial. I am especially discouraged at the difficulty of trying to penetrate the social cliques that more stable students have formed around their private little worlds. I want friends desperately, but because of our vagabond existence I have little confidence in my ability of finding them. I am certain that very few of the eight hundred students who will graduate from South in June will have been handicapped as I have been. No wonder, then, that my social life has been nil! I haven't gotten to know a single student except for one very flirtatious girl in Chemistry class named Donna, who only wanted to be friendly and not necessarily to stir up my hormones as she did. Or did she? There will be no need for me to attend future reunions of the class of '39. I have been in the same building with three thousand students, but hardly a one of them knows me, and I don't know anyone of them except Donna.[8]

A severe sickness. In general we had been a healthy family. When I was younger I contracted what Dr. Sickafoos called scarlet fever. The family was quarantined and I was confined to bed. Poor Dad, he was not allowed to enter the house and had to stay with one of our relatives. I remember him greeting me through the closed window. How fond a sight it was to see his smiling face! A happy surprise ending to this episode was that the doctor decided that I didn't have scarlet fever after all, just some kind of rash.

In my second semester as a high-school senior I am felled by a severe attack of another kind of sickness. I become feverish and nauseated, unable to hold down any kind of food. Doctor Sickafoos puts me to bed, predicting that I won't get out of it again for more than a week. What I have is peritonitis, an infection of the lining of the body underneath the skin. I am a very sick boy for more than a week, as the doctor predicted.

[8.]I have heard that a child's social psychology developed during high school is a virtually sure prediction of how he or she will function in social groups as an adult. In my case this has been very true. In later life I have done well in groups that I have been able to dominate -- for instance, as pastor of a church or professor in a classroom -- but I have never been able to relate as creatively with peers as I would wish. In other words, I have never learned the politics of social interaction on an egalitarian basis.

An experiment with eating undercooked beans. I got better soon, and during the ensuing summer, before I found work, I found occasion once again to enjoy my old kind of adventure with my bosom friend, Arvin Roos. As I have narrated, he and I had not been able to convince our parents that we should be allowed to go off to British Columbia to live in the wilds and evangelize the Indians and trappers. The truth is that we had not convinced ourselves, either. We proposed an experiment: let us go off into the Rockies southwest of Denver -- in the same general direction as Turk's Head but beyond it -- and stay two or three days, living off things like biscuits, beans and bacon. If we did well, that would be a start.

Having gained our parents' permission, we head out on our bicycles loaded down with supplies. The experiment is basically how well we will do with cooking staple items under wilderness conditions.

It is a long, hard climb up U.S. 285 to Shaffer's Crossing at Elk's Creek. Arv and I take advantage of slow trucks grinding in low gear to make the steep grades, towing us along as we cling to the back of these vehicles. Once we arrive at Shaffer's Crossing, we ride our bikes several miles west by northwest on a dirt road and then hide them near a fence belonging to a nearby ranch. We decide to take no chance of making ourselves known to the ranch personnel. Shouldering our heavy packs, we follow a trail that leads in the direction of Mt. Evans, about ten miles to the northwest.

We do have a lot of enjoyment. The best is when we climb to the top of a prominent mountain[9] lying above timberline in the vicinity of Mt. Evans. Up on top, we see that great peak so near that we can almost reach out and touch it. It is gigantic and awe-inspiring. What a view! What an inspiration!

When we come down from this high perch we realize that things have not been going well in the commissary department. The pot of beans we set to soak are still hard. Since we must have food and we are ravenously hungry, we set them over a fire anyway, trying to cook them just as they are -- trying to defy nature. Stupidity is the offspring of desperation. It doesn't work, of course. The beans are still hard after two hours of cooking! Besides, they are now half burnt. After another six hours they are burnt black and completely

---

[9] Probably Meridian Hill, 11,490 feet above sea level

74   The 1930's: An experiment with undercooked beans

inedible. We are forced to survive on raisins and cookies, which had not been intended as staples.

That was just the first day. We hung on for a second day, trying to cook new batches of beans. Fortunately we had made an appointment to be rescued on the third day. Both sets of parents were at the rendezvous point with lots of our two moms' delicious cooking!

So much for our chances of living on beans and bear meat! British Columbia will have to wait.

I get headed towards the ministry
At Arvin Roos's house, where I often go, we listen to good gospel music on the radio. We are both thrilled at the kind of spiritual songs that mention the joy of being saved and spending eternity in heaven. We also enjoy singing these songs ourselves. The ones that soar up high are our favorites, such as "When they ring those golden bells" and "The lost chord."

Years ago Uncle Gerrit, who was a Presbyterian minister, said to me that I had great aptitude and intelligence for the ministry. I had not forgotten that, in fact I thought of it often. Although Arvin Roos and I had made an early confession of faith, this did not in itself imply that we began thinking of ourselves as future ministers. On the contrary, our "magnificent obsession" about becoming woodsmen-evangelists up in Canada implied just the opposite. We certainly did not think of ourselves as leading church services and doing things that ordained ministers typically do. We were less in love with lost souls than with the threatened ecology. What we actually wanted was to save forests, not people. When we tried to persuade our respective parents to back us in this, they very wisely refrained from ridicule and used our forwardness as an opportunity to get us interested in actually going to school and studying to become missionaries or evangelists. More than that, they led us away from the idea of going to a school like Moody Bible Institute and turned us to the idea of college and seminary within our respective denominations. Thus Arvin and I meekly accepted a plan that would put us on parallel but separate paths.

If I ever obtain funds for it, I shall be headed for Calvin College and Seminary, Arv will go to Central College and New Brunswick Seminary. The phantasy of paddling our canoe through remote northern lakes is beginning to dissolve. We won't be in any canoe, we won't even be in the same schools! The fact is that Arv and I are committed to some sort of Christian ministry through our parents' decision. I say this as a tribute to our two sets of godly parents rather than as criticism of what they have done. They have shown us the pathway that they could identify as the pathway of God's covenant.

Children are often led to follow a special vocation of Christian or other altruistic service through what their parents say and do. Both Arvin and I had a worthy role-model within our respective family circles who had previously been committed to the Christian ministry. Arv's grandfather Rev. Frederick Dekker was a well-known RCA minister, and I of course had Uncle Gerrit. It was true that Uncle Gerrit gave me the impression that he was not happy with being a parish minister. It was not even clear that he was more satisfied with ministry in the Presbyterian Church than he might have been in the Christian Reformed Church, in which he was brought up. Uncle Gerrit could not have taken the path into ministry that he took except for two factors: (1) he must have deliberatly rejected the idea of going to Calvin Seminary and becoming a Christian Reformed minister, and (2) he must have been strongly influenced by some person unknown to me whom he deeply admired and respected.

It is a striking coincidence that Uncle Gerrit received his bachelor's degree in theology at Princeton Seminary and then stayed another year to get an S.T.M. in Old Testament -- a pattern I was destined to repeat in my own future studies, though entirely without foresight, planning, or even awareness on my part.

Be that as it may, Uncle Gerrit had not fitted very well into the Presbyterian denomination. He seemed unhappy in his Golden congregation -- discouraged and unfulfilled. He certainly would have desired the support and approval of his brothers and sisters living close by in Denver, yet they never said anything, at least in my hearing, about his being a Presbytertian minister.

I would very much like to learn sometime why and how Uncle Gerrit left the CRC, went to Princeton rather than Calvin, and became a Presbyterian minister. How did his parents accept this? No one ever talks about these issues in my hearing, and I get the impression that everyone is too embarrassed about it to discuss it. Is Uncle Gerrit a shining white knight gone astray? I would say that our mother is closer to this brother than the other brothers and sisters are. She shares a variety of social activities with him and often seeks his company. Perhaps she is more sympathetic with his separation from the CRC because she and Dad once took a similar step in joining, and then remaining in, First Reformed Church.

It was during my twelfth grade at South High School that I came under another kind of influence, that of Rev. Rens Hooker, pastor of the newly formed Second CRC, of which our family had become members. Rev. Hooker persuaded me to join his advanced class in Christian Doctrine once a week in the Christian school. As I have mentioned, this was just across the alley from our house. I did distinguish myself in this class and delighted in it as a special spiritual opportunity. In effect, Rev. Hooker became my private tutor, seeming to enjoy as much as I the discussions we had about the church and the world.

All in all, I have become ripe plucking in God's garden, but as yet with no one to pluck me. The present prospects for my going to college are dismal. The Great Depression is still going strong. Many heads of families are still out of work, hence there is little place for the young people just now coming into the labor pool. Few, however bright, will make it into college. Nevertheless, momentum has been building toward something new that God may have been preparing for me. It is hard for me to believe that I have come so far to no purpose.

A summer job at a mountain mink ranch. Graduating from South High School in June of 1939, I had no prospects whatever of going to college for the foreseeable future. My parents had no money for this, and I had no money at all. Nevertheless I had to find gainful work to do. First I worked two days at a nearby farm helping to cut and stow away baby's breath (a whole field of it!) in a barn for eventual sale to florists. Then I worked a week in tandem with my brother Hank digging a huge hole at a rendering plant on Denver's north side; it was for a large scale for weighing trucks that would come into this unbelievingly vile-smelling place carrying sick hogs to be made into serum. I then worked a week at Bethesda Sanatorium. Uncle Gerrit had resigned his parish and had taken a temporary job as business manager, and he had employment for me, writing lists of donors to the institution. But that job, like the others, did not last. Uncle Gerrit was at the moment considering, and soon accepted, an appointment to teach Bible at Pike College in Pikesville, KY.

I was next rescued from unemployment through my mother's effort and with the help of Uncle Gerrit. The Ritchie family, members of his church in Golden, owned a mink ranch in the mountains above Golden. Mrs. Ritchie happened to be in love with Uncle Gerrit, which may be one reason why he quit his parish. Of course this had nothing directly to do with my job. Maybe Mom had been making use of her friendship with the Ritchies, maybe it was a matter of their having had a bad conscience over Uncle Gerrit. Anyhow, they gave me a job for the remainder of the summer. I was to clean the cages of a small army of mink and do other chores as needed. For this I received a small wage plus meals with the farm manager and his wife, who lived on the premises. My own lodging for the summer was a wall tent with a cot and a few other articles of furniture, pitched away from the animals in a stand of pine trees on a hilltop.

I do very much enjoy the solitude and beauty that go with spending my evenings in pristine and inspiring surroundings. I become like a hermit, reciting Scripture and singing hymns for my own entertainment and edification. Almost every night, coyotes come near my tent, howling at the moon and stars. I am not afraid of them. I actually like them. I cannot say as much for the mink I have to attend to day by day. "Perhaps they know they are going to be made into fur coats," I think, "and are mad at the world, and especially me. That may be why they are always trying to bite me." Mink truly are vicious animals. I have to wear heavy leather gloves in handling them, and often get bitten in spite of them.

My job terminated at the end of August. I returned home with bitten fingers, to be soaked in epsom salts. I was glad to be home, but there was change and unrest in the air. Germany had just invaded Poland. My brother Henry had enlisted in the Marines. I wondered what was to happen to me now.

The 1930's: I arrive at my apparent destiny

I arrive at my apparent destiny. Just when I had returned home from the mink farm, and without any prospect for further employment, God intervened in the person of Rev. William Haverkamp, who had been preaching and lecturing in Denver for several days. Something led Dad and Mom to attend one of these occasions, where they had the opportunity to speak to him about me and got some advice on how to proceed in getting me enrolled in Calvin. They could not have chosen a better situated or disposed person. It so happened that Rev. Haverkamp was a close friend of Uncle Jack, our mortician uncle in Grand Rapids. This led him to suggest that Uncle Jack might have a room for me in his house, or might know of one. Rev. Haverkamp promised, if this should work out, to take me as his companion on the train to Chicago and then drive me in his car to Grand Rapids, where he had to attend a meeting. Dad and Mom jumped at this chance. They got Grandma De Vries to accept me as her boarder at a very minimal price, one that they could manage to provide. They also got me to agree.

So I set out for Grand Rapids in the company of this kindly and distinguished Christian Reformed clergyman. We talked religion and theology all the way to Chicago and beyond. Good as his word, Rev. Haverkamp brought me to Grand Rapids, introducing me first to Uncle Jack and Aunt Alice, then to my grandmother, who had been living alone in a small house since Grandpa died in 1932. The following day Uncle Jack drove me to Calvin to get me enrolled. I did not know which courses to sign up for and meekly accepted the advice to take those that were required in the Pre-Seminary program: Latin, English, History, Public Speaking, Reformed Doctrine.

A family all together for the last time

I have now got through most of this first semester, and my studies are going well. However, I still feel lonely in a strange new environment. I don't have any close friends at Calvin because I am so new. Grandma is very kind to me, but her way of life is very plain and austere. There is no entertainment for me, nothing but study, study, study. I do enjoy Uncle Jack and his family, who occupy a stately mansion at the corner of Eastern and Hall. This is their funeral home as well as their private residence. I enjoy especially the children of the family, Betty and Con, along with their pet dog. I am invited to be part of all that goes on in their home. They are probably just as pious as my Grandma is, but they are more open-

minded and manage to get more enjoyment out of their simple manner of life. To be sure, the special reputation with which I have come here gives them high expectations of me. It has also played into Grandma's hand perfectly. She is extremely pious and also very rigid in her way of life. For example, I am allowed to write letters on Sunday, but forbidden to mail them.

Dad and Mom send Grandma five dollars each week for my board and room. In addition, I am obligated to help Grandma in every way I can. I do not yet have a good job, but the Calvin authorities employ me as janitor and general maintenance person, paying me the grand sum of thirty-five cents per hour under the NYA (National Youth Administration) program. I will also be making application to my classis during the spring for the student subsidy they have made available for worthy pre-seminarians.

As the year 1939 draws to a close I find myself on Christmas vacation in my parents' home on South Ogden Street. The tumultuous decade of the thirties is about to come to an end. My older brother is in the Marine Corps and no doubt will see plenty of fighting. He is here on furlough. I have enrolled in the college that will prepare me for ministry in the CRC.

Heavy snow has fallen to make it look like Christmas, yet we all feel that our close little family, which has come through so much together, may now be together for the last time. Hank must go off to sea duty after leaving here, and it seems very probable that the war that has started in Europe will draw him and many other young men like him into the conflict. How proud we are of our brave brother dressed in his Marine blues! My future is less apparent. If our country stays out of this war, I will likely be able to complete my college program within the next four years and avoid entering the war altogether. After that will come seminary. Hank seems better adjusted to his role than I am to mine. How it came about that I am now a freshman at Calvin College in Grand Rapids, MI must certainly be recognized as an act of special Divine providence on my behalf.

So I am on my way! Things are still hard, but looking up. How interesting that the Calvin basketball team is called the "Knights!" I'll never get into basketball, I have no training for it. But I have great faith that God will open up the future so that I may become what I am certain he wants me to be: his own shining white knight!

4
The Nineteen Forties --
When I Become a Man

New experiences and influences. One will be able to tell from the unusual length of this chapter that the 1940's must have been the most momentous decade of my life, and that is true. Going away to college and then seminary, with a hitch in the military service in between, made a man out of me and prepared me for an unusual career.

I have read that many of the returning veterans of the Civil War, having been recruited from dull lives on farms or in small villages, and having returned to a dull life afterwards, were quite sure that their entire lives -- at least the only part that mattered to them -- had been lived during those few months and years while the nation was covering itself with blood and glory on the battlefields of that war. I can understand the feeling, even though neither my life before I got involved in World War II, nor my life afterward, could be described as dull and uneventful. The way I would put it is that my war experience -- even though I was not directly involved in fighting -- gave meaning, perspective and poignancy to both my previous and my subsequent years. By interrupting my progress towards a life as a minister or missionary, it put my entire sense of calling into a broader framework of understanding.

Others might think that my being called to war would have seemed to me a contradiction of what I believed to be God's call to the Christian ministry in general, and to a career as missionary in particular, but that is not how I interpreted it. Instead I took the broader view that God knew what he was doing and would eventually set it all straight. All I could do was follow duty and maintain integrity, and leave the rest to him. I was so fortunate that I did not have to solicit counsel from super-pious people like my Grandma or some of the professors at Calvin College. Instead I had Betty, with her strong sense of moral purpose and her willingness to stand by my side even to the point of participating in some of the anxieties, unheavals and discomforts that came especially for the wives of servicemen during the War. God did definitely use her as my guide as well as my intimate companion, both during the War and afterward.

I had never been quite sure that I did wish to become a missionary. That notion had been a peripheral element in the scheme that my friend Arvin Roos and I had earlier conceived. It was in fact my parents and his parents who seized upon our mention of evangelizing somebody as an offer on our part to actually become evangelists or missionaries, and of course my super-saint grandmother and her flock in Grand Rapids took it over without further discussion as the career that I had definitely chosen. A young woman who boarded at Uncle Jack and Aunt Alice's place naturally heard of this and immediately took me off to the Mission Society at Calvin College, of which I was eventually elected president -- a heady experience for me!

Grandma De Vries was meanwhile subjecting me to her all-encompassing grasp of Christian piety. From her example of absolute devotion I was inclined to give God one-hundred percent of all my own thoughts and aspirations. This unrestricted consecration made my life like that of a monk in his convent or a hermit in his cell.

There was, as a matter of fact, something soothing and therapeutic in this sharply focused pattern of piety. When I first came to Calvin as a freshman, I was dispirited, confused, and inwardly troubled. Spiritually speaking, I was already a weazened old man. I had missed much of the opportunity for personal and social growth that is normally experienced when one passes through adolescence. Boarding with my grandmother away from my parental home delivered me from many of my previous perplexities. My Grandmother was not perplexed or mixed up -- not at all! She knew perfectly well *who* she was and *whose* she was, and she believed that nothing else mattered. She offered me this possibility in her routine of an austere Christian life. By example and precept, she encouraged me to live a life without question or uncertainty, a life on the way towards complete and perfect sanctification!

Nevertheless, I was not ready to be the saint Grandma wanted to make of me. There was still the adventuresome little boy in me, still the tough little kid fighting to survive against odds, searching in the dark and hoping to break through to the light.

Three important things happened during my Junior year at college that radically modified my own image of how I was to render service to God in this world. The first was relatively trivial when measured by its impact on my external way of life, but it did have a profound effect on my personal sense of worth and calling. This was the disappointing and embarrassing experience of my miserable failure in selling Bibles. *Bibles, mind you!* They should be the easiest for a true man of God to sell. But in an entire month of trying I had actually sold only one Bible! I was so ashamed that I bought three

New experiences and influences 85

additional copies for myself or to give to others, just to make my pathetic sales record look better. All the same, I could not fool myself. I knew I had failed -- I, Grandma's little saint and the rising star of the foreign mission field!

I shall never know whether I might have done better as a Bible salesman under more favorable circumstances, but if I was to fail, it was good in the sense of forcing me to come to grips with the question whether I actually did possess the gifts and determination necessary to succeed in this very difficult task. Certainly it was better that I disappointed the Kirkbride Bible people than that I should disappoint my Lord Jesus Christ in bringing his cause to shame and ruin somewhere on an actual mission field! This sobering experience taught me that I was no guaranteed, automatic success as God's shining white knight!

The second drastic change that came about during my Junior year at college was the rising of Betty Schouten as a brilliant daystar on the horizon of my expectations. No more than a month or two after I had hitchhiked home from Iowa like a dog with his tail between his legs, Betty came into my life, and from that moment up to the present, she has filled all my days with purpose and a sense of completion. She took me out of my isolation. She rescued me from Grandma's overpowering piosity. She helped me get a broader view of the career that God might have in store for me. One day, after she had introduced me to her parents, Betty asked her dad to tell her whether he thought that I was perhaps too orthodox Christian Reformed to allow her to be happy with in marriage, and to this question her father's answer was both perceptive and timely: "Just be patient with him. He has very good stuff in him, and I know that he is going to turn into someone you will be proud and happy to be associated with!" I have always been grateful for that trust and insight.

The third drastic change that came about during my Junior year was our country's entrance into World War II. Betty and I both remember vividly what our thoughts were as we listened fearfully to the announcement on Sunday, December 7, 1941, that Pearl Harbor had been bombed by the Japanese. When President Roosevelt announced a Declaration of War against Japan, Germany and Italy, we felt deeply within us the inchoate dread that this war could -- and perhaps would -- separate us from each other, frustrate our plans, and throw our future into confusion.

The 1940's: New experiences and influences

In what is to follow I shall tell about the War -- that is, the part that affected me. Suffice it for me to say that I am proud that I did well as a Marine officer and certainly never conducted myself in such as way as to bring discredit on myself or on those associated with me. The War helped me do some of the growing up that I hadn't gotten around to. When I returned to civilian life after the War, I was fully able to take on a man's duty to my wife and child, as well as to be both serious and competent at the seminary and in the church with which I was to be affiliated. No longer was I content to let others call the shots for me or allow myself to fall back into someone else's accepted mode of orthodoxy and piety. That would not be because I was some kind of rebel, but because I was now my own man. It seems strange to hear myself saying this, but so it was! God remained supreme in my thoughts and in my allegiance, but no one was going to tell me how I was to serve and obey him.

My life with Grandma De Vries

After four years of eating Grandma's food, the most charitable thing I can say about it is that it is unpalatable and hard to digest. Largely by necessity, she skimps on her food budget in order to get by. For instance, she sends me to the meat market on Saturdays with instructions to buy the very cheapest ground beef in the case, the one with 40% fat. Or the cheapest roast, the very tough one, full of bone, gristle, and fat. Fresh vegetables are rarely included in our Sunday dinner, and there is never anything resembling salad. We do get lots of good potatoes. The Dutch always insist on this; and besides, Grandpa used to import potatoes from the Netherlands in large gunny sacks when he had his grocery store in Denver. Grandma always cooks potatoes the same way: in large chunks and by boiling. To go with this she prepares a gravy which is clear yellow except for a very thin layer of brown material on the bottom, where it is hard to get. Actually, Grandma considers it impolite to fish around for the brown stuff. If you want some, you have to take a lot of yellow fat with it. My mother told me that it is pure suet. I wonder if it was because of eating lots of it that Grandpa died of phlebitis and coronary thrombosis when only 65. Grandma herself is grossly fat and has diabetes as a result, which means that she does not eat cakes or pies, and therefore neither do I.

I would have improved my diet if I had accepted Grandma's offer of a thick porridge which she regularly prepared. It was made with oatmeal and buttermilk, and laced with corn syrup. Grandma consumed this in great quantities. The southern Netherlanders call it "botermelksepap" and the Frisians call it "soepenbrei." Whatever the etymology, both words have the same meaning.

Occasionally Grandma would also serve "krentebrei," made from barley and currants, or "riesenbrei," made from rice and milk. I used to eat both of these at home and loved them, so I rejoiced when Grandma put either one on the table. She never, never made coffee. Her tea was virtual poison because she allowed it to set percolating all day on a small warmer, covered with a tea cozy or "theemuts," as she would call it. Generally I got enough milk because it was reasonably cheap, and I absolutely lived on fresh apples, which Grandma bought by the bushel at one dollar or one dollar-fifty in order to make sauce of them. Another nutritional source was Aunt Alice's cooking, which was varied, well prepared, and nutritious. I should add, "delicious." At least once a week she would invite me to her place. She probably realized that Grandma was virtually starving me.

Grandma's house at 1346 Butler Avenue, SE was cluttered and shabby. She and I shared the downstairs. Upstairs were a kitchenette, a bedroom, and a shared bathroom which she rented to a married couple, and another bedroom rented to an aging bachelor, George Wierenga.

My bedroom-study was tiny, just large enough for a single bed and a small desk. It also had a small closet that was adequate for my wardrobe because I possessed hardly any clothes. There was a small bathroom between my bedroom and hers where once a week I was permitted to take a bath. Grandma never used the tub because she was so obese.[1] Instead she gave herself sponge-baths. She thought she was clean, but she wasn't. Evidently she did not do a thorough job on her "smelly parts," with the result that it was more pleasant to be in front of her than behind her!

Grandma's bedroom had windows on the side and front. Opposite it was a small living room with a sofa, an overstuffed chair, and sun-

---

[1] An outrageously funny story -- evidently true -- tells that her sister Djoke, twice as big as she, got stuck in this bathtub and was pulled out by Uncle Jack, who had to come in through the window.

dry other pieces of furniture. That was where she kept her one pet, a canary. Behind the living room was the kitchen, where Grandma spent more than fifty percent of her total time. It had a stove, a refrigerator, a round oak table with four straight chairs, a sink and some cupboards. All of this was very old fashioned, even for the 'forties. There was also a cluttered basement which contained a coal furnace that I was called upon to stoke with low-grade coal during the winter. Outside there was a one-stall garage. There was space for a garden, but Grandma planted neither vegetables nor flowers.

As I have said, all was shabby and drab. There were no bright colors anywhere and no white. All was the color of clay or dirty sheep's wool. There was a musty smell everywhere. Long ago, apparently, Grandma gave up trying to keep this house clean and attractive, and I did not volunteer to take over the task. Nothing was ever repainted or freshened up. Every article was kept until the paint wore off or the fabric became threadbare. To be sure, I did sweep the floors with broom and carpet-sweeper. There was no vacuum cleaner. I also washed the windows for Grandma, inside and out, once each year. I mowed the grass, cleared the sidewalks of snow, and took care of the storm-windows.

During the entire period in which I boarded with Grandma, she was reasonably ambulatory for an overweight person in her seventies. However, this involved little more than getting in and out of Uncle Jack's car when she would be taken to his house for something special, plus walking back and forth to church ever so slowly, with her hand grasping my arm, twice on Sunday. She also went regularly to the weekly meetings of the Ladies' Bible Class with the help of other members. Fortunately, Oakdale CRC was only three short half-blocks away: a half block at our end of Butler Ave., then a half block on Temple St., and again a half block on the eastern half of Butler Ave., beyond where it separates into two parallel streets. For a person who was rather grossly fat, Grandma was surprisingly healthy. At least she appeared so, though appearances could be deceiving. For a while she suffered from a painful palsy in her cheek, which had to be operated on at the University Hospital in Ann Arbor. As I have said, she was diabetic and needed to take medicine to control it.

I am not aware of Grandma's finances. I have the idea that Uncle Jack helped her keep her records straight, and for all I know, he may have given her a small amount on a regular basis to help her out. I am not aware whether the officials at Oakdale church were assisting her from their Deacons' Fund. I suppose that she had a small savings account, and of course she owned the house, clear and free, unless she had a "reverse mortgage." After all, she and Grandpa were not destitute. Grandpa had been engaged during his latter years in acquiring and selling real estate. But one should realize that very little profit was to be made from old houses during the Depression years. Certainly, I had no reason to think that Grandma was able to make a profit from the pittance that she received for my keep.

Although I would be away during the summer months, Grandma did not become lonely. Besides Uncle Jack, who came to see her almost daily, there were Mr. Wierenga and the other renters upstairs. She often invited Mr. Wierenga for afternoon tea, and he was always good company. He existed on perpetual church assistance because he had a neurological condition that prevented him from working. He would trap the numerous fat squirrels that inhabited the large trees outside our place and turn them over to Grandma for her, me, and himself to feast on. They said that this was illegal. I was inclined to say that it was a virtual necessity. Anyway, I enjoyed the squirrel meat.

For a man as timid as George Wierenga was, it was a small wonder that he actually dared attack these animals. He had a gunny sack which he placed over the opening of his trap when he had caught a squirrel. He would hit the trap with a stick to scare the animal into the sack and would then tie the opening. He would head to the upstairs bathroom where he would beat the squirrel to death, after which he would skin and dress it. But one time he did not beat long or hard enough and the squirrel revived. It leapt out and started running up the walls. When Mr. Wierenga tried to catch it, it slashed him with its claws and drew blood. Eventually it was driven out an open window, and thus survived for another day. But not to be caught in another trap because Mr. Wierenga was so shaky and disturbed from this violent experience that he was instantly converted to a no-squirrel diet.

In addition to regular visitors, Grandma had relatives from far away who visited her on occasion. There were cousins and nephews from the East, and in addition one or another of her children from out west, such as my father and mother, who occasionally visited her. When he came, my dad was always in a hurry to go again. He was "antsy" about participating in Grandma's daily routine. Not at all so restless were two of Dad's siblings, Aunt Trina from California and Uncle Joe from Denver. When they came, it was for "a time, two times, and a half a time," as the Bible puts it. In other words, they came to stay, not to visit, just as in the old days at home when they were children. No wonder, because from my observation these two of my dad's siblings were the worst-adjusted and immature of her offspring, age notwithstanding. Aunt Trina usually drove Grandma almost crazy with her complaining. Uncle Joe was a hopeless hypochondriac. And of course, both were great spongers. After weeks or even months of this, Uncle Jack would generally have to throw them out.

The reason why I am mentioning these rather unsavory facts is their bearing on my own situation as a paying guest in Grandma's small house. It was always I who was obliged, in the name of Christian charity and out of reverence for my elders, to give up my room and my bed while this went on. Meanwhile, I still needed a quiet place to study and just a bit of privacy. I usually ended up studying overtime at the Calvin library. Where I slept was on the sofa.

I have been painting in this background in some detail in order to prepare for my main subject, which is how Grandma and I related in daily commucation with each other. Grandma was a great talker -- not quite gabby, but full of thoughts and words of solemnity and worth. We talked Christian doctrine. We talked Bible interpretation. Most of all, we talked old times in the Netherlands. Grandma grew up in the quaint city of Bolsward in the west of Friesland. Because its canals often freeze hard in the winter, it was one of the "eleven cities" visited on the annual ice race, in which Grandma herself was once a female champion. As she would tell me things like this, I began to see the vivacious and pretty girl in the flabby old woman. She told me that her father refused to attend church during her early childhood, but later underwent a profound conversion experience, following which he had a special zeal for the Lord and his church. Her father became, in fact, the full-time "koster" or custodian of the local Gereformeerde Kerk.

Grandma informed me of how she met Grandpa, who worked as a house-painter in Workum, his home town in the province of Friesland. She told of falling in love with him and becoming engaged; of waving him off on a ship to America; of her own sea voyage a year or so later, and of their wedding the next day after her own arrival; of her children at home as they grew up. But most of all, Grandma told me of her profound love for Christ and of her happy assurance that she belonged to him forever.

My grandmother was unusually intelligent -- even brilliant in her untutored way. She read constantly. She thought theologically. Most importantly, her God was no abstract Power, but a living person with whom she lived in intimate, trusting fellowship. Her fifteen-minute audible prayers as she knelt beside her bed at night were a wonder to listen to.

If I have inherited anything at all from my Grandma, it is her godly intellect and her power to grasp theological meaning in all of reality. Another positive trait is her very loving concern for, and cheerful intimacy with, her family, her neighbors, and her fellow church members. Her Calvinistic doctrine may have made her a particularist, but this love for other human beings makes her an universalist. This is another trait that I covet for myself.

Thus the good side of my living with a very unusual sort of grandparent will surely be that I have been given a marvelous example of Christ-centered life and thought. This is bound to affect the career that I have chosen for myself. But there is a negative side, also. I am too tightly tied to her. She dominates my life too much. In a way of saying, she places her scent on everything that is important in my existence. People who see us walking solemnly to church together suppose that I am entirely like her, that I am just her shadow, that I am her grown-up "little man." There is praise in this, but also blame. In short, I am being created in her image in ways that I am not comfortable with.

Maybe the most negative effect of the kind of life I am living with Grandma is the fact that my opportunity to socialize with other young people has become stunted, narrowed, and truncated. After all the insecurities and disruptions of my teen years in California and Colorado, I need to be more with people my own age. I need others like myself who can share with me the experience of changing from a boy into a man! In effect, I am being robbed of my youth.

I have had no chance to mingle with teen-agers in a normal way or become interested in teen-age things. First I am a juvenile who is too much burdened with the adult cares and worries of getting through poverty and joblessness; now I am placed in daily contact with a super-pious grandparent, skipping an entire generation.

I should have been allowed to live in a dorm, co-op or lodging house, where I could have mingled every day with my peers. But of course that would have been impossible! I had to go to Calvin if I were to go to college at all; I had to board with Grandma because we couldn't afford anything better. In fact, I could not have gone to college at all had I not been preparing for the ministry -- that or nothing!

This should not be taken as complaining. I am not griping or finding fault. I fully realize that what I got is far, far better than the nothing I would have had otherwise. But facts are facts. I am getting to think like an old person rather than like a teenager. I know, that is exactly how my own father had to grow up, in his case straight from grade school into supporting himself as an adult.

When I say that I need companionship with persons of my own age, I have mainly in mind young men. In matter of fact I have chosen the company of a few such as my special friends: Harry Vander Aa and Douglas Paauw, for instance. But they are actually loners like me. We mainly serve to confirm each other in our mutual isolation from the main stream of social events. In this respect, these friends are replicas of what Arvin Roos once was for me and I was for him!

But God, knowing my deep need for stimulating and vital companionship, sent me someone special to lead me out of isolation and social abnormality -- another female! Suddenly, Betty and I encountered each other, and from that moment forward the problems that I have mentioned began to fade into relative unimportance. When I introduced Betty to Grandma, Grandma immediately sensed that a female of even greater potency for forming my mind and personality had entered the arena! I would gradually begin to think more like Betty and less like my grandmother. But in matter of fact, I consciously strove to take from each the best she had to offer: from Grandma, an all-encompassing piety; from Betty, a vivacious engagement with life. To me, God was present in the one as well as in the other. Both the one and the other remained part of me.

Financing my studies. It was rough going for me financially when I started my college courses. Fortunately, I was charged an incredibly small sum, only $17.50 per semester, because I came from far-away Colorado. The college had a sliding scale of charges that took into account the relative remoteness of members from far-away churches, who paid their synodical quotas equally but failed to benefit as members of nearby churches could from the relative proximity of the college to their homes. Local and nearby students therefore paid full tuition, and non-CRC students like Betty Schouten, my future fiancée, paid a surcharge. My dad paid Grandma $5 weekly for my board and room until I started receiving student support from the classis. I was paid thirty-five cents per hour by the NYA for cleaning the boy's and girls' lavatories and for washing windows. I did the first with all the dignity I could command under the circumstances, and the second with a flair. My working buddy, a guy with the unbelievable name of Karel De Waal Malefyt, and I paired off with each other using a jury-rigged balancing platform; the outside worker would wash the outside of the panes while the inside person sat on the inner extension of the platform to balance it. We took turns at this. Passing students would kid us about whose obituary they should expect to read next in the *Grand Rapids Press*. After a while I got a more substantial and dignified job as a salesman in the college bookstore under the gracious Ruth Imanse as manager. Ruth was a swell girl and we got along just fine. She later married Professor Thedford Dirkse.

Somewhat later I sold sporting goods for Sears Roebuck and waited tables for conventioneers at the Pantlind Hotel Annex -- a job I soon lost because I got caught soliciting tips for our group of waiters. They put me up to it -- said it was my turn -- but I paid for it by losing my job.

During my senior year I was to work four hours 5 days a week at Keeler Brass, which was manufacturing metal articles for the military. I just dreaded the first job I had there: working the mammoth punch presses. I would place the piece to be fabricated on the die, then trip a pedal with my foot to bring the hammer crashing down. To make sure that the operator's hand would be out of the way, a movable guard would sweep by just before the hammer struck.

I would have died of jangled nerves if I had been forced to stay on that job! Fortunately, I was soon transferred to more interesting and lucrative work that involved painting and finishing manufactured articles, also for the military service. Over the whole country, small factories like this were working steadily to supply the needs of our national war effort, and I was glad to make good money while contributing in this way.

I was not allowed to preach in churches, as I was later to do while in seminary. The work I did in missions was of course *gratis*. I therefore needed to get a good job each summer in order to get by during the schoolyear ahead. After the Freshman year I was being supported partially by the student-aid fund of Classis Pella in the amount of $850 annually, but this was far from adequate for my needs. I had to sign a promissory note to repay this subsidy in full in the eventuality of my not becoming a Christian Reformed minister, or failing to remain such for a minimum of five years. Of course that was no worry since I had no intent of becoming anything else.

Visiting my friend Arvin Roos at college. This took place in 1940, and it was not a social visit that I was making. I was taking advantage of Arvin Roos's hospitality while I checked in with the classis that I belonged to as a member of Second CRC in Denver, Classis Pella. The classis was in its spring session at Leighton, IA, a few miles southeast of the city of Pella. I had to appear before them to apply for student aid as a preseminary student at Calvin College. I had been able to find a free ride from Grand Rapids. Arvin graciously invited me to lodge for a night or two in his co-op, and I got my meals at the Central College dining hall as a guest of Arvin.

Arvin Roos and I have been staying in touch through regular letter-writing. We compare notes on the courses we are taking, such as Greek. Arv still claims that we should both remain woman-haters, and thus far nothing has changed sufficiently in my life to make me want to drop this cardinal point of our ideological self-definition. As I spend these few days with Arvin, I recognize though how good it was of our parents to squelch our wild scheme and encourage us to go to college and seminary -- separate colleges and seminaries, as it turned out. We definitely did need to get away from each other and cultivate other friendships, both with boys and with girls.

A change had to come when we inevitably discovered that we actually did enjoy the company of women too much to hate them. And sure enough, we both got into dating. Arv discovered his

Augusta and I discovered my Betty. Arvin and Augusta became parents of four children. They both graduated from Central College and he studied for the ministry at New Brunswick Theological Seminary following an intervening stint as a waste gunner on a B-17, with thirty missions over German controlled territitory.

Looking back, I recognize that we had been confused. We didn't actually despise women, we despised the plundering of nature, which we rationalized in typical adolescent fashion as a consequence of human population expansion. The way we wished to protect nature would be to discourage uncontrolled human reproduction. If truth be told, we were not as much concerned with doing the work of the church as with saving God's great and good creation, a far more difficult assignment.

My first date
I am so out of it socially that I do not even try to date a girl until my freshman year at Calvin is almost past. I am wondering whether I will end up celibate the way Arvy wants us to be, but it so happens that Uncle Jack and Aunt Alice's student boarder, Dorothy Westra, introduces me to a pretty local girl named Mildred Gritter, and I wind up asking her to accompany me to a Thespian play at Ottawa Hills High School. The Thespians are the Calvin drama group. We both enjoy the play, but this will be our last date because neither of us apparently cares enough about the other to continue the relationship.

I wonder whether I shall dare tell Arvin this when I write. It is probably best that I don't. He is the last person I want to have scolding me!

I become active in the Mission Society. Again it was Dorothy Westra who got me into a social group at Calvin, the Mission Society, and at the last meeting of the year I was elected vice-president. I suppose I deserved the honor because I did have a zeal for missions. The Mission Society often invited missionaries to speak or show slides with what we called the "Magic Lantern." The club sponsored charitable visits to such institutions as the Kent County Infirmary and encouraged its members to become active in local mission work.

The kind of girls that I meet at the Mission Society tend to be daughters of ministers or daughters of missionaries. I become very good friends with Jean and Connie Dykstra, and with Eunice Smith, whose respective parents are veteran missionaries in China. The only one of these three girls that I try to date is Eunice. She is very blonde and very pretty. We actually do go on one date together, but no more because she is far less infatuated with me than I am with her. When she refuses further dates with me I become irrational. I am fiercely jealous when she dates another boy, and I bawl her out for it, which she very understandably resents. All is in vain, so I try to forget her. Ironically, I later find out that she is not doing very well in playing the field and becomes resentful towards me for "throwing her over." Just who is throwing whom over? Mysterious are the ways of woman!

Social groups at Calvin College

It has taken me some time to figure out why I have not been elected to more prestigious social groups at Calvin. It is mainly because of a rigid caste system. I was of course eligible to join certain groups, such as the Pre-Sem Club, by virtue of my chosen career. Similar groups are the Pre-Meds, the Pre-Laws, and the Engineers. Other groups which anyone may join involve special interests of one kind or another. The Mission Society is of that category to some extent.

I may not have got involved with the Mission Society had it not been for an invitation from a member and friend of mine, Dorothy Westra, who had heard that I was interested in missions. Once I joined and was first elected vice-president, later president. I was stuck with this label and felt obligated to uphold the image by spending a lot of time doing actual mission work. I think I was trying to convince myself that missions is what I actually intended to choose as my career.

Still other social groups chose their recruits by election or special invitation, which is to say that to get in, one had to be previously identified as being specially qualified. This was the way it was with one group I belonged to, the Plato Club. Professor Henry Stob had organized this club when he joined the faculty a year or two previous to my coming. I was elected to it in my sophomore year, after I had done superior work in his courses in philosophy, and I remained active in it throughout college. The total membership was twelve, with three new members being elected each year. This was a real working organization in which the members took turns reading original papers on assigned sections in a book that was chosen for discussion, such as Plato's "Republic."

The social groups I have mentioned so far were based either on interest or on merit, or on both. Entirely different were what I would call "prestige groups," which were filled mainly by reputation and/or prior affiliation. Definitely this label applied to the A Capella Choir, the *Chimes* and yearbook staff, the Thespians drama society, and the student government, all of which carried a high level of prestige. One had to have previously established his or her place in a dominant clique in order to get into one of these. I call them "mutual admiration societies." There was a carry-over in their membership from tutelary societies at the high-school level. Thus, if you had been in plays in Chicago or Grand Rapids Christian High School, you were automatically invited to be a member of Calvin's Thespians. I had no chance to get near these kind of activities for the simple reason that I had never had the privilege of attending a Christian high school. There was none in any of the places where I had lived during my high-school years.

Finally, I mention varsity athletics, particularly the basketball program, as something I had no possibility whatever of entering.[2] One had to come to college previously prepared in high-school athletics to be considered. I suppose that this was not only the way it *had* to be, but the way it *ought* to have been because it was after all a system based on skill and merit. On the other hand, there are probably many students with latent athletic skills who never get to develop them because, like me, they have no standing on the ladder of recognition and patronage.

My work on a construction job and my first kiss. I spent my first summer home from Calvin working for the Tamminga Construction Co. as "water boy" at thirty-five cents per hour. I was working at the site of Denver's future Second CRC. Officially it was my task to bring water to the laborers and craftsmen, but I wound up doing

---

[2]Certainly I was never going to be the athletic kind of Knight!

heavy work such as helping erect forms for concrete. This was good for my muscles as well as for teaching me some basic construction skills that would later be useful. While working at this job, I had opportunity to become better adquainted with my Uncle Sid Tamminga, my mother's oldest brother, who worked as finish carpenter. I found him always smiling and cheerful, just like my mother. No doubt he benefited from having less stress and responsibility than my Uncle Bill and Uncle John, who had the worries of running the company. These two uncles donated their entire profit to the church, which ended up paying only $35,000 for a commodious and beautiful sanctuary.

It was while I was on summer vacation that I met a girl who wanted to kiss and neck, the first warm-blooded female I had thus far encountered. When she enrolled at Calvin in the fall, she was interested in continuing the relationship, but I wasn't.

Following the evening service on Sundays, the young people my age hang around together, and sometimes we go to one of our homes to sing hymns around the piano. One Sunday, however, there is a new girl attending our church service whose name is Arloa. She catches my eye and I end up in a car learning what it is like to be with a girl who wants to do more than just talk. Arloa is visiting from Kansas, and I am sure she will make some good Kansas boy very happy by marrying him. She wants to hug, so we hug. She wants to kiss, so we kiss. We keep it up until we both get sweaty and realize that we must stop. The next few days on the job, I can think of nothing else than the sensation of kissing Arloa.

Participating on Calvin's debate team
Debating may be counted as one of the English courses that are required for graduation. Students may earn one unit of credit for it. I probably would have done better to have taken another course in English as such, but my choice is to go for Debating.

Anything that would train me in extemporary speaking would be extremely useful in my future career of preaching, teaching, praying, and whatever else a minister does vocally. After I signed up, I was told that there was a debate handbook which defined the one universal debate proposition for the current year, around which all

Participating on Calvin's debating team

debate teams were to shape their affirmative and negative arguments. This handbook outlined the general pro and con supports for this proposition, but the students were themselves expected to do research on their own initiative.

I sign up as a Sophomore and continue as a Junior and Senior, thereby achieving certain status among this special group. There is a debate coach; in fact our debate coach is Harold Dekker, a seminarian who has been acclaimed for his skills as a public speaker. Once we have been assigned a partner, we stay with him (or her) for the entire school term.

A poor partner often pulls down a good partner, but a good partner may not be able to help a poor partner, so they both go down together in the eyes of the judge who hears their speeches. I had an able partner, Gordon Van Wylen, who went on to become a Science dean at Michigan and President at Hope College.

In general I had to be satisfied with being judged just average as a debater. The kudos went to fair-haired boys on our team such as Fred Baker, Bernie Pekelder, and Alex De Jong, all sons of renowned preachers in the Christian Reformed denomination. This was another example of the truism, "It's not what you know, but whose kid you are!"

The enjoyable part of being on a debate team is that one gets to go to other college campuses, such as Michigan State, Western Michigan University, Goshen College, and the like. Calvin's team generally does well, and on the bus driving home, we are usually in a

high mood. A novel but delightful experience for me is getting to eat dinners in nice restaurants, something that until now has been all but unknown to me.

I test my wings as a fledgling missionary
It is my Sophomore year at Calvin. As vice-president of the Mission Society, I must set an example for others. I accept the role of going out on Sunday afternoons on behalf of the Madison Square Mission to contact, and hopefully convert, persons who have written in or called. I try to explain to individual prospects what it means to accept Christ as one's Savior and become a member of his church. The results of these pleas are generally disappointing. As long as I work for this mission (gratis, of course), there is not even one person who agrees to come to services at our mission, let alone join the church (let alone join the Christian Reformed Church!). I begin to doubt whether I actually possess the abilities needed to convert sinners to Christ, after all.

This stands as a corrective and a rebuke to Arvin's and my juvenile notions that we could go off to Canada or somewhere and become some sort of evangelists. Faith in my own prowess to persuade has grown apace, fertilized by this exotic belief, but has now been effectively rebuked.

The trouble was that it had not been possible heretofore to put this confidence to the test in any pragmatic way, and while in high school I certainly did not receive any such training, although I do remember that during our junior year in high school, Arvin and I attended a downtown church where the renowned radio evangelist, Charles E. Fuller, was proclaiming his much admired version of the gospel. He was conducting, in matter of fact, the actual radio broadcast right there and then, with his beloved "Honey" reading the enthusiastic letters. Arv and I were so moved that we signed on for a class on the book of Hebrews conducted by a man from their team. Although I did not understand this biblical book any better after having taken this course than before, the zeal and enthusiasm with which these folks were promoting their views led me to think that, if only I had their level of enthusiasm, it should be possible for me or any Christian fully committed to the gospel to persuade just about anybody to be saved and become a Christian. This is what really lay behind all my puffery about being mission-minded.

I have to give credit to my negative experience at Madison Ave. Mission for getting my head screwed on right on this issue. I still have no clear notion of what it means to be a successful missionary for Christ, but I am beginning to discard some unworkable alternatives that have stood in the way.

My failure as a Bible salesman
Tony Hoekema and John G. De Kruyter came back at the end of the previous summer telling of making up to a thousand dollars selling Bibles for the B. B. Kirkbride Bible Co. in Indianapolis. I have tried to follow their example, but apparently I have been sent into the wrong territory. Those two fellows were sent down south, into the "Bible Belt"; I have been sent to Calhoun County, Iowa, and have made hardly any money at all. Things are going so badly that, if I had not signed a note for $300 promising to continue for a minimum of sixty days on the job, I would just pick up and go home.

It was the summer of 1941, the end of my sophomore year. I went in early June with five or six other Calvin students to take the Kirkbride training course, staying at the YMCA in downtown Indianapolis. We were not taught anything about the technique or psychology of selling, beyond the sales pitch, which was to be repeated word for word in the presence of our clients. The product we were to sell was the renowned Thompson Chain Reference Bible, costing from $8 to $24, depending on the paper and the binding. While still in Indianapolis, I purchased my own personal copy, the one with the India paper and the cordovan leather cover. At the end of the course I was ushered in for an interview with the president of the company, who asked me first to sign a promissory note, after which he gave me my assignment. I had been hoping to be sent to a southern state, but received this assignment instead. When I muttered something about hoping for easier territory, Mr. Kirkbride smiled and patted me on the back, saying, "Sure, Iowa is harder, that's why we picked a man of exceptional ability such as yourself to go there."

We had not previously been informed that there would be a note to sign. In desperation to get done with a tedious week of training and to spend time making money on the road, I was not mentally prepared to haggle over this matter. Mr. Kirkbride's genial smile and outstretched hand were calculated to inspire me to trust in him sufficiently to assume that everything would be all right.

I have reached my territory and have in fact been here for four weeks. I started in a small town near the southeast corner of the county and have been working westward. Very systematically, as you can see. Though I have approached as many as five prospects each day (Iowa farms are far apart), the results have been dismal. There has been only one actual sale; which is to say, a bona fide sale to another person for which I stand to receive a commission. However, if I count others for which I have myself paid, there are a total of four. This includes the one I bought for myself, another that I gave to my first landlady in lieu of rent, and a third that I traded to a kindly Baptist preacher in exchange for a study Bible that he had. I remember so well the scene: this preacher's wife takes pity on me and treats me to a hearty meal, topped off by gooseberry pie with whipped cream (my first-ever taste of this wonderful confection!). Otherwise my daily diet consists of two meals a day, both of which consist of a quart of milk and a package of sticky buns from the grocery.

I should explain my one bona fide sale. This lady bought the Bible with the rough buckram binding, the cheapest on my list. Its price was $7.95, so at ten percent commission, I earned seventy-nine and a half cents. That is my total earning so far this summer: less than eight dollars! And to think that I still have to pay for the three expensive Bibles I have bought on my own!

I have been writing to my parents, and a few times I have telephoned them collect. Although I try to sound optimistic, I cannot disguise from them the fact that I am becoming increasingly despondant, trapped in a situation that I cannot control to my own advantage. In desperation I finally mention to my mother the real reason why I have to stay here whatever happens: the note that I have signed. If I do not stay the sixty days, I will have to pay the $300, it's as simple as that! Mom says, "Call back tomorrow. I am going to ask Uncle John [Tamminga] whether they can do that to you." When I call again she says, "Your dad and I want you to come home immediately. You can find a job right here in Denver. Uncle John says that because you are a minor your signature is not binding. Obviously it is just a ploy to keep you at a rotten job!"

A great burden was lifted from my heart. Immediately I headed for home in Denver, hitchhiking all the way, as I had done travelling to Iowa from Indianapolis. I was to work the rest of the summer at Schwayder Brothers, the factory that made Samsonite luggage and card-tables, but the best part was that I was home, where I got to eat as much good food as I wished.

It hardly needs be said that I had learned some important things about myself and the world I lived in. I was terribly disillusioned about my own abilities to motivate other people and felt that this debacle was all my fault. But it wasn't all my fault. The Kirkbride people had sent me without transportation and with meagre financial resources to a territory where one positively has to have a car, or at the very minimum, a bike, to get around to prospective buyers. I absolutely could not reach a significant number of farm families on foot and had to restrict my soliciting to folks who lived in the small towns -- mainly retired farmers, who were the least likely to buy my expensive product, no matter how much they might admire it!

I was outrageously victimized by this situation. The fault lay with Kirkbride rather than with myself. The promissory note which they required was sufficient indication of their negative expectations and exploitative designs; they expected me to fail, and wanted me to persist in failure out of fear of having to repay it! Certainly the greatest damage was done to my youthful psyche, and over time the damage might have been far greater, were it not for the marvelous stroke of good fortune that lay just ahead in the entrance of Betty Schouten upon the stage of my existence, a perfect cure for my crestfallen and bedragled spirits.

Hitchhiking back to college. It was early September, 1941. The summer that began with the Bible fiasco had ended well in a steady job, tailing a buzz-saw at the Schwayder factory.

Classes will start soon, so I now have to get back to Calvin. In view of my relative impecunity, I know that I must again rely on my thumb and a smiling face to get me there. I take the Greyhound bus to Cheyenne, WY, then walk a mile east to the city limits, where I get my first ride. I am taken as far as the easternmost boundary of the state. Here I stand for minutes and then hours, out in the midst of what was once called "the great American desert," where buffalo once ran in the millions and where Cheyenne, Arapaho, and Sioux hunted. Fortunately for me, the skies remain clear. Just as the sun is going down, a car stops to pick me up. I am welcomed aboard by a genial salesman on his way to Cleveland, OH. He offers to take me as far as I want to go. This means that I can ride with him all the way into Indiana. My kind benefactor is as generous as he is genial. Although he allows me to pay for my own food, he insists on paying for my lodging. It is in an Indiana town named Peru that I take leave of him and go my separate way to Michigan. I will never know what is to happen next to this gentleman, but I will pray that the good Lord who sent him to help me will also bless him on all his future journeys.

Very soon my life's pathway was to turn in an unexpected direction. The callow young man who could not sell Bibles to Christians was to come upon an unanticipated turn of the road, following which in enthusiasm and self-confidence, he was destined to open up broad and splendid horizons of personal development.

My first date with Betty Schouten, my future wife. This was supposed to be the big social event of the year, the Calvin Soupbowl. It turned out to be very big for me.

Just to show how antisocial I have become -- or how impecunious -- I have not attended the Soupbowl event in previous years, but this time I am going because I have a date. And what a date she is! Her name is Betty Schouten, and she comes from Grand Haven, which is west of Grand Rapids on Lake Michigan. At first I thought that her name was "Benny," which is what I thought Irene Heyboer called her when she mentioned her availability, but when I looked her up in the college directory I saw my error and was reassured. Her name is Betty, as plain and simple as that! I might worry about dating a girl named "Benny."

I got introduced to Betty because I asked Irene for a date and she had to decline because she already had been asked, but offered, "My roommate would love to be asked." So I met Betty at Irene's locker, as agreed upon, and introduced myself, smiling warmly as I gazed into the uplifted eyes set in her lovely face.

There was a lot for each of us to do, once Betty and I knew who our date was to be. Betty asked her dad to bring her yellow formal, and I ordered a large matching corsage to be pinned on it, reaching from her shoulder to her waist. It turned out that my corsage for Betty was far larger and more beautiful than those received by the other girls who were residing in Betty's boarding house. I hired a taxi to transport us and I wore a borrowed tux.

When I called for her, I saw her in radiant glory, ready to descend the magic stairway, and I spontaneously spoke words that neither she nor her girl-friends and landlady could forget: "Just stand there and let me drink you in!" The girl-friends were shocked because they had heard that I was very shy, but it made a big hit with Betty, as did my little ditty, "Oh those golden slippers," in recognition of what she was wearing on her feet.

We are now seated at our table. Next to us are Angie Beukema from Grand Haven, who first encouraged Betty to come to Calvin, and her date, a pre-seminarian named John A. De Kruyter. They seldom smile and do not seem to be enjoying each other's company. But Betty and I are surely enjoying each other! We also enjoy the dinner, especially the desert. We laugh and laugh. Everything is funny. We smile and smile. A strange and wonderful feeling is coming over me: "Can this be the one I will love and want to marry?" I can tell by the way she raises those gorgeous big eyes to me that she is thinking the same!

Betty and I almost break up
It is still September, 1941, and we are on our third date together. Betty and I are at the Civic Auditorium in Grand Rapids, attending a concert by the famous English songstress, Gracie Fields. Betty doesn't seem to be enjoying herself and scarcely looks at me. Also, she doesn't say very much, which does not match the impression that I have received of her as a very talkative and outgoing person. A terrible question arises in my heart, "Is this to be our last date, so soon after we met, and just when I have begun to think that we are really in love?"

When the concert is over, we depart with the audience and make our way to the coupe that I have borrowed from my friend Jay Van Andel. I ask Betty whether she would like to go somewhere for a snack. After an unenthusiastic, "Whatever you want to do," I know something is wrong for sure. I drive to John Ball Park on the western edge of Grand Rapids and park the car where we can look over the lights of the city. Then I say, "All right, Honey, what is the matter? Tell me, what is wrong?" So she responds, *"What is the matter is that I have been getting to like you very much, but the girls at my boarding house tell me that you are nothing but a heart-breaker. You get a girl to fall for you and then drop her cold! I don't want to keep dating you if that is how you are. I've already had my heart broken too often."*

I am astonished at this -- not astonished that Betty should feel this way, but astonished that anybody would say this of me. "What girl or girls have I dropped cold?" "Both Angie and Irene say that you did this to Juliana Flietstra, and also to Eunice Smith." "As for Juliana," I respond, "I have never had even one date with her. She evidently has a crush on me because when I was at her father's church in Iowa I said that I would 'look for her' when she got to Calvin, meaning only that I would remember that we had met on this occasion and that I encouraged her to come to Calvin. I was only trying to be kind and polite. I did date Eunice once, and I wanted to date her some more, but she cut me off cold. If anybody's heart was broken, it was mine!" Because of the frankness and sincerity of my answer, Betty believes me. The evening ends with some warm hugging and our first kiss.

Thus a marvelous life together in deep commitment to each other began to grow. The tender sprout of our love was rescued from the harsh winds of unfeeling gossip and the scorching sun of intolerance. We learned two important lessons from this experience: (1) the necessity of frank communication as the lifeline of true love, and (2) the deadly potency of jealousy and slander coming from those who envy and seek to destroy the fragile flower of true love, if given the chance.

What I learn while off the road in a rainstorm
The car I am driving spins out of control and skids to a jarring stop in a ditch on the opposite side of the road. The three passengers and I are too stunned to speak, but after feeling our bodies to see if we are still intact, we all break out in a nervous laugh. Betty is in the middle, next to me, and the closest to the door is John A. De Kruyter with his date, Angie Beukema, on his lap. We are on our way to Grand Haven to bring Betty home when this misadventure occurs. I am taking her because I plan to spend my first weekend with her at

What I learn while off the road in a rainstorm

her parents' home. It was not my intent to crowd three passengers into this small car, but when John and Angie found out that I intended to drive Betty home they implored me to take them along too, gratis. This Oldsmobile coupe belongs to my friend, Jay Van Andel, and I am renting it from him.[3] *If anything bad happens to it, it is I who will be responsible and will have to pay for it. I am not prepared to call this event an accident. Until I check outside the car to determine if there is any damage, it is a misadvanture.*

Rain had been pouring down ever since we left Grand Rapids and the wipers were not able to give me a clear view ahead. At times I could hardly see the road. Being crowded so tight, four of us in a single seat, didn't help. At the top of a long grade up from the Grand River bridge I was blinded by the headlights of an oncoming car. As I veered to the right to miss it, my right wheels dropped off the pavement onto the gravel shoulder. To keep from going off the shoulder I jerked the wheel left a bit too hard. The car went into a spin and slid into the ditch on the left side of the roadway.

Everybody remains calm as I open my door, step out into the downpour, and grope around in the dark, without a flashlight, to check for any damage. My heart is in my throat, but thank God there doesn't seem to be any damage! No rocks, no trees, nothing but mud! So I climb back into the car, turn on the engine, and try to pull back onto the road, but the wheels only spin. I know that I shall have to go out on the road and try to get help.

All this time John De Kruyter remained completely silent. He didn't offer to push while I tried to pull out of the ditch. Nor did he offer to accompany me when I went to seek help. He just remained sitting in his place, with Angie on his lap. It was all up to me!

Good fortune takes me some five miles back towards Grand Rapids to a tavern where I may use the telephone to summon a wrecker. When it arrives at the scene of the misadventure, with me in the cab beside the driver, it has no trouble whatever towing Jay's car

---

[3]This was the same person who later joined Richard De Vos in establishing the highly successful Amway enterprise. Jay's father owned an Oldsmobile agency.

108   The 1940's: What I learn in a rainstorm

back onto the highway. I pay the driver, get behind the wheel, and drive on sopping wet to Grand Haven. After I drop off my "helpful" guests at Angie's house, I drive on to the Schouten residence. Betty tells me that the entire time I was away getting help, De Kruyter has been necking the dickens out of Angie.

Next day, Betty's Pa and I checked out the car and found no damage whatever. Nothing but mud. I didn't even mention what had happened when I delivered the newly washed car back to Jay.

Bad luck with cars. I had learned to drive on an old Chevy coupe that my dad had bought. I hadn't driven it on the road at first, just out in an open field where teenagers drove hotrods. What eventually happened to this coupe I don't know because I went off to college. When I came home at Christmas in my first year at college, Dad had bought a brand new sedan, also a Chevy, and he let me drive it. Unfortunately, heavy snows had fallen and I managed to crumple the left front fender against its equivalent on a car coming toward me, whose driver would not get out of my chosen path through the snow.

Too bad! Dad will never let me drive it again. He also will not make me pay for it. If he does, I won't be able to pay, for I am just barely existing at Grandma's house in Grand Rapids.

Soon after I met Betty in the fall of 1941, I purchased a beat-up old Hudson for $85 and called it "Buttercup." It did not have much longer to live. Betty and I took Buttercup to Dearborn, MI on an all day visit to the Ford Museum. This is a marvelous display of nineteenth-century technological triumphs. During the many hours we were in the museum, the weather turned very cold. Apparently there was insufficient antifreeze in Buttercup's radiator because the engine had frozen and the motor-block had cracked -- not badly enough to prevent our anxious return home, but bad enough to reduce its salvage value to $25. Sixty dollars was therefore added to the price of this trip to Dearborn, a heavy toll for an impecunious college student!

Despondency over my romantic attachment
I am so infatuated with Betty that I think of her day and night. I see her whenever I can. I walk to school with her and I walk home

Despondency over my romantic attachment

with her. Her roommates at her boarding-house on Henry St. are beginning to gossip about us. They say we are Romeo and Juliet; and they are half right: it is a real love-match, not an attachment of the moment. I don't like it that people are beginning to poke fun at us, but of course that can't stop us from wanting to be together because we both seem truly in love. But the realization grows upon me that I may be getting myself into something I may have difficulty handling.

What about the future? If Betty and I keep on this way, we will become engaged after a while, but without any possibility of setting up a home together. We are both poor. I have been poor so long, I can't remember when I had prosperity. I have to live with Grandma, eat her lousy food, and wear sweaters with darns in the elbows. Betty isn't as poor as I, but she has had it rough too. Her father got cheated by his two business partners a few years ago and had to close his factory and go into bankruptcy. Now they live in a tiny rented house. Betty can hardly afford the Calvin tuition, and I know it's a financial burden on her parents to pay her board and room in Grand Rapids. How can we ever save enough money to get married when we both find money so hard to get? I do want to marry her eventually, for I can't think of life without her. But how is it ever going to happen?

For several days now I had been in a state of depression like this. My mood was dark and gray. Betty soon became aware of this, and, bless her heart, knew just what to say! "Honey, I don't know what's eating you, but I want you to realize that I can't put up with gloomy people. If you keep on moping around like this, I won't want to be with you and I will break off our love-affair!" I knew she meant it, and she was too precious to me to risk losing, so I pulled myself up by my bootstraps, girded up my loins, and snapped out of my dark mood! Unfortunately, this was more than a mood, but a temporary swing into what was to become a clinical depression some thirty years later.

From this day forward Betty becomes even more precious to me. The destiny that has brought us together may not, and will not, be shunted aside or derailed by the shakiness of my very fragile self-confidence.

How we become engaged
Betty and I have returned to college following spring break. This evening we have been out walking, and right now we are seated on Grandma's sofa, expressing our thoughts and feelings to each other after being apart.

I made a very adventurous trip during the break, taking the Greyhound bus to New York to visit my brother Hank at the Brooklyn Navy Yard, then hitchhiking the entire way back home. While out east, I was introduced to Hank's fiancée, Louise Lorion, at her parents' house in Montclair, N.J. They met at a USO dance in New York City. The way they carried on gave me some ideas of what might be next in my own relationship with Betty.

It is now mid-March in 1942, and Betty and I have been practically inseparable since we met in September. We are very much in love, and spend as much time as possible together. We go out on dates, but in addition we walk back and forth to college together, and even study together. The fact that we walk hand in hand, plus the directness and intensity of our devotion to each other, has had a negative effect in giving certain super-pious and self-righteous people, including students and college administrators, an excuse for ridiculing our attachment. I am baffled as well as peeved at this ill-treatment. This has been my first, but it may not be my last, occasion to experience how petty moralizers take pleasure in persecuting the lovely and the loving ones in their midst!

Something else important that has transpired since last September is the Japanese attack on Pearl Harbor. I am not quite old enough to get drafted, and in fact preseminarians are getting deferred by being pre-enrolled in the seminary, yet our nation's being at war makes the future very clouded for me. Just the same, I have seen my Marine brother daring to become engaged in the midst of this war, and this gives me courage and conviction.

Kneeling down and taking Betty's hand, I say, "Darling, will you *marry me?" Sometime...some place...somehow! Who knows? God knows. Betty says Yes. It takes the rest of the evening and a walk in the woods to help us realize that we have actually spoken the magic words.*

Betty puts my grandmother in her place
Now that we have become engaged, I have invited Betty to spend a weekend with me at Grandma's house, rather than going home to Grand Haven. Grandma approves of this because she is anxious to learn more about my fiancée. To be sure, she would never have allowed it before we became engaged. She is a real stickler on propriety. Since both Betty and Grandma are kind and affectionate persons, they treat each other with warmth and respect. Betty manages to choke down some of Grandma's cooking; I have warned her ahead of time of what not to eat. When bedtime comes, I take over the sofa while Betty sleeps in my bed.

As we prepare for church on Sunday morning, Betty is about to go out the front door when Grandma notices that she is bare-headed. Grandma does not approve of this because St. Paul commands women to cover their heads when entering the house of worship. Grandma asks, "Where is your hat, Betty? Don't you have a hat? You mustn't go to church without one." When Betty replies that she has no hat and never wears one to church, Grandma says, "Oh, but in our church you must have one. Wait a minute, I'll get one of mine for you to wear." She comes back with a hat that is even more ugly than the one she herself is wearing. "Here, put this on. It's old, but it will do." Betty is aghast both at the idea of wearing someone else's ugly old hat and at Grandma's effrontery in telling her what to do. With a questioning but defiant gaze Betty calmly says to me, "If I have to wear this hat, I refuse to go to church. I'll just stay here while you go with Grandma." Then I say, "Honey, you don't have to wear it. Grandma is just trying to be nice to you." But Grandma is not, in fact, being nice; she is trying to make Betty conform to her standards, as she has been making me conform. She has to give in, though, because she would rather have Betty go to church without a hat than not to go at all.

What Grandma did simply shows how completely out of touch she was. I was glad that Betty was standing up to her.[4] I would not have

112   The 1940's: Betty puts Grandma in her place

allowed her to wear that ridiculous hat in any case.

Being beaten on by Oakdale Park Christians. This event was ironic because I had been attending Oakdale Park CRC for three years, also because just a month or two later I was to affiliate with the U. S. Marines myself.

I am a Junior at Calvin and Betty is a new Freshman. Usually we walk home, hand in hand, to her boarding house on Henry Street, but this time we are headed for Grandma De Vries's house on north Butler Avenue (this is where the avenue divides into two parallel streets to surround the block the church is on). Three young guys -- teenagers -- are in a car, slowly driving by us on the street, laughing and carrying on. I recognize them as youth from Oakdale Park CRC, where Grandma and I attend. As they pass us, this one guy who is going to become a marine makes an insulting remark about our holding hands. He also uses some derogatory term for Betty, and I consequently feel that I have to call him to task. He stops his car and we have some exchanges of fisticuffs. He is still defiant when I break it off, but I feel that I have defended my intended's honor. Soon we are at Grandma's place and tell her what happened. Instead of her being proud, she is shocked that a "Domine-to-be" would stoop so low as to brawl in public! She phones Uncle Jack to tell him, and he sternly reproves me over the phone. Soon the whole neighborhood of hyperpious Calvinists is abuzz. I am naturally quite perturbed. So too is Betty. She phones her Dad and he praises me, telling me that he would have done the very same thing.

That is how I was "beaten on" in Grand Rapids in the year 1942 -- not by a young punk, who would find lots of outlets for his aggressiveness when he would report to Marine boot camp -- but by the staunch representatives of puritanical morality who thought self-defense and honor were unworthy of Christian saints!

---

[4] Although I did not realize it at the time, Betty's unabashed independence turned out to be my main support when the time came for me to make my own stand against the unreasonable mores of the church and community of which we became a part. Betty turned out to be the prime support and enabler of me as a "shining white knight" when my time came to make my stand and take my blows!

Betty becomes the victim of a squeeze-play. Betty had already taken all her second-semester exams except the one in the Education curriculum on Latin American Geography. In general, none of her professors had discriminated against her for not being Christian Reformed. She became suspicious, however, when the professor started his first lecture by pointing to one or two students whom he already knew and said, "He is going to get an A. She is going to get an A. But the majority of this class are in grave danger of flunking out. I'll be keeping an eye out for you!" In other words, guilty until proven innocent!

Betty has the misfortune of coming down with the flu, and is so sick that her landlady phones the professor to get her excused from her exam. A few days later she reports at his office and requests another chance to take the exam. Professors are understandably wary of students giving them this kind of excuse, but Flokstra contrives to make the outcome doubly punitive. He hasn't liked Betty since the rumor began to circulate that she had been leading a certain pre-seminarian -- me -- into sin and temptation. He is probably influenced by the dean of women, who scolded Betty for holding hands with me. He responds to Betty's request by scheduling a time for a re-examination, but when Betty shows up, she realizes that all the questions pertain to sections of the textbook which he had explicitly excluded. He does not remain in the room, hence Betty can't question him about the reason for this switch. The end result is of course as he intended. Betty gets an E for the course in disregard of high grades she received in other tests. This certainly looks like persecution, but if the administration and faculty are determined to squeeze Betty out this way, what can I do?

When Betty told her dad what happened, she had to restrain him from going to the professor and busting him in the jaw. The whole incident was instrumental in getting Betty to drop out of college. She interpreted this experience as a second strong reason for finding a full-time job at this time in order to save money for our eventual marriage. I somehow did not realize at the time this happened, as I ought to have, that I was a target as well as she, maybe not consciously and explicity, but symbolically and by virtue of the fact that I too might expect to be squeezed if I became the butt of petty ecclesiastical politics. When this did in fact happen eighteen years later, I observed that rules of fairness did not matter when persons in power positions were determined to have one out of the way.

My summer job in Pando

I am back in Colorado for my third summer vacation, this time in a good-paying job. It is almost the end of August, 1942, and in just a few days I will be reunited with my fiancée, Betty, who is travelling to Denver in order to meet my parents, and will return to Michigan with me when it is time for Calvin's classes to resume.

My father presently has the best job he has ever had. The Army is building Camp Hale for training ski-troopers for mountain and winter warfare. I do not know why the site for this camp has the name Pando. It lies in a mountain valley between Redcliff and Leadville, CO. There are not any soldiers here, nothing but construction workers. Sturgeon Electric in Denver, Dad's company, has received the contract for putting in all the electric facilities, with Dad as supervisor. He has given me the job of grunt on the line crew, which means that I dig the holes and perform various kinds of menial labor for the linemen, the workers who climb up the poles once they are made secure in the ground in order to secure the power lines and transformers to them. Working at this job all summer, I am developing a good tan and bulging muscles.

The problem of finding housing for a gang of workers was a major one here because this was a primitive area with very meagre facilities. The hamlets that were in the vicinity had been built for, and by, miners. In Redcliff there was a boarding house where Dad and I got rough and ready meals that included such questionable dishes as kidney stew. There were about fifteen men who sat at the dining-room table with us. Where they all laid their heads at night, I had no idea. I heard that there were three shifts of men occupying most of the beds that were available, eight hours for each. Dad had it better because he was a boss. We had a separate room to sleep in, but had to share the same double bed.

It seems a little odd to sleep with one's own father -- a little Oedepusian -- but we get along fine. This is actually a very good time for me because Dad and I are able to have long, intimate talks during the evenings together. I learn that Dad takes a deep personal interest in my plans and ambitions, and is willing to support me in every venture that lies before me in the future.

A week before Betty's arrival, Arvin Roos, drove up to Redcliff in his father's car. He brought his brother Harold and my brother Bob with him, so the four of us spent the day climbing Notch Mountain, el. 13,237 feet, offering an unobstructed view of the magnificent Mount of the Holy Cross, approximately two miles away and 14,005 feet high. Arv and I were just good friends again. There was no more talk about being blood-brothers or hating women. In fact, Arvin was engaged, just as I was! This was to be the last wilderness experience for the two of us together.

When the time is near for my return to Grand Rapids, I quit my job and ride back with Dad to Denver for the weekend of Betty's arrival. Once she and my parents meet, they become fast friends. One thing they strongly disapprove of is that I rather innocently go into Betty's bedroom clad in my pajamas to awaken her for breakfast. Actually, I have not thought of this as a sin, but now I know in case I wish to commit one!

We four, Dad and Mom, Betty and I, drive back to Pando on the ensuing Monday to drop Dad off at his work, and then the three of us take a little sight-seeing trip as far as Glenwood Springs, where my mother again finds occasion for expressing strong disapproval of my behavior. This time it is for carrying Betty around on my shoulders while we are bathing in the warm pool belonging to this resort. Again I am shocked to realize that my parents react just like the Calvin blue-noses in censoring anything that involves touching a person of the opposite sex.

The climax of this week comes when I take Betty to the Lovers' Fountain in City Park in Denver in order to slip on her finger an engagement ring with a tiny blue diamond. I managed to purchase it on one of my previous weekend trips with Dad to Denver. Because the trains are awfully crowded, Betty and I take the Greyhound bus all the way back to Michigan, and enjoy the ride immensely.

We have never had so long a time to be in close contact with each other as we have now. Furthermore, no one on this bus seems to mind in the least that we do hug and kiss each other once in a while.

I am called to war

This is the fall of 1942. World War II came to our country on December 7, 1941, and now, less than a year later, it has reached me. I have just received a summons from the draft board in Denver, where I am registered. I registered for the draft on the sixteenth of February, 1942, but haven't been old enough until now to be called up for active service. However, on November 25 I received a notice that I had been rated 1-A, and on December 10 I receive an order to report for induction on the twenty-first. Until now there was some possibility that, as a pre-seminarian in good standing, I might be rated 1-D, a special classification for ministers and seminary students.

Calvin Seminary, to which I had been headed, had been following the example of Catholic seminaries in pre-registering prospective students who were still in the college Pre-Seminary program, with the intent of giving them an exemption from the draft. It all depended on whether an individual student's draft board would allow it. Since the Grand Rapids board did not want to "rock the boat," it went along with it, with the result that virtually none of the Pre-seminarians who lived in or near Grand Rapids saw military service. My Denver draft board, however, either had not heard of this practice or refused to go along with it. I could not restrain the thought that this was what fairness and equity should require, even though it would certainly affect me directly.

For a moment or two after receiving my draft notice, I feel sorry for myself. "What about Betty and me now?" I ponder whether it might be possible to appeal to my Denver board and try to get them to follow the example of the Grand Rapids board. But then I think, "No, I couldn't do that. My father was in the Army in France. My older brother Hank has been a marine since the fall of 1939. Even my younger brother, Bob, has been drafted and is in recruit training in the Navy. How can I refuse my duty when my father and brothers have gone to serve our country?"

My summons to report for duty was for a week hence, but my willingness to do my military duty did not prevent me from weighing the option that I had of enrolling in one of the officer-candidate programs offered by the Army, the Navy, the Air Force, and the Marine Corps. Each of these services allowed senior collegians like myself to remain in school until receiving the bachelor's degree, after which they were to report for active duty. While in college, such students were required to take correspondence lessons and, in the case of the Navy and Marine Corps, to learn how to swim in the event that they did not already have this capability. This was not the same as the Navy V-12 program, which sent men to college to learn specialties useful to the Navy, but one designed to prepare seniors for Officer Candidate School by keeping them in their own colleges.

Betty and I discuss this in a somber mood before I make my decision. This is a challenge both to our courage and to our faith as we face the dark uncertainties that threaten to interfere with our wedding plans and may prevent me from fulfilling my goal of attending seminary and entering the ministry.

My decision is to approach first the representative of the Marines, my reasoning being as follows: "I am almost certainly not good enough to get into the Marines like my brother Hank, but I should try them first just to measure how good I actually am. If they turn me down, as I expect they will, I will try one of the other services."

With this resolution I report to the Marine recruitment officer and within less than an hour am sworn in. My head is swimming as I take my leave. "Can this be true? Am I really going to be a marine? What have I done? Why did I have to try the toughest branch of the service first?" I cannot banish these thoughts from my mind, yet a deep feeling of pride and satisfaction takes over as I realize that my course is now firm and set. I know that it is a good and honorable thing that I have done this day! I will mark the day -- December 13, 1942.

Next day I write a letter to my Denver draft board informing them of what I have done. Later the same day I enter the office of Dean

118   The 1940's: I am called to war

Henry Ryskamp at Calvin College to tell him of my new status. I shall never forget the look in his admiring eye and the warmth of his voice as he says, "Simon John De Vries, I respect you!" Dean Ryskamp had been opposed to the exempting of pre-sems and admired one who might have stayed out, but chose not to do so.

Years afterward, my Marine buddy, Bob Dever, was to tell me that he had two reasons for admiring me: this choice and the fact that I continued to practice my Christian convictions while serving in the Marine Corps.

Some time after this I received the news that my brother Bob had been sent to the Fleet Marine Force as a hospital corpsman. Now all three of us De Vries brothers were to be marines!

Acquaintances from Denver who served in World War II
George Anema, Jake Baker, Fred Brouwer, Wilbur Brunger, William Byleveld, Jerry Bylsma, Jake Buschbach, Marion and Ralph Camping, Fred Cleveringa, Gary De Nooy, Henry and Robert De Vries (my brothers), Chuck Dykstra, Fred Haan, Bud Ham, Don and Harold Jeltema, George Keesen, Ed and Leonard Koeteeuw, Clarence Kronenberg, Eddie Leensvaart, William Lindemulder, George Lont, Edwin Noordewier, Melvin Redeker, Fred Ritsema, Arvin Roos, Alfred Schemper, Maurice Sikkens, Ed Stuursma, Will Suwyn, William Tamminga (my cousin), Harold Terpstra, Jim Vander Laan, George Vander Weit (married my cousin), Benny, Fred, Neal, Walter and Wendell Van Heukelem, Herbie and William Van Schooneveld, Kenneth (killed in action) and Tom Van Wyk, Bob Vonhof, Andrew and Richard Wassenaar, and Lawrence Zoetewey. (From *The Rocky Mountain Sentinel*, June 1944, listing once again as many servicemen from the Denver enclave whom I did not know, including two women and a doctor. My name did not appear on this list because I had transferred my church membership to a Grand Rapids church.)

My Senior studies at Calvin College

I am in my Senior year at Calvin College and I manage to foul up my one and only elective. With a view to choosing something that may help me when I enter the Marine Corps, I write down Trigonometry since artillery is dependant on it. Who knows, I may wind up as an artillery officer! Trigonometry has to do with force, angles and range -- where a shell will land if fired at a given angle from the ground. What I fail to keep in mind is that this is a very

My Senior studies at Calvin College 119

advanced course in the Mathematics curriculum and I haven't had any Math since leaving high school. Besides, Professor Albert Muyskens[5] is the kind who doesn't baby anybody. If you are too slow to understand and keep up with him, get out!

Well, that is precisely what has happened. Here I am in Muysken's class. His faithful followers are in the front seats, rapidly jotting down all that he has to say. If they interrupt his rapid-fire lecturing, it is to egg him on, not to request help.

At least I have enough sense to realize what is going on and why I don't belong here. So I am substituting Greek Culture, an automatic A for students who have already taken all of Prof. Ralph Stob's Greek language courses, as I have done. I ought to pick out a more challenging course to be my elective, but to tell the truth I feel a bit intimidated. The minute I stepped out of my field, I was in difficulty! Not a thought to make one proud of oneself, but in this case true.

I have actually kept up high grades in the courses I have taken, not always but quite often receiving A's. I am certainly not anybody's fair-haired boy, but I am a digger, and I come up consistently doing a creditable job.

There have been certain courses, to be sure, in which nobody could possibly earn a good grade, such as the two courses designed solely for pre-sems: Survey Chemistry and Survey Physics, which were really quite worthless because they consisted entirely of lecturing, without any lab work to prove and illustrate what was being stated, an utter fiasco as far as my learning anything worthwhile was concerned.

Everyone is supposed to take the required courses in English, Public Speaking, History, Economics, Psychology, Sociology, and Reformed Doctrine. I have done well enough in them but have seldom been inspired. The professors mainly just drone on and on. A happy exception, to be sure, has been Seymour Swets in his course in Public Speaking. I got a lot out of that course. Everybody laughed and applauded when I made my speech on "Why man will never be able to reach the moon."

The heavy stuff for pre-seminarians was languages. First, I needed a year of Latin because I had failed to take it in high school. Also, I took two full years of Greek, beginning with basic grammar

---

[5] Also our popular basketball coach

and going on to read Xenephon and Plato's Aeneas, as well as the Gospel of John. Also, we had to take either German or French. I chose German and did well in it. Besides all this, pre-sems were required to take Dutch Grammar and some advanced courses from Professor Van Andel. He was a dapper little fellow who served as the college's official organist. He wrote a not very good textbook for this course. "Yes, boys," he would say, "it was a very hot summer when I wrote it, and I did the best I could under the circumstances."

Can you imagine an author actually saying such a thing about his own book?

Pre-sems were required as well to take Professor Van Haitsma's Introductory Biology, plus his course, Biological Problems, which was ostensibly an effort to refute evolution. The Curators wanted to make sure that we would be ready to refute the heretics!

We were also required to take courses in Philosophy, taught by Professor Henry Stob. Many students were enamored of him, me included, only more so. I was so much inspired that I took no fewer than five courses from him. He cultivated a casual socratic method in which he dialogued with his students and got them to propose tentative answers for him to refute. He was the first person who actually taught me to think! Add to this his complete mastery of words. He always chose precisely the most effective and appropriate word to express his meaning.

All that is behind me now, and all that remains is this final semester. I will go ahead with Greek Culture even though I don't expect to learn much new from it. I won't be like the student in Van Andel's Dutch Grammar class who wrote his final exam, laid his bluebook on the professor's desk, and said to his fellow students while holding up his copy of Van Andel's book, "Would anybody like to have this book?" When nobody answered, he walked over to the open window and threw it out, saying, "I'll just have to throw it away then. It isn't worth keeping." Guess what kind of grade that brave fellow received!

Senior physical education
Am I lucky, or what? I just knocked Cornie Van Zee on his butt! Cornie is our phys.ed. teacher at Calvin and he has been teaching me

and others how to box. He didn't know that I had already learned some boxing from Frank Roubos when I was a young boy in Denver. Anyhow, I have boxing gloves on and am sparring with Cornie when I see an opening and Whammo! I catch him with a right uppercut and he goes flying to the floor, all 225 pounds of him! Cornie is very strong, but fortunately he is also very mild-mannered. He is the Iowa state corn-husking champion, but now he is also a preseminarian and plans to enter the ministry.

Physical Education at Calvin College was not a requirement for pre-sems. Apparently the church didn't mind if it got a lot of unhealthy domines. Nevertheless, the Marine Corps deferred enlistment program required me to be constantly enrolled in phys.ed. during this entire Senior year.

So here I am, boxing, tumbling, doing calisthenics several evenings per week. I am also required to report regularly at the YMCA downtown to swim in their pool so that I shall be able to pass the swimming test after I am called to duty. Every person entering the Navy or Marine Corps must be able to swim, at least a little bit. If not, he will be required to take special training after being called up. I won't have to worry because I swim quite well -- not a champion of course, but well enough to have a chance of surviving a shipwreck or similar disaster.

My weight is now 154 lbs. at 6'1". My eyesight is very good. My hearing is good. I don't have any physical impairments that I know of. I should do fairly well in Marine training even though I don't in any degree rank as a real athlete. My not being athletic does not reflect lack of interest, just lack of opportunity. With our family's bouncing around all over the country, I have never found enough stability or continuity to become involved in structured athletics of any kind.

My arrival at Parris Island

I left Grand Rapids three days ago and have spent only one night in a bed, in a hotel in Atlanta. We just got off the train and have been lined up by a tough-looking sergeant. "Straighten up that line and stand at attention," he demands. "What a bunch of misfits you are, it makes me sick to look at you! The Marine Corps is in real trouble if it expects to make officers out of you. Don't think you'll get special treatment just because you went to college and are PFC's. You are just plain old privates here. You'll be treated just like the rest of the crowbait that comes in here." I cannot help feeling shocked and intimidated by these rough words. It is clear that the Marine Corps means to drive civilian ideas out of our heads and cow us into unquestioning obedience.

It was an awful moment when I had to say goodbye to Betty at the Pere Marquette Station. What an abrupt way for my college education to end! What a cruel interruption of my budding romance! I had been well trained for adapting to drastic changes, but this had to be the worst interruption I had ever faced. As with warriors everywhere and in every age, there were two things that drove me: a sense of duty and a craving for adventure. Could this be the end of everything? Or was it to be the beginning of something good and worthwhile?

I have to go, of course; and I want to go. But beside the awareness that I may not make it back, there are two things that trouble me and give me a vague sense of anxiety. One is the question whether I have what it takes to become a good marine and a good officer. Another is an awareness of being a social misfit. Familiarity with what my brother Hank has gone through makes me realize that I am likely to have a tough time getting along with a profane, godless, and licentious bunch of marines. I don't swear. I don't have sex. I don't smoke or drink. Truly, I am what they call a Holy Joe. And now I am supposed to live and fight with men who live just the opposite. Will they mock and deride me, or will they accept me? Worse, will I give up my Christian convictions and become pagan like them? Am I strong enough and talented enough to be a true Christian and a good marine at the same time? One thing is for sure: if my family upbringing had not already toughened me and refined me like silver, I would stand no chance whatever of pulling off this double role. Living four years with an aged saint is no preparation for fighting with the Marines!

I was not supposed to be called up so early. It was only the fourth of May, 1943. There were still three weeks of classes before I was supposed to graduate. I had been given no explanation -- just go! Judging from the way the Marines had been getting slaughtered in places like Guadalcanal, they desperately needed more lieutenants as replacements for the ones the Japs were shooting.

I am glad at least that Calvin will allow me to graduate in absentia. I won't be standing in the graduation line in June, as I anticipated, but they will know where I am and what I'll be doing while the other pre-sems in my class go directly on to seminary! Much as I dread what I am about to go through, I am glad that I can hold my head high and not use a career in the church as an excuse for staying out of the war, letting other men do the fighting.

In Detroit I took a train bound for Atlanta. I had received travel vouchers along with my orders. This was a regular train that I was on, not a trooptrain, but I took note as we travelled southward that young, collegiate looking men like myself were getting on board and showing military orders to conductors. We soon began to introduce ourselves to the others. One strange thing, I thought, was that all of our last names began with the letters A through D, which made me think that we might be the first contingent of an alphabetically arranged roster, with men further down the alphabet to come later.

That's why I am so early; my name starts with D!

We stayed overnight in a hotel in Atlanta because there was no train available to take us eastward to Augusta and Parris Island, but next day we got on a new train and set out again. We kept on being shifted from one train to another. In a place called Yemassee they gave us a train right out of the Civil War era, with an old engine with a huge towering smokestack and old-fashioned cars with kerosene lanterns. We were haphazardly given food in dining cars, but there was no place to sleep, except in our seats.

We were a pretty cohesive bunch of guys by this time. We would talk with our seatmates. Some would tell jokes and make everyone laugh. Mostly we would just read or gaze out the window at the spanish moss.

As I begin to feel more and more a member of a group, I wonder about making friends. Whom would you make friends with, and how would you do it? I am not up to evangelizing anybody, I just want to get along and become what they become. Some men are playing poker, with small money as stakes, and they invite me to get into their game. "I have never played," is my reply. "Don't worry, we'll teach you." So I play a hand. I win. We play two more hands, and I continue to win. But this is just for dimes. The stakes are raised to quarters and soon I begin to lose. Then I lose some more. And some more. I realize I have been suckered, so I get out and refuse to play anymore. My experiment with being a good guy has not got me anywhere. I still don't have any friends!

We are now completely bushed. We are coming in view of a railroad station with the sign, "United States Marine Corps Recruit Depot, Parris Island, S.C." It doesn't look so bad with trees, grass, and flowers all around and tidy buildings everywhere. We get out of the train, carrying our civilian belongings, and are told to get in line. Since most of us are not yet familiar with close-order drill, our line is not as straight as it might be, so we get "chewed out," as the Marines say. We discover that the Marines have Navy words for everything, like "Aye, aye" for "yes, yes." They also have cuss words you never heard of and use them to good effect. After the sergeant's chewing out, we are marched to the barber, where we pay a quarter to get our heads shaved. It takes thirty seconds or less, so fast you don't know what hit you! We are marched to the quartermaster depot next to receive our field greens, white skivvies, piss cutter and pith helmet; also an ill-fitting pair of boondockers. Then we are marched to the mess-hall for supper, and finally we arrive at a quonset hut which is to be our barracks for the next four weeks. I have a great empty feeling inside me as I realize that the war has finally come to me; or I have come to it, either way.[6]

Feeling low in boot camp[7]

We have no time to sit down or simply do what we want. Our day starts at 4:30 when we are rousted out of our sacks[8] *and made to run*

---

[6]Skivvies are underwear; piss-cutter, also called cunt-cap, is a barracks cap; boondockers are rough unpolished field shoes, always two sizes too wide to accommodate for carrying heavy loads that will spread out the feet.

[7]Recruit depot

four laps around the parade ground. Then we shower, shave and get dressed. We hustle to get enough food before everybody scarfs it all up. Returning to our quonset barracks, we make our sacks precisely as instructed and straighten up our footlockers. At 8:15 we are out on the parade ground again, doing calisthenics marine style, with a minimum of fifty pushups, more if we screw up. Because some amateur boxer from the Bronx happens to be aboard,[9] our drill-instructors (D.I.'s) get the idea that we ought to learn to box along with doing everything else, so the first thing this guy gets us to do is strengthen our arms by holding them straight out from our bodies for ten minutes. "Don't drop your arms," he urges, "Keep them up, keep them up." I strain to keep mine up. "Groan, groan, will it never end?" At the end of the ten minutes my arms and shoulders are completely paralyzed.

That is just how the day begins. Pretty soon we learn close-order drill. We are marched up and down, forward and back, with the D.I. screaming at us, "Your other left, you idiot! Try to keep in step." In a few weeks we begin to do this with rifles. Then we learn the manual of arms, in which we go through a fixed routine of shifting the piece[10] to various positions while marching.

There is a short break for lunch. Part of the afternoon we are in classes. Much of this is boring and we fight to stay awake. An important thing to learn is what they call "General Orders," the Marine Bible. We have to learn these by heart and recite them upon demand. "Do not strike your superior officer.....Do not leave your post until relieved....Obey every lawful command...." What is a lawful command? What is an unlawful command? Am I being given any unlawful commands?

As the day draws to an end, we are supposed to have leisure time, time to amble down to the PX,[11] time to write home. But not we! We are the lucky platoon that has a D.I. who takes us out for an extra hour of drilling after supper while everyone else is relaxing!

We have to take turns practicing to be sentinels, marching up and down the dark corridors of the headquarters building for four hours

---

[8] Beds

[9] On the base

[10] A more delicate name for "rifle," with certain erotic allusions

[11] Post-exchange, borrowed from the Army. The Navy says "Ships-stores."

126   The 1940's: Feeling low in boot camp

at a stretch. I happen to be assigned one night to the 0200-0600[12] watch. Somebody awakens me at 0145 and gets me pointed in the right direction. I relieve a grateful marine and start marching, up and back, up and back. There is no one for me to try my "General Orders" on. Nothing happens. I get so tired I almost fall asleep while marching. Never in my life has a night passed so slowly! Eventually my relief shows up, just in time for me to get breakfast and hurry out to the parade ground.

Something we are taught to be very particular about is our rifle. We are married to our M-1. Every day it has to be taken apart and cleaned, whether or not it has been fired. One thing we must never do is call it a "gun." "The Navy has guns on ships, you have rifles," we are taught. Pretty soon they make us take our rifles apart and put them back together in the dark. We can appreciate that this is a useful and necessary skill for when they get jammed up while one is fighting in the jungle at night.[13]

I could take this all in stride were it not for extra duty such as policing the grounds for cigarettes and wrappers, cleaning the head[14], and helping in the galley.[15] The head has to be kept as clean as we can get it. This is certainly important because contagious diseases can wipe out a fighting force. That is why certain facilities are marked off for guys who get V.D.[16]

I think I have just hit bottom. We are supposed to get extra food on Sundays, which is supposed to be good for our morale. But today is Sunday and we have received hardly anything to eat the whole day, nothing but some semi-sour milk, sliced baloney, dry bread, and vanilla wafers. Somebody tells me that this has happened because messhalls are given supplies for a month at a time, and this is at the end of an extra-long month. This information does not make me feel

---

[12] Universal military time-equivalents for 2-6 a.m.
[13] Not an idle metaphor. This is exactly what the marines and G.I.s had been doing for eight months on Guadalcanal.
[14] Latrine
[15] Dining hall, not just where food is prepared
[16] Everybody knows what V.D. is. In Officer Candidate School I learned that any officer who contracts syphilis or gonorrhea will be court-martialed.

any happier. It's probably a prophecy of how bad food can get, and therefore will get, in the Marine Corps!

I do manage to get letters off to Betty regularly, and of course I am receiving hers. A good thing, for there are no books and no time to read; no music to listen to and no time to listen to it; no movies to go to and no time to go to movies. Also, I never once during the entire time I am in boot camp get to go to Sunday services at the post chapel. I don't know why -- that's just the way it is. It seems that someone is hassling us, but what can we do about it? It's a good thing I have plenty of stamps and writing paper because we are not even allowed to go to the PX, not one single time in the entire eight weeks!

Learning to shoot straight

A change that comes about at the end of the first four weeks in boot camp is that we are shifted to new barracks -- still a quonset hut -- and spend most of our activity time on the firing line rather than on the parade ground. All attention is now drawn to the M-1 (Garand) rifle, a semi-automatic weapon in the firing of which every marine must be proficient, whether or not he ever gets into infantry action in the field.

Every marine must be ready and capable to be so placed if the occasion should arise. Keep in mind that on the average there are nine men in the rear echelons to back up each man on the front line, but if an enemy force so chooses, it can always put all ten men in peril through unanticipated aggressions.

During the first week of the final four, we spend a lot of time learning each of the firing positions: prone, kneeling, sitting, and standing.

The rifle is equipped with a leather sling that can be shortened or lengthened to suit the person or the purpose. It is used for carrying or for keeping the piece steady while it is being aimed and fired. It is not easy to keep a rifle steady. That is why the most stable position is the prone -- unless there is some handy prop to use while in one of the other positions. The position they are the most anxious to have us learn is the standing position. It is the quickest to get into. One should stand with outstretched legs for good balance, place the left arm around the sling so as to steady the barrel, then place the right hand on the grip with the trigger finger on the trigger. The trigger is not overly loose. It must not be pulled in a jerk, but very smoothly and steadily. Holding one's breath is recommended.

Other things to pay attention to are the trigger lock, which must always be kept on until one receives the order to release it, and the sights. There is a rear sight, which has a slot on its top and is adjustable up and down or from side to side, and a front sight, which is a small upright rectangle to be viewed through the slot on the rear sight. In getting ready to fire our pieces, we first have to "sight them in," meaning, adjust the rear sight so as to make the bullet strike the bullseye, neither too high nor too low. The practical reason for having this adjustment available is that longer distances from the firing line to the target require that the rifle should be raised to a higher angle than for a nearby target. It all has to do with trajectories. The bullet coming out of the muzzle has great velocity, but it also has weight. The farther it travels to its target, the more it will drop vertically.

Anyhow, we know the distance to our large paper targets on frames raised and lowered by pulleys, and adjust for that according to our instructions. This is considered to be the average or default setting and the shooter keeps it on this setting until, and unless, it shows it has to be changed for improved marksmanship.

Day after day we practice shooting from each position. We do the same things we will do when we shoot for record on the final day. With the rifle in correct position and under absolute control, we sight down the barrel to align the sights centering on the bullseye. We hold our breath and squeeze. A few seconds after the shot goes off, we are given a signal indicating its effect. This is in the form of a numeral on a round placard, the numerals being one through five, five for perfect -- a bullseye. If we miss the target completely, a red flag called Maggie's Drawers is waved from side to side, as if in mockery. For the benefit of the shooter, the numeral is supposed to be placed just where the shot has struck the target.

Who is it that does the signalling? It is we ourselves, taking turns with our fellows. We hunker down behind a high dirt wall and watch where each bullet strikes. After the assigned number of shots have whizzed through (or past) the target, we lower the target, count the score, paste paper patches over the holes, and signal the results to the shooter. After having gone through this procedure twice a day for a couple of weeks, we are ready to shoot for record. There are different names for the levels of shooting skill that will result: Marksman, Sharpshooter, Expert.

First I must signal scores for the other echelon. When it is my turn to shoot, I am very much keyed up, but still under control. Certainly not wild. I very carefully take my shots and add up my scores as I go along. I begin to notice that many of my shots are not going where I think they should be going. My cumulative score is dropping down enough to keep me from being an Expert. I still hope to make Sharpshooter, but I panic a little when I see that I may not even make that. I must have 192 for Sharpshooter. I begin to get nervous and confused, a bit careless. My final score is 191.

This is a considerable disappointment to me. It is hard for me to accept because I felt fairly certain of making Expert at one point in my shooting. At the end of all the shooting I am surprised to learn that my team of signalers has been giving me the wrong scores. They have shown the position of impact correctly, but have somehow failed to send me the correct numerical score, showing me instead one or two points too low each time. This is, of course, what put me in a panic and made me careless, so that I gradually began to shoot less accurately than I might have. Within this scenario it was impossible for me to excel. I got screwed and as a consequence I screwed myself! Anyway, I will be proud to wear my Marksman medal on my jacket pocket!

Cutting through military bluster

The name of our D.I. is "Sergeant De Lisle." He is impressive because of his snappy manner and striking looks. His uniform is always perfect. He has a handsome face and commanding presence. Even though he is a non-commissioned officer -- not a commissioned officer -- he makes us call him "sir," and I would say he deserves it. You have to respect him. But of all the marines I have met so far, he is absolutely the most profane. He cannot seem to speak a sentence without at least one vulgarity or swear word. He makes it appear that you cannot be a marine who amounts to anything without swearing. Also, he brags of all the women whom he goes to bed with, and I believe him.

130   The 1940's: Cutting through military bluster

We wouldn't have any complaint against Sgt. De Lisle, were it not that he is trying to be recognized as the best D.I. on the base by making us be the best-trained platoon. He does get us to snap-to and hustle, we do try harder because we know he wants us to make him proud. If he is happy, we are likely to be happy. If we don't make him happy, he will see to it that we aren't happy. That's the sum of it! Nevertheless, he has been going too far in taking us out on the parade ground after supper each evening to make us march some more. Just to make us perfect! Just to make us snappy, like champion dogs in a dog show. Just to make him look good.

Inevitably Sgt. De Lisle gets caught. An officer happens to see him drilling us after hours and puts him on report. The result is that he is ordered to quit, not because it is inhumane to us, but because it isn't fair to the other D.I.'s, who have been observing the standing rule against drilling recruits overtime. Typical marine reasoning! All the same, he continues to keep us from going to chapel or the PX. While on Parris Island, we never get to go to either of them.

In spite of all this, I am not afraid of Sgt. De Lisle. He is so colorful that I decide to take his picture with my brownie camera. But I don't dare ask him if I may do it, for fear of his refusing. One day as we are lined up for mail call, I wait until he has a letter to hand me, then, steppng up to him, I snap his picture with his arm extended toward me. Having done so, I take my letter with a thank you! Conceivably, he could chew me out, though I don't know of any rule that I have broken. He doesn't chew me out, but instead smiles and says, "If you get that developed, do you suppose I could have a print?" Like one human being to another human being. "Aye, aye, sir," I reply. I do get the film developed, and I do give him a print. He thanks me for it.

This might have tended to make us buddies except for the barrier of rank and position that remained between us. It was still important for him to keep his mystique and to make us respect his absolute authority for so long as we were in his charge. All in all, I would not mind in the least having a non-commissioned officer like him in my platoon.

A week or so before the end of boot camp, I have a somewhat different ice-breaker with a less admirable figure, a corporal named Young, who has just joined Sgt. De Lisle's staff. I don't like him at all. He is all bluff and swagger. One day he has us in open-order march, going somewhere as usual to wait awhile. "Open-order" means we don't keep in step and are allowed to talk. Cpl. Young has a big wad of chewing tobacco in his mouth and keeps spitting juice. I want to kid him and also to let him know that I'm aware that he is breaking the rule against chewing anything while marching. "Corporal Young," I say, "don't choke on that big wad you're chewing!" His eyes pop open and he almost does swallow his wad. He remembers that he is supposed to frown and growl, and he blurts out, "I'm putting you on report for talking to me like that!" But nothing happens. It is all bluster.

Soon afterwards Cpl. Young seeks an opening for breaking the ice with me. I am surprised that he wishes to have words with me in private. It is the day before our recruit training comes to an end. He comes up and tells me to follow him to his quarters. Then he lays a photo before me and asks, "What do you think of that? Pretty good, don't you think?" It is a shot of a woman's genitals. I am supposed to be gratified by this crude gesture, but instead I am shocked and angry. Cpl. Young continues, "I have picked you out because you've got some gumption. I want you to go around and ask the men in your platoon for a little love-offering for Sgt. De Lisle and me." Without a word I walk out. He knows he can't stop me. He does not get any love-offering. The following day we leave for Quantico.

I would say that the good and the bad were unevenly mixed in men like these, just as in the human race as a whole. Sgt. De Lisle had it together. Cpl. Young was a vile toad. I think I know now the difference between a lawful and an unlawful command. Cpl. Young wasn't actually ordering me, but he was attempting to suborn discipline and put improper pressure on me. This was certainly not the kind of discipline that keeps men fighting together in the crisis of battle!

My arrival in Quantico

It is early in the month of July, 1943. We are sleepy and exhausted. We have just got off the train.

132   The 1940's: My arrival in Quantico

All the platoons that had been undergoing training in Parris Island were now mixed together indiscriminately, but we would soon be sorted out alphabetically. In Parris Island my own platoon consisted of men from the midwest and south, but now those from the east were mingled with us to form new platoons.

As our names are called, we march off, led by NCO's to one of three stately brick barracks that look identical. They are labeled A, B, and C. D and E are behind them, and that is where the new class of lieutenants who have just graduated are now entering the Platoon Leaders' School in which we in turn are destined to be enrolled if we pass Officer Candidate School. We are scheduled to be commissioned Second Lieutenants at the end of August, eight weeks from now.

It had been a rough experience getting to Quantico. We marines from Parris Island took up most of the seats on the train we were travelling on. There were civilians on board, but they had to be satisfied with the seats that were not needed by us marines. We would all line up to be fed in the one lone diner. I didn't get my turn until after 10 p.m., 2200 as we would say. Not that we had anywhere to go. We were just trying to keep from starving, that is all! After returning to my seat, I tried to sleep but found it impossible because of the chatter and the crowding. I found a place on the floor of the lounge car where I could lie undisturbed, and got some sleep that way. My uniform became rumpled and filthy, but so did everybody else's. We had no chance to wash ourselves or shave.

Our train started out at Beaufort, SC and passed through Yemassee on the way to Charleston. After standing in the station at Charleston for a while, we sped on through the night through the states of South Carolina, North Carolina, and Virginia, to arrive in Quantico, forty miles south of Washington, at this early hour.

We have been given no breakfast on the train, so the first place they march us to is the mess-hall. We cannot believe our eyes at what we behold on the tables: food of considerable variety and of a quantity sufficient for satisfying every one of our hungry bellies! Eggs, bacon, sausage, toast, grits, oatmeal, dry cereal, fruit, even ice cream! Ice cream for breakfast? You had better believe it! The Marine Corps knows what it takes to make a half-starved bunch of survivors from Parris Island feel welcome!

Our barracks are going to be far more comfortable than those we have been living in during the past eight weeks. Everything is arranged to confirm my feeling that it is an honor to be here as a candidate for promotion to Second Lieutenant. We will still have to sleep in double bunks as in Parris Island, one man above another, and we will have to make up our own sacks. But the floors are tile and we have standing steel lockers along the walls to take the place of wooden lockers standing on the floor next to the foot of our sacks. Also the showers and toilets are attractive as well as commodious.

We will be kept under as sharp a discipline here as at Parris Island, but it will have a different focus and quality. In boot camp we were virtual automotons because what we needed was discipline. Here we will be given more responsibility because an ability to accept responsibility will be a major test whether a candidate deserves to become an officer. We will be under close supervision. We will be allowed to go anywhere we wish here on the base, once our daily schedule is concluded, but we may not leave the base without permission and we must be in our sacks for bed-check at eleven p.m (that is 2300) sharp, without exception.

We do not yet know all this. For most of the morning we are allowed to shower, catch up on sleep, and arrange our gear. Each platoon is assigned a place within one of the three buildings, A, B, and C. I am in Building A, which is no surprise because I am near the beginning of the alphabet. The platoons are divided into squads of eight men each, and bunks for each squad are assigned alphabetically, which means that I am located near the main corridor. We have no choice of up or down, it goes alphabetically. Dever is first, then De Vries, next Dewey and Dougherty, Drinker and Duckworth, Duncan and Erickson. Odds are down, evens are up. With most of these men I am still unacquainted, but we are certain to know one another very well by the time this course is completed.

Officer Candidate School

They have been marching us everywhere on the map. When we haven't been marching, we have been in some kind of class. When we haven't been in class we have been shooting something.

No more M-1 rifle. The main weapons they were now training us on were the .50 cal watercooled and the .30 cal aircooled machine guns. Each morning following breakfast we reported to the basement floor of our barracks to load bullets into the ammunition belts that we would be using. Then we boarded trucks for the machine-gun range. Forget about the .30 cal aircooled, it isn't used very much in combat because it overheats and is too light to be effective. It's the .50 cal watercooled that the marines depend on. The water in its cooling chamber does get very hot during a sustained battle, but as long as there is water in it, it keeps firing as long as you supply ammunition to it. It is reported that once on Gaudalcanal the .50 cal machine-guns had been used so long while repelling a Jap attack that the water had all evaporated and there was no other water handy to replace it, so the marines urinated in it to keep it firing!

It turns out that I am very skilled in this particular weapon, and this is good because it too has to be fired for record. Since there is so much vibration from automatic firing, the target has to be sighted in and the trigger locked. To change to another target, one adjusts the range and direction mechanically by a rachet in the trigger, a flat lever for your thumb. I do well enough with this weapon to make Expert.

Besides this and the rifle, there were no other weapons that one had to qualify for, but we were taught many others that are important in infantry fighting. There was the carbine, a small rifle used by non-combat personnel such as chaplains and medical corpsmen; the 81mm mortar, which hurls an explosive projectile into a high arc so that it will come down on enemy troops who may happen to be out of eye contact. There was the BAR (Browning automatic rifle), which was a longer and heavier weapon with two short fold-out legs to give greater stability to the end of the barrel. One BAR is assigned to each squad, whose members take turns firing and carrying it, a week at a time. Men don't grumble very much about having to lug it around because it is a very effective weapon in a fire fight.

One time I had to carry the barrel portion of an 81mm mortar while another man carried the large steel base. I also carried some mortar rounds, my M-1 rifle, and my 75 lb. field pack. This was on a rather challenging exercise, a practice amphibious landing. We marched to the Potomac and went aboard a scow. Upon reaching the designated place downriver, we climbed down cargo nets into landing craft and approached the shore, ending up wading. Then we marched a mile inland carrying all this gear.

That is how it has been the entire time in OCS. We have been constantly pushed to the limit, both mentally and physically. They have been keeping score on us, and it may seem that they actually want us to crack up or drop out. Actually, they don't want anyone to crack up and they don't want any but the unfit to drop out. Long before a graduation list is posted, certain individuals who aren't making it turn up missing. When this happens, you are given two choices: (1) you go directly to a fighting unit as a Pfc. (meaning probably joining marine operations in the Pacific) or (2) you go to the F.B.I. school which is right next door here in Quantico and become a G-man. Realizing this, I had to correct my previous notion that the very best kind of men got to become G-men. The very best get to be Marine officers and the next best, maybe, become G-men!

Quantico, VA is where the Federal Bureau of Investigation had its school. They actually used our firing range; this is, the pistol and tommy-gun parts of it. Which reminds me of our having to form a special honor guard on one occasion for J. Edgar Hoover and the Duke of Windsor as they left the train at the Quantico station on their way to an inspection of the F.B.I. facilities. Hoover really looked tough. Edward had huge bags under his eyes.

During this entire period there has been little relaxation for us, but we have received weekend passes, the main reason being that our supervisory personnel want a leave for themselves as well. As I have said, one restriction has been that we might not wear dress shoes, on the base or off. We may go anywhere we wish, but we must be back in our bunks by one a.m. sharp Sunday night.

It is the 21st of August, 1943, and I am on bicouac deep away in the boondocks behind Quantico. We are about to make an all-night march into our barracks. I am at the moment chopping some firewood. A sergeant named Luther has seen this as his opportunity to speak privately with me. He comes up and says in a confidential tone, "Why can't we get along, De Vries? I haven't had anything personal against you. I would like in the future to be friends with you." "O gee, that's swell, Sgt. Luther," I reply, "I'd like to be your friend too. I actually have high regard for you."

What this was all about is that about ten days ago I was with three other officer candidates learning how to use the bayonet. Sgt. Luther was our instructor, but he wasn't doing very well. First he had tried to teach us judo, but from his instructions I had not been able to get the hang of it, nor had the other men. So he went on to the bayonet, but he wasn't much better with this, in fact I thought he was rather awkward about it. This made me raise my eyebrows and throw a knowing smile to another candidate. Unfortunately Luther caught me doing it and took it as a personal affront. Shades of Mr. Jump! I wasn't actually making fun of him, anyway; I was just taking note of his humanness in spite of his bluster. Anyway, he looked me in the eye and blurted out, "All right, De Vries, I'm going to see to it that you don't get your name on the graduation list when it comes out next week!" Well, it turned out that my name was on the list. Either he did nothing to prevent it, or his request was not supported by the persons who made up those lists.

Sgt. Luther is afraid that I will find some way to get even with him, and that is why he wants to make friends. He knows that after August 25 I will be a second lieutenant and he will still be a sergeant. He is just mending his fences. You never know.

This kind of thing kept happening to me. A few weeks earlier I had had another run-in with a junior NCO. It was a hot Saturday afternoon and my feet were really hurting from a thirteen-mile hike with full field packs. I had purchased a pair of beautiful cordovan dress shoes for the day when I should graduate, and they were in my locker. But of course I had not worn them. As I drew off my hot boondockers and placed them in the locker, the sight of the dress shoes gave me the idea of putting my feet in them to keep them off the bare floor. I didn't wear them as shoes, I wore them as slippers. But wouldn't you know it? Our company sergeant (not Luther) saw this and immediately censured me. "Don't you know you are forbidden to wear dress shoes, De Vries?" "But Sarge," I replied, "I am not *wearing* them, I'm just using them to keep me from getting athlete's foot." "No damn excuses, you hear? Evidently you are not as familiar as you should be about school rules. To make sure you do know, I want you to get some paper and copy down every single notice on this bulletin board by morning. You'll be too busy doing that to worry about shoes." My face fell a mile. I knew that it wouldn't do any good to argue. "He won't listen to what I have to say. There must be a hundred notices on the bulletin board. It is huge! I'll never get finished." All the same, I didn't have to do what this sergeant said because when our Gunny Sergeant[17] learned of it he countermanded it. While I was standing in formation, Gunny came up to me and said, "Don't you worry, De Vries, you don't have to do it. He was way out of line."

My most momentous week. I took advantage of the opportunity to spend some Saturday nights in Washington, usually at the YMCA. I occasionally went to the USO, who gave me free tickets to concerts and plays. I joined a small Christian Reformed group of servicemen calling itself "Young Calvinists" who were holding Sunday afternoon services in the Western Presbyterian Church on H St NW, led by Rev. John Verbrugge, a CRC Army chaplain stationed in the Washington area.

This brings me to say something really big: Betty and I are going to get married! It will be in Washington because I won't have enough leave time to go to Grand Haven. I may be given a furlough after we complete the ROC Course in November, but that is not guaranteed. Betty and I have decided to get married next Saturday, which is August 28th. I have obtained permission from the church to have the ceremony in their sanctuary, and Chaplain Verbrugge has agreed to solemnize the event free of charge.

With this in mind, Betty has travelled alone and is right now in her hotel room in downtown Washington. Her parents and sister will arrive sometime next week. Grandma De Vries will travel with them and be at the wedding too. Also, my mother and my sister Ruth will be coming all the way from Denver.[18]

---

[17]To be a "Gunnery Sergeant" one had to be an outstanding leader in the field.
[18]Mom and Ruth covered approximately 2000 miles each way going at the speed-

138   The 1940's: My most momentous week

So two big events are in store for me in this week: on Wednesday morning I will be commissioned as an officer in the U.S. Marine Corps. On Saturday evening I will be married to the most perfect woman God ever created! I am going to meet Betty tomorrow and then we will go to the D.C. courthouse and get a marriage license.

I don't know what condition I'll be in because we will have to march home tonight from bivouac, and I don't know whether I'll get any sleep at all before I go to meet Betty.

At midnight we started our fifteen-mile march with rifles and full field pack. The going was terrible because the night was very dark and we had to stumble through a forest filled with slash timber; that is, cut-down trees that had not been removed and made into lumber. We spent the next two hours climbing over these trees and brush. After that it was slog, slog, slog, mile after mile on a dusty road. My stomach had been upset all day, and I was very gassy. My regular place was at the head of our file because I was the tallest, but after standing me as long as they could, the other men demoted me to the end of our file and called me "Goat."

Back in our barracks about 8 a.m., we got breakfast, showered and shaved, then spent the rest of the morning working on our gear. We were not allowed to leave until noon, but when the hour arrived, I was on my way.

Oh, what excitement, what thrill, to think that I will be seeing my sweetheart once again this very day! Too bad I am so exhausted and sleepy!

My train arrived at Pennsylvania Station. By bus and on foot I made my way to Betty's hotel two blocks from the White House. My sweetheart was there waiting for me. The moment we had long been waiting for had come!

We obtain our marriage license and then spend the afternoon and evening together. Since we are not married, I depart to a room in the YMCA, where I should be able to get a good night's sleep, but do not. Just as I am dropping asleep, a drunken sailor, my room-mate,

limit of 35 miles per hour. Bless them!

stumbles in and goes noisily to bed. Later, I have almost dropped off when I hear a flapping noise and discern a dark shape hitting the walls and ceiling. It is a bat, a wandering bat that has entered through the half-open window and perhaps intends to bite one of us! Both of us stumble to our feet and wave towels at it until it flies out the window. By that time I am all wrought up and have a difficult time getting back to sleep, even though I am now even more exhausted.

Next day, Sunday the 22nd, Betty and I go sightseeing together. Sitting in the park with her, I drop off for a short nap, but it turns into a long nap, a very long nap. Finally Betty gets me awake, but I feel groggy and listless the remainder of the day. Betty and I have supper together and then go back to her hotel room. After going over our wedding plans with her, I lie down on her bed to sleep until midnight, when I shall need to hurry to get back to Quantico before bed-check at 1 a.m. When midnight arrives, Betty calls me and tells me that it is time to go. I hear her voice far, far away, as in a distant room. Betty calls me again. She begins to shake me. At last my eyes go half open, but I am not awake. Desperate to get me on my way, Betty helps me put my shoes on. I am still asleep when I stumble out the door, through the corridor to the elevator, down the elevator and out into the street. I begin to come to about a block before reaching Pennsylvania Station.

I receive my gold bars. Betty stayed all week in her hotel except on Wednesday morning, when she travelled to Quantico on the train to attend my commissioning at noon. This was held in the post theater, which was jammed. The Secretary of the Navy and the Commandant of the Marine Corps signed the certificates of commissioning as new Second Lieutenants. "I want you to know," says the Commandant of Marine Corps Schools, "that you are now the best of the best of the best! We Americans have the best armed forces in the world, you are part of the elite fighting service out of all our American armed forces, and you as commissioned officers represent the cream of all the Marines." It was stirring to hear him speak it, and though it sounded like heavy propaganda, I wanted to believe that it was true.

140   The 1940's: I receive my gold bars

It really is different when you become an officer! You are not just recruited; you are given a sort of contract to do a special work for your country. With the certificate of commissioning you gain the right to wear gold bars on your collar tabs and shoulders. You also get considerably more money in your hand, plus an allowance for dependants.

I could not have lunch with Betty after my Commissioning ceremony because we were due back immediately in our old barracks in order to transfer our gear over to the new barracks, D and E, which we were to occupy while attending Platoon Leader School during the coming ten weeks.

From my end, all the wedding arrangements had been made. My dress greens were fresh and new, my new shoes were polished like a mirror, my squad-buddy Dougherty was primed for his part as one of my male attendants. I had tried to get my brother Henry to come from Camp Lejeune to be my best man, but it had been impossible for him to get a leave, so I asked a sailor named Frank Dieleman, whom I had met at the Young Calvinists' worship service, to play this particular role.

Our wedding night
The big day has finally come! All the guests from Michigan and Colorado are in their hotels. Betty's mother has arrived with Betty's gorgeous wedding dress and will help her put it on and get herself ready for the moment when she marches down the altar at the Western Presbyterian Church.

I could not do anything to help because I was being kept most of that last Saturday afternoon of August in classes. The wedding ceremony was set for eight o'clock, but I was due at Betty's hotel at six in order to have supper with her and her family.

In order to meet this schedule, I take off the minute we are allowed to leave and run the half mile into the town of Triangle, next to the Quantico base, where taxis are waiting to hustle the first batch of marines to Washington. Because I am wearing Marine greens in this ninety-degree weather, I sweat profusely while riding in the cab, but I cool off a bit by the time I reach Washington and work my way over to Betty's hotel. She and the other relatives with her have started to eat their supper by the time I arrive. Betty and I savor this happy moment together, then go our separate ways in order to be ready on time for the wedding. I was thinking of just hanging around at the church, trying to get myself cool, but instead I gladly accept Frank Dieleman's invitation to come up to his hotel room and freshen up. I arrive back at the church just on time for the rehearsal. Chaplain Verbrugge has been here a while and is adither because I have not yet presented him with the marriage license, which he insists he have in his possession before he can proceed with the ceremony.

I don't remember much about the wedding, mainly because I was just plain uncomfortable in my Marine greens in the summer heat and humidity of our nation's capital.

Everything seems to swim before my eyes. There are a few people in addition to my relatives sitting in the pews. There are candelabra and flowers. The minister is standing facing the congregation. My attendants and I are in our positions. An organ is playing. The bridesmaid and maid of honor are in their places. Then the grand entrance, Betty adorned in her gown and a long veil, her face obscured with a shorter veil, and on her father's arm. She seems ecstatic and her father has a proud grin on his face.

What precisely was said I do not remember. I do remember that Betty promised that she would "obey," but I know she had her fingers crossed!

Finally come the words of solemnization, the placing of a ring on the bride's finger, and the invitation to kiss the bride.

When the ceremony was concluded we went to the lower level of the church for a small reception. We were surprised to see, standing on a table, a three-tier wedding cake with the figurine of a sailor and his bride on the top. That was not what Betty ordered. She had requested a decorated sheetcake, no more. Before the ceremony the church custodian had offered to pick up Betty's cake at the bakery, and when he did so, he was handed this particular cake with the explanation that it had already been paid for. By the time the wedding was concluded, it was too late to bring it back, so we just enjoyed our free wedding cake, laughing at the little sailor and his bride!

While some guests lingered, those who were in the wedding party -- the bride and groom, two female attendants and two male attendants -- had to be excused to go to the photographer's, but were forced to wait in his studio for what seemed an interminable time while another wedding party had a lengthy array of pictures taken. We just wanted one or two! When our turn finally came, we were sweaty and all out of sorts. This turned out to be the part of our wedding that we disliked the most! Somebody taking advantage of us again!

It is almost midnight. Exhasted from the heat and humidity, and from our long intense day and evening, Betty and I approach the front desk of the Roger Smith Hotel in downtown Washington, where we have reserved a room.. The clerk greets us with, "It's a good thing your marine buddy showed up here and advised us to keep your reservation because you are getting married today, otherwise I would have given your room to someone else because you are so late getting here." Who is this good friend? The hotel clerk doesn't know. I would like to think, not just my marine friend but my Friend in heaven as well![19]

So, finally, here we are at our hotel and we are late -- very late -- just the two of us together, ready to discover the joys and mysteries of holy matrimony. I have no trouble whatever carrying my bride across the threshold. I am as brown as a nut and as strong as a tiger! After showering and getting ready for bed, we kneel together to thank God for making this blessed thing come to pass.

I cannot even imagine what our wedding night might have been like if we had had no hotel room to go to!

Our so-called honeymoon

Betty and I are determined to stay together as long as possible before she either has to go home to Michigan because there is no lodging around for her, or I am sent into combat or further training.

---

[19] When I got back to my barracks I discovered that it was a squad member named Dewey, whom I profusely thanked.

The latter doesn't seem imminent because I am just beginning the ten-week Platoon Leader's Course, but it does seem at first that Betty may have to go home. To stave off this unwelcome possibility, we have checked her into a guest room at the Post Exchange for the maximum of four nights (Monday through Thursday). We have also made arrangements for her to take a job there as sales clerk beginning on the following Monday, which will allow her to spend Friday night on the post in a rustic female barracks located in the attic of the PX. She is allowed to sleep there Friday night even though she has not begun work. Actually she doesn't intend to take this job on Saturday. We are going down to Fredericksburg VA, scene of the bloody Civil War battle, on Saturday in order to find a room for her there.

On Saturday afternoon I got my weekend pass and we took the train to Fredericksburg, twenty miles south of here. We spent Saturday night in the wonderful Stratford Inn,[20] then on Sunday we located a nice room in a private home, paid a week's rent in advance, and returned to Quantico. I kissed Betty goodnight at the entrance to the female barracks, explaining to her that if she did not find a room somewhere near Quantico by the following evening, she would have to take the last train back to Fredicksburg and stay there until I got another weekend pass the following Saturday. This did not seem very ideal, and I was sure that Betty would become very bored and lonely.

I have to be in my own barracks Sunday night for bed-check, and am kept busy all day Monday in the classroom and on the parade ground. There has even been an evening class to keep me from checking on Betty. Finally -- it is about 10 p.m. -- I manage to get away and hurry on foot to the railroad depot to see her off on the train. While on the way I decide that I should also check to see if she is possibly in the PX. Just as I start up the steps, I see a frantic figure coming down. It is Betty! She is weeping and almost hysterical. "Oh Honey, Honey," she cries, "I have been looking all over for you and I didn't know what to do, and now it is almost time to take the train to Fredericksburg and I don't know if I should take it. A nice sergeant in the Post Exchange told me where there is a

---

[20]Subsequently renamed "George Washington Inn."

room that we can rent, but it is two miles outside the town. He offered to take me in a taxi to look at it before someone else gets it, but I didn't dare because you told me never to trust a serviceman."

Kissing away her copious tears, I reply, *"Honey, we'll just have to forget the train, no matter what, and go to see this house right now."* We hire a taxi, see the room, put down the rent, and place Betty's bags in the room. It is a mess, but cleaning it up will give Betty plenty to do. Since it will soon be time for my bed-check, I cannot linger, so I take my fond departure as we promise each other to meet tomorrow evening at the Officers' Club in Quantico. Before I leave, we kneel down together once again to express our thanks to God for providing for our great need in a crisis of dire circumstances.

Betty and I still saw each other almost every day. Some may attribute this to luck. I attribute it to a lot of pluck on the one hand, and to the benevolent guidance of benign Deity on the other hand. The part in which we had no role to play was Mrs. Walker's just happening to get a vacancy at the moment of our desperate need. Also, we had no role in causing a compassionate Sergeant to be in the PX who knew about Mrs. Walker's room and really cared. The part that Betty was responsible for was to keep on looking and asking for help. When she got that help she was in a dilemma, not daring to accept the offer to go and look at the room with the sergeant, yet realizing that she could be stranded all night in the Quantico railroad station if she did not succeed in finding me, which would cause her to miss the last train.

This brings us to my part. It seemed pure happenstance that I met Betty late on Monday evening on the front stairs of the PX when I expected her to be on her way to Fredericksburg. I don't believe very much in coincidence; I am certain that divine providence is what led me to that place and at that time. God certainly knew how desperate Betty was, and that she might wind up in serious trouble if she were unable to find me. God was also caring for her -- and for me -- so he caused us to find each other at the most crucial moment. My role extended further. It involved responsibility and responsiveness. I had to decide forthwith that we should take a taxi to Mrs. Walker's home in the country, not knowing whether the room would still be available and whether it would be suitable. I was quite certain that there was zero chance of getting Betty on the Fredericksburg train if we did this. What I was in fact doing was taking responsibility for a possible mishap of considerable proportions on the chance that it would turn out well and not ill. Call that faith, call it grit, call it skill in adapting to necessity and opportunity. All would be correct. God uses the best that we have, the greatest sacrifice we are willing to offer if this is required. God had surely been directing the course of our daily circumstances, and we trusted him to bring us onward as we faced new challenges and new opportunities.

Mrs. Walker's large old farmhouse is a dump, but Betty has made her decision and has adapted to what is required of her. She has cleaned up her room and is living in it. Since she has kitchen privileges, she makes her own breakfast and lunch. In the afternoon she walks two miles, or takes the taxi, to the base to watch us march or do whatever interests her. When I finish in the afternoon, Betty and I enjoy dinner at the Officers' Club. This is very nice; we are impressed by the difference a pair of gold bars make! After dinner we take a taxi out to our room and spend the evening together, then I run the two miles back to Quantico in order to be in my bunk for bed-check. My running partner is a former track star from Ohio State. After a while my squad buddies catch on that I have a sweet little deal going, and they make me pay for it. More than once I find broken glass in my sheets or coke spilled on my pillow.

Platoon Leader School. The acronym for "Officer Candidate School" is OCS, while ROC stands for "Reserve Officers' Class," which is what I was in now. It was also called "Platoon Leader School." I don't know why there were two names for it, but the second name identified more accurately what we were being trained for, which was to lead platoons of marines in infantry combat. Most of us would end up in the Fleet Marine Force fighting somewhere on a Pacific island. It was quite appropriate, accordingly, that much time was being spent with the weapons we and our men would be using, besides the ones already mastered. We learned to shoot every kind of weapon used by ground forces in combat, and others besides, such as the .45 caliber pistol and the tommy gun (a useless and unmanagable weapon). We learned to use hand grenades and grenade launchers. We learned to use dynamite and plastic explosives. We fired antitank guns and antiaircraft guns. Besides this, we found out new ways of firing our M-1 rifles, such as from the hip, John Wayne style. One purpose of this training was to acquire greater accuracy; another was to make us confident in using these weapons.

An undesired effect of all this shooting, but one that I can hardly avoid, is that my ears are often set ringing. They probably are undergoing permanent damage since we have no way of protecting them. The Marines won't worry about that because we may not live long anyhow.

Getting more directly into our specific training for platoon leadership, we were immersed in techniques for handling troops in combat. This was something that I enjoyed immensely, and in which I received praise for my special skill. We were taken in trucks far out to a wooded area that had been prepared with charges to be set off as we simulated advancing over it. We were given maps and aerial photographs of the area, and were tested on how well we could devise an attack upon a certain position, or prepare a defense against attack by the enemy. We prepared all sorts of defense works, from rifle pits to timber barricades. We often had to sleep out at night in pup-tents constructed from two poncho halves, our own and our buddy's, sometimes in a pouring rain. Towards the end of the course we were actually out in the frost, wearing sheepskin coats. Things were not always serious; one of our instructors had a public address setup in his vehicle for playing snappy music for our enjoyment.

We were also taught about military organization and administration. We learned military etiquette. We continued to march and drill a lot, but the emphasis was now upon controlling large units of men -- platoons or companies -- on the parade ground.

This too I enjoyed, with the exception of one embarrassing moment when I called out "Column right march" when I meant to say, "Column left march."

I have been doing just fine and feel very proud of myself as I march at the head of an entire platoon of my fellows. There has been no mishap as I have maneouvred my platoon around the parade ground in the view of the staff officers and assorted spectators such as my wife. Given the order to bring the platoon in line with others marching and then bring it to a position in front of our barracks for dismissal, I prepare to wheel them to their left and march left myself, but I call out "Column right march!" and so they start to go right. Immediately perceiving my error, I call "Halt," and then "About face," "To the rear march," "About face" again, then "Forward march," and finally "Column left march." When the men are in the correct position I command, "Halt," "Right face," "Order arms," and "Fall out!" For a moment I wonder if it will be worth living. I am too chagrined to look anybody in the face. But most are kind, knowing that they could cut the same caper, and say nothing.

Such mistakes cannot be disguised; they are there for every eye to see. My colonel immediately sent for me, and I entered his office with trepidation. I need not have feared. Actually he thought it a very amusing incident and certainly not one to jeapordize my prospects as a Marine officer in any way. When he asked me whether I had learned an important lesson in this mixup I replied, "Most certainly, Sir! And I won't let anything like it happen again." But I was certain that my mistake would eventually tally in how I would be rated.[22]

[22] Although I otherwise scored high in virtually every exercise, I ended up about one third from the bottom of my class when my instructors and peers voted. Each man was given a list with the names of all his fellows and was asked to rank them all numerically. This was then averaged out alongside a similar list that the instructors had filled out. I thought it all but certain that my fellow trainees would look upon me as something of a klutz for my screwup in this instance, although another probable factor may have been their envy that I had managed to find a way of keeping my wife close by, while they had to do without. Because of my lower than average standing in my class, I made First Lieutenant a month later than others ahead of me and missed out by just a week of making Captain before the War ended. Not that that mattered once the War was over and most of us headed back to civilian life!

Soon ROC will be finished and I will probably be sent into combat to practice what I have learned. I will have to send Betty home, and I may not see her again until the war ends -- if it ever does end! Sometimes I am unmindful of my blessings and start to feel sorry for myself. Why am I here, at the very point of being placed under enemy fire somewhere far away, when I could be safe back in Grand Rapids, studying in the seminary and preparing to become a minister rather than a platoon leader?

I shall have to search my heart on this, but I am certain that I don't think like this because I am a coward -- far from it! What I regret is the denial of personal freedom and the threat to the realization of the goal I always thought God was preparing me for. I will have to leave this up to him. He has not yet forsaken me, and he won't do it now!

Our Arrival in Columbus, Georgia. It was about a week before the end of Platoon Leader School that I found out about my next assignment. It was not as I had assumed all along, to be sent directly to the Fleet Marine Force and combat in the Pacific. This is what happened: Shortly before graduation, a notice was posted with a list of military specialties for which there are appropriate schools, and one that I applied for was communications. Recalling that I had helped my dad in electrical installations while he was working in construction in Denver, and that I later helped erect power lines at Camp Hale at Pando, I realized that I might have some kind of head start in this specialization. After a few days, the news came through that my application had been approved. A set of orders followed. I was to have a ten-day furlough, and after that was to report to the Infantry School in Ft. Benning, GA to attend a special course in communications for Army officers. The government was to pay for my travel down there, but of course we ourselves would be responsible for Betty's fare. I would also be paid a subsistence allowance, and we hoped that this would be sufficiently generous to partially pay Betty's expenses as well, in spite of the fact that, according to the orders I received, she was not supposed to be accompanying me there.

We said farewell to Quantico, where I had been since the beginning of July, and Betty since the end of August. We travelled together to Grand Haven. At home with Pa and Ma Schouten, we were able to hold a proper reception for our wedding, with Uncle Jack De Vries as Master of Ceremonies. All my Grand Rapids relatives were invited, along with many on Betty's side, mainly from Grand Haven and Muskegon. The days of my furlough flew by, and we soon found ourselves about to set out on our trip to the southland. We naively supposed that we would have no difficulty finding a room in Columbus, as we had done in Quantico. Columbus, GA is after all a far larger place than Quantico!

It is a Saturday night in mid-November, 1943. Betty and I are about to be punished for our brazen persistence in sticking together in disregard of the automatic order that there will be no quarters provided for dependents, and they are not to be taken along. At Quantico I received this same notification when I was sent to the Platoon Leader School, but in spite of some hairy moments, it worked out after all. But this time it looks as if we may be stopped cold. We are both very weary from our long train ride from Grand Haven, MI to Columbus, GA, a trip of at least a thousand miles.

When we leave the train and enter the station, we are informed that all the local hotels are jammed with servicemen on weekend pass. Fort Benning is a huge establishment. We had of course counted on being able to get a hotel room over the weekend, and afterward to find a room somewhere for Betty to stay in while I am at the Infantry School in Fort Benning. But the sight of soldiers sleeping on the floor and every chair filled makes it look as if we are finally out of luck. We probably will end up sleeping on the floor of the station like the others.

Arriving in a town like Columbus on the very worst day of the week, Saturday, is not a smart thing to do. Soldiers are lying on the floor and occupying every seat. Prayers are therefore in our hearts as we make our hopeful way to a desk marked "Travelers' Aid," behind which a kind-looking middle-aged lady is sitting. We ask her about the availability of rooms, but she shakes her head and says, "I'm terribly sorry, there is nothing whatever available on a weekend like this." Just as she says this, the telephone rings. She picks up the receiver and motions for us to wait. After a moment she puts her hand over the receiver and asks, "Are you Christians?" Of course we are, but why should she ask? The kind lady passes this information down the line to the person on the other end, "Yes, they are Christians, a Marine lieutenant and his wife." After further interchange she hangs up and reports, "This is a minister whose wife and daughter happen to be away for the weekend, and knowing how difficult it is for servicemen to find lodging, he wishes to welcome a service couple into his home. But of course he doesn't want anyone who is rowdy or incongenial. That is why he is asking for a Christian couple."

"Are you Christians?" Was it a good-hearted preacher who wanted to know this, or was it God? Was I still a genuine Christian even while wearing the uniform of a U.S. Marine? Yes, maybe we hadn't been as good Christians in practice as we professed to be, but that was what we were and intended to be in spite of our faults. So if this was to be God's way of helping us out of yet another grand mess, we were glad that it could come to pass because we are Christians -- not the getting into the mess but the getting out of it. Getting into trouble can happen to all kinds, worthy or unworthy. But God has his mysterious ways of bringing about the good of those who fear him and love him. Some would call this luck or happenstance, I chose to call it divine leading. How ungrateful we would seem if we did not give God the credit for allowing two people very much in love with each other, and very much committed to his service even in and through service to our country, to find a way of remaining with each other yet a few more months before going off to what might be a long separation!

A taxi drops us off at the manse of the Rev. Dr. John Calvin Reid, pastor of the First Presbyterian Church of Columbus. We are warmly welcomed inside. Dr. Reid shows us to our room and introduces us to his black maid, who will make some meals for us. We are told that we must leave, however, on Monday since he expects his wife and daughter back home then. But he assures us that some rooms in private homes in the city are available for servicemen, if one only looks for them. He promises to chauffeur Betty around this section of Columbus on Monday morning to look at what might be available, while I am away at Ft. Benning.

Learning Army communications at the Infantry School. It gave me a measure of satisfaction that I was able to remain in command of

Learning Army communications 151

my destiny to the extent of having Betty with me part of the time while I served in the armed forces. It was also gratifying that I could exercise an option offered me that might give me a role in the Marine Corps that would draw from my special gifts and talents. By receiving advanced training in a specialty, I would be in a position to offer a strategic service toward the functioning of the military unit to which I might eventually be assigned.

I am at Ft. Benning, attending a three-month course in communications for Army officers. The connection between infantry operations in the U.S. Army and infantry operations in the Marine Corps is very close, and that is why the latter relies on the former to provide this schooling. There are some duplications here with what I have already learned in Platoon Leaders' School back in Quantico, such as a third course in map reading. While here we will receive no training in weaponry or infantry leadership as such. There is plenty of that going on elsewhere on this large military reservation, but it is all for Army personnel and not for us. I am particularly intrigued to observe the paratroopers as they practice jumping from a high steel tower. Nor do we have contact with enlisted personnel in this particular school except for the few who have support functions. It is specifically for officers, preparing them for the specialty, Communications Officer, in order to be assigned to a combat unit of battalion or regimental strength.

As far as we marines were concerned, this anticipated that we would be functioning within the headquarters structure of a Marine battalion or equivalent unit. There are four distinct specializations within the headquarters of any such unit, corresponding to four distinct functions or responsibilities: (1) intelligence, (2) operations, (3) communications, and (4) supply.[23] Being placed in such a unit did not mean, to be sure, that we would have little or no contact with enlisted personnel. On the contrary, we would have direct command over NCO's and privates who would be assigned to specific tasks within the unit, depending on its size and mission.

There are two special things that belong among the responsibilities of communications personnel in a combat situation.

---

[23] In military jargon these are respectively as G-1, G-2, G-3, and G-4.

152   The 1940's: Learning Army communications

One of these is the special kind of "language" that military units have traditionally relied upon, Morse Code. We learn how to receive it and how to send it. In receiving, we listen with earphones as we write with pencils on special message pads, which would then be presented to the communications officer and passed on by him to an appropriate officer for information or action. For several weeks we are in class morning and afternoon learning Morse Code. We practice it over and over again until it becomes as familiar as the language we speak. In fact it becomes a habit so tenacious that we catch ourselves speaking in code ("ditta-da-da-ditti, da-ditta-da-da-dit," etc.). Or we will be tapping it out on the table-top with our fingers, as though using a telegraph key. Because I can hardly stop myself from doing this, Betty calls me "code-happy."

In infantry operations, telegraphy had been mainly superseded by the field telephone and the backpack radio, but we still had to be familiar with Morse Code in the event that these more modern devices should fail in particular situations. Of course, to have telegraphy, combat forces needed also to have electric wire strung from superior to inferior units. How to prepare and maintain this system was another of our major areas of training.

Here I have opportunity to exercise the familiarity with field wiring that I gained at Pando. Just as the civilian linemen did there, we put on cleats and safety belts and go out into the woods to climb the trees that will carry our communication lines. We are reminded that under combat conditions we may expect to be doing this while the enemy are shooting at us with rifles, but we think it is great fun anyway.

To some extent we were familiarized also with the technology of the field telephone and the backpack radio. In combat units there are enlisted personnel having specialized knowledge of how to repair them and keep them working. The field telephones are fairly reliable once the lines are strung and remain intact. But they are most useful in static and defensive situations. They are relatively useless in offensive operations, which must rely on the radios carried by front line and rear echelon troops. These can be rather crucial in making a successful attack, including a situation in which the attackers are forced to resist a counterattack by enemy forces.

Apart from our small contingent of Marine lieutenants, the student-body in this class consists entirely of junior Army officers. There is no rivalry; we are all in this together, and we all respect one another. It might be different if we were obnoxious Marine grunts, but we are officers and as such are conscious of our responsibilities as well as our privileges as prospective members of combat staffs.

To be sure, no one stands on his dignity. We enjoy fun and horsing around. One particular Army guy is a regular riot. He is both a ski-trooper trained in Pando and headed for the Italian campaign, as well as the only son of the man who owns the Dixie cup organization. He just loves playing practical tricks, such as starting fires in folded maps sticking out of back pockets.

There is a lot of standing around. During such periods of idleness the dice are brought out and a crap game begins. I won't be getting involved in things like that!

I don't sleep in barracks that are available to me, but I do receive my noon-meal, such as it is, in the Army mess-hall. It is awful food! The Army must assign its very worst misfits to duty as cooks! The only way I can down this vile stuff is by smothering it with ketchup.

Although I am entitled to sleep in barracks on the post, I sleep instead in a double bed in the room that Betty and I have rented from Carey and Muriel Joiner, a lovely Southern middle-aged couple with one child, a ten-year old son.[24] Dr. Reid helped Betty find this room and we are very comfortable in it. We are allowed to use the kitchen for making our breakfast and Betty has her lunch there. In the evening, after I return from the base, we take a bus into downtown Columbus, where we often have our supper at the famous S. & S. Cafeteria. We enjoy this cheap, good, and plentiful food.

The Joiners were Baptists, and they showed true Christianity in their very gracious hospitality toward us. Once they treated us to a home-cooked dinner of genuine Southern-fried chicken. They also treated us to a concert of the famous Grand Old Opry, a four-hour production that they evidently relished far more than we were able to do.

A Marine lieutenant named Bud Chesley[25] has brought his

---

[24]Carey Joiner, Jr., who later distinguished himself as an Air Force colonel.
[25]Chesley was very severely wounded during a Marine landing in the spring of 1944,

convertible with him. Since he also lives in town with his wife, he is able to provide convenient transportation for us to and from the base. I don't get to know him very well in spite of this daily contact; he was with us in Quantico. The one marine whom I do get to know very, very well is Bob Dever, my old bunkmate from Quantico. We discover that we have very much in common, particularly the coincidence that he got married to his wife Dotty on the same weekend when I got married, August 28. Dotty did not go down to Quantico, but she does come to Columbus. She and Bob have found a pleasant room to live in close to us, with the result that Betty and Dotty see a lot of each other and become fast friends. Bob and I become closer than we were in Quantico. He is very much interested in what I have to say about religion and theology.[26]

One other person deserving special mention was our first host, John Calvin Reid. As I said, he was pastor of the First Presbyterian Church in Columbus, distinguished looking and a fine preacher. We both enjoyed his sermons, and especially his innovative talks for children which he called, "Bird Life in Wington."[27] It turned out that ten or twelve Christian Reformed army personnel from Ft. Benning also attended his church. I helped organize this group into a "Young Calvinist" Bible study class, with myself as teacher. This experience proved to be more satisfying to Betty and me than attending chapel services had been in Quantico, which we had found rather cold and unappealing. I was experiencing that there is room for a profession of Christianity while serving in the military services.

Still together at Harvard

It is springtime in 1944 and we have moved north to Cambridge, MA, where we have found a room in a large frame residence a few blocks from Harvard yard, the central quadrangle of the great university founded in 1632 by John Harvard. Since marines are solders, we have been sent to an Army school for communications

shortly after he left Ft. Benning.
[26] Bob and Dotty went to teachers college in upstate New York. Bob and I remained colleagues in Marine training until June, 1944, when he joined a fighter squadron bound for Okinawa. After the war he enjoyed a brilliant career as teacher and administrator in a public school system on Long Island.
[27] This was eventually published as a very popular children's book.

officers. Since they are also naval personnel, the powers that be have now sent us to a Navy school for communications officers. As in the Army school, this is to be a three-month experience.

When I received new orders in February I was again told that there would be no provision for dependents. We would be required to live and sleep on base, which in this case would be the yard, dormitories and dining halls ordinarily used by Harvard underclassmen. However, we did not allow ourselves to be scared away in this new situation. I did send Betty home on the train while I journeyed on alone to Philadelphia for two weeks at the Marine Supply Depot. There was nothing for me to do or learn at that depot; it was just a fill-in. All I had to do day after day was show up and be dismissed. Growing bored and lonely in such circumstances, I asked Betty to shorten her vacation and join me in Philadelphia for the remainder of the two weeks. We shared a room in the YMCA, then took the train for Boston, with a one-night stay-over in New York. This was memorable only in that Betty was very sick in New York from drinking the Schuylkill River water of Philadelphia. Oh, yes, it was memorable also because the hotel manager in New York required us to show our marriage license before he would allow us to share a room together.

Once in Cambridge, I reported in at the naval school headquarters. Then, with the assistance of a housing bureau, we two searched on foot for a room and finally found a room that would do. It was not as nice as our room with the Joiners in Georgia, but very much more attractive that the room outside Quantico. It came with kitchen privileges, which meant that Betty and I were allowed to make some of our own meals. We would have been perfectly content with this arrangement, were it not for the grouchiness of our landlady, Mrs. Paine (who seems very well named)[28] and one of the other residents, a navy lieutenant commander who tried to pull rank by usurping our kitchen time. Some of the other residents who were naval personnel made up for it by being especially nice to us.

In this new experience, Betty is determined to make more profitable use of her time, so she goes to work at the great Widener Library as a page. She is able to meet some lovely people on this job.

---

[28] Appropriately, we referred to her as "Mrs. Ouch."

The stacks hold over twelve million volumes, so Betty feels almost lost when deep in the bowels of the library searching for books for the scholars who are asking for them.

On week-nights I am supposed to be sleeping in the dormitory room assigned to me, but after bed-check each evening I take off and spend the night with Betty instead. Then I report in after breakfast for roll-call. Most of the students are, of course, junior naval officers. They are the ones the school is designed for. This makes it unavoidable that some of what is taught should be irrelevant for Marine officers, such as signalling with flags aboard ship and navigating sea-vessels. Yep, I have learned how to figure a vessel's precise position in the middle of the ocean, though I'm sure that as a marine I shall never be called upon to practice it!

There is only one skill taught here that promises to be permanently useful to me, taking down Morse Code on a typewriter. I get good enough at this to receive eighty words per minute. This is superfluous for me as a Marine officer, even if I were aboard a ship, because enlisted men would be doing this work. Well, perhaps, if every other officer and enlisted man on board a ship had been killed off and only I were left! But typing as such is a skill that will always be useful.

One other skill that I learn here at Harvard that has some potential usefulness, though hardly for a combat marine, is the deciphering and decoding of garbled messages sent by shortwave radio from one naval ship or station to another. The Navy has developed super-secret coding/decoding instruments, and we are privileged to operate them. Our classes are held in a secret place, deep in the bowels of one of the laboratories.

Boston and environs were, to be sure, interesting for their historical significance. We seized the opportunity to see Lexington, where the Revolutionary War began, and Plymouth, where the pilgrims landed. For Sunday worship we sought out churches such as Ockenga's Park Congregational in downtown Boston and that of the Whitinsville colony of Christian Reformed dairymen. The Whitinsville experience was an adventure in itself because of the unlimited food that was offered by a uniquely hospitable membership to visiting servicemen. For breakfast they served guests eggs and sausages, steak, home-fried potatoes, apple pie, cereal cooked or dry, and plenty of toast and jam.

Bob Dever is also at this school, though his wife Dotty has returned home. Because our names are closely adjacent in the roster, he is again my roommate. One night we have the watch together, which means nothing at all except that we must run a record playing taps at sunset and reveille at sunrise while we lower and raise Old Glory in the campus yard. We have the duty all night, but nothing happens. We take turns sleeping, first Bob for two hours and then I for two hours.

There is a live microphone in our watchroom rigged up to a P.A. system. Being quite bored, we decide to try it out. It just so happens that a group of pretty girls are passing through the Yard just in front of us. I let out with a magnificent wolf-whistle, "phew-e-roo, phew-e-roo!" Actually I do not intend that the objects of my admiration should hear this. It is just an expression of my private enthusiasm. But they hear it. Do they ever! The P.A. system carries the sound throughout the Yard and far out into the city of Cambridge. Everyone, including the young ladies in question, is startled, even terrified. The girls stop and look around in vain to discover from where this menacing sound has come. Bob and I hunker down out of sight, not wishing to be identified as the cause. We fully expect to be called in for a reckoning on the following morning, but apparently the officer in charge of the school never learns of it. Discipline is very slack at this school.

Hanging on in Greenville, North Carolina

It is June 4, 1944. Travelling up here on the bus, I heard that the invasion of Europe has begun! Maybe it will be over soon in Europe, but I am certain that the war in the Pacific will last many years yet. I have arrived in a small city in the lowlands of North Carolina named Greenville. No doubt about it, it is very green here -- lots of water, lots of foliage. But it is also hot as blazes. Not much seems to be going on in this town. It does have a teachers' college. On the north end of town there is a landing field and a small military base presently occupied by VMSB 343,[29] a Marine dive-bomber squadron about to be sent overseas. I am one of the last personnel they have been waiting for in order to complete their roster.

---

[29]V stands for "aviation unit," M stands for "Marine," SB stands for "scout-bomber." Originally these units were called either S or B, depending on their primary mission.

After more than a year of training, I had finally been sent to permanent duty. In true military tradition, I was assigned duty for which I had previously received no training whatsoever: a Marine aviation unit! I had learned marching, leading combat units in the field, shooting all sorts of weapons, map reading, field communications, signal flags, naval navigation. But I knew nothing at all about aviation, Marine or otherwise. How did I get into this? The answer is perhaps simple: someone higher up looked at the roster of lieutenants just completing their training as communications officers. Marine Aviation needs communications officers just like everyone else. If they wanted four or five to fill a special quota, the first four or five were checked off at the head of the roster, stopping probably after "Dever" and "De Vries." It is hard to believe that we were picked because we were the best qualified, but maybe that is the reason.

Many years later, Bob Dever told me that in discussing this with his new C.O. at Cherry Point Marine Air Station he was advised that we had been selected for Marine Aviation because we had received high grades in our previous training. It is flattering for me to accept this as the correct explanation. Either way, God's leading is not ruled out. He uses whatever means he chooses, a bureaucratic checkoff or a record of superior performance in training as a prediction of a higher level of competence in dealing with the operation of highly technical war machines. As my old grandmother used to say, "De Heere kan recht slaan met een kromme stok (The Lord can hit straight with a crooked stick)."

We were both to report to the Cherry Point, NC, Marine Air Base. Bob Dever joined a fighter squadron there, but I was sent to an isolated squadron at a small airstrip fifty miles or so northwest of Cherry Point. That was the last I was to see of Bob Dever until long after the War.

After reporting in for duty I was excused to make arrangements for some place to live in the town of Greenville. To be sure, I could sleep at the airfield if I were unaccompanied, and that is what I would ordinarily expect to be doing. But I wanted Betty with me, through thick and through thin, and she wished to be with me. There would not be much more time. We knew it!

I had little to choose from. After renting an upstairs room in a large Southern mansion, I drove a service vehicle via New Berne to

Hanging on in Greenville, North Carolina 159

Camp LeJeune. Having come down from Washington on the train with Betty, I had left her at Hank's and Louise's small apartment at LeJeune while I reported in and found a room, so she had been the guest-of-honor there for those two days. Saying farewell to Hank and Lou, we drove back to Greenville, not expecting that Betty would be able to stay with me very much longer because this squadron was scheduled to go overseas. But until that should happen, we were willing to try to make the most of those last precious days or weeks together, whatever God should give us.

I am sure that Betty will be glad when the time comes for her to return home. The summer climate in tidewater North Carolina is very hard to bear. It is almost always 100% humid, and every day the temperature rises over 90 degrees, or even 100. Trying to cope with this extreme discomfort, Betty spends each afternoon in the town's single air-conditioned theater watching the same movies over and over again. We routinely eat supper together in the local cafeteria and find it inferior to the S. & S. in Columbus, GA. Then we sit up for a while and afterwards try to sleep. All we have to keep us cool are a small fan and some wet towels. If we survive this, we can survive anything!

I receive an idea of what may lie ahead for me as a member of this squadron when I accept an invitation to ride in the rear seat of a Douglas Dauntless dive-bomber (SBD) to Cherry Point and back. It is a fast ride, most of the way within 100 feet of the ground and sometime winding only yards above the surface of the Tar River. Betty is a bit shocked when I tell her of this. Glad that she has made me promise not to become a pilot, she makes me promise that in the future I won't fly unless required to do so.

Our squadron is put on alert for a possible assignment to Iceland. Iceland? What for? Is this just some more idle scuttlebutt? Anyway, the alert is called off. But one day in early July we receive definite orders. We are to board a trooptrain that will take us to the west coast, from where we will be sent to the Pacific. Betty and I take final leave of the hot old house in Greenville, journey by bus to Kinston, then say a sad and final farewell. The train is crowded. Betty must transfer in Washington. I worry how it will go with her. I do hope and pray that all will be well on her trip and that she may arrive safely at home. And on my own trip, wherever that may lead!

I have never heard anything about Marines being stationed on Iceland, though I did know that the Allied forces were occupying it to prevent it from falling into the hands of the Germans. The powers that be might very well have been considering stationing a Marine dive-bomber unit there. But it was not our destiny to be sent there. Like almost all Marine ground and air units, we were to be stationed in the vast Pacific area for the duration of the war.

Betty walks like a zombie. When our squadron arrived at Camp Miramar, the west-coast shipping depot for Marine aviation north of San Diego, we learned that our squadron was to be delayed for three weeks in shipping out because the CVE (carrier escort) which was to provide our transportation to Hawaii was to be dry-docked for repairs. When I phoned Betty to tell her that we could occupy an apartment at this post for those three weeks before I was to ship out, her dad borrowed gasoline ration stamps from his friends and drove her to Chicago, where he got her on a train for Los Angeles, where she would catch a bus for San Diego.

I am standing in the bus station in San Diego waiting for Betty's bus to arrive. When the L.A. bus comes in, I watch the passengers as they step out, and soon I see a young woman who looks a great deal like my Betty but walks like a real zombie, one of the living dead worshipped in the Voodoo religion. Her hair is disheveled, her clothing is rumpled, her skin is grey, her eyes are hollow and vacant. This is my Betty! Have I put her through this? My heart skips a beat to see her like this, but as I recover from my astonishment and dismay, I immediately realize what an ordeal she has been through. Approaching her, I take her in my arms, kiss her, and say, "Betty darling, it's me, John! I know how desperately tired you must be, and I've come to take you to a hotel to get clean and have some sleep." We take a taxi to the hotel where I have reserved a room. I undress her, put her in the bathtub and scrub her, then put her nightie on her and put her to bed, where she sleeps like the dead for half a day. In a day or two, when she is a little recovered, we will go together to Miramar, where we will enjoy being together in our own little apartment for the next weeks.

Once Betty is rested, she tells her incredible story, explaining why she has come to me looking like this. She has been three days on the train out of Chicago, standing or sitting on her suitcase the whole way. No one on the train has been able to wash during the entire journey because people were sitting and standing in the washrooms. They had to struggle to use the toilets. As for meals, they were hard to get to. Once she arrived at the L.A. station she had to stand in line all night in order to get the last seat on the San Diego bus. Sitting in the rear seat of the bus, she fell dead asleep and had to be awakened when she arrived in San Diego. "Awakened" is hardly the word for it. A soldier sitting next to her called to the driver, "Please, wait for this lady to get out! She can hardly move and doesn't realize where she is!"

From this grim adventure I learned two lessons that I shall not forget as long as I live: (1) that our women have suffered bravely in this war alongside their men, to the extent that they have had opportunity; and (2) that I will never, never forsake the one who was willing to endure so much personal discomfort in order to be with me, even if it was for only three precious weeks!

To anyone who has difficulty understanding this, let me say, "No one can escape the feeling that our servicemen may not make it home again, and many of them never will, you can count on that! That is why time together under difficult circumstances like these is so precious!"

"Temporary training" on Midway. A day after Betty left for home on the Santa Fe Chief, our squadron boarded the CVE that was now ready in Coronado harbor. The officers, including all the pilots, were given comfortable bunks and ate with the ship's officers. The enlisted personnel, meanwhile, were assigned to five-tier bunks in the hanger deck below and ate in the mess-hall. Our new Helldivers were lifted onto the flight deck and fastened down for the voyage. This is the precise purpose of the CVE's. They do not participate in battles, they carry planes and personnel to advanced bases or to regular aircraft carriers.

The voyage to Hawaii took about a week. Upon reaching Pearl Harbor, we were transported directly to Ewa (pronounced "Eh-vah") Field, a Marine airbase a dozen or so miles west of Pearl and adjacent to the large Barber's Point Naval Air Station. One of our enlisted men, a Gunny Sergeant, had been right there at Ewa working as a

162 The 1940's: "Temporary training" on Midway

radioman when the Jap planes flew overhead on their way to Pearl Harbor on Dec. 7, 1941. They also bombed and strafed Ewa Field and Barber's Point.

We did very little while at Ewa except get organized for further transport. Our pilots had to fly regularly, with or without a mission, in order to keep up their flight eligibility. After two months, our squadron was transported a thousand miles farther west to Midway, where we replaced another squadron, on its way to the combat zone. We were to remain at Midway for two months of further training. Of course, we realized that "training" was just a euphemism for "waiting." We were stacked up behind someone else. We were now in the "ready slot," expecting to leave there soon to an advanced combat area. Midway was to be only a temporary assignment.

We arrived at Midway with our new airplanes, SB2C's or Curtis "Helldivers." We had left our old SBD's in the States because they had been made obsolete by this superior warplane, but it turned out that there would be serious problems with the Helldivers after all. They flew farther with a larger bomb load and were deadly accurate, but the Japanese Zeroes were knocking them out of the sky. In any case, Midway was a good place for our pilots to be since they could practice flying them and diving with them on any of the deserted islands lying within a hundred miles.

Midway Island is almost as renowned as Pearl Harbor as a crucial site in the struggle with Japan. In matter of fact, it partly made up for Pearl Harbor, a strategic victory in the place of a humiliating defeat. In the spring of 1942 the Japs, having knocked off Pearl, thought that it would be easy to occupy Midway and then use this as a forward support base for their grand aggresssive strategy. But they did not know about two crucial factors: (1) that we had broken their code and knew their plans in advance, and (2) that we had a number of aircraft carriers ready for them. There was at the time a Marine fighter squadron on Midway with antiquated planes. These were inferior but they could and did fight back when the Japs attacked. They in fact forced the Jap carriers into the unwieldy maneuver of shifting from the launching and recovering of dive-bombers to the launching and recovering of fighters, making sitting ducks of them when the dive-bombers from our carriers hit them.[30]

---

[30]For details of this battle see Hugh Bicheno, *Midway*, London: Cassel, 2001

Two years after the battle there are no visible scars of the Japanese attack. Our squadron, VMSB 343, possesses in its executive officer, Maj. Schlendering, a personal memento of that fight since he was a Marine pilot on the island at the time of the attack. None of our other officers has had combat experience, but this does not mean that they are not good. After two years of intensive training, our pilots are hot and ready to go. I find out just how good they are one day when I accept an invitation to occupy the rear seat in one of these new Helldivers. My stomach is turned inside out and my ears are left ringing from a fast climb and a number of rapid maneuvers, including a sudden, 10,000 foot dive on target.

Here on Midway our squadron has been assigned to facilities on Eastern Island. There are two islands separated by a deep channel through which ships may pass. There is a fringe of reefs forming an atoll, with fairly shallow water inside this fringe. Eastern Island has runways, hangers, and revetments where our planes are placed while waiting to be flown. We share this island with a PBY-5 (Catalina patrol plane) squadron. Because they can land at sea if necessary (but cannot take off from the water), these fairly large craft range out as far as a thousand miles in search of Jap warships and submarines, a mission shared by our squadron, though we have the far shorter range of about 600 miles. We expect soon to be restationed on Sand Island, where the main air facilities and a submarine base are located. Along with other Marine aviation units stationed on this atoll, we are part of the Twenty-third Marine Air Group and Third Marine Aircraft Wing.

Our squadron had several hundred enlisted men and half a hundred officers. This would be a rather drastic disproportion in an ordinary combat unit, but in our case it was appropriate because we had so many pilots, most of whom were Second Lieutenants or first First Lieutenants. The C.O. (commanding officer) was Major Gregory. Another Major served as executive officer and the operations officer was a Captain. All were Marines, as were the so-called ground officers, with the one exception of our only purely naval officer, the squadron doctor, a naval Lieutenant (= Marine Captain).

The pilots had been trained at Pensacola or one of the other naval air-stations. They had been commissioned as Ensigns in the Navy but were allowed to elect the Marine Corps, which they did at an

164   The 1940's: "Temporary training" on Midway

advanced stage of their training. They were little different from ordinary Navy aviators. Our Marine fliers did, in fact, have to keep up their qualification for taking off from and landing upon the flight decks of aircraft carriers, but they did this on a marked area of one of our airstrips. The officer in charge of the entire base, including the submarine facility, was a naval Commodore (= Brigidier General).

Besides Marine fighter planes such as the F4F, we regularly see other warplanes since this is a half-way station to the Orient. Like the old Clipper planes, B-17's, B-24's, and B-29's stop here on their way to the Philippines or the Marshall Islands.

In addition to aircraft personnel, this island has another Marine unit, a so-called Ground Defense Battalion with nothing to do but man the air-defense weapons. The men assigned to this unit have been here since prior to the battle of Midway in June of 1942, and they will undoubtedly remain here until the war is over. Some say that they are the culls from the Fleet Marine Force. As a matter of gossip it can be told that their C.O. has been sent here permanently because he got caught having sex with a colonel's wife back in Pearl. For him, it was either Midway or Leavenworth.

I live here with the other squadron officers in what is called the

BOQ, "Bachelor officer quarters." Few if any of us are actually bachelors, but then again, it is not only bachelors who get Bachelors' degrees. Still, we might as well be bachelors because our sex partners are far away and we won't be seeing them for God knows how long! We take our meals in an officers' mess served by surly black stewards -- the first black personnel I have seen thus far in the military service. Our food is just one step above sheer awful, yet it is not as bad as the enlisted men's food, which I had to taste one day

when I took my turn as Officer of the Day.

The Comissioned and Warrant Officers in VMSB 343 were the following:

Lieutenants (Marine) Alarik, Barry, Covington, Crutcher, Davis, Deines, DeVries, Donovan, Edwards, Ernest, Haughton, Henry, Hicks, Holloway, Inman, Israel, Jungbluth, Kalmoe, Laney, Lange, Magill, McDermott, Nash, Peterson, Roe, Scruggs, Shellito, Skotvold, Smith, Spurlock, Stevenson, Studt, Vehon, Wase, and Watkinson
Lieutenant (Navy) Hawks (doctor)
Captains Brogan, Glen, Janson, and Simpson
Majors Gregory (C.O.) and Schlendering (Ex.O.)
Warrant Officers Blevins, Burke and Curtis

One thing that displeases me very much is that there is no real job for me here. My specification, earned after more than six months of special schooling, is "Communications Officer." The published Table of Organization shows me as the chief of all communications personnel within the squadron. It also shows that I have another Marine officer, the "Radio-Radar Officer," serving under me, along with the entire contingent of radio and radar technicians who are required to keep our warplanes ready to go into battle. In disregard of the Table of Organization, the radio-radar officer is a First Lieutenant, while I am just a Second Lieutenant, and he surely is not going to be taking any orders from me. It won't be any different when I get promoted to First Lieutenant because he will still outrank me. Bill Covington does his job, and does it well, under the direct supervision of the C.O. I as Communications Officer am supposed to have certain other areas of supervision, but they are all covered by my counterparts at the Group and Wing level. Thus I am essentially functionless in my assigned classification.

The C.O. has his eye on this and tries to keep me busy by giving me fill-in jobs, such as "Inventory Officer," "Ground Defense Officer," and "Education and Training Officer." I do these jobs in one-tenth the time I would expect to take in my proper specification. Hence I still have a lot of time on my hands. This places a heavy burden on my morale and self-esteem. I find myself questioning why I have to be here at all. "Why all this special training when I can't use any of it?" I try to comfort myself with the realization that a great many servicemen are finding themselves in a similar situation. It certainly does beat actually leading a platoon of marines against enemy forces in a steamy jungle! Now I understand what the poet meant when he wrote, "They also serve who only stand and wait."

The birds of Midway. This seemed a magical place because of the teeming birds. Midway is a major bird sanctuary, and we tried to do everything possible to protect them while we were there fighting a war. Aviators who were landing or taking off always watched out for them landing and taking off. Most of the birds were off somewhere during most of the year, but in the winter they remained close to the land or on it, breeding, hatching eggs, and rearing their young. It was a delight to watch their courting rituals and the way the parents fed their babies. All their food came from the ocean and they were expert fishers.

There were the awkward looking boobies, the ubiquitous and elegant terns, the mean and ugly frigate birds, and the magnificent Laysan albatrosses, also known as gooney birds. It was the goonies that we loved the most. Large, graceful, and coming in two colors, black and white, they would land like airplanes, fairing their wings to slow their speed and then touching down with their webbed feet extended. When they took off, it was by running at full speed into the wind until they were airborne. After courtship, the female laid one egg, and then she and the male took turns sitting on it until it hatched. The babies looked like frightened tar-babies, with hairy down sticking out on all sides.

I love these marvelous creatures! Without the diversion of watching their antics, my life would be very boring. At the very least, living here among them reminds me that the Creator has a wider scheme than ours. We will fight for a while and then go away. They will go on living here forever. May the good Father who watches over them throughout their hazardous existence watch over me and all the lonely men in the middle of this vast ocean!

Innocent and not so innocent fun. Our total overseas time turned out to be fourteen months, the standard rotation of fliers for avoiding combat fatigue. We ended up being on Midway almost ten months.

The employment of our Curtis Helldivers turned out to be less lavish than anticipated because they were very vulnerable to the Zeros and were getting shot down. Their mission of pinpoint bombing on tactical targets was no longer as essential as it had been two years previously at the battle of Midway when Navy SBD's (Dougless Dauntless, superseded by our Helldivers) from our carriers destroyed four Japanese carriers and won a great victory.

This restraint in utilizing the Helldivers proves to be a serious morale hazard for our fliers -- mainly the pilots, but the rear gunners as well. Mind you, these guys are trained to a peak and armed to the teeth! They can drop a hundred pounder right down the throat of a sealion on the beach at Kure Island! Not getting to do what they have been all psyched up to do is harder on them than my non-job is on me. More and more they are overindulging in the hard liquor that is available to them at the officers' bar, to the point of being badly hung over when summoned to dawn patrol the following morning. It gets so bad that one of the rear gunners has made a formal protest to the C.O. about his life being placed in unnecessary peril by having to fly with a half-inebriated pilot. And then the worst happens: a rather fuzzy-brained flier lets his plane be caught in the tailwind of the plane in front of him and loses control, causing him and his gunner to perish in the ocean. This sad tragedy brings everybody to their senses. A stern warning against the misuse of liquor is raised by the C.O., who threatens that all booze will be locked away if this state of affairs continues. This is when the squadron doctor gets us all together for a quick course on alcoholism, based on his previous work with alcoholics at Bellevue Hospital in New York City.

I am not directly involved because I don't drink. I have never drunk beer, wine, or alcoholic beverages of any sort. This rule does change just a crack somewhat later when I am invited to a party by the enlisted men working in Communications. They are all drinking beer, and they invite me to do the same in full knowledge of my reputation of being some sort of a puritan. Just to be polite, but out of curiosity too, I accept a bottle and enjoy it, for better or for worse. I do find that a drink of beer now and then helps relieve my depressive mood.

I eventually found myself wondering about this decision because of the gross drunkenness that I witnessed at the squadron party on

Memorial Day.

Beer by the bucket, plus hot dogs and hamburgers, is the fare of the day. Everyone is in a high good mood, enjoying a typical marine contest in which volunteers climb up a ladder and clamber onto the corrugated metal roof of a shed. They are given bottle after bottle to drink, and the referee keeps count to make sure they stay equal. They fall off one by one, and the last man to remain sitting on the roof wins the contest. The ones who fall off are too numb to feel the impact of hitting the ground. Good, clean marine fun!

Waiting out our time until rotation. All the squadron officers were involved in censoring personal mail. Things that I was likely to be found doing on any given day was censoring the letters of enlisted men and writing my own daily communications to Betty. These were also censored -- by my fellow officers.

Betty's regular letters to me are my daily food and drink. Incidentally, I have contrived a clever way of bypassing the strict rule against mentioning anything like gooney birds. I won't divulge what it is, but I have managed to communicate to Betty where I am. No harm is done; if my censor cannot notice it, the Japs won't know either!

There were no organized athletics, not even calisthenics. Apparently no one cared if our bodies went to pot. I walked a lot along the seashore, picking up seashells to make into a necklace for Betty. Also I swam and snorkled within the reef, looking out for sharp coral spikes and stinging portuguese man of wars.

We have happy times and sad times. Something very funny that happens is a boo-boo that I commit very similar to my faux pas with the P.A. system at Harvard. This happens while we are getting used to our new layout following our move to Sand Island. In my function as Ground Defense Officer, I go with two enlisted men one day to inspect some bunkers that have remained unused since the battle of Midway. We enter the door and go down some dark steps. I grope around in the dark, feeling for the light switch. When I find it, I snap it on. The immediate consequence is a loud wail that surges louder

Waiting out our time until rotation   169

and louder. Realizing that I have hit the switch of an air-raid siren, I quickly turn it off, but the effects have been heard far and wide over Sand Island. As with the incident at Harvard yard, I expect to be called down for this, but nothing happens except that the enlisted men now have a great story to tell about their lieutenant.

Something especially sad is the death of one of my enlisted men. He was standing in a wet spot when he turned on an electric drill that he was holding. He got electrocuted. Appropriately, I fulfill my duty by riding along on a naval launch as his body is taken out to sea to join the dead heroes of the battle of Midway. It is a solemn moment when his flag-draped coffin is tipped up to allow his body to slip out and drop into the heaving ocean. The water is so rough that my own stomach is queazy. It had been that way before the committal, but this grim sight makes me so sick I have all I can do to keep from tossing my lunch overboard.

I must mention also that I made a determined attempt to find something more valuable to do with my time and training. Aware that the facility had a code-room, I called upon the commodore himself with the request that I be put to work there. He was glad to give his permission. For some weeks I used my wits resolving garbles in the messages that came in over the shortwave radio.

Also worthy of note was the acquaintance that I struck with our Navy chaplain, a Southern Baptist from Texas. When I revealed to him that I was planning to enter the ministry, he gladly used me as his liturgist in the Sunday services. One particular Sunday I went along to sing hymns at the ocean shore as one of our Marine pilots was baptized in the surf. Betty received a letter from Chaplain Flint in which he spoke very warmly of my Christian consecration.

What a strange sight it is to behold Chaplain Cort Flint dipping Lieutenant Edwards in the salty billows of the great Pacific!

Everyone was sad about the death of our revered president, Franklin D. Roosevelt. I had scarcely even heard of his successor, Vice-President Harry S. Truman. Will he be able to carry on Roosevelt's policies?

This event made us wonder even more when the war in the Pacific would end. To be sure, we were glad enough to know that the war in

Europe had come to an end. V-E Day had finally arrived and Hitler was dead! I heard that many American troops from the European theater were being transferred to the Pacific in preparation for the final assault on Japan. Some were saying that the war could continue on to the end of the 40's. The Japs had been putting up a fierce resistance on Iwo Jima and Okinawa, indicating that it would probably take a long and bloody campaign to crush them on their home terrain.

Marine aviation units are rotated to the States on a fourteen-month basis. This means that by October or November we will be out of here and won't be eligible to be sent further west for the final assault on Japan. Although I certainly do welcome this prospect, I regret that vast numbers of Marine, Army, and Navy personnel will need to remain out here until the finish.. I have no reason to be ashamed that I have not got into the ongoing combat any more than I have. Although I have escaped being under direct fire from enemy guns, I have certainly been "standing in harm's way." I am serving with willing devotion to my duty. If I am personally spared being in the worst situations, this has been due entirely to the vagaries of military command and not to any choice of my own.

Because our squadron was still listed as being on temporary duty, it was impossible for the enlisted personnel to get replacements for their worn-out garments. The C.O. was obliged to issue an order allowing worn shirt sleeves to be hemmed above the elbows.

R. and R. on the big island
It is July 3, 1945 -- two years to the day since I first arrived in Quantico, and I am on R. and R. -- "Rest and Recreation" -- in Hawaii, having flown here on a DC-3, ubiquitous workhorse of the armed forces. Inside one of these planes, it is pretty basic -- nothing but a few rows of pads along the bulkheads to sit on. The flight from Midway takes about four hours to cover more than a thousand miles.

At Ewa field on Oahu I stayed in the BOQ, as previously. I had the week to do as I might wish. As one may imagine, most Marine officers and enlisted men make their way directly to the brothels. My roommate boasted of standing in a line that wound halfway around the block. It disgusted me to hear this, more because it was exploitative of women than because it was degrading to the men who boasted of it. I did go into Honolulu, but it was for a different thrill, that of talking to Betty on the phone.

I had to reserve this call before coming here, and it is for two minutes, no longer. It also goes out over shortwave radio, requiring that it be censored. They will cut you off after two minutes and they will terminate you for saying anything not allowed by official censorship. No telling where you have been! But Betty already knows where I have been, so there is no temptation to mention it. Ahead of time I jotted down what I am going to say, but in the excitement of the moment I forget. All of a sudden Betty's voice is on the line and my mind just blows! Same thing with Betty. It is all tears and emotion. It is as if my brain is aglow with dazzling white light, the same as during our marriage ceremony. I could never have imagined the powerful yearning that I feel during these two precious, wonderful minutes.

There might have been a variety of things for me to do during the rest of the week I was to be in Hawaii, but what I chose to do was take another DC-3 down to Hilo on the big island on the southeastern end of the chain in order to look up my brother Henry. He was serving as First Sergeant of the Headquarters and Reconnaissance Company in the Fifth Marine Division. That I knew, and I knew that this division had just returned from Iwo Jima with fifty percent casualties, and was presently resting and regrouping at Camp Tarawa in a former cattle ranch located in the northwest quarter of the big island. The outlook was that it would be needed in the final assault on Japan. It had taken one and a half months to subdue Iwo Jimo and two and a half months to conquer Okinawa. Each of these operations had cost thousands of American lives and tens of thousands of Japanese lives. There was no doubt but that it would take a gigantic effort to crush the homeland territory of Japan itself.

I am enamored of the scenery as I fly south from Oahu. One by one the major islands, as well as some of the very small ones, come into view. The prettiest sight is the high eastern escarpment of the big island named Hawaii, with rank vegetation and beautiful high waterfalls peeking into view along the way. Upon landing at Hilo, I join several other marines in a 75-mile taxi ride to Camp Tarawa. The road follows the eastern fringe of the island, repeating in reverse much of what I saw while flying south over the water. At lunchtime we enter a native Hawaiian cafe in which crowds of local people are celebrating Independence Day -- Fourth of July. They graciously include us in their revels. The native Hawaiians love the marines. It is the tourists they hate.

At the end of the journey I am taken to a group of tents near the sign, "Headquarters and Reconnaissance Company." Hank is completely surprised since I have not been able to reach him on the phone. Delighted to see me, he introduces me to all the officers, including the C.O., and many of the NCO's. I eat with Hank in the NCO messhall, but sleep in one of the officers' tents. Hank seems unconcerned about the ambivalence regarding the protocol of where I fit in. He is very relaxed toward the officers, and they to him. For some reason, officers and non-coms all call each other by their first names, a seeming abandonment of all the military etiquette that I have learned.

Hank told me details of the Iwo Jima battle. His division definitely did suffer heavily, no doubt about it. Hank himself had to be taken off the island and brought to a naval hospital on Guam because he couldn't keep his food down. Nervous stomach, just like me! Hank told me also of making his way over to the sector occupied by the Third Marine Division for the purpose of looking up our younger brother, Bob. Bob did not recognize Hank at first because he was wearing a heavy beard. Probably Bob was pretty dazed. His division also suffered heavy casualties. It is only the Japs who suffered more heavily than these two Marine divisions.

I join in on some of the company's night exercises, the most interesting of which is an offensive crawl (not march) in pitch darkness over terrain occupied by scorpions and other squiggly creatures. Hank and others invite me to a lovely beach on the island's western shore for swimming and picnicking.

On my final day I say godspeed to Hank and get aboard the mailtruck, which travels directly overland through the rugged lava fields between Mauna Loa and Mauna Kea. Neither Hank nor I can guess that we will be seeing each other again within half a year.

My war draws to a close

It is September of 1945 and I am on a transport ship sailing from Midway to Oahu, effectuating the first leg of the rotation of our squadron back to the States. Our fourteen-month duty is up. Nevertheless, this is to be, not our penultimate but our ultimate return home. The war is over and Japan has signed the articles of surrender.

How suddenly this has come! Just as I am wondering how long yet this awful war will last, we hear the unbelievable, incomprehensible news of a first and then a second atomic attack on two Japanese cities. To those who have been long in the struggle with Japan, it truly seems like an apocalyptic judgment direct from heaven. That fierce nation has finally received just retribution for all its atrocities over many years, from Nanking onward.

As our forces crowded it farther and farther back into its island fortress, we had long foreseen Japan's approaching end, but had dreaded the enormous human loss, both to Japan and to the Allies, that would inevitably be exacted before Japan could be brought whimpering to its feet -- and now all that had been made unnecessary and irrelevant. The atomic bomb had done it for us! Let those who have not participated in this struggle cavil over the ethicality of using this frightful weapon. We who have participated know that Japan itself made this kind of cataclysm both necessary and logical.

This is a slow ship that we are on. It takes six days crossing from Midway to Oahu, about 165 miles during each twenty-four hour period. We don't care, we are not in a hurry! We have nothing more to do and wish only to go home. The red-hot dive-bomber pilots with their rear gunners will never get a chance to drop a bomb on a Japanese submarine. I, with all my training in communications and other military skills, will leave with no regrets the so-called job that exacted so little from me. We have filled our spot, we have manned our station, we have done our duty. Bored to death with inactivity, we certainly have made our contribution to this victory. At the very least we have made it possible for other squadrons and other divisions to carry on the bloody conflict. All of us return together to a victorious and grateful country. We have now been at war so long that we cannot imagine what it will be like to be at peace again.

174   The 1940's: Hitchhiking home

Hitchhiking home on a destroyer escort
Through great exertions I have literally hauled myself aboard this little DE (destroyer escort), the U.S.S. Bangust, for a quick ride home, and now I can relax and enjoy the gorgeous sunset as we travel through the mouth of Pearl Harbor and sail out into the ocean.

Things were not going well at Ewa. I was getting more and more stressed waiting for our squadron's turn to board a ship for the States. The problem was that we ran into heavy traffic once our transport reached Oahu. All the marines, sailors, and army men stationed in the Pacific were being dumped off the military rosters as quickly as possible, which meant that every ship going eastward, large or small, was jammed to the gunwales with men on their way home. Our squadron had been forced to join the general rotation. Everyone was part of the same enormous flow.

I sent a telegram to Betty to tell her that I was coming home, without being able to say when. Two months had passed and we were still at Ewa Field, but on account of our prior outstanding orders, we were told that we still had priority to go aboard a suitable vessel as soon as it became available. This meant another CVE (carrier escort), the kind we came out on.

WESTERN UNION SEP 16 1945 - TO BETTY DE VRIES GRAND HAVEN MICH: EXPECT ME HOME SOON ADVISE YOU RETURN WITH DAD LOVE JOHN

From a fellow marine I learned that individual servicemen had been making their own arrangements and not waiting for their turn to come up. One went to the destroyer base at Pearl Harbor and asked to be taken aboard as a supernumerary passenger; i.e., above and beyond the total number of passengers that were assigned to each ship by the harbor master. I got a sergeant in the motor pool to drive me to the destroyer base, and as he waited I rode over in a skiff to a group of destroyer escorts moored together some hundreds of yards away in the water. Climbing aboard the nearest vessel, which turned out to be commanded by a naval Captain in charge of the entire division of small ships, I made my request and received his letter of permission. The five ships of this division were to depart together at 1800 (6 p.m.) and I was warned to be aboard by then or be left behind. I thought there would be plenty of time, but my driver

Hitchhiking home on a destroyer escort

insisted that I hurry. Hastening back to Ewa field, I roused a major from his afternoon nap to get him to sign my orders, then quickly packed all my belongings into two foot lockers, and returned to the *Bangust* with fifteen minutes to spare. Still, I needed every minute, every second. Even my high degree of promptness was barely sufficient to get me on board because the Captain had decided to depart early. Even as I reached the dock, the vessel was preparing to weigh anchor. I could see the anchor dripping water and mud as it was hauled from the harbor bottom. Luckily for me, one skiff from the *Bangust* was at the dock just about to depart. I jumped in with my two foot lockers and the skiff arrived at the ship's side in time to heave my lockers to the deck above and scale the ladder.

What a wonderful feeling of relief and satisfaction! I have done it, I have really done it! I am aboard ship and will soon reach California, where Betty will be waiting. My sergeant driver promised to telegraph her that I am on my way. Neither of us had any idea of how fast this ship can travel.

WESTERN UNION OCT 13 1945 - TO BETTY DE VRIES DENVER COLO: EXPECT ARRIVE WEST COAST NINETEENTH OR TWENTIETH LOVE JOHN

The voyage was slower than one would expect. It actually took six days and seven nights to reach California. I did not know that; I thought destroyers -- even destroyer escorts -- were fast.

Everyone on board the Bangust is cordial and kind. I eat supper with the ship's officers and share stories with them. One problem remains for me to solve: where shall I sleep? Most definitely this ship's captain has obeyed his orders and has taken on board his full allotment of passengers, all navy men from Hawaii. As darkness approaches, I begin to look about for a place to lie down, but men in white uniforms are lying everywhere, on the decks, in passageways, in gun emplacements. I was warned of this, but with my characteris-

tic make-do attitude I assumed that I would somehow manage. But where am I to lie? A junior officer gets me an army cot and a poncho, suggesting that I lie against the aft bulkhead (rear wall) of what is called the forecastle, the above-deck structure that houses facilities for operating the ship, such as the bridge, and has cabins for the senior officers. I lie down under my poncho and try to sleep, but one thing disturbs me, the sweet greasy smell that wafts over me from the stack ventilator just behind. Our wind happens to be a following wind, with the consequence that the sickening odors blow forward instead of backward. No wonder no one else has chosen this spot to lie!

I started to get nauseated and could not sleep. The ship pitched and rolled, and I became a little seasick. Rain fell and partially freshened the air, but it soon became foul again. In the morning I was a walking wreck. Not intending to go through another night like that one, I searched the ship during the morning for an alternative, giving special attention to the area afore the forecastle -- that is, up front.

Anchors are here and all sorts of weaponry. There is a 90mm antiaircraft gun, with a magazine for its ammunition just abaft it. Close scrutiny reveals that I can just get my army cot into this magazine if I keep the door open.

That is where I lay down the second night, again covered by my poncho, and went fast asleep. I had not told anyone of this venturesome move because I suspected that it might be an infraction of the rules and I didn't want to get caught. Good thing, too, because during the night a storm hit the ship and set it apitching, with ocean spray flying into the open door of the magazine. Not knowing what else to do, I just lay there and let the salty spray blow in. As I awoke in the morning I furtively removed all evidence of my visit and closed the door fast, leaving an inch or two of salt water to wash about on the deck of the magazine. I hardly dared look at the 90mm shells, still stacked in their holders.

When I do take a furtive glance, I notice that they are wet, dripping with sea water. They are probably ruined! Is this to be my court-martial?

What was I to do now? In desperation I mentioned my plight to a junior officer, not disclosing that I had been in the forward magazine. He responded by inviting me to place my cot in his cabin down in the bowels of the ship. For some reason, his four-person cabin was missing a fourth bunk, and I was just able to place my cot where this would have stood. This proved to be the end of my ordeal, with no further mishap to report except a big black eye that I acquired by bumping my face against the steel bulkhead in the dark.

But I was still uneasy about the ruined ammunition. Towards the end of the voyage I took a nonchalant amble up forward to inspect whether there had been any changes. I started at the sight of seamen handing ammunition one to another to be pitched overboard. They were taking it from the very 90mm magazine where I had been sleeping.

Is it ruined? Can it no longer be used? Is that why they are throwing it away? Someone must have reported that water had gotten into the magazine. I try to seem casual as I ask the nearest sailor, "Why are you pitching the ammunition overboard?" His reply allays all my fears: "We have received orders from Washington to jettison all our ammunition because the war is over and it must not be kept any longer. As it gets old it becomes very volatile and dangerous."

Saturday morning, October 20th, came. Our DE tied up to a pier in San Pedro harbor. There were ships of all descriptions at the docks, including a CVE, Carrier Escort. Retrieving my personal gear as it was unloaded on the dock, I made my way into the terminal. The first person I met in the terminal was a man I knew -- Chief Warrant Officer Blevins from our very own squadron back in Ewa! "What are you doing here?" I asked, "I left you back at Ewa a week ago." With a triumphant smirk on his face he replied, "Our CVE came into Pearl last Sunday. We left on Monday and got into San Pedro two hours ago. That's our ship tied up to the wharf. Too bad you didn't wait for us!"

Three Marine brothers return home from their wars. Betty was not in the San Pedro terminal because she did not know when, or even where, I would arrive. Dad and Mother had been in Michigan and were glad to bring Betty as far as Denver. While there at my parents' home, she received the telegram from my sergeant and immediately took a train for Los Angeles. This time there was no problem for her because all the servicemen were returning home, mostly travelling east rather than west. By prearrangement my cousin Betty Sterk took my Betty into her home in Artesia, and this was to be our rendezvous point.

In San Pedro I tried to telephone Betty Sterk but no one was home, so I took a bus to the town of Artesia and was just beginning to look around on the street to see if I could find a taxi to the Sterk residence. My eye fell upon two women walking in my direction. It was they, the two Betty's! What a surprise for me -- and what a surprise for them!

Betty and I were guests in the Sterk residence over Saturday night, but the next day, Sunday or not, we had to leave in order for me to check in at Miramar. This lay a few miles north of San Diego, but of course the train took us directly to San Diego, where we checked in at the U. S. Grant Hotel, the same as the one where I had rescued Betty from the zombies more than a year previously, paying $10 for two nights. During the following two weeks Betty and I were able again to occupy a quonset apartment at Miramar. Here we revived our latent passions while planning for the future. There was nothing for me to do except show up at roll call each morning. I filled out papers needed in order to be released as soon as possible from the service and begin studies at Calvin Seminary in January.

When I received permission to go, I realized that I should immediately have arranged for travel assistance from the Miramar transportation office, for now they had more requests than they could handle. We were on our own. The result was a long, crowded, tedious trip that might have been made easier had I acted with greater alacrity. Calling in at the San Diego railroad depot, we were told that it was impossible to get on a train out of L.A. heading east. Instead we took a train all the way north to San Francisco, where there was less competition for travel accommodations. Nevertheless we barely managed to get reservations and then had to share a single upper berth. Also, the train we took seemed much slower than it should have been and all the facilities, including space in the dining car, were taxed and overcrowded. Thus -- for me, at any rate -- our last wartime train trip turned out to be the worst. To be sure, even this was far superior to Betty's three-day standup trip to San Diego the previous year -- and that had been all the way from Chicago!

What a happy and God-blessed reunion is this! Here are Mom and Dad De Vries at Denver's Union Station to take us, their dear second son John and his pretty wife Betty, off the train from California. We two are excessively weary from a difficult train ride that took much longer than it was supposed to. Anyhow, we are home at last! We have much to tell one another. How excited we all are! I am back from my war.

Betty was returning to my parents' home after having left it less than two weeks previously. I was returning to it for the first time since June of 1944, while on furlough between my schooling at Harvard and my assignment to Marine aviation.

Dad is approaching the curb just in front of his house on South Ogden Street. This happens to be Aunt Jen's former residence, where I was privileged to board many years ago. As Dad turns off the ignition key, a taxicab pulls up just ahead of us. As we step out of Dad's car, a man in a Marine uniform gets out of the cab. He has sergeant stripes and some hashmarks for length of service. He is Hank, our brother Hank! He too is back from his war! But who would have thought that it would be on the same day -- almost at the very second -- of my own arrival?

Hank stayed overnight and the next morning continued his trip eastward to New Jersey and his wife and son -- Louise and little Peter. Our own plan was to stay in Denver about a week and then go on to Michigan. The next several days were spent reviving the far-famed Tamminga cordiality. Then on Wednesday we had a surprise as wonderful as the one preceding it. Our brother Bob arrived home from the Pacific! Bob was home from his war too! If Hank had stayed here a few days longer, we would all three have been together in an unimaginable reunion. We were all three home from our wars more or less intact, all from the same branch of service, and almost at the same time. This coincidence of virtual simultaneity was beyond belief, but to be preserved whole -- all three of us -- has to be written down to a kindly and very special divine providence!

I was discharged from active duty on 29 December, 1945, having been in active service for two years and eight months, and the resignation of my commission was accepted a few months later. Counting the time from my enlistment to the approval of my resignation, I was under military discipline for a total of three years, one and a half months, stretching from late 1942 to early 1946.

Now a great gap in my preparation for Christian service has been traversed and I am back where I was in 1939-1943. But it isn't the same as before: I have changed and my academic environment has changed. All of the pre-sems whom I left behind when I departed for Parris Island in May of 1943 have completed their seminary course and are out in the churches. I doubt that any of them are better for having been excused from helping defend their country. Being in the armed services has been hard on me even though I have been spared the worst. Still, I have come to know who I am, and to like and respect myself, and I am glad I am not like them -- Domines without much sense of what goes on in the world outside the church!

Trying to make ends meet as a civilian. During the months prior to the beginning of my course of studies at Calvin Seminary, Betty and I did not see an immediate improvement in our financial situation. I had sacrificed the fairly good salary that I had been receiving, and Betty had resigned her position; she would have been unable to return if she had wished to do so because the war goods that had been manufactured were no longer needed and many persons had been laid off. Many businesses and factories were in transition from war production to supplying a civilian market, and it was generally quite difficult for veterans returning from World War II to find work.

When I was sent home in early November, my letter of resignation was sent to Washington and was promptly accepted. I had urged that I needed to get out of the service as quickly as possible in order to enter Seminary in January. Marine Headquarters in Washington acted on the information I gave them and dismissed me from active service before Christmas. They were no doubt glad to be able to oblige me because they needed to get rid of thousands and millions as soon as possible.

I had not anticipated that I would have to find a civilian job because I expected to enter the seminary early in 1946. As I had read in *The Banner*, the denominational periodical, the seminary had been kept on an accelerated calendar so long as the war continued. Its effect was to make successive school-years fall at different times of the year, with the summer vacations dropped. Once the war was over, however, and I was on my way home, this arrangement was abandoned and the seminary went on a long vacation in order to recommence on its usual schedule in September of 1946. I was completely naive about this and perhaps should have known better than to expect the war calendar to continue after the war. The point is that I did not know it.

This deprived me of a paycheck and put me in the position of needing to find a civilian job in the interval. After I learned that I would not be going immediately into the seminary, I began to feel a little sorry for myself and wished that I could continue to receive my Lieutenant's pay for six or seven months longer. But no, I wouldn't want it that way anyway, because then I would have to go somewhere on military duty and either leave Betty behind or face the same old hassle of trying to find lodgings for the two of us.

In Grand Haven, Betty and I were able to lodge free of charge with Pa and Ma Schouten. Mr. Bill Viening, an elder at Second Reformed Church, where the Schoutens were members, offered me a job clerking at his men's clothing store until after Christmas, but in the new year he had to lay me off. I then found a job at Grand Haven Brass, which manufactured bathroom faucets. Understandably, I was given one of the least desirable jobs, that of electroplating those brass faucets after they had been cast, buffed, and polished. This was done in highly concentrated sulfuric acid. First a coating of nickel was applied and then a coating of chromium, to make a nice looking and hot-selling item. For my part in this process I was receiving the grand sum of eighty-five cents per hour.

The plating job was hazardous to one's health, so as soon as I had the opportunity to get a different one, I quit. My new job was carpenter work, building apartments for veterans. The locale of this project happened to be directly across the street from the Schouten residence on Griffin St. in Grand Haven. Very convenient for me -- or rather, too convenient! After a couple of weeks on this job, I got fired. The reason I got fired was for taking my coffee breaks at home. I never could figure out why the boss didn't like this, because I was very conscientious about being back to work on time. Maybe it was just an excuse. He could probably tell that I was not an experienced carpenter, as I claimed. It depends on how one defines "experienced."[31] I was miffed that as a veteran I was not good enough to help build apartments for veterans.

Getting off on the wrong foot with my brother-in-law to be
It is hard for me to get over some of the attitudes and habits of service life. We all know that it is typical of men in the various branches of the military to josh each other and call each other names. This is a way of establishing camaraderie, not of putting someone down. For instance, marines call sailors "Limies" or "Swabs"; they also call Army men "Dog-faces." There is no need to take umbrage at this. The Army and the Navy had their own pet names for marines.

Soon after Betty's and my return to Grand Haven, her sister Minnie comes home with her new boy friend, Paul Luytjes. He is an ex-Army sergeant with service in France. "I want you to meet Paul," says Minnie, "He has just been discharged from the Army." "Ah," say I, "It's good to know a true Dog-face." I do not say this in derision. It is just joshing, but Paul's face flushes and he casts down his eyes. He barely says anything, and after a few minutes he leaves. He is evidently angry at what I said.

I am sorry that I have offended Paul, if that is what I did. I hope I will soon have the opportunity to apologize and become friends with him. If he and Minnie get married, I will have to get along with him on a permanent basis.

The arrival of our first child. Of course Betty and I used birth-control while I was in service. A pregnancy would have put a quick end to Betty's determination to travel with me. When I was released from the Marine Corps at the end of 1945, Betty wanted to continue using birth-control, at least until I should actually enter seminary, and ideally until I should be ordained and settled in a church somewhere. But here is where my theology took priority over common sense. I thought it would be sinful to continue using birth-control just for convenience or out of personal preference. At my insistence Betty agreed to let nature take its course, and very soon nature did just that. It took its course and produced a wonderful new life! A baby was on the way and was due about the tenth of October.

---

[31] I seem to be inclined to be continually testing the limits of what is allowed.

At the end of the summer I quit work in order to get ready to enter Calvin Theological Seminary. We had urgent need of an apartment of some kind in Grand Rapids, preferably one convenient to Calvin, but as the summer progressed we received no leads. Then unexpectedly I heard of the coming availability of apartments to be built for veterans in the remodeled Pantlind Exhibition Building, adjacent to the Pantlind Hotel on Monroe Avenue in downtown Grand Rapids. I put our name on the waiting list for one of these, but learned that they would not be ready until October. This was okay with us because Betty would not be able to move until after the baby was born. This put me in the position of having to hire a room for myself in a private home for about six weeks. I commuted by bicycle to and from Calvin Seminary each day, and by bus to and from Grand Haven, where Betty and little Judy were, on each weekend.

Betty was very healthy throughout her entire pregnancy. She did a lot of walking and carried her baby high in her tummy. The tenth of October arrived, but the baby refused to appear, or to give any hint of wishing to do so. She did not in fact come until the nineteenth. I was on hand to bring Betty to the rather primitive (at that time) Grand Haven Municipal Hospital when the birth became imminent. Unfortunately, every room in the hospital happened to be filled, so Betty was forced to wait on a cart in the second-floor vestibule, with persons coming and going. Because of this invasion on her privacy, she declared that she intended to return home and wait there; but soon after her arrival at home the labor began again, and we barely had enough time to get her into the labor room. She had certainly fooled her doctor, who had gone to bed and arrived back at the hospital after the baby was born. I was initially in the labor room with Betty and was able to see a little human head, covered with dark hair, striving to push its way into the outside world. I was not allowed to stay for the grand climax, but soon I did hear the baby's wails and was told that we had a little girl -- a very little girl, one who weighed only five and three quarters pounds. That is what she weighed at birth, but she dropped down below five pounds next day because there was difficulty in getting her to nurse or take formula.

This little girl's name is Judith Kathleen. We like the ring of that. Our intention is still to honor the grandparents -- or, rather, grandmothers -- Janet de Fijter Schouten and Catherine Tamminga De Vries. Neither Betty's mother nor mine cares about namesakes

The 1940's: The arrival of our first child

and they simply adore their first granddaughter.

Betty's non-part in her sister's wedding
It is November 2, 1946, and I am a member of Paul's entourage at his wedding to Minnie at Second Reformed Church, Grand Haven, MI. The thing I shall never forget about this wedding is Betty's total absence from it. She is neither in the wedding party nor sitting in the pew.

Since Minnie had been maid of honor at Betty's wedding, Betty had counted on being maid, or matron, of honor in Minnie's wedding party. After all, the two had been inseparable during the years of their growing up. Wherever Betty went, Minnie went. But Betty had been pregnant during this past summer and early fall. Paul insisted that he would not have anyone in his wedding with a big belly (his terminology!), so, even though Betty delivered Judy on October 19th and was already back to normal size, she was not permitted in the wedding party. Paul and Minnie thought she would still be too fat and had invited someone else to be maid of honor. Even though Betty was now back to normal size, and even though it was her sister's turn to have her as maid (or matron) of honor, she was out!

But that was not the worst of the matter. Betty had at least counted on being a guest in a pew, but was deprived of this as well. My Aunt Trina Martens, who had been staying with my grandmother for a while, promised that she would come to Grand Haven and take care of our newborn baby while Betty went to her sister's wedding. But this was not to be.

Aunt Trina arrives at the Schouten home all dressed up and declares that she intends to go to the wedding, promise or no promise, and too bad for Betty!

So here I stand hurt and confused as part of the ceremony that Betty is barred from attending. Is this how it is always going to be whenever Betty tries to have close relations with her sister? As for Aunt Trina, who needs her kind of help?

A snug apartment for "Baby and We." Because the baby was so tiny, Betty and she remained in the hospital for ten days and returned to the Schouten residence just a few days prior to Minnie's wedding to Paul Luytjes on November 2. This occasion brought a large number of noisy guests to the house and made it impossible for the baby to remain asleep, which led in turn to more and more crying. Betty and I were unable to enjoy the party at all. Judy did not fall asleep until the wee hours, after the last guest had departed. The following day, a Sunday, I was in complete nervous collapse. The war had left me in a semi-depression anyhow, and I had been tense and troubled ever since I got home to Michigan.

On the following day, a Monday, Pa Schouten brought us to the veterans' apartments in Grand Rapids. The apartment that we were to occupy had become available while Betty and Judy were in the hospital, and I had immediately put down rent money in order to hold it. I took the savings that Betty and I had individually accumulated during the War and with her acquiescence went out to shop Grand Rapids for furniture. What I purchased would certainly not have been my or Betty's first choices, but I bought simply because nothing else was available: a powder blue sleeper sofa; a gas range with six burners; a mahogany drop-leaf table to serve as our dining table, with two straight chairs; an upholstered rocker; a barrel-back easy chair; a veneer bed-room outfit; a Maytag washing machine. In addition, a friend of the family gave us an old icebox. That was to be our Fridge for the next year.

Our apartment is on the fourth floor of the Pantlind Exhibition Building and is reached by stairs or by freight elevator. Because the walls are very thin and not sound-proofed, there is very little quiet or privacy. We'll just have to try keeping our sanity! We share a cavernous laundry room with the other guests. Our apartment is like all the others and has two rooms, a kitchen-living room and a doorless bedroom. Ah, to be sure, there are a toilet, a wash-bowl, and a bathtub. We call it heaven! As we settle in, we three kindred souls begin to enjoy the exciting new adventure that lies before us.

Judy had been very tiny at birth. When she went home with us to Grand Rapids, she began to cry a lot, especially at night. We took turns feeding her with the bottle and were trying to do all that our Grand Haven physician had told us to do, but things did not always go well. When Aunt Alice got to see her soon after our arrival, she informed us that there was a free baby clinic in downtown Grand Rapids that we should make use of. Intending to do so, we entered the waiting room, where a nurse immediately took Judy in to the doctor because she was so small. He came to the conclusion that her problem was her formula. It was too thin a mixture and needed to be strengthened. Otherwise, said he, she was in fine health and there was no need whatever to worry about her. The doctor's name was Dirk Mouw, M.D. He was a good Christian man and real life saver to us. We were invited to call him at his home at any time if there should be any emergency. Dr. Mouw took a special interest in us because I was a veteran and a seminary student as well. Betty took Judy to see him once every week.

My daily routine was to ride the bus from Monroe Avenue, N.W., to Calvin Seminary. While I would be at the seminary, Betty and Judy would of course remain behind. Betty would take Judy on regular strolls in her baby carriage. I found this new regimen very fulfilling and calming. My nervousness and stomach irritability were gradually disappearing. I had what they now call "post-traumatic stress disorder," for which there was no better remedy than to have a wonderful little family and the occupation of studying regularly and quietly for a worthwhile goal.

My new academic venue. There were six regular professors and some adjunct instructors at the seminary. The students were organized in three classes: Junior, Middler, and Senior. Our Junior class was very small -- only seven -- and four of us were returning veterans. None but I had been a pre-seminary student at the college.

I might have felt very lonely when I arrived at Calvin Theological Seminary except for a bond of closeness in our unusually small class and the fact that three others beside myself were veterans. The war experience had evidently been a large factor in turning each of them towards the ministry. Dick Van Halsema had served as chaplain's assistant in New Guinea while Bill Ribbens and Louis Dykstra had been infantrymen in the European campaign. Lou was regularly receiving government compensation for severe frostbite received in the Battle of the Bulge.

The remaining three students in my seminary class were non-veterans: Harry Vander Aa, who had been kept out of service because of epilepsy, Gerrit Vander Plaats, and John Peterson. The latter two had small children. All seven of us were married and lived in apartments. We DeVrieses, living in downtown Grand Rapids, were the farthest from the seminary.

We veterans were supported by the GI Bill. This included a living allowance for us but not our families, plus tuition, fees and books. Because of the three-year gap caused by my being away in the War, I was not well acquainted with the middlers and seniors. They did not include any of the former college classmates who had been deferred from the draft, who had already graduated and were serving churches. Our middler and senior men were older, and several of them had children.

My seminary professors were William Hendriksen for New Testament, Martin Wyngaarden for Old Testament, Diedrich Kromminga for Church History,[32] Clarence Bouma for Ethics, William Rutgers for Dogmatics, and the president, Samuel Volbeda, for Preaching and Practical Theology.

I regularly get A's in all these fields except Preaching, and that is because Volbeda believes that no one should ever get A's in Preaching -- that no student is ever good enough for that!

During the three years in which I was to be enrolled at Calvin Seminary, I would be allowed only one elective. All the rest of the courses were prescribed and were accordingly attended by the same group of men. This could be -- and was at times -- very boring. There were no new persons to stimulate or challenge us, either among the students or among the faculty. Yet I always maintained good decorum and worked hard to learn all that the faculty would allow me to learn.

My interview with the Home Missions Board

I have just walked out of a meeting with some of the highest eminences of the church. My first year at Calvin Seminary will soon be completed, and I have intended to do summer work on the home-missions field, wherever this might be compatible with the needs of my little family.

After all the hardships I put Betty through during the War, I think she needs and deserves some comfort and security. I am hoping that I may receive special recognition from the board, and perhaps special treatment, for two good reasons. One of them is that I am a veteran of World War II and deserve it; the other is that I have previ-

---

[32]Professor Kromminga, who was well regarded, died of pancreatic cancer during my first semester in his course.

188   The 1940's: My Home Missions Board interview

ously shown a strong devotion to mission work while a student at Calvin College, serving even as president of the Mission Society and going out almost every Sunday to do evangelizing in one place or another.

Before coming to the board meeting, those of us who applied were informed of our provisional assignments, and I was not happy with mine. I was to be sent out to a god-forsaken place in Alberta called Burdett, to minister there to a tiny settlement of immigrant wheat farmers, and to live in with a farm family without my wife and seven-month old child. I went into the meeting intending to change this. Gerrit Vander Plaats and I proposed that we be allowed to exchange our assignments. He would have preferred to go into a rural setting while I would be better off in Chicago, where Gerrit was being sent. But the all-knowing board members turned us down flat, sternly scolding us for thinking that we knew better than they knew as seasoned clergymen! I wouldn't take this and really told them off.

This is what I tell them: "Evidently you are accustomed to ordering seminarians about like puppets. You think everyone should be so glad to have a job that they would not question your judgment. However, I am different. I have been a commissioned combat Marine officer accustomed to bearing heavy responsibility and to have others obey my orders. I want you to know that I have been away from my wife for 14 months during the War, and I have earned the right to have her with me now, wherever I may go. Besides, she needs me, as does my infant daughter. You can keep your job!"

It was hard for me to say this because I did urgently need to earn good money and did not know where else to look for a job. But I knew crap when I saw it, and I wouldn't take it!

Just as I close the door behind me, another person opens it. It is Rev. Edward Visser, the pastor of the church where the board is meeting. He has heard what I said, and observed how I said it. He is smiling and pats my back as he says, "I congratulate you on how well you conducted yourself in that meeting! Don't worry, I can get you a summer job working at the Ferrysburg Chapel." I know that this is just outside Grand Haven. To be assigned there means that Betty and Judy can spend the summer at her parents' home while

I commute daily to Ferrysburg. Truly, God blesses the brave and the true-hearted!

Moving to better quarters. In the late spring of 1947 one of the middlers, an older man named Harry Vander Ark, let us know that the upstairs apartment in the house on Alexander St., SE, where he lived and which he owned, would become empty. He wished to offer it to us at an attractively low rent. We were very glad. This would be a much more suitable place for us because it was fairly large and was in a quiet residential neighborhood where Judy would be able to play safely out of doors. It had a kitchen, a bedroom where the three of us would sleep, a living room, a dining room that would serve as my study, and a bathroom that would double as a laundry room. All of this was reached by a long covered stairway on the side of the house. A space heater would keep us warm. We bought a better second-hand icebox to serve as our refrigerator and Betty did the wash in the bathtub.

As we were preparing to move into our Alexander St. apartment, my brother-in-law, Paul Luytjes, went with me to the Continental Motors plant in Muskegon where veterans were being allowed to purchase left-over office furniture. As an important facility during the War, it had employed numerous persons who had used this furniture, but now that they were gone, the furniture they used was to be sold. I was able to purchase a large walnut veneer desk for $17.61 and a hardwood swivel chair for the ridiculous price of 47 cents. These were placed in my study, which they shared with Judy's playpen and our space heater. I studied while Judy played at my feet.

As Betty and I begin two quiet and happy years in this old -- yet new to us -- house, we manage problems that arise and contentedly make do with what we have. Our dearest treasure is our little girl, who grows cuter by the day. Judy has begun speaking and walking ahead of schedule. She sometimes plays outside with Betty or me, and has neighborhood playmates besides. She is still rather small for

The 1940's: Moving to better quarters

her age, so much so that strangers are often amazed when they hear such a tiny tot speaking in complete sentences, as she does. One time she and Betty are riding together on the city bus when she notices a black lady on a seat ahead of her. "Look, Mommy," she says, "that lady has a dirly face!" Betty is a bit shocked and worries that the lady will be offended, but she just laughs.

It was at this time that we had a lot of contact with Aunt Alice and Uncle Jack, who lived only four blocks away. Betty was especially dependent on Aunt Alice for advice on raising children. Aunt Alice had had a lot of experience; she now had five of her own. Other relatives little Judy got to meet at this time were my Grandma, still living in her old house on Butler Ave., and my dad and mother, who had moved into Grandma's house during the winter of 1948 to search for a new job in Grand Rapids. Dad had abandoned an attempt to become an independent electrical contractor in Denver. Predictably, he was too restless to remain long in Grand Rapids. Unable to contend with the heavy snow that fell that winter, Dad went off to California to look for a fruit ranch and soon summoned Mother to see what he had purchased. He had bought a fruit ranch, residence included, a great bargain! A gas explosion had partially destroyed the house, which is why the former owner was offering the property at a sharp discount. The thought of having to clean up such a mess completely devastated Mom, and she soon flew back to Michigan to enter Pine Rest Sanatorium with severe depression -- her third hospitalization. She recovered with the help of electric shock therapy -- something new at the time -- and was a guest for some weeks in the home of the Schoutens in Grand Haven.

A "new" car

Now that I have begun my second year at Calvin Seminary, I will definitely need some kind of car in order to get to teaching and preaching assignments. A year has passed since the War ended. The manufacture of new vehicles has just begun. That is what has freed up the pastor of Spring Lake CRC to purchase a new car for himself and sell his much-used Lafayette to us. It is not in very good shape, *and I fear that I may have lots of expenses with it. If I have ever needed some good luck, it is now! Betty and I won't take a chance on giving this new car a pet name because that is what may have jinxed our long-departed Buttercup!*

Social life at Calvin Seminary

The members of my seminary class have elected me president, but this does not involve much responsibility or bring any kind of prestige. It might make me their spokesman, but we do not actually need a spokesman because the students have no communication with the faculty beyond what goes on in the classroom. The one exception to this is the special effort on the part of Professor Cecil Bouma to be our mentor. He invites our class to his home and takes us into his study, lined on four walls with books, an awesome sight to budding theologians! He uses this occasion to give us helpful suggestions about which books to buy. He also outlines the interrelationships between the various theological disciplines, "Theological Encyclopaedia," as he calls it. He is definitely one seminary professor I respect and esteem -- a real teacher and not just a bag of wind!

Cecil Bouma was also the mentor of an honorary discussion society named *Nil nisi verum*, "Nothing but the Truth," in which various topics of interest were discussed. I was elected president of this society.

Since there were only seven persons in our class, we enjoyed frequent evenings together at one another's homes. At potluck suppers we would take turns as hosts so as to spread the work evenly. Another thing that we did as a class was hosting the morning coffee-break, a regular ritual for students and teachers alike. One of us had to be dismissed from class a few minutes early in order to start the coffee in a large urn. We would all help lay out the cups and saucers and open up packets of donuts and rolls. Afterward we would share the cleanup work. For all this a pittance was charged, but our fund grew through our senior year into a significant sum of money. Our intent was to purchase a splendid memorial gift for the school. We decided to donate our coffee fund to the purchase of a stained-glass window in the seminary chapel. It was to have a plaque with the words, "Gift of the Class of 1949."

"Guess what! The faculty have refused to follow our wish and will instead spend our money to purchase new hymnals." We have no expectation that these songbooks will memorialize our gift as our window would have done. This is a completely authoritarian system and has no democracy in it! Now we fully realize how little we count in a medieval-style theological seminary like Calvin.

Professor Hendriksen censors conditional election

"Look here, Simon, it won't do to speak about election being conditional, as you say in your paper! It is one of our cardinal Calvinistic doctrines that election is unconditional -- just the opposite." "But Professor Hendriksen," I reply, "You have assigned me Ephesians 1:3-4 as my text for New Testament exegesis, and that is what the text says. Doesn't the biblical word have a higher authority than church doctrine?" "It doesn't matter," he says, "The Bible cannot possibly contradict true doctrine. I want you to change what you say about Christ being the condition of election."

> "Blessed be the God and Father of our Lord Jesus Christ, who has blessed us in Christ with every spiritual blessing in the heavenly places, even as he chose us in him before the foundation of the world, that we should be holy and blameless." Eph 1:3-4

My line of argument is as follows: "Does not Paul expressly state that God the Father chose or elected us in him (i.e., Christ) before the foundation of the world (i.e., in eternity, before the beginning of time)? So what Paul must be saying is that "in Christ" is the condition for the Father's choosing. In other words, the Father does not just choose the saved at random, he chooses them in and through the Lord Jesus Christ. They are elected to be saved in and through Christ! Is that not sound Reformed doctrine as well as sound biblical theology?"

What Professor Hendriksen was anxious to avoid was the impression that he was allowing one of his students to even sound as if he might be challenging Reformed doctrine, as set down in the Canons of Dordt.

What do those Canons say about election? Do they not state that our election is unconditional? Yes, but that only means that God does not elect a person on any other ground than his sovereign will. God does not look for any prior basis, such as human merit. What the Canons claim, then, and rightly so, is that God has absolute priority in our salvation.

Perhaps the professor had been so shocked at my opening statement that he failed to continue reading. In my explanation I had defended it as I just have. I did not deny election; I did not deny "unconditional" election; I was simply stating that, according to no less an authority than St. Paul, our salvation happens only in and through Christ.

But of course I see the wisdom -- indeed, the inevitability -- of my doing as the professor says, especially since I want to get a high grade in his course. Professor Hendriksen cannot afford to have a budding heretic on his hands![35]

Practical training in Calvin Seminary. In Calvin Seminary there was no supervised field work. The only out-of-class experience that we were receiving came as a response to the requests of individual churches for catechism teachers or pulpit supplies. It would have been wrong to have called this "training" because no one prepared us for it or debriefed us after our experience. It was performance without preparation, without analysis, and without application. It was learning by doing -- whether right or wrong.

Often the trouble was that we didn't really know whether we were doing right or doing wrong, and so just kept on doing what we had been doing. This presented us with little opportunity for experiment and growth. In the catechism classes it was merely a matter of hearing the pupils' responses and correcting them; the smart ones knew better than to play games with the teacher. In the worship setting, where there was a set liturgy to follow, the only real opportunity for innovation would be in the sermon. The members of the congregation would have been delighted to hear a powerful sermon, eloquently presented, but they did not expect this and they seldom received it. If the sermon went badly, many members would

---

[35]It is significant that Hendriksen wanted election to be seen under the traditional rubric of *De Deo* ("Concerning God") rather than *De Christo* ("Concerning Christ").

be sure to be away, visiting a neighboring church or staying home, the next time the student in question would come round, but nobody was improved by that kind of haphazard exposure.

I was now almost at the end of my final year, and what I remember about my experience during those three years was not the sermons I preached, but the difficulties I often had in getting to my appointments on time. I remember, for instance, being on a train all day Saturday, and then again all day Monday, in order to lead divine services on the Sunday between these two days at a small church in far-off Cincinnati. The remuneration I received barely covered the train fare, hence I retained only a pittance as my compensation for the three days I was away from home, not counting the time I had spent preparing my sermon before starting out.

My worst experience came when I sat all day one Saturday on a train to Chicago and on another to Fulton, IL, lying on the Mississippi River. Because the train out of Chicago was held up by a blizzard I failed to reach my destination until 3 a.m. Sunday morning. Imagine how nervous and fatigued I was!

I should at the very least be allowed to drop into bed in order to be fresh for the morning worship service at 9 o'clock. Instead my hostess is insisting categorically that I do something with the large dinner that she has prepared and kept warm for the past six hours. If the congregation in Fulton receives a poor impression of my preaching abilities tomorrow morning, it will be through no fault of mine!

Fortunately, most of my pulpit appointments were within 100 miles of Grand Rapids. This often involved my sleeping overnight on Saturday at the home of my host, but not on Sunday night. The powers-that-be had wisely ordained that seminary students needed to be fresh for class on Monday mornings and therefore would not be violating the Sabbath by travelling home directly following the Sunday evening service.

There were unpleasant pressures on this issue too. Once, I took a plane to Wisconsin in order to lead services on a Sunday, but I subsequently encountered severe and vocal opposition to my plan to fly back home that same Sunday evening. I decided however not to "wimp out" on this and insisted that, reluctant or not, these Wisconsin legalists were obligated to drive me back to Milwaukee in order for me to catch my plane, as planned. I would stand ready to accept responsibility before God's judgment seat if necessary -- I assured these good people -- for what I was doing.

During my Middler year I conducted a catechism class at Oakdale Park CRC in Grand Rapids for 11-12 year-olds. In my Senior year I travelled a few miles to Hudsonville, MI to teach a class of teenagers. As much as I was able, I got both age-groups to interact with me in discussing the lessons. I was flabbergasted one evening to find, as I stood before the students, that my trousers and my jacket were from two different suits, one grey and the other brown. I was flustered and embarrassed, but the pupils acted as if they did not even notice. Always the catechumens were docile and entirely unwilling to cause any stir with objections or unorthodox opinions. I was glad in the sense that it was preferable to have them unresponsive than to have to cope with unruly students. I too could be mercenary and ruthlessly pragmatic!

I am glad enough at these opportunities to earn extra money. I cannot say that I am ever paid enough in consideration of the time expended. What I receive is perhaps adequate for the actual time I spend in the acts of teaching and preaching, but certainly not for the many hours, and even days, of preparation for them and travelling to far away churches.

My worst regret was that I learned very little from this kind of church work. I blame this partly on the seminary's poor policies with regard to outside involvements, but mainly I blame it on the miserable classroom teaching that I myself received from the professor of Practical Theology at this institution. I learned virtually nothing from him either in Homiletics (preaching), or in Catechetics, or in Liturgics, or in Church Administration. In Homiletics all that I learned that was lastingly helpful was the sound rule of sticking to a single theme in sermonizing. I learned nothing at all from him about educating young Christians or conducting public worship. I also learned virtually nothing from him about the administration of church affairs. He always preferred to lecture on and on about something else that had taken his fancy! Thus we ended up with reams of notes from his classes, but with virtually nothing to help us function well as practicing ministers of God's word.

I shall have to rely mainly on my own good judgment whenever I am faced with these duties in my coming role as a pastor, preacher, liturgist, practicioner in Christian instruction, or church administrator. My classmates and I have been victimized by a lazy, showy and hypocritical man posing as an orator and saint!

Stuck in the mud on a preaching engagement. There was a Christian Reformed church in countryside near the small town of Grant. I had been asked to lead their Sunday morning service on a particular Sunday in the spring of 1949. Their own minister had to be away on what was called a "classical supply," which meant that the church to be visited by him was vacant and was being served round-robin by the ministers of the other churches within the classis.

Winter had definitely come to an end and a general thaw had set in. City dwellers do not realize what a trial this brings for farmers. At least in this area, all the country roads were gravel, or just plain dirt. When the frost went out, these roads turned into quagmires. Of course, being a city dweller, I was not especially aware of this and as a result had set out confidently, but got stuck in the mud.

It so happens that my father-in-law, Gerrit Schouten, wishes to accompany me on this assignment in order to hear me preach, and he has offered to take me in his car. But he does not get his chance. A quarter mile off the pavement, his car finds itself completely stuck in mud. We are still three miles from the Grant church. What are we to do? What will the worshippers think when their guest preacher fails to show up on time? Is there perhaps an experienced elder who will at least start the service while we try somehow to get there?

Well, look here! A farmer on a tractor is approaching. Yes, he is willing to pull the car out of the mud. As a matter of fact, he tows us all the way to the church. Profusely thanking him, Pa Schouten and I enter the church building to the sound of hymn-singing. The congregation is going at it as if nothing is wrong. Furthermore, the minister is right there, sitting in his high-backed Domine's chair, and when the singing ceases he rises to deliver his sermon. Nobody pays the least attention to us, so we sit down in a rear pew and listen. Everything proceeds in regular fashion up to the final hymn and the benediction. As the people depart, the minister approaches us. He is amazed to see us. "How did you make it through the mud?" he asks. "I thought it would be impossible to get to my classical appointment, and I never expected that you would make it. So I decided to stay here and take care of the service myself." He shakes hands with us and departs, but not before I find my voice and say, "Rev. -----, Could you not have phoned me and asked me to go to that other church? It lies on a paved highway, and I could easily have made it there if I had only known. As it is, the vacant church has lacked a preacher while I have been idle."

A seminary choir tour to California. During my Junior year I had participated in a choir tour in the east. It was a lot of fun being with a fine bunch of seminarians, most of whom were middlers and seniors, as we sang our repertoire in places such as Detroit, Celeryville, Cleveland, Rochester, Palmyra, Prospect Park, West Sayville, and Whitinsville.

I was now in my Senior year at the seminary and I was president of the choir, with Art De Kruyter as business manager and Dick Van Halsema as conductor. We worked hard to learn a challenging repertoire. Our plan this time was to visit Denver and then various churches in northern and southern California. We could not go by bus on this tour, but had to travel by rail because the distances were great and the time short. As in previous years, we would rely on freewill offerings from the churches where we were to concertize in order to make up our travel expenses, and our members would be distributed to private homes for their meals and lodging. The novelty of our undertaking had the potential of putting us in financial difficulties arising from unseen contingencies, hence we decided to ask select Christian professional and business persons in the Grand Rapids and western Michigan areas to underwrite our expenses up to $200 to $500 apiece in order to make up any deficiencies that might arise. I took upon myself most of the responsibility for soliciting likely individuals, resulting in total backup support to the amount of $2,500.

In Denver I made a speech in which I mentioned that my family had lived in a dozen different Denver houses. Dick Van Halsema, the big clown, followed this by saying that the De Vries family were forced to move so often in order to keep ahead of the bill collectors!

198   The 1940's: A seminary choir tour to California

Ha, ha, if he only knew how conscientious my father had actually been to pay all his debts! No, he was not sneaking out of past obligations, he was simply trying to get a grasp upon the future.

After we had sung in Modesto, CA, we were treated to a picnic in a marvelous coastal redwood forest. When we sang in Bellflower, my cousin-in-law, Henry Sterk, and a group of prosperous dairymen treated us to the best obtainable filet mignon dinner. Everywhere we were enthusiastically received. What marvelous publicity and good will this was bringing to Calvin Seminary! The faculty would perhaps have liked to take credit for it, but it is we students who conceived it, planned and arranged it, and carried it out. It was our gift to the school and the church. To be sure, we were personally gaining a great deal of benefit from this direct contact with CRC churches far away from Grand Rapids, and it stood to affect our future careers in a positive way.

I have successfully managed the potential problem of having a dark-skinned student along as a choir member. My roommate is from Ceylon, where the native people tend to be dark. His name is Lionel Felsianus and he comes out of the centuries-old Dutch Reformed mission. In addition to taking course-work at our Seminary, he comes along on our choir tour. Before we depart we have a session to decide on roommates and nobody chooses him, so I take him. My prior experience in the South during the War has already made me an outspoken advocate of racial equality, and here is my chance to put it into practice. Felsianus and I have a great time together.

-- ---------------------

We are presently in Redlands, CA, and have just finished singing our last concert. But perhaps this will not be our final concert. In a few hours we will be on our way to Chicago unless we make a small change. Someone with close contacts in the Navaho mission field has suggested that the Christian Indians at Rehoboth, NM would very much appreciate our stopping there and giving a concert at their mission school. It is right on the Southern Pacific, so we could get off there and catch another train the following day. The trouble with this plan is that there would be an extra charge for having the railroad do this.

We talk this up within our membership and all but one person agree to it. The holdout is a dour fellow named Bill Flietstra,[34] who has the reputation of always being negative. When I explain that we are entitled to draw from our contingency money in order to finance this charge because this is a very excellent and fully authorized project of the CRC, Flietstra remains adamant and will not agree. I finally have to say, "Flietstra, you have not raised one cent of our contingency money. Since I personally have raised all but $200 of it, I am overruling you. I say we go! If we come short, it is I who will accept the responsibility for figuring out how much to ask from each contributor, and I will go out and get it myself."[35] General applause greets this statement, and that is what we decide to do. Here at the San Bernardino train-station we change our tickets. The Santa Fe Chief will be along in a few minutes and we'll be on our way to Rehoboth! This is a fine group of men, and I am proud to be their president!

Casting my line free to another vessel of theological learning. My intellect and my personal qualities were by this time perfectly apparent to the six professors presiding over theological education at Calvin Seminary, but only one of them, a newcomer, took sufficient notice of my promise to do anything positive about turning me in the direction of graduate study. I had learned all that I was going to learn from them, which was not a great deal. Because I had never given any one of them any trouble or raised embarrassing questions, they were ready to recommend me along with the other Seniors as a candidate for the ministry in the CRC. That was the most they could be counted on to do; they were not prepared to stick their necks out by helping me reach a higher personal goal. I would have to be content with my lot as a neophyte CRC pastor. Special recognition would not come from them. It would have to come from the church or churches that would be interested in calling me to their pulpit.

On the other hand, I was still amazingly incognizant of my own promise. True, the students had shown me some recognition by electing me to be president of just about everything. There is little

---

[34]Reportedly the same fellow who threw his Dutch book out the window in the presence of the professor.
[35]I immediately made my calls and collected $200 each from willing donors.

doubt that I would have done very well in the CRC ministry, had I left my special theological destiny undeveloped and competed on an equal basis for attractive churches and generous salaries with all in my class and those of many classes, past and future. Being one pastor among others is indeed what I confidently expected to be doing. Becoming an ordained missionary was one possibility among others, but I never dreamed of becoming a scholar or a professor.

Even at that late moment, the mere possibility of going on to graduate school had not so much as entered my mind. When it did, I had insufficient confidence in my seminary professors to seek advice from them -- except from that one new person. Neither did I seek him out nor did he seek me out; it just happened by chance and opportunity. This new professor, Diedrich Kromminga's replacement as Professor of Church History, had come to our seminary just in time to take us through his course in Christian Reformed History. His name was George Stob -- the third one of my Calvin professors by that surname[36] -- and he had grown up in Chicago, served some churches and as an Army chaplain, and was currently enrolled as a Th.D. candidate at Princeton Theological Seminary, where he was preparing his dissertation on the history of the CRC.[37] He was definitely of the progressive school and a strong believer in the true potential of the Reformed theological tradition as America's best hope for the future. He had been called to the seminary because the Synod apparently thought it needed someone who was an expert on the denomination's history. I benefitted from his course even though it was one of the few in which I did not receive an A as my final mark. This man fulfilled the role of being my earliest beacon into safe passage beyond the shallow harbor in which I now found myself.

This is one of the few occasions on which I am returning by train from a Sunday preaching engagement. I have been in Chicagoland, and seated here in the lounge car with me is George Stob. This is a good opportunity to talk, one I have not enjoyed yet since his arrival at Calvin Seminary. First we compare notes about our war experi-

---

[36] The three were cousins. Henry Stob had been my professor in Philosophy; Ralph Stob had taught me Greek.
[37] Some years later I was a guest at his graduation, and afterwards he attended mine.

ences. *He seems to think I am special because I have been overseas in the Marines. He has not gotten to know all the seminarians as yet, but he knows us Seniors as students in his CRC History course. He is aware of my rather remarkable academic record at Calvin Seminary and is a little amazed that I have given no thought, with such credentials, to going on to study elsewhere after graduating.* "I have a wife and a three-year old daughter to think of," I explain. "I have been studying on the G. I. Bill and my eligibility is almost used up. I do, it is true, have another year. It's not that I am tired of studying, but that I have gotten so little out of my work at Calvin. I have learned so little from certain members of the faculty that the subject matter remains fuzzy in my apperception. Even in those few courses where I respect the professor, it is seldom possible to carry inquiries to the roots of the problem. In some fields, including Practical Theology, I'll definitely have to improvise when I get out in the parish. We have learned Hebrew well enough, perhaps, but the courses in Old Testament Exegesis haven't helped us understand the biblical text better -- at least the difficult passages; the same with New Testament Exegesis. You might recommend that we try to find good books in these fields to improve our understanding, but Wyngaarden and Hendriksen behave as if it is one hush-hush secret. They won't let us know about important books in the field, and seem to prefer keeping us ignorant.[38] Rutgers's courses in Systematic Theology are just plain awful; all he does in class is read his synopses of the points of doctrine found in Louis Berkhof's book, which is itself a synopsis of Herman Bavinck in the Netherlands. Once in a while men like these do mention certain prominent opponents, which somewhat surprises us when it happens, but it is hard to follow through and become engaged in what it's all about. I wonder whether it's just a sham to fool us into thinking that they are actively concerned about them. But most of these vaguely tantalaizing books are not to be found in our library; one would have to scratch around Lord knows were to find them. That's the way it has been these past three years. I am not only disappointed, I am benumbed and disspirited by the whole farce. We'll all draw a deep sigh of relief when it's over and we can go out trying to be competent ministers in spite of all the miseducation we have been receiving."

---

[38] Just as likely, they themselves did not know.

The newly appointed professor, George Stob, had at this point in time only a few short years to teach at Calvin Seminary, for in 1952 he was to become a casualty along with Harry Boer in a mad upheaval of reaction and resentment that swept four professors from office: them along with Hendriksen and Rutgers. Thus he was not long in the strategic position for guiding students in which he found himself at this moment, but he used this moment well and I will always thank him for it. He not only opened up a door for me, but employed the very modest self-confidence I had gained from doing so well at Calvin Seminary as the moral ground upon which I should move forward. He believed that a student who had demonstrated a high level of ability in his seminary work had a divinely imposed obligation to explore further at the level of graduate studies in order to discover precisely where God was actually leading him, and the special role that God intended for him in Christian ministry.

"But Professor Stob," I protest, "Where should I go for such study? I have no idea. No one has ever given me a hint of where to go." "Don't call me 'Professor,'" he responds, "It's just plain George to you." "Thanks, and please call me John. That's usually the name by which my close friends call me, although since the Service most call me Simon."

He continues, "One good answer to your question would be to try Princeton, where I am still enrolled for the doctorate. Out of experience I can heartily recommend it. In fact, a significant number of previous scholars coming out of the CRC and the RCA have gone to Princeton for their graduate work in theology. Also I could suggest good contact persons at Princeton for you to take advantage of. Otherwise you could go to the Free University in Amsterdam, though that might pose some serious problems for your family." My question to this is, "But do you suppose that Princeton might have a place for my family, that's a pretty serious consideration for me."

Since he had always been a commuter, Stob could not give me specific information about housing at Princeton, but he did urge me to make immediate contact to find out whether they would admit me and whether there might be accommodation for my family. The first thing I did on Monday morning was write a letter of inquiry. In less than a week I received the welcome news of my acceptance into their graduate program in theology. However, they had no accommodations for the families of graduate students since all available facilities had been assigned to undergraduates. Like theological schools everywhere, they were being flooded with returned veterans. As much as I regretted being denied, I understood that theological undergraduates, especially veterans, should have first attention.

Wonderful! It looks as if I will be going to the same school where Uncle Garret attended. Princeton has a very high reputation and is actually preferred by graduate students from the CRC. Too bad that I will not be able to have Judy and Betty with me there! This poses a very serious problem for me because I need them and they need me. I have already had too much of separation from my family during the War, darn it! I can't accept the idea of going off to study somewhere while they remain virtually as wards in the home of Betty's parents. Besides, where will I get the money to support them at one residence and myself at another? My G.I. Bill allowance is not sufficient for that. Maybe I should wait until I've been a pastor for a while and have been able to amass some savings. Also, if I can get a call to a church out east somewhere, I may be able to commute to the seminary and have them safely provided for in a nearby manse. I've been told that that is what the majority of Princeton graduate students are doing.

I tried out these ideas with my Betty and her parents. They were appreciative of the recognition I would be receiving, but had trouble getting their minds around the idea of separation and the uncertainties that seemed to confront us as part of this grand opportunity. I did not trust in or rely upon my fellow students sufficiently to seek out their opinions, nor did I discuss my plans with any of the faculty members save Stob. But while I was thus in the midst of much perplexity, a beam of light unexpectedly shone upon my pathway. My old debate coach from Calvin College, Harold Dekker, revealed to me another, perhaps better, possibility.

I am about to depart for the day from the seminary building and enter the cloakroom to get my jacket. I am suddenly face to face with an old acquaintance, the Rev. Harold Dekker, a former Army chaplain and presently pastor of a small CRC congregation in Englewood, NJ, which is in the Palisades just across the Hudson from New York City. He seems as delighted to see me as I am to see him. It has been a while since we have been together. There was college debating, and early in my seminary years he taught a clinic in vocal declamation and another in parliamentary procedure.

I tell Harold about my application to Princeton and the difficulties concerning family housing. He replies with an unexpected new possibility: "Well, if you are open to the idea of graduate school, why don't you apply to Union Theological Seminary in New York, where I am taking some courses. It has great scholars as professors, such as Paul Tillich and Reinhold Niebuhr. They will probably be glad to accept you, given your excellent academic record, and it may be that they will have housing for your family. If you do decide to go there, I might have some work for you to do in my church and you could earn something extra to help out your G. I. Bill."

I immediately mailed an application to Union and receive an almost instantaneous reply: They would be glad to have me. I was accepted as a graduate student, program to be decided upon later. They did indeed have housing available for me and my family, though not in the Union quadrangle or its immediate vicinity. It was located in a small village up in New York state, just north of the Jersey line, at a place called Orangeburg. A former Army transit depot called Camp Shanks had been converted for family living. As a veteran and as a graduate student, I would be assigned to occupy one of these units. The place was now called Shanks Village.

I am ecstatic upon receiving this good news. Immediately I send in my acceptance of this excellent offer, and during the remaining months and weeks Betty and I make busy preparations for our move to New York. Still I refrain from sharing this with my Calvin Seminary professors. The ones whose opinion I would not be likely to accept in any case are kept in the dark. Professor Hendriksen learns of it and speaks to me briefly as follows: "Princeton is where I am enrolled for my degree," he says, "but I'd rather that you went to Union because at least you can recognize the devil there. You can see it plainly in all the heresy that is taught there -- at least you will be able to, if you are willing." Thank the good Lord I do not have to depend on such outrageous caricaturing as the beacon of my future!

I did not tell our President since I was quite certain that he would give me a hard time, but he inevitably learned of it. Near the end of the semester he stopped me after class and requested that I report to a small conference room adjacent to the main entryway; he had something to say to me. I dreaded the confrontation, for by that time I had lost all respect for the man and had no reason to think that he had sufficient respect for my integrity. There was no reason to believe that he had my best interests at heart because he had never taken the trouble to discover what those interests were. I needed to be careful about what I said to him because he and the other professors still retained the power to recommend or not recommend me as a candidate for the ministry.

"Mr. De Vries, do you realize what you are about to do? I am told that you have gone ahead on your own volition and have enrolled in one of the most liberal theological seminaries in the country. Of course I take this as an act of disrespect, for why have you not consulted me? I certainly would have squelched it if I had known about it before you had committed yourself. You can still get out of this, you know. I counsel you to do so immediately. By this act you have cast an aura of suspicion on your potential candidacy for the ministry. After you have spent time at that school, no one will trust your soundness."

"President Volbeda," I reply, *"what is so suspicious or objectionable about Union Theological Seminary? I know their reputation as a liberal school, but this does not bother me. I want to go there to find out for myself just how liberal a school they are, and make up my own mind whether their teachings are objectionable. Great and world-known scholars are teaching there: Paul Tillich, for instance. Reinhold Niebuhr is there as well; everybody knows his high reputation as a leader in Christian society. There must be some good reason why the school is so popular, and I want to find out why. I'm not going to yield to heresy so easily. You know very well how high I have ranked as a student here, and you should be aware of my maturity as a committed servant of Jesus Christ. I have come here to Calvin from service as a Marine lieutenant, and I have shown you that I am worthy of all confidence and respect -- more than you seem willing to grant me."*

Up to this point in the interview, I managed to remain cool and calm. I refused to show any emotion. There was such picayune basis to the President's fear of my obtaining some of my theological education at a school better than the one I had been at that it scarcely required refuting. Why was he making this fuss? I would soon find out. The man began to cry. His voice trembled. He said he was afraid. Afraid of what -- that the devil would get power over my soul? Or afraid that I might learn so much at Union that I would come to despise and decry what was passing for theological education at Calvin Seminary? Was there some danger that I was going to destroy the CRC and its institutions by getting somebody else's viewpoint? Was he afraid because he considered me stupid, or because he considered me too smart? If too smart, what was I likely to figure out, once I had stepped outside the circle of his influence and control?

With tears welling from his eyes, he began to plead, "Please don't do this, don't you know how dangerous it is?" He sank to his knees. "I beg you, Mr. De Vries, I beg you. Stop what you are doing and put your name in for candidacy, then all will go well with you. Of course I am thinking of the church's wellbeing, but I am thinking most of all of your own."

The blood is draining from my face. I have the sensation of the room turning pale and white, all the color vanished. I have been in this state before: as in another state of being, in another world. I am so shocked to hear this dignified man pleading and to see him kneeling and weeping that my mind refuses to stay focused. As he goes on and on in the same fashion, I am no longer listening. I am only trying to imagine why everything has gone so crazy.

At a pause in the President's pleading, I stand up and say, "I've heard all I want to hear. Please stop it. I promise you right here and now that I will never become an apostate from the true faith. You can believe this or not. I am not responsible for your doubts, for your inability to trust one of your best student's high ideals and fidelity to what is true and worthy in what he is being taught. I'm not going to be afraid. I am going to follow the Lord's clear leading to go on into a wider world of learning. The opportunity is there, and I am ready. When I come back, I am going to be a better man and will end up being the better minister as well.

"One more thing I have to say. You have revealed something to me in this interview that you may not have intended to reveal. You

have shown me how little you respect me, but most of all you have shown me how little you believe that the entire system of doctrine you hold so dear cannot be competently defended when it is compared to other points of view. You know very well that there is no basis for mistrusting my intellectual ability or my moral commitment, so you must be afraid that your house of cards will fall if somebody blows upon it. Is that what it all is -- a house of cards? I hate to think that it might be true, but if it turns out that it is true, your cowardice and your trepidation will have been instrumental in giving me the clue.

"Oh yes, another thing I have to say is that if you somehow bring your faculty to refuse me a recommendation for the ministry one year from now, I will find some means of demonstrating how miserably poor my education at this place has really been. We are not yet at the place in the CRC where a person may be condemned purely on suspicion!"

I had never been so clear about following God's will for my life as I was at that moment. The president's outrageous behavior had the direct effect of convincing me that I had a clear obligation to go on to further schooling, if only to discover what I had been missing, what I had been robbed of, what they were afraid I might find out!

Now I see God's design in having me spend three years in the Service before continuing my training for the ministry. It was to make a man of me, which I have desperately needed at this awkward and embarrassing moment. I know I can't stop here.

Maybe the analogy is not entirely appropriate, but it was as if God had placed some high cards in my hand and now expected me to play them intelligently and with courage!

Rough passage to Shanks Village. As soon as my seminary graduation was finished, I initiated the onerous process of moving lock, stock and barrel to Shanks Village, enlisting the very welcome assistance of my brother-in-law, Paul Luytjes. He was at this time extending himself rather noticeably in trying to help me further in my career progress; he gave a full week of his time, but in such a way as to cost me a great deal of money and labor.

Paul had his own ton-and-a-half stake truck, and in addition borrowed a two-wheeled trailer from a neighbor. He had a hitch welded onto the back bracket of his truck, but apparently not securely enough to eliminate the possibility of breakdowns. Thus prepared, he arrived at our place on Alexander St. and we began loading. I had packed my books in a dozen wooden orange-crates,[39] which fitted so neatly on the trailer that we didn't think of the weight. The rest of our goods went onto the truck bed. We were well prepared with pads, tarps and ropes.

It is the first Monday evening in June. We will be all week on our way to and from New York, but I need to be back early enough to get myself ready for filling a preaching engagement in the First CRC of Grand Haven[40] this coming Sunday. It begins to rain as we head south on Kalamazoo Ave. Our plan is to drive on U.S. 16 to southeast Michigan and points beyond. But our high expectations are dashed by a series of minor disasters.

Before we are well out of the Grand Rapids city limits, the tongue of the trailer begins to make sparks on the pavement. It has been bent to the ground under the weight of the books. We are forced to take two hours getting the tongue strengthened at a welding shop that is still open, but are on our way again as night falls upon us. It is soon pitch dark. It has been raining, but the rain has stopped. We cover about fifteen miles when Bang! a tire on the trailer blows out.

This time I hitchhike in the dark and all alone into the town of Lowell, where I find a place to buy a new tire and get it mounted on the rim. I begin to realize that this may become a very expensive trip if we keep on having mishaps like these.

Back at the truck, we mount the new tire and continue grimly onward. It is now past midnight and we are exhausted. Arriving at Ionia Corners, a large truckstop, we try in vain to hire a motel room. The owner won't get out of bed to accommodate us. We park truck and trailer on a rear area of the parking lot. Paul goes to sleep in the front seat (the only seat!) while I crawl under the tarp and fall asleep on a rolled-up rug and pad. When we awaken, we first get

---

[39]The reason for not storing my books at the Schouten residence was that Betty's parents were talking about possibly selling their house, in which event they would have had to empty it entirely before turning it over to new owners. As it turned out, this was not to be the case. I ended up having the added problem of getting my library transported from out East to my first parsonage, farther away in Iowa.

[40]Formerly served by Rev. John Verbrugge, the chaplain who married us.

breakfast and then go to work transferring the dozen crates of books to the most forward position on the truck bed, reserving the lightest goods for the trailer.

It is now Tuesday. We travel on through Lansing and Jackson, reaching the Toledo area about five o'clock. We are just through the city of Maumee and are beginning a long, gradual grade through the outskirts of Perryville when Bang! the trailer hitch breaks off again, this time dropping the tongue of the trailer to the pavement. What to do now? The same as before; only, while we are disconnecting the trailer hitch, one of my fingers somehow gets mashed. I try to ignore the pain as we drive the truck back into Maumee, find a welder, get the hitch rewelded, pay the tab, and return to Perryville by seven p.m. About 11 o'clock we reach central Ohio and decide to put up for the night in a motel. I don't sleep very well because my finger is throbbing and I don't have even a single aspirin to control the pain.

I am now getting seriously in arrears with regard to sleep; and my pocketbook is hurting too. All day Wednesday we ride on through eastern Ohio and western Pennsylvania, managing to reach Pittsburgh just at five p.m. It looks as if a jinx is on us! Deep trepidation seizes us as we make our way slowly through the downtown rush-hour traffic. And wouldn't you know it? Just at the busiest and most inconvenient place in downtown Pittsburgh, the trailer hitch breaks again!

We are forced this time to drag the trailer with the use of ropes to find another welder, again paying overtime rates to get the hitch strengthened even more, hopefully now for the last time. While the welding job is being done, I walk to a nearby doctor's office to get my throbbing finger lanced.

We were now so far behind our schedule that we decided to drive all night to reach New York. We followed the Pennsylvana Turnpike, recently completed from east of Pittsburgh to west of Harrisburg, until we turned off onto U.S. 22, which we followed through the eastern sections of Pennsylvania, and drove on through New Jersey and portions of New York state, to arrive at Shanks Village in mid-afternoon on Thursday.

Both of us are now half-dazed from lack of sleep. For the first time I notice that the weather has turned hot. Finding the housing office, I sign papers and receive my keys. Returning to the truck, I find that Paul has fallen sound asleep on the grass and cannot be awakened. After frantically shaking him, I manage to get him into the truck and drive to our apartment. Inside is a glowing furnace. I throw open the doors and windows. Then, because Paul still cannot be aroused, I singly transfer all my goods from the truck and trailer save for the sofa and the boxes of books. I finally get Paul sufficiently awake to help me carry the sofa into the apartment. Leaving everything just where I dropped it, I then drive the truck some fifteen or twenty miles to Englewood, NJ, where we reach the Christian Reformed parsonage occupied by Harold and Fran Dekker. Again all by myself, I carry my dozen crates of heavy books up the thirty-nine steps into the sweltering Dekker attic.

Understandably, we do not make very good company for the Dekkers. We eat the supper Fran serves us with as much appreciation as we can manage, but we are now in a daze of exhaustion. I long for my bed, but first I have to go with Paul to get the truck lubricated and then load the empty trailer onto the bed of the truck, where it should safely ride without further calamities all the way back home to Michigan. We raise the trailer by positioning it on an outside hoist, then raising the hoist to the level of the truckbed and wheeling the trailer onto it.

Back at the Dekkers', I telephone Betty to tell her where we are and ask her to inform the church where I am supposed to preach that I will definitely not be able to make it back there on time. Maybe we will make it back on time, but I will not be in any condition to do any preaching. The responsible thing for me to do is to alert the church of our situation in order to allow them to get another preacher to take my place.

Early Friday morning we thanked the Dekkers for their hospitality and were on our way home. We drove all day and all night without mishap or delay, taking turns driving. We arrived in Grand Haven at about noon on Saturday. I ate some breakfast (or lunch, whichever it was supposed to be), took a bath, and dropped into bed for an all-day and all-night snooze.

Before I fell asleep, Betty mentioned that the elder at First CRC was rather huffy and ungracious about accepting my excuse. He told her that I was being very inconsiderate in making him scramble for a substitute pulpit supply at this late occasion.

I may be quite certain that this church will not call me to be their pastor. Should I be sad, or glad? At the moment it did not matter because all I needed was sleep.

A new home and a new school

It is a few weeks later and I am riding in a carpool from the rendezvous point near Columbia University. It is a pleasant drive along the Hudson and over the Washington Bridge on our way to Shanks Village, which is at Orangeburg, about five miles into New York state. There are usually drivers eager to get passengers for the trip in either direction. It costs each rider twenty five cents. The passengers are students from New York University or Columbia. I am the only one I know of from Union. These institutions cooperate in setting this up because without something like it, it would hardly be practical for their students to live so far outside the city.

Today was my first visit to Union Theological Seminary. Until now everything has been carried out by correspondence, but now I put in an appearance in order to arrange for my veterans' benefits and register for the summer session that is to begin tomorrow.

I later learned that the cordial young man in charge of the veterans office was George (Bill) Webber, who was destined to become director of the innovative East Harlem Protestant Parish.

I signed up for Old Testament Theology with Professor Samuel Terrien and Pauline Doctrine with Professor John Knox (talk about Presbyterian influence!). Because I had fairly well decided to specialize in biblical studies, I intended to concentrate on Old and New Testament courses. I would decide later which of the two to choose as my major.

We had never expected to have so difficult a trip from Michigan. In the first place, it was extremely hot and our car did not have air-conditioning. In the second place, the trip seemed longer and more difficult than we had anticipated. Our old Lafayette held up pretty well, at least we had no flat tires or mechanical trouble. It was stuffed full with our belongings, save for a bit of space in the rear seat where Judy could play and take her naps.

Judy is ordinarily a very contented child, but having to stay in a hot car for so many hours at a stretch has made her cross. No wonder! She fusses and cries a lot. The only way to keep her a bit content has been to take her on our lap, but she gets tired of that too. We open all the windows and let the breezes blow, but the wind is hot and does little to soothe her or us.

It took the greater part of two days to travel to New Jersey. We did not go directly to Shanks Village because we had an invitation to stay at the residence of Herm and Josie De Young in Prospect Park, outside of Paterson. Josie was the daughter of Trina Youngster, a niece of Grandma De Vries. I had met her previously on our 1947 seminary choir trip to the East. Josie and Herm gave us a cordial welcome and promised to take care of Judy for us while we went on to Shanks Village to open up our apartment. We thought that this would be an ideal arrangement and planned to spend several nights with Herm and Josie, but when we returned to their home after our first trip to Shanks Village, we found Judy crying and very unhappy because she had been mistreated by Delores, their little girl. Delores was a spoiled child who did not make a good playmate. Observing that Herm, and especially Josie, seemed to approve of Delores's bad behavior, we packed up the following day and took Judy with us. We were confident that this would turn out to be far better because once we got settled, Judy would be able to play outside our apartment and would soon find more compatible friends for company.

Betty and I had arrived in Shanks Village with Judy the following day and immediately had set to work cleaning up the place and arranging the furniture and our other belongings. There was a lot of work for us to do because when Paul and I brought our belongings there in June, I had been forced to carry virtually everything into the apartment from Paul's truck all by myself and I had had no energy left to do more than dump things down in the first convenient spot. Now we had the task of straightening everything out. I knew that between working to make this a comfortable home and keeping up with my course work at Union Seminary, I would be very busy.

The car arrives at the rendezvous point in Shanks Village, I hurry to the converted barracks that is to be our home for the next year. I find Betty piteously weeping and almost hysterical, demanding to be taken home to Michigan. When I ask her what the matter is, she blurts out that she can't stand the heat and that she hates this ugly, cramped apartment. After I soothe her, she begins to feel better. I reassure her that things will be better, once we get things arranged as we want them.

Before long Judy met a little friend whose mother invited us into her apartment and showed us what she and her husband had been able to do to make things more cheerful and convenient. She also told us where to get free paint, as much as we might wish. Her husband had made a little play-yard for their daughter. With this encouragement and good example, Betty and I got to work in the days that followed, painting every room, putting up screens on the windows, and installing spring-wound window curtains in front of the open cupboard shelves. This did not make things easy for us, but it did make them possible. Betty managed to store our Maytag in a closet, where it would remain until being wheeled into the kitchen to be used. I set to work putting up a picket fence for Judy to play in and installed aluminum screening and a screendoor on the sides of the front stoop so that we might sit together and watch the gorgeous sunsets over the mountain to the west, unmolested by mosquitos.

Judy seems to consider the disshevelled condition of our house an adventure. How cute she is, trying to help with the dishes and arranging her little things in what is to be her bedroom!

Soon after we settled in Shanks Village we received word that Grandma De Vries had passed away. Having attained the ripe old age of 83, she had been ushered by God's angels into glory!

If it were just not so blamed hot!

A summer semester at Union Theological Seminary

I do not know whether I really belong here, but at least I know that I can do the work. Professor Knox has given me an A for a paper on "Paul's understanding of salvation." This faculty is challenging to me for two reasons: (1) it confronts me with a point of view and a methodology that was barely mentioned at Calvin Seminary, let along explained or advocated; (2) I am finding a far broader coverage of courses here than at Calvin. As long as I sift out the modernist factor in what is being taught, I can learn a lot. I am keenly aware of the superiority of this faculty over that of Calvin. They challenge the student and do not waste his time. I certainly do not detect any special pleading of the sort that I have too often seen in Wyngaarden, Hendriksen and Volbeda at Calvin, nor do I encounter the blundering incompetence of Rutgers.

I was happy to find fellow Christian Reformed students who were taking summer courses at Union. I encountered my mentor, Harold Dekker, and he introduced me to Harry Boer, Clarence Boomsma, Nick Beversluis, and Alexander De Jong. We tended to gather in the quadrangle and have lunch together while discussing theology, and of course we often spoke of the CRC and its future. These men were critical of various shortcomings of the denomination but were also optimistic about accomplishing some significant changes in the near future. Dekker and Boer, as former military chaplains, were especially determined to see progress towards bringing the denomination into the twentieth century.

I see men like Clarence Boomsma and Harry Boer as intellectually superior, with a broad mind along with a wide tolerance in non-essentials. It stands to reason that they and I will be able to learn much here. Knowing them and conversing with them gives me courage and direction for my own program.

This was my very first exposure to liturgical grandeur such as I found here at James Chapel. No one could spend time in it without being inspired by the stately architecture and aesthetic arrangements. Scottish Presbyterianism provided the model. Worship services were held every weekday in James Chapel. The chapel had gorgeous stained-glass windows and dark walnut wainscoating. I was most deeply impressed by the very large golden cross that hung above the chancel, making the reality of Christ and his suffering absolutely central. Often I found my soul "high and lifted up" in praise and adoration. Just being there taught me far more about liturgy and worship than I ever learned in Volbeda's dismal course in Liturgics. As often as I could, I was in attendance, and I generally did so with profit and delight. The School of Music that was established there at that time provided a splendid choir. The faculty members would take turns leading the liturgy and delivering meditations or sermons.

Since I do not live on the premises, I find little occasion to become acquainted with the students, whether graduate or undergraduate. As I learn from the bulletin boards, there is plenty for them to do besides studying. Maybe they are doing some things that are questionable, such as holding dances. Since I have never learned to dance and have had little exposure to it, it is inevitable that I should be negative towards it.

Many of these students are infected with an unbiblical theology, and they seem to be generally intolerant of conservative Christians like myself. This is probably what explains what I observed one day while standing in line to enter the refectory. Some persons who were obviously from outside were trying to hand out gospel tracts, and the students were laughing. They were laughing because who would think that seminary students would need gospel tracts and would be candidates for being saved? Maybe they do need to be saved, I don't know; but I think everyone should be willing to listen to other points of view.

I sometimes find it rather difficult to process all that I am hearing inside the classrooms and in discussions with the Union students. For example, I am not entirely satisfied with my construal of the word "virgin" as a translation for the Hebrew word עלמה in Isa 7:14. My staunch defense of this passage as a prediction of Christ and his virgin birth seems to shock some students not expecting to have that view advocated here. On the other hand, I am set to wondering how I might come out on this question if I applied the same rigorous linguistic and historical standards to the exegesis of this passage that they claim.

I found Samuel Terrien, one of the Old Testament professors, to be a very appealing teacher. I liked his way of exhaustively scrutinizing the biblical text and bringing the Bible to life. I also appreciated his habit of beginning every classroom session with prayer -- something that I have not observed in any other professor, here or at Calvin Seminary.

Betty and I were honored one evening by the visit of the president of Union, John C. Bennett, and his wife. The two dropped by at our Shanks apartment to become acquainted. How delightful and gratifying it was to receive such attention!

No faculty member at Calvin Seminary, I am certain, would ever stoop to such sensitive pastoral nurturing. Certainly the Union professors are better pastors to their students than the Calvin professors have been to us! Better pastors, better scholars, better teachers, better preachers, better examples as Christians -- that is what they truly are!

President Bennett and his wife did not stay long, but while they were here they clearly communicated their deep personal concern for me as one of their students. Another thing that came across clearly was Dr. Bennett's evaluation of my personal library, and I was glad he was so frank. He was not happy to find on my bookshelf a well-worn copy of Louis Berkhof's *Reformed Dogmatics*. He didn't go into why. I on my part was not interested in defending it.

I have never approved of Berkhof's method of prooftexting doctrine from Scripture. Berkhof does not take the trouble to actually exegete the biblical texts that he uses as a prop for his doctrine. Too bad that I will be forced by and by to sustain my examination for candidacy in the CRC by boning up on Berkhof! Under the circumstances, that will be the smartest thing to do, but once that is finished, Berkhof will go onto a high shelf where it won't be required.

Dr. Muilenburg tells me I am "honest"

It is now fall semester of 1949-50. I am enrolled in a S.T.M. degree program that is heavily concentrated on Old Testament theology and other biblical subjects. I have found myself strongly attracted to a brilliant and world-renowned scholar in the person of James Muilenburg. What is the most striking about his appearance is his probing yet reassuring eyes. He knows all about me. He realizes the soul-searching that I am presently undergoing as I try to adapt what I have learned at Calvin Seminary to biblical exegesis and theology as he teaches them. He can identify and empathize with my struggle because he is himself of Dutch Reformed (RCA) derivation, although presently a member of the Congregational Church. He went through his own purgatory when he tried to reconcile what he had learned at Hope College with what he later learned at Yale University. I have already found myself admiring him deeply, while remaining on my guard against wholesale adoption of his "liberal" Bible exegesis.

After class one day I accept from Dr. Muilenburg's hand a paper he has just graded. It is marked A, which makes me glad and gives me reassurance. He pauses and his penetrating eyes search my face for my reaction, then he utters a few words that will be destined to change my entire future development as a biblical scholar: "Simon, I now know that you intend to be thoroughly honest."

At first I was a little puzzled when Dr. Muilenburg gave me a compliment that I did not think I needed. I had always held personal honesty as a high ideal. Yet I sensed that Muilenburg was not commenting on my moral character, but on my intellectual integrity. From this moment onward I would ever be measuring all that I should think, say and write according to this high standard. Liberal or conservative -- it makes no great difference so long as one is thoroughly honest in the way he treats Scripture -- honest, that is, to the intent and design of Scripture itself, honest to God himself.

This word spoken by a revered teacher has been a vision of pure light breaking upon me from above, which I dare not disobey. Saul of Tarsus was turned into Paul the apostle of Jesus Christ by a vision from heaven. I have been transformed by this model of what I was in my better self and of what I ought to be as a projection of this better self. Dr. Muilenburg was relying on a virtue that he saw in me as a prediction of what I could become and therefore would become. I must most certainly have exemplified a high level of personal integrity in my scholarship before he spoke to me, otherwise he would not have been able to recognize it in my paper. Doubtless, he saw more than I could see. He saw the clear signs of authenticity, still unfocused in my own self-awareness. But once he pointed this out, I had to accept this as my transcendant goal and sublime ideal. I was forced to acknowledge that what he was able to perceive was my true self in the confused and uncertain student that I then was.

Standing at the turning-point of my career. If I had never returned to Union, this extra year at the halfway point of the twentieth century would have been memorable for the perspective it brought upon my chosen career. Out of the experience of studying at a world-class seminary, I actually acquired an optimistic attitude concerning the salvability of the CRC, confidently expecting and working for sorely needed reform to bring it forward into the twentieth century. My Union exposure was revealing to me how urgently necessary reform was in the CRC, but it also gave me hope for its possibility, if not its likelihood. It made me aspire to be part of a new effort in the CRC to live up to the true heritage of the Protestant Reformation and the gospel of Jesus Christ, applying them more forthrightly to the problems and needs of modern-day America.

The half century that I was about to embark upon was, nevertheless, destined to witness retreat and retrenchment, rather than renewal, in the Christian Reformed denomination. A strong iridentist influence from neo-secessionists among Dutch immigrants into Canada and among refugees from so-called "apostate" churches in America, in particular that of Cornelius Van Til and his followers at Westminster Theological Seminary, was to emerge triumphant. By my inability at this stage of my life to discern the true nature of this struggle, I was then and in the decade to come wasting valuable opportunity for professional advancement outside the CRC. A new signpost had been set upon my life's path, showing me another way than the one I had been travelling, but at the moment I lacked the wisdom and the courage to follow in the direction this signpost was pointing.

5
The Nineteen Fifties --
When I Become a "Man of God"

Top, Mom & Dad, ca. 1937.   Middle L, Denver, 1931: Ruth, John & Bob with bunnies.   Middle R, Bellflower, 1934: Hank, Bob, John, Ruth, Betty Sterk.   Bottom, Littleton, 1937: Sparky & Ruth, Bossie & me, Tiddles & Bob.

Top L, Grandma De Vries, 1941. Top R, Betty at Calvin, 1941. Middle, Leaving for Parris Island, May 3, 1943: Uncle Jack, Grandma, me, Betty, Aunt Trina, Ma Schouten. Bottom L, sight-seeing at Cambridge MA, 1944. BottomR, Young Calvinists at Dr. Reed's church, 1944, with Betty and me in the middle

Top, swimming with VMSB 343 officers off west shore of Oahu, Fall, 1944; Bottom L, Hank & me in California before shipping out; Bottom R, Hank & me at Camp Tarawa, July 1945

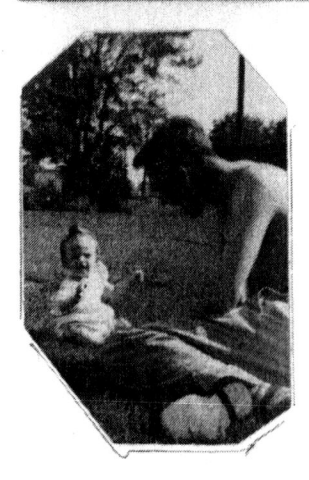

Top, Home from the War, 1945: Aunt Alice, Bob's buddy, Aunt Trina, Bob, Grandma, me, Betty, Ruth. Middle, Calvin Seminar class, 1948, G. Vander Plaats, Harry Vander Aa, Bill Ribbens, Leon Wood (Baptist), Dick van Halsema, me, John Peterson, Louis Dykstra. Bot\tom L, Judy with her dad, 1947. BottomR, Judy & Leslie, Shanks Village, NY 1950

Top, Prairie City, 1950, Paul, me, Mom De Vries, Judy, Minnie, Betty, Ma Schouten. Middle L, PrairieCity, 1953, Judy, Garry & Ma Schouten. Middle R, Me in my study; Bottom, Pa Schouten and me shortly before his death, 1952

Top L, Passaic, 1954, John Wisse, Garry &Dad. Top R, Passaic. 1956, Garry, Betty, Judy, Dad & Mom De Vries. Bottom L, Spring Lake, 1952, Shep, Ma & Pa Schouten. Bottom R, Boarding the *Zuiderkruis*, 1956: Ma Schouten, Betty, Judy, me & Garry

Mid-century: a hinge in my budding career. If participating in the War helped me grow up morally and intellectually, my decision to continue my studies outside the institutional program of the CRC broadened my understanding of theology and the Bible as I learned also to embrace the entire Judaeo-Christian tradition. Here again, it had to be from God that this came about, for it certainly did not arise out of my own ambition. I had been much relieved, as a matter of fact, when I had been able to glimpse the completion of my academic program at Calvin Seminary, which I initially viewed as the suitable end of study for me. So many pitfalls had lined the course I had run -- the intimidating prospect of insufficient funds to begin college work, the long detour of war experience, the need to provide well for a wife and child, the disappointment at the quality of education I received at the seminary -- that I naturally felt immense relief that it was almost over and I could go on to be ordained, receive a call, and serve a church somewhere as pastor. However, the Christian Reformed ministry was not where my story was to end.

My initial literary effort

I have been in a two-semester seminar with Professor John T. McNeill on John Calvin, the reformer. McNeill is an acknowledged expert in this field of study. It seems to have attracted some of Union's very best students, such as Richard Niebuhr, the son of Professor H. Richard Niebuhr at Yale and nephew to Professor Reinhold Niebuhr at Union. Harold Dekker, pastor of the Englewood CRC and my mentor, is in the seminar along with an RCA minister by the name of Garry Roorda, who comes from my hometown, Denver.

The course is based on weekly presentations by the seminar participants, followed by the professor's comments and general discussion. Each student is required to select a topic from a list offered by Dr. McNeill. One that especially intrigues me is "Calvin's Attitude Toward Art and Amusement." In choosing this topic, I am motivated partly by an apologetic impulse, which is to investigate whether the reformer is to be blamed for all the rigidity and abstemiousness of the Puritans and other Calvinists, such as the Christian Reformed.

I discovered that, though frugal by necessity, the reformer John

Calvin did not censor art in any way, and this in spite of the fact that some of his professed followers did smash a few church windows. I also discovered that he did not frown on "innocent amusements," although he certainly did condemn their abuse and misuse. The fact of the matter is that he had neither the time nor the means for indulging in joyous pursuits -- what we would call recreation. He was much too driven by constant demands on his time to have any energy left over for optional activities of any kind. Calvin's lack of energy did not in itself render his lack of attention to the development of his aesthetic sensibilities censurable.

The paper that I read to the seminar was the first lengthy research paper for me since I wrote one on the morality of gambling for Cecil Bouma's Ethics course at Calvin Seminary. Bouma had at the time offered to publish my paper in the journal, *Calvin Forum*, which he edited, but I had declined out of modesty and a lack of self-confidence. I was not ready yet to think of myself as a scholar and author. Now McNeill made a similar offer for my paper on Calvin. He was willing to send it to *Church History*, the most prestigious journal in this field of study, with his endorsement. Again I declined, and for the same reason. I eventually came to see the folly of rejecting opportunities like these. I was certainly hobbling my own professional potential, but I had no sense at the time of my fitness for entering the field of scholarship and the theological professorate. Once I began to serve as a full-time pastor I had my Calvin paper published in *Calvin Forum*.[1]

Another term paper that I prepared for a Union course was one on Luther's opponent, Thomas Münzer. I was flattered when a Union student requested to be allowed to duplicate it for a communist study group. The communists in East Germany were making much of Münzer because of his radically populist program. I was interested in him only because of his apocalyptic radicalism. As I shall tell, I later did publish this paper as two separate articles.

An impromptu interview with a disillusioned Christian Reformed scholar. Martin J. Wyngaarden, our Old Testament professor at Calvin Seminary, was fond of warning us never to say or do anything that might be suspicious to "consistory, classis or

---

[1] January 1952, pp. 101-7

synod." Lacking the background to comprehend what motivated him to keep saying this, I gave little thought to it at the time. I was vaguely aware that Wyngaarden's predecessor, Ralph Janssen, had been deposed by the Christian Reformed synod of 1924 for his mildly "modernist" views concerning Scripture, but at the time I was not informed enough to realize the connection. The truth is that Wyngaarden was not warning us, he was *threatening* us. Since Synod had entrusted him to make up the supposed deficiencies and correct the errors of Ralph Janssen, he had appointed himself as inquisitor-general over his students and we didn't even realize it.

To be sure, once I entered the refreshingly different climate at Union, and especially when Professor J. C. McNeill made casual mention of the fact that one of Janssen's students, Quirinus Breen, had earned his Chicago doctorate under him, I began to link things together. Breen had resigned his church in Grand Rapids, Broadway CRC, in protest against Synod's high-handed action against Janssen.[2] After a period of searching out alternatives, Breen had gone on to earn a Chicago Divinity School Ph.D. in Church History, and for some years had been on the History faculty at the University of Oregon. It was just at this time that Breen happened to be lecturing here at Union as a guest of his teacher, Professor McNeill. He spoke to our seminar about Calvin's humanism, concerning which he had published an important book.[3]

Not managing to catch Professor Breen after class, I take my opportunity to approach him while he is sitting in the library reading room. I identify myself and then go on to request whatever advice he might be able to give me as a potential biblical scholar who also intends to be ordained in the CRC. The frank answer that he gives is that I don't stand much chance of bringing these two together. "The church that deposed Ralph Janssen on flimsy grounds has not changed for the better," he says, "and I cannot encourage you to become a Christian Reformed minister if you adopt the stance toward

---

[2] See David E. Holwerda, "Hermeneutical Issues Then and Now: The Janssen Case," *Calvin Theological Journal*, vol. 24 (1989), pp. 7-34.
[3] Quirinus Breen, *John Calvin: A Study in French Humanism*, Grand Rapids: Eerdmans, 1931

the historical criticism of the Bible that prevails here at Union."

That was a wise and understanding word that I disregarded to my own great disadvantage. I assumed that I would somehow find a way to resolve this problem even as a CRC pastor in good standing.

Paramus Chapel and the Jackson Whites

I have driven my car into the Ramapo mountains of northern New Jersey, where I have been trying to communicate the gospel to a bunch of filthy little kids, the incestuous offspring of the Jackson Whites, a small group of hill-billies descendant from early Dutch settlers, escaped negro slaves, and Delaware Indians. The intriguing thing about these people is that they all have the same last name, De Groot. They are tawny of complexion and have kinky hair. I have tried to talk to the adults who live here in their dilapidated shacks. They are all ragged, ignorant, and destitute. They are also too lazy to look for work. When they get some money, they squander it on booze. No one knows which kid is his. I am shocked at this sight of squalor and utter hopelessness.

The mission committee of the Midland Park CRC assigned me to do mission work among the Jackson Whites. That was one half of what they were paying me to do, and God knows I needed the money. But how was I to do it? As I saw it, all the churches had given up on the Jackson Whites. So also the welfare agencies and boards of education.

This was the first half of my part-time job, which I handled on the side along with my graduate courses at Union. The second half was Paramus Chapel, which was some tens of miles distant from the Ramapos. The Midland Park church had established evangelistic work at a small chapel near the town of Paramus, and I held regular services in this chapel each Sunday. Besides this, I spent one day per week calling in the community, for which I had had some previous experience from my work at the Ferrysburg and Hope chapels in Michigan.

Quickly I was recognized as pastor in this community, visiting the sick in hospitals and performing all the work of an ordained minister except administering the sacraments of baptism and communion. Betty and Judy usually accompanied me to the worship services on Sunday. This part of my job I liked because the people were approachable and I knew what to do. But nothing was going to enable me to evangelize the Jackson Whites. You could not talk religion to them. They would like you to do favors and give them handouts, but they didn't want anything to do with God or Christ.

On the one occasion when I actually succeed in gathering a small group of children to listen to what I have to say, I have to settle for getting these snotty little kids to hold up their finger and sing, "This little light of mine, I'm going to let it shine." But they have no idea what this is all about.

These animal-like people are not only on their way to hell, they're already in it! Although they remain fixed to one spot, they live worse than Gypsies. I believe that the good people of the Midland Park CRC are wasting their mission money by occasionally sending persons like me to "do something" about them. There is little chance of saving their souls unless we save their bodies and change their entire way of life.

I am attacked by a Paramus rooster
I didn't see chickens in front of that house when I just passed in front of it. Where did they come from?

I was making a house-to-house survey of the entire surrounding territory on behalf of the Paramus Chapel. A narrow gravel road leading out of thick trees and bushes had brought me to this deserted gravel pit with the old two-story house in the bottom of it. I wanted to check on who lived there and possibly talk to him or her (or them) about church affiliation, as I had done elsewhere on this survey. Some of my contacts had brought new people to the chapel, or had the promise of producing a good effect later.

After I speak to whomever lives in this gravel pit, my survey will be virtually complete.

But nobody responded to my knock and there was nobody outside. Actually, the house looked deserted, so I continued on through the gravel pit to a second house standing on the far bank of the gravel pit. But nobody responded there, either.

Oh well, I'll just leave a tract with the chapel's address, as I will also do at the first house.

At that point I began to feel eery, even a bit frightened. Those chickens were acting very strangely. They hadn't been there before. Why would they have been let outside? They were proof that somebody had to have been in that house. One of these birds was a great big rooster with flaming red wattles and long spurs on his legs, and he was coming directly toward me as if he were approaching a foe in a cock fight. I decided to stay as far as possible from him by making a semicircle around the house, maneuvering to find my way back as fast as I could.

The big rooster comes closer and closer. I begin to trot and then to run. He runs faster and faster, menacing me with loud squawks and flapping wings. He gets so close that I have to turn and kick at him. He won't give up. I keep kicking until I land a solid blow that sends him flying. End of fight.

This was the weirdest house-call I had ever made or ever would make. Why did whoever was hiding in that house wish me out of there so badly? I shall never know because I am not coming back.

Church-extension work in Harlem
The CRC home-mission board is not forgetting about me. They still expect to make a full-time ordained home-missionary out of me.

The "Back to God Hour" broadcast would send to the home-mission board the names of persons in the New York area who responded to their messages, and it in turn would send someone like me to check on those names. Since I was presently doing graduate work at Union, they turned over a dozen or so names to me of persons living in Manhattan. Most of these people proved to be in Harlem, just down the hill beyond Morningside Heights, where Union and Columbia are located. I decided to make the calls not so much from denominational loyalty as from the need and desire to make the money that the board offered as a stipend. This decision brought me, not to one of the main streets of black Harlem, but into its darkest alleys and dreariest corridors.

I observe various signs of poverty, moral decadence, and despera-

tion. Drunks and dope addicts are lying in the streets. When climbing a staircase, I almost stumble on a man who lies unconscious. I don't wish to know what violent and resentful thoughts may be lurking behind the black faces which I pass on the sidewalks!

So far as I could see, only one of my visits would bear fruit in terms of direct future contacts with the CRC.

I have a card with a Dutch name. How come someone from Holland is living here in the heart of Harlem? A cheery and intelligent black face welcomes me inside in response to my knock. I enter a roomy and well-furnished apartment. This man is not actually a Hollander (i.e., from the Netherlands). Instead he comes from Curaçao, a Netherlands dependency in the Caribbean. He has responded to the Back to God Hour invitation because he is Dutch Reformed, like most of the people in Curaçao.

If I were intending to stay and work here, I would certainly have wanted to get in touch with the Rev. Bill Webber, my veterans' advisor at Union and later to be senior minister in the East Harlem Protestant Parish, which carried out some effective programs in reaching the people who lived there. He did not only preach the gospel and bring the gospel; he *was* the gospel!

I now see clearly that I am not going to be a missionary in the mode of my adolescent dreams -- one who calls the heathen to salvation. My work in New Jersey and New York, added to that in western Michigan, is actually nothing but church-extension -- establishing a denominational presence. I have some experience in this, and have been fairly successful. But it shouldn't be called "mission work." Those who are really fallen, like the Jackson Whites and the street people of Harlem, certainly need Christ, but we must not make the mistake (or pretense) of missionizing those who are already Christians. Maybe the Lord will bless my work. I have sown the seed, and who knows what the harvest will be?

My S.T.M. thesis on "the fear of God"

I am in a committee room with my oral examiners, who include Professors James Muilenburg and Samuel Terrien. This examination is more perfunctory than what they give for the doctorate, but still it is done in seriousness and with some rigor.

This is my final month at Union, May, 1950. Ideally I should go on to get my doctorate. It would be a great advantage to me to do so here at Union and/or Columbia because my work on the master's would count as the first year on the doctorate. However, there are two strong arguments against it: (1) I am broke, and (2) I am scared. On the first point: my eligibility for G.I. Bill support will not last out another full year, and I do not dare request more material sacrifice from Betty and Judy. Besides, there is another baby on the way. On the second point: I am theologically confused and fearful of the consequences for my aspiration to become a Christian Reformed minister.

I have done well in all my courses here at Union. Muilenburg has been a constant support to me. He knows in his heart what I am going through and does everything he can to show me that the Bible demands to be interpreted with historical rigor along with pious assent to its message. As for Terrien, he admires me. He himself studied at the famous Huguenot seminary in Saumur, France, before he went on to the Sorbonne and eventually to Union Theological Seminary in New York. What he likes in me is my conscious identification with a pure strain of recognizable Reformation belief. But for him too, this will mean little unless I show that I am willing to put the Bible ahead of dogma.

I began work on my S.T.M. thesis back in the fall when I looked at a list of recommended topics which Muilenburg handed me. I was reluctant to choose a topic that demanded the literary analysis of a particular Old Testament passage. What I had learned at Calvin Seminary had failed altogether in preparing me to deal with such an assignment. So I chose a broader topic, "The Concept of the Fear of God in the Old Testament." The first thing I did was to read Rudolph Otto's classic, *The Holy*, a work on the nature of the religious encounter which was recommended as well by Professor Paul Tillich. What was so important about that work was that it bases religion not on a set of beliefs, but on the personal and immediate experience of confronting transcendental holiness in the presence of God. All religions worthy of the name go back to this in principle. The worshipper is filled first with dread for stupendous majesty, and then with fascination with the object of his devotion. Numerous occult beings are absent from biblical religion, which has only one infinitely personal God, whose aim is to draw us to himself.

I reviewed other books as well. My thesis began with a chapter on the phenomenon of fearing God. It continued by identifying the various Hebrew roots which are needed for expressing this fear of God in all its nuances. This brought me to some important philological and theological conclusions, including an arrangement of the texts chronologically and an attempt to correlate and interpret them in the light of Old Testament theology.

My professors are very well pleased with what I have accomplished. They do not find it necessary to ask me numerous questions about it. Just for fun, they throw in a few irrelevant questions, such as how the account of the circumcision of Moses is to be understood. As if I knew!

At a lodging place in the way the Lord met him and sought to kill him. Then Zipporah took a flint and cut off her son's foreskin, and touched Moses' feet with it, and said, "Surely you are a bridegroom of blood to me!" So he let him alone. Then it was that she said, "You are a bridegroom of blood," because of the circumcision. Ex 4:24-26

They do not expect me to know, nor do they offer me their own explanation(s). The hour concludes with Professor Terrien announcing that the grade on my thesis will be A.

I shall attend the final graduation ceremony at Riverside Church, just next door from Union. Soon thereafter I shall pack up our belongings at Shanks Village and be on my way, with Betty and Judy, to the Schouten home in Grand Haven. Early in June I shall have to appear for examination by the Christian Reformed Synod in Grand Rapids as a candidate for the ministry.

Thus a year has been spent establishing Old Testament exegesis and theology as the main object of my graduate endeavor. Will anything come of it?

Why am I choosing this particular area of concentration? Is it entirely the attractiveness of my professors in this field? Or is it possible that I am choosing this field because I feel the need to prove to myself how wrong a fossil like Wyngaarden has been? He has tried to make it so dry and boring, and at the same time so unpleasant and unattractive, that no one will choose it. But I find it lustrous in its splendor. Here in the Old Testament is the very heart of biblical religion!

Nursing Minnie. Our family life at Shanks Village was disrupted for two weeks in the spring of 1950 because of Pa Schouten's urgent request to Betty to return home to help nurse her sister Minnie back to health. Minnie could not overcome a serious bladder infection that was keeping her bedridden.

Minnie's husband Paul could not handle this and turned her over to her parents. They took her into their home, but she was not responding to their care, either. In desperation Pa and Ma turned to Betty by long distance phone. Reluctantly Betty agreed to come. I took her and little Judy to Grand Central Station in New York to put them on the train. To save money, they reserved only a single berth, an upper. Although the two of them were challenged by the ladder and were very crowded when they tried to sleep together, they did have lots of fun riding together on the train.

When Betty arrived in Grand Haven, she immediately went to work nursing Minnie, who gradually responded. Neither then nor later, however, did she seem to appreciate the sacrifice Betty and I had made toward her wellbeing. Paul scarcely took notice of Betty's and Judy's presence. I meanwhile managed to take care of myself without my two girls.

After the crisis was over, Betty and Judy returned. Rejoicing in one another, we spent the few remaining weeks until the semester ended at Union and then packed up to return as a family to Michigan, where we were to spend the summer.

The evening before we were to depart for Michigan, Judy was injured, and as a consequence did not enjoy the trip.

Alas poor little Judy! The Dekkers and we are having a farewell picnic together. While playing with Gordy and Danny, Judy catches a swing on her collar bone, knocking her down. This causes her immediate pain and distresses her during our entire trip to Michigan.

Judy was not diagnosed and treated until we were at home with Betty's parents. Sure enough, her collarbone had a break in it, and she had to wear a harness until the bone was healed.

1950, a summer of transition. This year was widely celebrated as the midpoint of the twentieth century. During the first half of the century, we had already been through two world wars. Winston Churchill was being acclaimed as "the man of the century." This might be true for the first half of the century; we did not know whether someone would outshine him in the second half. This year marked as well the separation between my years of learning and preparation, and the beginning of the career I had been preparing for. I had no idea that my formal education was far from finished.

Examinations, calls, and the birth of a little son. Three times during the summer and early fall of 1950, I made a roundtrip to Prairie City, IA, more than 500 miles each way. The synodical and the classical examinations were alike in covering many of the points of theology and ministry. Both required the candidate to preach a trial sermon. It was a strange coincidence that I was examined anew by the same classis that had examined me back in 1940 for student support. I had fulfilled their trust!

The biggest difference between the synodical and the classical exam was that the former had a number of examinees -- the entire graduating class, plus any who had delayed their examination, as I had done -- while the latter had only such examinees as had accepted calls within the classis of ordination, in this case only myself. I preached the same sermon before each body, "Finding the Pearl of Great Price." I do not recall any particular question that I was asked at either gathering except one by Rev. Henry Vander Kam at the classical examination: "Do we have the truth, or are we seeking for the truth?" I answered, "both," but I could see that this did not satify him, and suspected that he might hold it against me in the future. Vander Kam was a great patron of Westminster Seminary and the Orthodox Presbyterian Church -- Machen's vexatious offspring.

-- -- -- -- -- --

It was nice to see my name appear in *The Banner,* official publication of the CRC, in the list of candidates for the ministry. My expectation was that I would be top choice and would accordingly receive more calls than anyone else, but this was not to be, and I think it was because I had not appeared for an entire year as a pulpit supply in the Michigan area. Prospective calling churches -- those that were vacant or intended to expand their staff -- were not thinking of me, only of those who were just graduating as seniors. Be that as it may, I did receive two calls, one from the Home Missions Board on behalf of a newly formed congregation in Milwaukee, and one from a decades-old church in Prairie City, IA. The compensation offered by each of them was roughly the same, but the Iowa salary included a $300 "bonus." It was not until later that I understood what that meant.

Of course I had to travel to both calling churches in order to become acquainted. Not to do so would have been taken as an affront. Rev. Harry De Blaey, the denominational home missionary-in-chief, accompanied me on the plane to Milwaukee. He was very eager for me to take this call, in fact counting upon me to do so because of my special interest in missions.

Here is where I had to decide whether my previous strong identification with missionary work would be allowed to determine my future career. Milwaukee might have been a better place for me to ponder and test what I had been receiving in my graduate year at Union. On the other hand, there was no manse or parsonage, so the Board would have to rent something for me and my family temporarily. My family, I felt, needed to settle down and begin to live normally for a change, especially now that a second child was on the way. What defintely decided me against Milwaukee was my observation of how one prominent local woman domineered the group of church members who were meeting with me. I felt that I certainly did not need to come to Milwaukee to cope with that!

Before I gave Milwaukee my answer, I took the train to Iowa and was met in Ottumwa, southeast of Pella, by an elder, who then drove me to what was called Prairie City -- though it was no city at all, just a town or village of approximately eight hundred persons. It lay midway between Pella -- the heart of the Dutch community -- and Des Moines, the state capital. The "prairie" part was very accurate. To the north and south, to the east and to the west, as far as the eye could see, was rich undulating farmland. Since I came to it in midsummer, I saw it in rich green. Prosperous farmsteads were to be seen, near or far, spaced two or three to the mile.

I ask my host a question about the roads in this part of Iowa, "Are any of the roads in the coutryside graveled?" I am thinking of the situation in the Paramus area of northern New Jersey, where virtu- virtually all the roads are paved or blacktopped, except for a very

Examinations, calls, and the birth of a son

few remote roads to places like the Ramapo mountains or the gravel pit with the chickens. My host proudly replies, "Yes, the situation has improved a lot. We now have one gravel road for every three that are still dirt or mud. We are really seeing progress!"

I led divine services the following day, and the members seemed glad to hear me. There were two services on Sunday, one at 9:30 a.m., and a second at 1:30 p.m., with Sunday School in between, allowing the farmers to get back home on time to milk the cows. There were approximately 95 church families -- that is the way the denomination prefers to count its constituents -- but many had a fair number of children belonging to them. There was a two-room Christian School, with kindergarten through eighth grade, directly across the street from the church building. Next to the church was a large white frame two-storied house, which served as the parsonage.

On Sunday night I was lodged at the home of a prominent church member living some distance to the north of Prairie City, who would be able to bring me to the large town of Boone in order to catch the Union Pacific for my trip back home to Michigan. I later learned to my regret that this person was watching my words and chose some unguarded statement of mine to be used later to get me in bad with the elder who had been my first host.

By the time I reach Grand Haven, I know that this will have to be it, but what a humbling thought it is! Here I am, one of the very best graduates from Calvin Seminary since it was founded, an ex-Marine officer, the recipient of a master's degree in Old Testament from the most prominent seminary in the nation, forced to take a call from a very ordinary and moderately small congregation, and in Iowa of all places! In Iowa, where I almost starved to death ten years earlier while trying to sell Bibles! Will Iowa be any more accepting of me this time? Can I succeed, even here?

What I came back to was a job I had gotten at the beginning of the summer, serving as a laborer at Rycenga's lumber yard in Grand Haven. The pay was minimal and the work was heavy, but it was a job and it was steady. I was also called upon to take occasional Sunday services for Ferrysburg Chapel, which I had established in the summer of 1947.

Betty and I were looking for the birth of a second child in the

234 The 1950's: Examinations, call, birth of a son

beginning of September. It had been my hope that the classis would meet late enough in the fall so that I would not have to make two more trips to Iowa, one to be examined and another to move into the Prairie City community and be ordained and installed. I was actually brash enough to request this, but it was doomed to failure. Nothing could have induced this august body to change its date of meeting, not even the second coming of Jesus Christ! Certainly not the installation of a neophyte minister.

It is the end of August and I am on a train on the way home from my just-completed examination by Classis Pella. The classical examination does not cover the same ground as the synodical examination, which I had sustained already in early June. The synod examines a candidate to determine whether to certify his fitness for candidacy; the classis examines him as the prospective pastor of a particular church, and ministerial member of its own body. That is what I have just been through. Now there remains only my service of ordination and installation, which will be on October 5.

Garry Peter De Vries, our new baby boy, is born in the wee hours of Sunday, September tenth, 1950. The birth is easier for Betty this time. It occurs in Hackley Hospital in Muskegon, and the attending physician is an obstetrician rather than a general practioner, as with Judy. We are thankful that Garry is strong and healthy.

I arrive back in Grand Haven about 3 a.m. and tell the grandparents the good news. I fall in bed for a few hours of sleep before arising to go to the Ferrysburg Chapel to lead the morning service. One can understand that my sermon should make poor sense. I am too tired to think! The one lasting effect of my performance is the congregation's general feeling of joy and celebration of this special gift from God.

When I return to Iowa in early October, it will be with my wife, my two precious little children, and all my earthly belongings. It should be easy because the congregation will be paying for a moving van to pick up our belongings from Rev. Dekker's attic in New Jersey and then pick up the rest of our furniture -- such as it is -- from Grand Haven.

We arrive as a family in Prairie City. I cannot imagine ever being busier than I was since our arrival in Prairie City, Iowa, in late September, 1950. Our furniture and my books were placed in their approximate places by the movers, with assistance from the custodian, Mr. John Schut, and Mr. Gerrit Vander Kieft, vice-chairman of the consistory. No problem there; I also had help arranging the furniture and placing my books on the shelves in my study.

There were two factors that were putting extreme pressure on us, however. First, we had made a long-distance move with a new baby, who was a good little boy but needed constant attention. He and our little Judy had been good travelers. Judy was not in the way here because she was outside playing with her little friends most of the time. The second factor was that there had been a severe drought and our well had dried up, just as we had need of extra water to do the baby's laundry. The chairman of the building committee ordered water brought in by tank-truck from Mitchellville, about ten miles away, but a tank-truck of water did not last long with such extra drain on it.

This stressful situation was aggravate by a third, the necessity to entertain in our home several guests who had arrived from afar to witness my ordination. They needed to be fed and beds had to be found for them. There were eight extra guests, my dad and mother from California, Betty's dad and mother, the Van Voorthuizen's from Muskegon Heights, and Paul and Minnie Luytjes from Muskegon.

On Tuesday, before I was installed, I was summoned to perform a funeral for a church member who had passed away -- my first. I would scarcely have known what to do without the indispensable help of Rev. William Roozeboom, my neighboring Reformed pastor.

Thursday evening was the time set for my service of ordination and installation. Two designated ministers from classis were present. At my suggestion, the consistory had invited Rev. Rens Hooker, my old pastor in Denver, to preach the sermon and lead the service. He had come from the Chicago area where his present parish was, and he was being provided for in the home of one of our members.

Following the service these special guests and all interested persons were invited to come to the parsonage to pay their respects. Naturally, everyone expected to be offered refreshments. My relatives and friends from California and Michigan were kept busy either finding chairs for guests to sit on or making more coffee and washing dishes. I was enjoying this moderately when the word was passed to me that Betty had suddenly begun to hemmorhage. A quick telephone call brought Dr. Herny, the local physician, to our house.[4] He immediately ordered Betty to bed, and she was obliged to relinquish her office as hostess-in-chief to the mothers and other female guests.

Two days of relative calm brought us to Sunday, which was guaranteed to be extra busy because I was to preach my first sermon and also administer baptism on behalf of my son Garry. Think of it, a father performing the rite of entrance into the covenant on behalf of his own child!

---

[4] Dr. Peter Herny was a crusty but kindly physician whose wife was a veterinarian. When summoned, he was likely to humiliate his patients by demanding to know whether their complains were serious enough to require his attention. It was always difficult for parents to be sure whether their ailing children were actually sick enough to meet his criterion. Nevertheless, he acquired hero status by such exploits as one in which a young woman of our church, Marjorie Monsma, came down with acute appendicitis at her farm home about five miles east of Prairie City. Dr. Herny, realizing that she needed prompt surgery, drove his car to the point where springtime mud prevented his coming closer. Marjorie's father brought her, bundled to her ears and sitting with him on the tractor, through the mud to where the car was and he drove her to a Des Moines hospital for surgery.

A stupid mishap in the parsonage kitchen

It is now Monday morning following my first Sunday as pastor. The guests will soon start their individual journeys homeward. I don't know how Betty and I have survived! In the flurry of many things happening at once, I have had no opportunity to reflect on my new situation. Almost in disregard of misgivings, I have become a Christian Reformed minister. I have abruptly terminated my academic career and taken on a role that would seem to make little demand upon my special abilities, such as they are. What can Union Theological Seminary have to say to these second- and third-generation Dutch farmers deep in the heart of Iowa? Has it all been a bypath that leads to nowhere? I have always believed that God is surely leading me; is he leading me still? Am I being obedient to God's design or disobedient? Until the answer emerges, I shall try to do this job as faithfully as I can.

A stupid mishap in the parsonage kitchen

My head is stuck and I am yelling for Betty -- or anyone -- to help me. Something on top of the new refrigerator has dropped down behind it, so I have mounted a chair and have pushed my head sideways as far as it can reach, but I still cannot see anything. Then, as I try to pull my head back out, my left ear gets caught behind the edge of the cabinet, preventing me from drawing my head backward far enough to release it. The space between the bottom of the cabinet and the top of the refrigerator is just too narrow. I never should have tried this!

A refrigerator was one of the few things in our parsonage that was brand new. The building committee bought it for us when they learned that we had been getting along with an old icebox, and we were delighted to have it! Also in the kitchen were our relatively new stove six-burner gas stove and kitchen set. They were four years old, having been bought when we moved into the Pantlind apartment. In the living and dining room, only two felt rugs were new. They were not woven, they were just thin pads of compressed fiber that had been imprinted with a formal design. The color was gray on gray, and I did not know why we ever bought anything so ugly.

To continue with the furniture inventory: Judy was still in her crib, but we planned to get her a regular bed when Garry should need the crib. He now slept in the dining room in his basinette, but this wouldn't be for long. There was no additional furniture there, just our old gateleg table and two upright wooden chairs. When we would have dinner guests, we had to bring in the kitchen table and chairs and combine them with these. Upstairs, our old bedroom set was for guests since we had bought a new set for ourselves. In the study or office, my big old desk and swivel chair from Continental Motors had been placed.

This inventory explains why a brand new refrigerator, which we did not even have to pay for, was so special to us. Not that this has anything to do with my head getting stuck!

Betty is on the phone to summon the custodian. It does not take long until John Schut arrives on the scene. He cannot restrain himself from laughing when he sees my plight. His wife Maggie, who follows him through the door, lets out a little scream, then joins in the laughter. I am in no mood to participate in the fun, I just want to get free! Getting up on another chair, Mr. Schut presses my ear flat against the side of my head, which I then draw to safety.

This uncouth event went the rounds as the very first joke -- greatly magnified, of course -- about the new minister.

Support for the pastor. I was making $3,200 per year, with a "bonus" of $300, as stipulated in my letter of call. $3,500 was thus my *de facto* official compensation, but the congregation insisted on designating part of it that way because of their resentment of a former pastor who went to court during the Great Depression to force them to pay his entire contracted salary when the congregation was experiencing difficulty raising it.

They have no trouble at all paying my salary, but I certainly have trouble living on it. Being able to meet our financial obligations month by month is a constant worry to Betty and me. We never know ahead of time whether there will be anything left in our bank account at the month's end. It is like my end-of-the-month cole slaw and vanilla wafers in Marine boot camp!

Ma Schouten's becoming a partial dependant of ours upon her husband's early death was to add to our financial burden, although she more than paid for her keep by helping Betty with the children and working around the house.

We are pleasantly surprised with gifts of food that are sporadically bestowed upon us by farm families in our midst: a chicken, some thick cream, some eggs, a piece of meat. All the farm families rent lockers in the local freezer plant in which to store large quantities of meat from a slaughtered cow or hog. What they are unable to cram into their lockers, they are likely to bring to us. At the annual Thanksgiving Day celebration we are delighted to be led down to the lower level of the church, where we behold a large variety of seasonal gifts from the congregation, either fresh or in jars, enough to fill the fruit cellar in our parsonage.

The congregation paid our electric bill, but we had to pay for heating, provided by our furnace. I had to shovel the coal, take out the ashes, and regulate the heat -- altogether a big chore in winter time. Iowa coal, from the southeast part of the state, could be purchased for $5 per ton, but it was very dirty and filled with clinkers. I preferred a better coal from Illinois that could be bought for $8 a ton.

I paid for my own books and office supplies. I paid as well for the fuel and upkeep for our car. Since our old Lafayette was on its last legs by the time it made it this far, I found it necessary to borrow sufficient funds from an elder to purchase a late-model, heavily used, Studebaker from one of our farmer members, who was disposing of it in favor of a new one. It already had lots of miles on it because farm families are always on the road.

In spite of believing that God is with us still, I wonder whether I have perhaps dug a grave for myself. It is impossible to save any money. It is almost unthinkable that I should be able to persuade my family to accept a new period of living on the edge of starvation in order to give me a further opportunity to extend my graduate studies. At the moment, the future seems closed to all expectation and imagination.

Chicken chasing. Our parsonage with garage stood approximately fifty yards from the church. A parking lot and driveway separated the house and garage from the church. Gravel roads or streets were on three sides and a Christian school with its playground was opposite the church and parsonage.

240   The 1950's: Chicken chasing

School children are playing in the schoolyard when a lady parishioner drives up and hands me a gunny sack. "Here, Domine," she says, "I wanted to give you a chicken, but decided it would be fresher if you killed it yourself." As the woman departs, I take the sack with flopping chicken inside to a place behind the garage that has been officially designated for poultry executions. A block of wood is there and I have a hatchet for severing the chicken's head. I reach into the sack to get a grip on the chicken, but it flops around so wildly that I lose hold of it and it comes jumping out into the open air. I grab at it, but it gets away. I run after it but cannot catch it because it is too fast for me. (I'd run fast too if I were about to get executed!) After circling the house twice I discern that I will never succeed without some outside intervention, so I call out to two schoolboys who happen to be catechumens of mine, "Please come and help me catch that chicken. It got away and is too fast for me." This ploy succeeds and the two boys come grinning and triumphant to present the bird to me.

The boys also stay to watch me do the execution. First, though, I tie the chicken's feet with twine. Forcing its head upon the chopping block, I go Wham! and in a moment the chicken is dead. Its head falls bloody on the ground. I remove the twine around its legs and lay it for a brief moment on the ground, long enough for the headless body to jump up and resume running around. A hilarious sight it is! This time I do not chase it. I just wait until it falls over. When it stops twitching I carry it into the house to clean it.

My schoolboy assistants returned to school with one of the best stories they had ever had to tell.

Mud cars. Iowa farmers -- from this region anyhow -- lived mainly on dirt roads, as I have previously stated. These roads were dusty most of the year but became muddy in the springtime, when the frost melted. It was impossible at that time to drive most automobiles on these roads. They just sank down to their axles and got stuck. One had to have a horse to get through, or a tractor, or a model T Ford. The model T's could make it because they had high axles with narrow tires. That was why one would see dozens of such cars in town and in the church parking lot at the time of the spring thaw.

Having been carefully instructed in this circumstance, I watch carefully where I drive, first my old Lafayette and later my not-so-new Studebaker. Drive only on pavement or gravel roads, I know! But one day, when it appears that the roads have fairly well dried out, I do attempt to make an urgent call at the home of a parishioner who lives on an unimproved road. I start out carefully from the gravel road on which I have been driving, easing my car down a gentle hill towards the farm dwelling in question. I slither and I slide, and before long I am completely mired and immobile. Abandoning the automobile, I arrive at the house with great gobs of Iowa mud on my two feet.

At the conclusion of the visit the farmer takes me to the model T that he has parked in a shed behind the house. With the transmission in second gear, he manages to pass my car stuck in the middle of the road and bring me out to the gravel, and then over the intervening miles to my home in the "city."

The following day one of the farmer's sons pulled my car out of the mud with a tractor and drove it to my home. One has to wonder why Henry Ford ever bothered to introduce the model A.

Golf. I drove my car to Waveland Country Club in Des Moines with a newly purchased set of golfclubs. Johnny Medendorp, my colleague at the Des Moines CRC, who was himself an accomplished amateur golfer -- shooting regularly in the low 80's -- had offered to teach me.

We start out together from the first tee. Johnny tees up his ball and swats it straight out into the fairway as far as I (or "eye") can see. Then he tells me to do the same. I tee my ball. Johnny shows me how to grip my driver and how to swing. The first time I miss the ball completely. I try again and strike the ball too high up, making it bounce a few times and then stop twenty-five yards ahead, "All right," says John, "now you will have to use your number three wood and hit your ball as it lies on the fairway, instead of on a tee. You swing at it the same way. I'm going to walk on ahead to find my ball, and I will meet you at the first green, where I will show you how to putt."

This is a sample of how it goes all morning. Johnny leaves me mainly on my own as I chop and slash to get my ball to the first green. When I arrive there, he has already holed out. "I didn't do well," says John, "I got a five." A five! I got a fifteen -- up to the green, that is. John teaches me the rudiments of putting. I catch on to this better than I do to driving. Another five strokes brings my ball into the hole.

It is clear by this experience that Johnny Medendorp is a good golfer -- a very good golfer. But he is hardly a good teacher. Or maybe I am not a good learner. Anyhow, I am not a quitter. I keep on hacking and slashing, hole after hole until the ninth, and by then I know I have had enough. My score is already 125 and I am pooped. So I thank John for his help -- such as it is -- and drive back home to Prairie City.

I did slowly learn, and golf became an occasion for exercise and relaxation every Monday morning, when clergymen were allowed to play free. Besides Johnny, there were several Christian Reformed ministers in the area who golfed. I continued to play my erratic style of golf as long as I remained a parish minister.

The untimely death of Gerrit Schouten. It was early August in 1952, and we had just returned to Prairie City from a hectic two-week vacation with Betty's parents in Grand Haven. I badly needed that vacation, but did not get it. I was so tired and stressed that it seemed as if I had had no vacation at all, all because a few days after our arrival in Michigan Pa Schouten suddenly died of congestive heart failure. He was only 59. Pa had been seeing a heart specialist for some while, but he had not done him any good. Pa kept us all in the dark. Still I thought it strange that he would occasionally ask Betty and me if we would promise to take care of Ma if he should be taken away. We said Certainly, of course, but we should have known, in spite of his assurances that nothing serious was wrong, but we don't see what we don't wish to see!

On Sunday, the 27th of July, he attended the morning service at Second Reformed Church in Grand Haven as I served as guest preacher and Betty and Minnie sang a duet as special music. Back at home, he was beaming with pride. We had old friends, Cor and Vrouwk Van Voorthuizen, as dinner guests. We enjoyed our Sunday dinner together, but immediately afterwards Pa said he did not feel well and excused himself to go take a nap. I checked on him a few minutes later and found him in convulsions. I phoned his doctor, who came without delay, but she could do nothing for him. I followed her out the door to ask for a prognosis. She was crying. "There's nothing to do," she said, "he is dying."

This event puts everybody in turmoil and panic. I ask to be alone with him as he lies in the small guest room. I try to speak with him, but get no answer. I can hear the death-rattle in his throat. Ere long he lies quiet and is gone. Gone to his Maker, gone to his Savior.

Ma Schouten and Betty were absolutely distraught. Judy was all eyes and full of questions. I tried to give her all the answers she needed. She understood that she was losing her dearest friend. Betty and I took our little Garry to Aunt Alice in Grand Rapids, to stay until after the funeral. My brother-in-law and I went together to the funeral home to select a casket. With our awareness of the financial predicament into which Ma Schouten had now been thrust, we chose one of modest cost, but Ma was unhappy with our choice. She would have preferred a splendid funeral for her dear husband, but we felt a responsibility to help her spend as wisely as she could the small capital left her.

The funeral was held three days later at Second Reformed Church. The Schoutens' former pastor, Rev. Harry Bultema, preached the sermon. There was a reception afterwards at the Schouten home. That is when we discovered how widely loved and revered Gerrit Schouten had been. He had hundreds of friends in the west Michigan area, and scores of them came to the funeral. Pa was taken to the beautiful Grand Haven cemetery to be buried. The inscription on his tombstone reads, "He now sings above," referring to his popularity as a singer and his love of music -- especially the music about God and salvation in Christ.

Immediately the house in Grand Haven is to be put up for sale because Ma Schouten will have no financial resources outside a small stipend from Social Security. But before it can be sold, I am forced to finish a big job that Pa had been unable to complete -- painting the outside of the house. He managed to get two sides painted before he died. This climbing and stretching undoubtedly contributed to his death. It becomes my chore now to finish the remaining two sides and the garage. I push myself long and hard each day in order to get this work done before our vacation is ended. This is followed by another 500-plus mile trip back to Prairie City.

I manage to get through my two Sunday services the following Sunday. What almost throws me is a wedding I have to perform immediately after our return. The rehearsal goes well, but in the actual marriage ceremony I find that I cannot remember the bride's name when it is time to say it, in spite of the fact that I have known her and her family for two years. She discreetly whispers the name, "Geraldine Vander Leest," and I proceed. After the ceremony I apologize. I tell her that I am exhausted and distraught over our family tragedy, and she says that she understands.

Betty and I, and Judy too, might not have been able to cope with this awful loss, were it not for numerous expressions of sympathy and many deeds of kindness on the part of the Prairie City congregation. Soon we had to make another trip to Michigan in order to help Ma Schouten dispose of her belongings and bring her back with us to Iowa to live. She was emphatic about being unable to live alone in her home without Pa.

Pastoral duties. Being busy was partly my own choice and partly an inescapable condition of the office I had taken upon myself. Two kinds of work brought special pressures because I so chose: doing an extra-thorough job of pastoral visiting, and writing things for publication. These were in addition to the minimum that was required of me: (1) writing and delivering sermons twice a Sunday, and (2) the pastoral calling that went with parishioners' illnesses and with funerals and weddings.

I shall explain by starting with the last mentioned: visiting the sick and bereaved, and conducting marriages and funerals. These tasks had to be done, and with some people it was hard to know when one had done enough. Professor Volbeda never told us how to do this; I had to learn it all from other ministers, or by trial and error.

It is especially hard to know how often to visit shut-ins and the elderly, but it is imperative to be present with persons who are undergoing medical emergencies. Whenever hospitalization is required, the sick are usually taken to Des Moines, twenty miles away, and that involves me in driving back and forth as often as is needed. When parishioners require surgery I go to pray with them for divine help and protection, a good outcome, and sufficient courage to bear the stress and anxiety.

Sermon-making kept me occupied in my study four mornings per week, and more when there were special services to prepare for. I had a small "barrel" of sermons to fall back upon in emergency, but generally my sermonizing was fresh and original. I found myself relying on "canned" illustrations and poetry, available through the mail, but I always began a new sermon with fresh exegetical study and concluded with appropriate application and exhortation. I wrote out each sermon exactly as I intended to deliver it, and then memorized it as well as I could. The early hours on Sunday morning, and again an hour on early Sunday afternoon, required absolute solitude while I prayerfully went over the sermon I was about to deliver.

I must add that I was generally able to keep my congregation's attention, but this became difficult during the afternoon services because their bodies -- and mine -- were craving a good nap.

On one particularly hot and stuffy afternoon there are so many heads nodding that I pause in my sermon and say, "If you all want to take a nap, I think I ought to join you." This startles them, and their eyes go open. Temporarily, that is. Next Sunday afternoon it is almost the same.

One thing that I found helpful was an arrangement by which all the ministers in our classis traded pulpits one Sunday in each month. We went round-robin and eventually appeared in every individual church. This provided a precious little breathing space.

The visiting that I did beyond what was minimally required usually involved Betty's participation, and with two little ones at home, this would hardly have been possible, were it not for baby-sitters who offered their services free of charge, and at some periods as well the presence of Betty's newly widowed mother, who had come to live with us following the death of Pa Schouten.

From all the calling that I have done as a student, my judgment is that Betty and I need to get acquainted with every member of the congregation as soon as possible. This means that during our first year in Prairie City, we go out together two nights per week and visit three new homes each night. The schedule of names is printed in the Sunday bulletin. The families are generally prepared for our coming. We make this a short, friendly experience for all. We learn the names of the father, the mother and the children. We ask how much farming or other kinds of work they are doing. After completing this schedule, we have acquired a store of information in our minds that will serve a good purpose when later visits may be required. The families seem to appreciate very much the special attention we are giving them, and that makes it all worthwhile.

Also more than absolutely required is the teaching of various groups throughout the week. I cannot handle all of them, so it is a question of which deserves my attention. I opt to cover Men's Society, which engages in Bible study or the discussion of the Reformed confessions; also Young People's Society, which I think is crucial. Betty attends, but does not lead, one of the women's circles -- the one for older women, a strategic move -- and also functions as superintendent of the Sunday School.

During this period I wrote meditations for the *Prairie City News*. I wrote up the news from the Pella area for the denominational weekly, *The Banner*. I prepared, and received a small honorarium for, a series of special articles for this paper, such as "Faith Healing or Healing Faith." After some hesitation I also sent two scholarly articles to the *Reformed Journal* which I had developed from term papers prepared for Tillich's course on Mysticism; they were about the radical reformer and opponent of Luther, Thomas Münzer.[5]

I am receiving appreciative comments on my writing efforts which encourage me to remain involved in creative scholarship on this level, though without any prospect of applying it professionally. Never do I so much as dream that I may eventually find a teaching position at the university or seminary level.

Just the same, I have gradually been making assessments regarding future possibilities in this direction. What might be possible, I think, would be to take a church in an area where I could commute to graduate school. The best prospects for this are in the Chicago and the New York areas. With the notion that sooner or later I may wish to make such a move, I take upon myself the

---

[5]"The Radicalism of Thomas Münzer. A Chapter in the History of Anabaptism," August 1953, pp. 11-14, "Münzer's Separatism," September 1953, pp. 13-15

additional task of working through a correspondence course in Ph.D. French from the State University of Iowa This carries me over the grammar and essential vocabulary, but gives me no proper intimation of conversational French. Oh well, just so it will help me pass a Ph.D. level language exam, whenever and wherever that may turn out to be!

Johnny Medendorp, my golf mentor, acted as proctor while I took the final examination for this course while sitting in his study. I had no idea as I took it that I would swiftly be putting this learning to use in taking the French entrance exam at Union Theological Seminary.

I am now in my third year as pastor of the Prairie City CRC. I find that I am carrying an increasingly heavy burden of stress. The two measly weeks of vacation that I get each summer are scarcely adequate to make me rested and renewed, especially the latest one during the summer of 1952, when I have been busily occupied with the death of Betty's father and its after-effects. From excessive stress I have developed eating discomforts, sometimes also hives and rashes. I begin to feel more trapped than ever in busy work that makes excessive demands on my time and energy, while making very little use of my aptitudes and special training.

Pheasant hunting. I have never hunted until now. True, I did as a child fire BB shot, and later, .22 caliber bullets, at assorted small birds, but that wasn't actual hunting and I never hit anything. The truth is that I did not want to hit anything. I was just practising. But some of my young parishioners at Prairie City hunted rabbits and pheasants, especially the latter because they were out where the farmers are most of the time, in the cornfields. Our dear friend and favorite elder, Gerrit Vander Kieft, had three grown sons who farmed. One day they invited me to come along on a pheasant hunt, and I accepted. They even provided an extra shotgun for me to use. I knew how to use it because I used to shoot trap on Midway -- clay pigeons.

As I prepare myself for the hunt, Ma Schouten comes to admire my outfit and promises, "John, if you shoot a pheasant, you bring it home to me and I will take care of it. We'll have it for dinner." With this promise and implied admonition, I am on my way. One of the Vander Kieft brothers is driving. Our destination is a north-central area a hundred miles away. We drive so far because this area is said to be prime pheasant country. Parking on a country road some distance from any farmhouses, we start out across a cornfield that has already been harvested. Sure enough, there are pheasants here, beautiful birds with long tail feathers and gorgeous colors. We march around from field to field and find plenty of birds feeding on the ears of corn that have been left behind. One by one, the Vander Kieft boys get their pheasants. I too am successful. We have no dog, so we have to retrieve our birds ourselves, and between marching, shooting, and retrieving, we soon see three hours pass and start on our trip back home.

I enjoyed myself immensely. The camaraderie was wonderful. But I was thoroughly pooped. I was glad to just sit in the car as the countryside whizzed by. We made it to my home around 4 o'clock, early enough for my three hunting buddies to get home and milk their cows. I thanked them profusely and waved them goodbye.

I stumble up the kitchen steps with my prize and hand it over to my mother-in-law. "Here, Ma, you said you would take care of it. You had better clean it right away. I will certainly enjoy eating pheasant meat for supper." "Nee, jonge," she replies, "I did not mean that I would pluck the feathers or clean it. You have to do that yourself." So, dead tired as I am, I am stuck with pulling off the bird's beautiful plummage. This takes a full half hour because the feathers are difficult to remove, not like the feathers on a chicken. I even have to remove some of the feathers with a pair of pliers. When I have finished this chore, I also take out the bird's innards and hand it, thus mutilated, to my womenfolks' further ministrations.

Another hour passed before the bird was cooked and dinner was ready. Needless to say, I was famished. Also, I was almost too tired to eat.

A doubly perilous flight to Philadelphia
Flying east in a small private plane all the way from Pella to Philadelphia was a bit hairy, but flying back is even more hairy. It is downright scary. If I manage to get my feet safe on land, I'll never

get involved in anything like this again! It's worse than anything I ever experienced in the Service. I shall refrain from communicating these thoughts to my companions because I don't want to scare them any worse than they probably are already. I shall just sit and pray.

One of my companions is Henry Vander Kam, minister of the Second CRC in Pella. The other is the pilot, Gary Vermeer, who happens to be president of the Rollscreen Company, which manufactures the famed Pella windows and partitions. Gary is also a member of Henry's church and a big donor to Westminster Theological Seminary in Philadelphia.

We attended a banquet in a downtown hotel in honor of Professor Cornelius Van Til. I had been invited to ride along in Gary's plane because I had been indiscrete enough on one occasion to mention to Henry Vander Kam that I was considering enrolling at Westminster while working on my doctorate at Dropsie College or at the University of Pennsylvania, schools at which I might have been able to pursue advanced studies in Hebrew and the Ancient Near East. The private reason I had for mentioning Westminster was, in fact, that it might offer living quarters for me and my family while I pursued these specialties at either of these schools. Of course, Westminster would have to be involved in the deal to make this possible, and I mentioned it to impress Henry, but I was not particularly happy about this prospect because I had very little regard for their Old Testament professor, Edward J. Young.

I am fully aware of the game that is being played by their inviting me for this plane ride and banquet. I am evidently a hot prospect in the eyes of these two ardent promoters of Westminster and its rationalistic brand of ultra-Calvinism. I am expected, no doubt, to be both happy and grateful to have been taken to this "holy place," where one of its chief high priests is being feted. Can there be any more efficient way of recruiting top prospects than this? The truth is, it isn't working! They have been trying to trap me and suck me into their orbit, but it is in vain. Sure, I have tried to be very polite and say all the right things, such as, "What an honor it is to meet you, Professor Van Til! It is very impressive to see at first hand how highly you are regarded by your admirers."

But that is behind me. Right now I am on this flight back to Iowa and our weather is far more hazardous than it was when we came east: lots of dark clouds with flashes of lightning to steer around. We experience extreme roughness combined with sudden drops down low and rapid surges up high. Piloting this plane in weather like this must be like trying to stop a bull by holding on to his horns. I can see Gary strain and sweat. He's not thinking of Professor Van Til right now.

A thousand miles of this wears you out and sets your nerves on edge. I am praying under my breath, "Lord, lead us not into temptation and deliver us from these present forms of evil -- both kinds of evil, the meteorological and the theological!"

My week in the Des Moines Veterans Hospital. When I slipped on the ice while shoveling the late-spring snowfall, I felt immediately that something had snapped in my body, and before long I was admitted to the Veterans Administration Hospital in Des Moines to receive surgery for an inguinal hernia. I told the admitting doctor that I was also suffering from chronic stomach discomfort, and because of this I was scheduled to undergo an upper GI examination after I had sufficiently recovered from the hernia operation.

Coming to the VA hospital for this is the logical thing to do. I cannot afford to go anywhere else and the VA is sincerely glad to have me. I'm poor enough, that's for certain! This hospital isn't at all elegant. No doubt the operating area is adequate for most of the procedures performed here, but the patients are in rooms of four each, one towards each corner. Unless one is a bed-patient, he has to go to the dining room for meals, and I do not find the meals appealing. Yet a cheerful attitude of general helpfulness and consideration characterizes most of the persons who work here, from the doctors to the orderlies and laundry workers. I am especially struck by the kindness of a middle-aged lady who gives me an enema the evening before the operation. I discover that she is the widow of an M.D. who worked here before he died. The best way she knows to remain on the optimistic side in her bereavement is to keep on doing humble things like this for the patients.

I think I am a toughy and insist on having a spinal anaesthetic so that I may watch the operation while it is going on. That is what I do. I watch my image in the large reflective mirror overhead as they cut and sew away. But I really can't tell very much of what is going on. At one point the surgeon asks me a question, "Is it all right if we don't try to remove your appendix, as we planned to do? I can't seem to find it." "Yes, Doctor, whatever you say. You know best." Think of that, a surgeon who does not know where to find a patient's appendix! Doesn't matter anyhow. It wasn't infected.

After a short while in the recovery room I was wheeled back into my room of four and was swung over onto my bed. At this moment I was beginning to feel a lot of pain. I was also nauseated and uncomfortable. For relief I took my pillow and folded it in two to serve as a prop for my head. After lying like this for some time, I was discovered by a nurse who sternly reprimanded me with "Now you've done it! You are really going to have a terrible headache. Didn't anyone tell you that you have to lie completely flat while recovering from spinal anaesthesia?"

I do indeed feel a lot of pain, with the result that a nurse comes in with a bottle of alcohol solution, to be administered by intravenous feeding. Gradually I become relaxed, then more relaxed. As a matter of fact, I become downright cheerful and begin to gab at a furious rate with my three roommates. As I become more and more hilarious, they laugh and guffaw at the sight of the inebriated parson. Betty finds me in this glorious condition and joins in the fun. Erelong an elder from our church arrives. We are careful to explain to him just what happened.

It didn't seem that recovering from a hernia operation should take six days, but that was how long it was. I was getting sick and tired of being in that place. I wanted to go home!

When my surgeon makes his final examination and is ready to dismiss me, he asks the question, "Shall we keep you here for your upper GI series?" "No, thank you, Doctor," is my reply. "I feel so good and so relaxed that I don't think I will have any need of it."

A roundabout route to Synod in Grand Rapids

After driving approximately three thousand miles, we five, including Ma Schouten, have safely arrived at Paul and Minnie's house in Spring Lake, where we plan to continue our vacation with such means as are available to us. Minnie enjoys our two children, especially Judy. Garry has lots of sand to play in and the lake to paddle around in. I meanwhile will be spending most of the coming week at the Christian Reformed Synod, to which I have been delegated from Classis Pella. Going to Synod is to be a new experience for me. It is much bigger and more important than going to Classis.

I had regularly been the Prairie City church's ministerial delegate to the biannual classical meetings, which were held in the different churches belonging to the classis. Usually these were those in the Pella area, but the classis did meet one time in Denver and then again once in Alamosa, CO, requiring a lot of driving or -- in the case of Alamosa -- a long ride on a chartered bus. But after less than three years as a ministerial member, I had been elected as the Classis Pella's ministerial delegate to the Christian Reformed Synod, held annually and at Calvin College in Grand Rapids. My way was to be paid, but I decided to take advantage of being relieved for two weeks from my Prairie City responsibilities to first take a much needed "sidetrip" to California to visit my parents and siblings.

Since we had driven southwestward on the outbound leg, on the return trip we decided to go north from Modesto, where my parents lived, and drove eastward from there. On the first day on this return trip we crossed over the Sierra Nevada and drove on into the far reaches of Nevada on US 50. We tried in vain to have a night's rest in Elko.

Elko is a small place in the midst of nothing, yet it can make a lot of bother for anyone who attempts to spend a quiet night in it. This is the month of June and the days are long, so by the time we reach Elko it is late towards evening, but still light. We can still see well enough to pick out a decent looking motel on the east edge of town. We have our supper in a restaurant next door. We are in our beds by 10 o'clock, ready to rest our aching bodies and get a good night's sleep. However, the noise of activity at the restaurant never subsides. People keep coming and going. They talk loudly and keep slamming their cardoors. We begin to hear the sound of drunkenness, but added to this is the noise of transcontinental trains as they keep on chugging and grinding just a few yards behind our motel.

The railroad track is directly in back of the motel -- directly! Why didn't we see it? We are practically sitting on the main Southern Pacific rail line! The great diesel engines pulling long strings of cars send out loud blasts, shaking us right out of our beds. The one who is troubled the worst by this is our little guy Garry, who repeatedly jumps up and cries. By 2 a.m. I realize that we are not going to get our rest in this place. I get up, turn on the lights, and begin to dress. "We're not going to stay here any longer," I say. "We are better off getting on the road. I will drive while the rest of you try to sleep in the car."

We got on our way again in the middle of the night. At Wendover, on the Utah border, we got breakfast. I drove on eastward over the salt flats. Betty took her turn driving. In early afternoon we arrived in Salt Lake City, where we took a few moments to visit the famed Mormon Tabernacle. We didn't have much enjoyment in this because we were so darn tired. We drove on into eastern Utah and then through most of the state of Wyoming. At Casper we found a nice motel that lay several hundred yards away from the railroad. There we enjoyed a long, uneventful night of sleep. We spent one more night in a motel, this time in northern Iowa, and continued on until we reached Minnie's house in Spring Lake. The following day I drove to Grand Rapids and reported in at Synod.

Frustration and disillusionment on a synodical committee

I feel disappointed and ashamed with the role I have played in the 1953 Synod's shabby handling of Harry Boer's appeal of his wrongful dismissal from the Calvin Seminary faculty in 1952. It has been an education for me.

Two young progressives, Harry Boer, the new professor at Calvin Seminary in Missions, and George Stob, my teacher in Church History, had been swept out of office for no more grievous offense than protesting against the rough handling the Eastern Ave. consistory, and subsequently the majority of the seminary faculty, had given a senior student in connection with his sermon, "Does God change his mind?"

"Thus says the Lord, 'Set your house in order; for you shall die, you shall not recover.'"...And Hezekiah wept bitterly. And before Isaiah had gone out of the middle court, the word of the Lord came to him: "Turn back, and say to Hezekiah....'I have heard your prayer, I have seen your tears; behold, I will heal you....I will add fifeen years to your life.'" 2 Kgs 20:6

In that sermon the student had forthrightly endeavored to make sense of the statement that God gave Hezekiah fifteen more years of life than he at first intended. He raised the possibility that in certain circumstances God does change his mind. At least in Hezekiah's case this seemed to have been true.

Ever since Stob joined the faculty back in 1948, troubles had begun to stir. The faculty members were at the point of no longer being able to speak to one another in a polite and brotherly fashion. When Stob and Boer defended the student, moves were instituted to get them fired. The trouble went outside the faculty. Those defending Stob and Boer called attention to the far greater shortcomings of such men as Hendriksen and Rutgers. When this whole mess came before the 1952 Synod, all four professors were summarily dismissed.

The Synod of 1953 was now forced to deal with a polite but incisive letter from Dr. Boer protesting the illegality of his dismissal. My thought was that he was entirely in the right in protesting his dismissal and now in asking to be restored.

And here I was in the middle of the mess, for I had been appointed to serve on the advisory committee that was first to deal with this matter. Hours and days were consumed discussing it. I made my views heard, but failed to convince the committee to do as Boer had requested. I considered the advisability of preparing a minority report but in the end was persuaded by the chairman against doing so. I thereby lost a lot of my respect for the chairman, Dr. Gerrit Heyns, who was a man of some repute. He was the son of a former seminary professor and had been around a long time. He was highly regarded in his office as Superintendent of the Ionia State Reformatory.

Heyns said that Boer had put himself in jeopardy by leaving an official meeting. Besides, trying to give him his job back now would be impossible because the whole seminary was in turmoil. It was in such a mess that four new professors must now be found who would be able to work together. Making Harry Boer one of these four made no sense, he said.

I am very disillusioned with my seminary and my denomination. They cannot seem to tolerate men who are both outstanding and independent. They always appoint the candidate who shows the least intelligence, initiative, and originality.

In the end I was swayed by this self-serving illogic to the point of admitting that justice could not be done to Boer in the present circumstances, but I thought that it might do some men's souls good if they could admit the wrong that had been done, by themselves or by others, and apologize for it!

I do not feel good about this wretched matter. I don't like myself very much, either, nor do I like the church for tolerating such outrageous politicking. I wish somehow that I possessed the clout and influence to force others to do what is right, but I haven't. This all makes me begin to wonder whether my days in the Christian Reformed ministry are numbered. I have already decided that I am going back to graduate school, the only questions being where and how. I am coming to see with increasing clarity that in 1950 I should have remained at Union Theological Seminary and gone on for a doctorate. My denomination has only gotten worse since I was ordained into its ministry.

Dr. George Stob was on hand at Synod. On one occasion he gave the advisory committee his recommendation on how to handle the Boer protest. It seemed clear that he at least was not trying to get his job back, as Boer was, but he had plenty to say on controversial issues.

I am shocked to the core of my being by the outrageous behavior of Rev. Chris Huysjen, one of the radical right-wingers. While Stob makes his speech before Synod, Huysjen takes off his shoes and begins beating them on the table in front of him, Kruschev-style. The worst thing, though, is the fact that the president of Synod does not reprimand him for this! Absolutely no one is safe if those professing to be Christians treat one another with such flagrant disrespect!

Deciding which call is from the Lord. It was fall, 1953, and I was entering my fourth year as pastor of the Prairie City church. My salary had gone up by $100 annual increments, to the lordly amount of

$3,500, in addition to the usual $300 "bonus." I was getting on famously with these good folk, and my little family were comfortably situated in the community. Nevertheless, I had made up my mind that we should move to a church where I would have a good opportunity to continue my graduate education.

Just when it seemed that I might have to wait a long time for a call from a church offering me good opportunities to expand my education, I received a call from the Willard CRC in Celeryville OH, promising a minor increase in salary over what I was getting in Prairie City.

Of all things, the call from Willard receives support in a personal letter to me from my ex-seminary president, Samuel Volbeda! I do not consider this to be much of a recommendation, since I thoroughly despise this pompous and pretentious man, and certainly I have no inclination whatever to move to another rural parish.

Just when I had reconciled myself to staying longer in Prairie City, I received three more calls, almost simultaneously. All three were from city churches, one of which was in the New York area. Recognizing that this might be my big chance, I intended to visit each of these three churches as soon as I could get away.

Packing up the family in our Studebaker, we drove first to Highland, IN, which is in a truck-farming area close to Chicago.

Second Highland CRC is the church that is offering me one of my calls. We are cordially received and are assured that the consistory would approve of my entering a graduate program in the Chicago area, so long as this would not interfere with my church responsibilities. Both Betty and I slaver over the modern, well-appointed parsonage that comes with this job. Quite a contrast to our Prairie City barn!

The next stop was Grand Rapids. The Dennis Ave. CRC in the northeastern quarter of that city had also given me a call. Salary, parsonage, and other amenities were comparable to those of Second Highland.

It appears that a dear friend of former years whom I knew as Ruth Imense has had an influence in the church's offering me this call. She was my boss in the Calvin College bookstore and has put in a good word for me, probably through her husband, Dr. Thedford Dirkse, a professor at Calvin and a member of the Dennis Ave. consistory. These good folk, too, are hearty in their cordiality. I think the main reason why vacant churches like these are suddenly interested in me is a number of articles I have recently written for The Banner, *which reaches virtually every member.*

Our family was welcomed as guests in the new home of Paul and Minnie Luytjes on Spring Lake. Naturally, they and Ma Schouten were heartily desirous of our coming to pastor a church close to them, but I took the liberty of advising them that Dennis Ave. would probably be out of consideration for the simple reason that the area offers no opportunity for the graduate education which I now considered so imperative.

While we are in the West-Michigan area, Betty and I drive a few miles to Muskegon Heights to make a call on Oom (Uncle) Kees and Tante (Aunt) Anna Schouten. As we usually do, we arrive unexpected at their small home. We ring the doorbell and Tante Anna opens the door. Her eyes bulge wide in fright, her mouth drops open, and her cheeks turn ashen. For a moment she stands there speechless. Finally she stammers, "B-Betty, is it you?" After we assure her that Betty is real, she admits us. Why Betty? Hesitatingly Tante Anna asks, "Aren't you dead? They told me that you were electrocuted by your radio when it fell into the bathtub while you were taking a bath!" "Tante Anna," we respond, "who told you that? We just got here from Iowa." It turns out that another Betty De Vries, one living in the Chicago area, suffered just such a dismal fate, and that this was subsequently reported in a radio broadcast which someone heard and told someone, who then told someone, and so on.

We were sorry for the Chicago lady but were very thankful that it wasn't this Betty, our Betty. Still, how strange it was that the report should come out of Chicago at a time when we had just been in the Chicago area! Was this meant as an omen to us?

----

258   The 1950's: Deciding which call is from the Lord

Leaving Betty, Judy, and Garry in Spring Lake, I next took a flight out to New Jersey to check out my third call, the one from Northside CRC in Passaic. This city borders on Clifton, which in turn borders on Paterson; thus I would be surprisingly close to my own father's birthplace. Passaic, with its Indian name, was an old mill town with a changing population. Some Dutch were still there, but many had relocated to Clifton and new towns beyond. The neighborhood where we would live was at a major crossroads in a distinctly urban setting. The Puerto Ricans were there in goodly numbers. The blacks were there; the Italians and eastern Europeans were there. It was not yet a ghetto, but it was on the way to becoming one.

The members of the Northside church were especially eager for me to become their pastor because they had been vacant a whole year. They were entirely accepting of my request to be allowed to enroll in graduate classes while I served as their pastor.

I discover that a certain elder called Nick Prins is a Passaic city alderman and also one who remembers me very well from last summer's synod as the enterprising young minister who knew how to get a traffic ticket squelched. Some recommendation! Yes, I did go to the downtown traffic bureau in Grand Rapids to explain why I thought the ticket I had received was unfair. But I don't particularly want a story like this to get around. Maybe he's kidding? Yes, if you know affable Nick Prins, you know he has to be kidding!

The return by air to Grand Rapids, and then the return by car to Prairie City, proceeded without incident. By the time I saw Betty I was able to inform her that I knew which call was the one from the Lord. He was placing me back in the New York metropolitan area expressly for the purpose of bringing me once again to Union Theological Seminary, where I should now bring my studies for the doctorate to their completion.

How do I know this? When all factors converge to make sense, this has to be God speaking to you!

A difficult move to Passaic. The distance from Iowa to New Jersey is approximately 1200 miles, therefore my calling church would receive a large moving bill for transferring our meagre belongings to the new parsonage. I took up someone's hint about the best and most economical way to do this -- a choice that I soon regretted. We engaged a mover from Holland, MI to come out to Iowa to pick up our load and then bring it cross-country to Passaic.

We wish, understandably, to coordinate our own motor trip with the van's departure from Prairie City and its arrival in Passaic, but we overlook the information given by the van company to the effect that, since a weekend will intervene between these two events, our driver has the option of stopping somewhere on the way for the Sabbath. Theoretically, we are in no position to object to this, but, unknown to us, the driver does not stop over in Holland, MI, where the van originated, but in New York City, where, instead of going to church, he apparently enjoys a wild vacation as we sit in an empty parsonage. When he is good and ready, this driver appears in front of our parsonage on Myrtle Ave. and requests that we obtain a man from the church to help him unload. I ask around and obtain some men to help. If this were a nationally franchised van company, there would be none of this nonsense! Some of our things turn up broken and some are lost, never to be seen again. We are just glad to have what we have received, safe and sound, and to begin this entirely new phase in our life and career.

Within a few weeks, everything that was going to arrive was in its new place, as if the disruption of moving had never happened.

Ministering in an urban environment. My Passaic parish had about a hundred families. Many of them worked in offices or factories. There were enough Christian Reformed congregations there to make up two separate classes (what the Presbyterians call presbyteries), Classis Hudson and Classis Hackensack. Hackensack was by far the older of the two; in fact some of its constituent churches had already been established before the CRC as a denomination came into existence back in 1847. One thing that I accomplished while serving Northside church was to get the two classes to realign themselves so as to achieve greater fraternity among their constituencies.

The RCA was there too; in fact this was original Knickerbocker country. Most of the eastern RCA churches, such as the First Reformed here in Passaic, went back to the early Dutch colony centered in New York City and the Hudson valley. I worked to bring the three CRC churches in Passaic into greater fellowship with their counterparts in the RCA churches; also to get the Northside church to affiliate with the National Council of Churches.

A lot of the inspiration for such moves came out of my association with Union Theological Seminary, but it also resulted from the leadership of certain rarely gifted and determined ministers, such as Dr. George Stob, my previous Church History professor at Calvin and now pastor of a sister parish in Passaic, Prospect CRC. Men like Stob actually believed that the time was ripe for the CRC to fulfill its "manifest destiny" -- that of providing solid theological leadership in the American church environment.

I for one sincerely hope that the CRC will not surrender the ship to fundamentalism. It is this vision that enables me to believe in, and work for, a place of theological leadership for our denomination. We must strive to keep it from becoming another Orthodox Presbyterian Church, devoted to supernaturalistic rationalism and little more than an erratic sect upon the American scene.

Our Northside church and parsonage were located on Myrtle Avenue, which joined Main St. at an angle near the city's northern boundary. All the houses and stores were old and many were dilapidated. The Dutch had become a minority group in the neighborhood, as they generally were elsewhere in the metropolitan area. Our program was to answer the needs of our own constituency, and little more. We did indeed welcome everybody, but few strangers showed any interest in joining us, mainly because we were too obviously ethnic. We did operate a summer vacation Bible school which attracted children of non-Dutch and non-white extraction from the neighborhod, but afterwards these children returned to their own churches.

We faced challenges in trying to witness to the neighborhood around us. Functioning as superintendent of the vacation Bible school, Betty needed extraordinary tact in guiding those helping her.

One little black boy playing outside at recess falls and cuts his knee. It bleeds profusely. He comes inside crying and is consoled by

Betty and another teacher while they bandage his knee. After he goes off to play some more, the teacher confides to Betty, "I didn't realize that black people have red blood like that!" Betty on her part is astonished at such arrant innocence. Her reply is, "Did you think that their blood is green or some other color? They are exactly like us."

Another happening concerned a slightly retarded individual of Caucasion extraction named Jimmy, who was offended by a misguided attempt to keep him from receiving Communion.

Some of our members have succeeded in getting Jimmy to attend the Men's Bible Class, of which I am the teacher. He enjoys this so much that he is soon a regular worshipper at our church services as well. The tri-monthly communion service comes around. It is supposed to be "closed" in the sense that only professing, full-fledged members not under censure are invited to partake of the sacred elements of bread and wine (actually grape-juice). As the elders pass the bread, the plate is handed down the row to Jimmy, who does as he sees the others do and takes a piece for himself. The elder responsible for covering this particular row says sotto voce, *"Don't let Jimmy have any!" Jimmy's neighbor obeys. Jimmy is startled and confounded. Emotion floods his face. I do not know the ending of this incident. Maybe Jimmy gets a piece of bread, probably not. In either case he is upset and his future interest in this church is put in jeopardy. When I hear about it I am aghast. I make it my business at the next consistory meeting to introduce a general discussion about the appropriate way of exercising church discipline. John Calvin may have done much as our elder had done, but I am certain the Jesus Christ (a more authoritative "J.C.") would certainly not have turned away a sorely trouble "little one" in Christ like Jimmy!*

Sometimes I had to deal with tramps asking for food. I had not seen tramps since the Great Depression, when they were everywhere. A lot of these unfortunate people saw our church at its prominent corner, just off Main Street. We had to be alert that they did not steal clothing from our line, but we always gave them at least a sandwich.

An old alcoholic named Charlie comes sobbing to our front door. "Reverend," he says, "I am going to hell. I can't stand the rotten life I've been living, and unless I quit the booze, I'm going to die. Please, can you help me?" Our church does not have any regular program to help alcoholics like him, but by God's guidance I do manage to say the right thing. I tell him that he must check in with the Alcoholics Anonymous program in Newark, and give him the address, while fearing that my gesture of concern will turn out to be nothing more than a cheap way out for me, and no effective help for him. But some months later, Charlie appears back at my front door to show me that he is a new man, by the grace of God and through the assistance of the AA program.

There was an occasion when I feared that I might have put myself and my family in danger by being approachable to strangers. A wild-looking man in his twenties or thirties rang my doorbell and requested something to eat. Thinking it too severe to make him stand outside on the front porch while waiting for the sandwich Betty was preparing for him, I invited him into my upstairs office. But immediately fear and apprehension seized me. Had I done the right thing? I learned that this man had just got out of prison and was on his way home on foot. He requested some money -- what he called a loan -- so he could get home. He mentioned where, but I didn't recognize it. I was afraid to cross him, yet I did wish to avoid being "taken." A phone-call to the president of the deacons permitted me to offer him $20, which I then took out of my own billfold with the hope of being reimbursed. Seemingly satisfied that this was the best that he could expect from me, he departed. As I watched this strange and troubled man walk down the sidewalk and disappear into the distance, I wondered whether I had made the least little difference in what apparently had been a troubled existence. I would probably never know, unless this man should return to my door some day as Charlie did. Maybe he would -- in the form of some other unfortunate person!

Harsh treatment for one of Christ's humble followers
I shall always remember John Wisse. He is short of stature but physically strong. Although he is being paid just to be our church custodian, he is actually a retired mason, and in that function he undertakes, all by himself, to rebuild the parsonage chimney. Since

it has a slate roof, to do so appears to me to be quite hazardous, but Wisse knows what he is doing. He constructs a scaffold that is safe and functional for doing this work.

Because our members were part of a mixed community and showed the impact of contemporary mores on their personal lives, I was obliged to do far more visiting and counseling than I had done in Prairie City. The elders also had more work to do of a pastoral and disciplinary nature. Two or three of them, however, were accustomed to wearing an imperious air towards those under suspicion. One of them was that gentleman who kept the bread away from Jimmy.

I found myself chiding them and pleading for some persons who had been under censure, such as our custodian, Mr. John Wisse, who had made the mistake of entering into what turned out to be a troubled second marriage. His new wife threw him out and refused to be reconciled to him. He was forbidden to partake of the Lord's Supper so long as he failed to live with this woman who despised him. Mr. Wisse was a deeply pious man and a wonderful Christian. He was as sorry as anyone could be that he did not live with his wife, but he could do nothing to change this sorry state of affairs, and he couldn't. I had made a call on his wife and understood why.

Every three months we have Communion and Wisse always shows up at the consistory room, asking to be allowed to partake, but always the answer is the same. "Please, Brothers, I have such a strong desire to partake of the Lord's body and blood. I love Christ so very much. It grieves me that I cannot receive these tokens of salvation, because I am a saved man -- a sinner, yes, but saved by the blood of Christ!" He says this with tears in his eyes and a tremor in his voice. I am myself ready to shed tears, but my advocacy is in vain; the elders will not open the door of the sacred sacraments to such a sinner! They were willing, even eager, to pretend that he was worthy of being penalized for something he was unable to change.

Social life for the pastor. Social activities while in this pastorate were limited and sporadic. We hardly went out in the evening to entertainment of any sort, but on one occasion George and Joan Stob persuaded us to go with them to the marvelous movie, "Marty," -- my first movie since the Marine Corps. We were discreet enough to go to a theater in Newark, far from the prying eyes of parishioners.

Much of our socializing was connected with church functions. It was, in fact, a policy that we as ministers should avoid having special friends in the congregation in order to avoid the appearance of favoritism. We did make a point of socializing with the young marrieds, with whom we had a natural affinity. There were some also, such as the Nick Fridsma family and the John Terpstra family, who were special friends and also served as mentors to us. One young lady, Cornelia Terpstra, became a special friend of our family through sitting with our children while we were absent from the home. Betty was in fact finding that she could confide in this young lady in certain matters. Unfortunately, Cornelia's own social life was somewhat hampered by the shortage of dates with boys.

In addition to the occasional dinner invitations that have been mentioned, there was only one time in our three-year tenure when we were actually invited to a purely social dinner at the home of members of our church, and this ended in disaster beyond remedy.

We do a pretty good job of outraging both the Dutch and the Italians. We are unwarily trapped in a social situation in which it is impossible for us to function according to our host's and hostess's expectations. A mixed Italian-Dutch couple without children, these two persons of ample proportions wish to do good towards us and therefore inquire after church one Sunday whether we like Italian food. In general I do indeed enjoy the taste of Italian cooking -- more I than Betty. I answer without hesitation, "Yes, we do." The next question is, "Would you like to come to our house for an authentic Italian meal?"

I know I should be cautious of accepting this invitation because as a young boy I was once made to sit through a four-hour Italian dinner in a restaurant in San Francisco, but in the circumstances mentioned it would be awkward to refuse. So I accept, hoping for the best.

Not the best, but the worst, happens. Will this couple take the small appetites of our young children into account? So we hope, but our hope turns out to be vain. As an appetizer, we are offered a huge bowl of spaghetti, all four of us receiving an equal amount. To set a good example for my brood, I struggle through the heaping mass before me while Betty and the two children pick at what is in their bowls and soon give up in despair. Meanwhile our host and hostess are wolfing down their spaghetti with joyful satisfaction. Then the real meal comes: a large capon with various stewed vegetables surrounding it on the platter. Not even I can eat this -- not even a little bit. I am already completely stuffed with spaghetti. Then the dessert comes: a fruit compote. We all take a bit of this under the censoring gaze of our hosts, whose own gustatory delight we are unintentionally violating.

Finally the meal was over and we got to go home, but we knew that we had made two implacable, lifelong enemies!

Pine Street Christian School. Judy went through grades two through four at the Pine St. Christian School in Passaic with some flourish and complete success, as was to be her style throughout her ensuing years of learning. She readily made friends, enjoyed her teachers, and learned quickly and well. Not so Garry, our little boy.

Garry's formal education began at this same school, but with considerably less success and little enjoyment. It happened that a Miss Cutler, a Southern Presbyterian of stern demeanor, was both principal of the school and teacher of kindergarten. She succeeded in completely intimidating our little boy, like all the other little boys and girls.

Betty and I receive our first misgivings about Miss Cutler when we bring Garry to school the first morning. As we approach the front door of the school with Garry, we notice a mother standing distraught and half in tears as Miss Cutler tows the woman's child, fighting and screaming, from the mother. "No, I don't need your help, ma'am," she is saying. "You just leave now, I don't want any

mothers in the classroom." Having been witness both to the student's terror and the mother's anxiety, Garry is shocked and unable to move. He too needs to be dragged by main force through the door.

Something really dreadful happens on Valentine's Day. All the children in this school enjoy giving and receiving valentines. Garry goes to school with a handful of them, intending to parcel them out to his friends during recess or after school. As I scarcely need tell, Miss Cutler hates valentines. I think she hates love and romance, probably because she isn't getting any love or romance in her own life.

Soon after the children are settled in their seats, Miss Cutler says, "All right, how many of you have brought your money for the Christian School fund? Come up now and put it in this box." Miss Cutler has told them that the money spent for valentines should be given to the Christian School instead. Knowing this, we have given Garry some coins for this purpose. He marches up with the rest of the children and deposits his money. When they are back in their seats, Miss Cutler asks, "All right, have any of you brought valentines?" Most of the little hands go up. Miss Cutler then says, "Bring them right up here and deposit them in the waste basket. I do not approve of valentines. They are worldly and sinful!" Garry does not cry, he is just shocked and puzzled. "How can anybody say that valentines are worldly and sinful?"

This was the worst instance I know of pedagogical despotism since my own encounter with the wrath of Miss Te Sla. I could certainly put myself in Garry's place. But I was now a grownup man and a former combat marine. Didn't I have the guts to march into this woman's office and tell her off? Apparently not. Being a Christian Reformed minister has often brought me into the position of holding back from defending myself or my kids as I thought I should. So resentment just kept building up in me. I feared that this would happen with Garry as well.

Progress toward a Union doctorate

This will be my final year of residence for my doctorate at Union Theological Seminary leading up to my written exams and then my research on a dissertation. Being no longer able to take advantage of the G.I. Bill, I am obliged to pay all my expenses, including tuition, out of the fairly modest salary I have been receiving from Passaic's

Northside CRC. I have lined up my courses so that I travel in to New York City two days each week, either on Mondays and Wednesdays or on Tuesdays and Thursdays. These trips are not cheap.

I catch the Erie Railroad right here in downtown Passaic and ride eleven miles by rail to catch the ferry across the Hudson River and then the westside subway uptown to 116th St. I then walk four blocks farther north to 120th St. and Broadway. I climb up the steps to the gothic doorway and enter the large entrance foyer. From here I may go down to the basement facilities or up to classrooms, library, and faculty offices. Both Professor Muilenburg and Professor Terrien are likely to be in their offices and will be glad to welcome me in for my conferences with them or for special academic exercises and tutorials.

Since doctoral students at Union are discouraged from taking most of their courses in their major field, I am often in class with students from other fields than Old Testament. This tends to minimize my opportunities for cultivating relationships with doctoral students in Old Testament, one exception being a course held at Columbia in Akkadian with Isaac Mendelssohn. By this time I have taken most of Muilenburg's and Terrien's courses at the advanced level; also a course in Textual Criticism with Arthur Jeffery, and four courses with Paul Tillich. I have also sat in on a course in Christian Ethics with the ever-popular Reinhold Niebuhr.

I was allowed to take student-initiated studies with my advisor, James Muilenburg. One thing I had been doing during the previous semester was preparing an original translation of 1QM, the Essene War Scroll from Qumran. I had gone so far as to produce the very first English translation of this fascinating document. There was a lot of interest in this translation on the part of students both in Old and New Testament studies, one of whom was Bill Farmer. Dr. Muilenburg offered to arrange having it published, but I demurred because I was not 100% sure of some of my renderings. I asked him if he would be able at least to check it over, but he had to decline because of other pressures on his time. I did not blame him; in fact, I wondered how I had the nerve to ask.

Dr. Muilenburg has been taking a lot of interest in the progress of my studies. He could have immediately sent my name to a number of interested institutions of higher learning, had I allowed him to do so.

268   The 1950's: Progress towards a Union doctorate

It really is a "seller's market" these days for Ph.D. and Th.D. candidates. On more than one occasion Muilenburg has come to class with a fistful of letters, asking, for instance, "Who wants to go to Bryn Mawr? Who would like to go to Howard?" Others speak up but I always remain silent. This results from my inability at this stage of my development to make the decision to trade preaching for teaching, a state of affairs almost unheard of among graduate students. They all want to teach, but I do not know yet for sure whether I do.

The same hesitation and uncertainty lead me to decline two further offers from Muilenburg that might have been of great advantage to me. One was to serve as his Tutor Assistant in Old Testament, with a sizeable stipend. Another was to apply for the Kent Fellowship, also at a sizeable stipend. I was strongly tempted by each of them and gave them careful consideration before declining them. Eventually I had to turn down the tutor-assistantship because it would conflict with my duties at Northside. I also declined to apply for the Kent Fellowship because I would have been required, if I did so, to state positively that my intent would be to enter the field of teaching religion at a college or seminary, and I simply was not prepared to make that choice. It was not timidity or confusion that made me so hesitant, but my strong commitment to the pastoral ministry. Yet I was able to see that I was already overprepared for such and needed to look carefully for God's leading into perhaps a modified form of the ministry. Also I perceived that I was becoming more and more orientated to a larger community of faith and no longer fitted theologically into the narrow confines of Reformed orthodoxy.

This is my final semester of course-work, and I am enrolled in Individual Study with another graduate student by the name of Joe Holbrook, reading the Hebrew text of Jeremiah with James Muilenburg. Holbrook happens to be pastor of an RCA congregation in northern New Jersey. Since I can handle Dutch and Joe can do quite well with French, Dr. Muilenburg has us take alternate verses in the Old Testament text and render the one into Dutch (me) and the next into French (Joe). This is fun for him. As a boy he heard the Dutch language at home. At college he learned French so well as to be able to serve as a liaison officer in the American Expeditionary

Force in World War I. This gave him the opportunity to serve at the headquarters of the French Army. As he is for many, James Muilenburg is a strong and eloquent model for me of what a working biblical scholar ought to be.

A rough trip home from an interview at Calvin College

I have just been through a most frustrating and exhausting experience. Rather than preaching as usual in my own Northside pulpit, I am trying to preach last Sunday's old sermon to the Ridgewood CRC, where Lewis Smedes is pastor.[6] Lew and I have been forced in desperation to exchange pulpits at the last moment.

Lew and I were both asked to visit Calvin College for individual interviews for a position (or positions) in Bible. Being aware that we were both being invited at the same time, we decided to travel together by plane to Grand Rapids. I did not sit in on Lew's interview, hence did not know how it went until he later told me about it. It apparently did not go well; he was found to be too liberal for them. In my own interview I apparently said some things that were suspect. For instance, I was lavish in my praise for J. T. McNeill's *History and Character of Calvinism*.[7] Also I was somewhat too free regarding scriptural inspiration. Thus these interviews were instrumental in closing certain doors, for me as for him. We were henceforward marked as unfit prospects for teaching Bible and Religion at Calvin College.

Unfortunately, that negative result of our trip was not compensated for by an easy or pleasant return to the normal. What should have been a quick and uncomplicated flight back home to New Jersey turned out to be a hell of frustration and disappointment. The interviews concluded Thursday evening, but we did not get home until mid-morning on the following Sunday.

Here is what happened. It was foggy in Grand Rapids Thursday evening, when we were ticketed to fly back to New York. Our flight

---

[6]Lew eventually entered an outstanding career of teaching and writing at Fuller Theological Seminary in Glendale, CA. Though popular among progressive groups in the CRC, he was never invited to a position at Calvin College or Calvin Seminary.
[7]As I have previously told, I had taken a graduate seminar with Professor McNeill at Union Theological Seminary in 1949-50.

270   The 1950's: A rough trip home from Calvin

had been cancelled. We were given a bus ride to Detroit's Willow Run Airport, but when we arrived there, it too was closed by the same thick January fog. The airline provided a bus ride into Detroit and a room in a hotel. On Friday morning another bus took us back to Willow Run. We waited all day and all evening, but the fog would not dissipate. Another night in our hotel. Another bus ride on Saturday morning to Willow Run, and still the fog held. In growing concern for our Sunday morning responsibilities, we made the decision to board the Empire State train for New York, leaving Detroit on Saturday afternoon. I telephoned Betty to ask her to get one of our elders to meet us in Grand Central Station at 7:30 a.m., so that he could bring me without further delay to Passaic in good time for the 9:30 service. Betty was also to alert Doris Smedes, Lew's wife, asking her to be at the Northside church in order to drive Lew home on time for his morning service, which fortunately was scheduled to begin a half hour later, at 10 o'clock. We slept well enough in our pullman berths and had finished breakfast when the train pulled into Grand Central, but our hope of being at last out of trouble came to nought.

It is precisely 7:30 a.m. We have taken our bags and have walked into the huge waiting room looking for someone from my church, but we can find no one we know. After wandering about in a vain quest for a half hour, I phone Betty again to find out whether someone has been dispatched and is on his way. Her reply is "Yes, Mr. Pete Hamersma is supposed to be there." Sensing that we are now in deep trouble, I tell Betty to phone Doris Smedes again and ask her to bring Lew's sermon from last Sunday with her so that he may preach in my church while I hasten over to his church to take his place there.

We wait until 8:45. We have Mr. Hamersma's name called on the P. A. system once, and then a second time, but he does not show up. In desperation, Lew and I take a taxi all the way to Northside Church, each paying $11. At 9:15 we pull up in front of my church. Doris is at the parsonage with Lew's sermon. He immediately heads for the consistory room with his sermon in his hand. I grab my last Sunday's sermon, but can not so much as glance at it while I drive my own car as fast as I can for Ridgewood, arriving at the church only five minutes before the beginning of the church service. I have time only to shake a few hands, mutter a few words of explanation, and mount the pulpit. I try to follow the liturgy as well as I can, but am forced to improvise the sermon. At the finish I apologize to the congregation and explain that I can do no better under the circumstances, and they seem to understand.

When I arrived back home quite exhausted, I was informed that Mr. Hamersma had indeed been at the Grand Central Station at 7:30 a.m., but left for home after ten minutes when he was unable to find us.

This wild week will always remain a blur in my memory, mercifully so. I feel utterly defeated and demoralized by all the impenetrable fog we have experienced: the fog that clouded the minds of the Calvin faculty; the fog that swallowed us in Grand Rapids and Detroit; the fog that confused Mr. Hamersma, our too-easily discouraged helper.

For years my recurring nightmare would be of driving frantically to an unfamiliar church on a Sunday morning, losing my way, arriving in a panic to a half-finished service under the direction of a layman and with a church full of angry and disgusted people.

Preparing for a study year in the Netherlands. The last step in a Union doctor's program before launching out into one's dissertation was to take the field examinations, consisting of six two-hour written essays in fields relating to one's special subject, as chosen by the candidate from a list of possible areas.

I choose Hebrew grammar, the Apocrypha and Pseudepigrapha, Old Testament textual criticism, Old Testament theology, ancient Near Eastern texts relating to the Old Testament, and the history of ancient Israel. As one would imagine, I have spent a lot of time preparing for these exams. Now I shall give account of myself as a mature scholar, coming back to the seminary week after week to take each new examination. After this is finished it will be summer, and then we will begin our preparations for our Fulbright year in Holland. I have received the good news that I have been successful as an applicant for a nine-month Fulbright grant!

During the previous school-year, 1955-56, I had been refining the topic of my doctoral dissertation, and I did so in such a way as to accomplish two purposes: (1) to explore the issues relating to the historical criticism of the Pentateuch by examining the theory and method of a group of famous Dutch scholars in this field of study, as seen in their literary output, and (2) to utilize my previous years of study in the Dutch language by locating this program in the Netherlands, the land of my own forebears. To meet these two goals, I applied to go to Leiden, the oldest (est. 1575) and most prestigious of the Dutch universities, where the famous school associated with Abraham Kuenen flourished from 1870 onward. Kuenen's own output was extensive, but what would be especially important for me to explore would be his wider influence in Holland and abroad.

In proposing this topic I shall be bringing myself to task with respect to the challenge that James Muilenburg put to me several years ago when he stated that I had satisfied him with regard to my own intellectual integrity: "Simon, I am now convinced that you intend to be completely honest!" I think that he of all persons well understands how programmatic my research topic will be towards convincing myself once and for all regarding the way in which my career should henceforward develop. Anything that I shall venture to present at the conclusion of this research project that is designed to convince him that I fully understand and rightly appreciate Old Testament scholarship in the country of Holland and under these auspices will most certainly place a heavy obligation on my own deep-seated value-judgment as to its scientific value.

Betty has been thoroughly consulted in all this. So also my children and Ma Schouten, who has been living part of the time with us in Passaic. They will all be going along. This will be a new life-experience for the children, something that will vastly enrich their own cultural development. Ma Schouten will also have a new chance to visit her sixty-six brothers and sisters, nieces and nephews, and we too will have an opportunity to become acquainted with them.

How to finance this was my biggest concern ever since I first started thinking about it. To tell the truth, I had not been able to save much money out of my very moderate salary. I thought about asking for a loan either from my father in California or from my brother-in-law in Michigan. Opting for the latter, I asked Paul outright one day last summer if he could -- and would -- lend me $1,000 for this purpose. At the time he said yes, and on that basis I proceeded to make my Fulbright application. Unfortunately, he said he could not lend it to me when I asked him for it. However, another door opened when this door closed -- a subsidy fom the Fulbright Commission.

Thank God, the Fulbright grant has come through! It will pay for my own passage to and from the Netherlands, for all my book and incidental expenses, for travel in the Netherlands, and for my own lodging and living expenses up to $1,800 for the nine-month period. Ma Schouten will share the rental cost of an apartment and will also pay her share of the groceries and utilities. Also she will pay her own passage each way. Of course I will be paying for that of Betty, Judy and Garry.

Something unexpected happened to help out our budget and make up for the money I would not be getting from my brother-in-law. At the suggestion of Lewis Smedes, the consistory and congregation were willing to grant us a subsidy in the amount of $1,000. This meant that we would have enough money to carry us through. The director of the Fulbright program in Holland located an apartment for us outside Leiden for F145 (about $50) per month rental, and we were able to book cheap passage on a Dutch immigrant ship named Zuiderkruis scheduled to leave for Holland in late August, 1956.

A "Southern Cross" crossing

We have been six days at sea and are close to the end of our voyage to Holland. The name of our ship is "Zuiderkruis," Dutch for "Southern Cross," a very appropriate name for a vessel with an Indonesian crew. The Southern Cross is a prominent constellation in the southern hemisphere.

The officers of this ship are Dutch. In fact, this ship belongs to the Dutch government, which is using it to convey emigrants to Canada and the United States. During World War II it served as a troop transport. Our fellow passengers include circus people going home to eastern Europe, some army wives with children on the way to join their husbands in Germany, and other assorted persons like

ourselves. We are one of two Fulbright families on board. With us four De Vrieses there are Betty's mother and her aunt, the younger sister of Pa Schouten, who has been in the States this past summer visiting some Schouten relatives in western Michigan. "Tante Marie" is a delight to have as a member of our entourage. She is as affable and gracious as was her deceased brother, Betty's father Gerrit.

In the cause of economy, this ship lacks most of the amenities of luxury liners; there are no lounges, no swimming pool, and no private bathrooms. All the adult passengers have their meals in the same dining room, along with the ship's officers. There are three large tables in the dining room arranged in a U; they have side and end boards to prevent the dinnerware from crashing to the deck during heavy weather, of which we have had quite a bit, especially during the first two days out of New York. There is no assigned seating at these tables. We sit wherever there is room. This facilitates our becoming acquainted with our fellow passengers and the ship's officers, including the captain. The children on board have their meals in the same dining hall, just prior to the adults.

There are some real characters aboard this ship. One of the strangest is a Hungarian seminary student clad all in black who continually wears his pajamas underneath his shirt and trousers. This substitutes for underwear. We laugh to see these garments poking out at the top and bottom when he shows up at the evening Vespers which I conduct.

Betty, I, Garry and Judy are together in one cabin, while Ma Schouten and Tante Marie share a second with a Belgian lady and her daughter Lillian. As I have said, there are no private baths or toilets. We have to find these in the corridors. Predictably, they become pretty smelly and messy when people get seasick.

Judy and Garry have great fun in the playroom and on the aft deck. They become good friends with the Belgian girl, who is just coming into puberty. Unbeknown to us, the teenage Indonesian boys in charge of the playroom are abusing these children by scaring them with ghost stories and making the girls sit on their laps, groping them.

An alarming thing happens. One of these Indonesian boys tries to get in bed with Lillian while she is alone in her cabin. She comes running to Judy for help, who finds us on deck to report what has happened. No more was seen of Lillian or of this young man during *the remainder of the voyage. Unmistakably, the Indonesian crew have been too long away from home.*

The final night at sea was for partying. We wore silly hats that the children had made. The kids put on a grand puppet show, with our inventive little Judy as director.

We all watch with great interest as the Zuiderkruis moves showly into the harbor at Rotterdam. At the dock there is a crowd of people waving. Ma Schouten and Tante Marie recognize many individuals in this crowd and tell us that they are waving for us. Ma spies two of her brothers and a sister, then also many nieces and nephews. They are all here together to welcome us to Holland. When we debark there is hugging, kissing, and hand-shaking.

We pile into cars brought by various persons in this group and head for the home of a sister of Ma, Tante Anna, who lives in the village of Hardinxveld on the north bank of the Maas (Meuse) River. We meet some new persons here. Ere long we get into the cars again and depart for the home of a second sister, Tante Sijntje, who lives in the village of Almkerk, south of the Maas in what is called "the Land of Altena." Anna's husband is a farmer, Sijntje's husband is a baker. It is in rooms above the bakery that we spend our very first night in Holland.

It looks as if we may count on many visits from -- as well as many visits to -- the homes of these enthusiastic relatives. There is a reason why they are so enthusiastic and generous. Pa and Ma Schouten sent numerous packages to them immediately after the end of the War, and they haven't forgotten. Although most of them do not have a great many material goods, they take every means available to demonstrate their gratitude and admiration.

Here we were in the countryside of Ma Schouten's childhood, a land of dikes and windmills, rich turf for growing crops in considerable variety to sustain the sizeable human and animal population. Three years ago this was all under sea water from a violent storm that broke through the Zeeland and South Holland seadykes. These folk remembered it vividly, but all was lush and peaceful now. The enterprising Dutch were in the first phase of a gigantic new plan to build a better diking system, the "Delta Plan," which was designed to prevent future calamities from the sea.

The 1950's: A meeting of world scholars

A meeting of world-known scholars in Strasbourg. Leaving my family in good and loving hands, I attended my first international conference of Old Testament scholars in Strasbourg during the first week of September, 1956. Dr. and Mrs. James Muilenburg from Union were there. So too Professor Samuel Terrien, who was on home turf, though he hailed from a different part of France. There were other prominent American scholars there as well, but they were far outnumbered by the Europeans: French, Germans, Swiss, Dutch, English, Scandinavians, and others. Père Ronald de Vaux from the École Biblique in Jerusalem acted as president of the conference. I noticed that there was a significant number of Roman Catholic scholars in attendance, a prognosis of what was to come in later meetings of this organization. The Israeli and Iron-curtain scholars were, on the other hand, noticeably absent. This too was destined to change.

This is a five-day conference held once every three years by the International Organization for the Study of the Old Testament (IOSOT), which Piet de Boer of Leiden helped organize immediately after the War. Besides sponsoring these conferences, it publishes the prestigious journal, Vetus Testamentum, *a quarterly, with de Boer as editor-in-chief. De Boer is the scholar with whom I shall be working as I do research for my doctoral dissertation.*

The IOSOT has previously met in Leiden, Cambridge, and Copenhagen. Here in Strasbourg, there are major addresses by leading scholars and shorter presentations by whomever wishes to present a paper on a topic relevant to the interests of the members of this organization. I shall not read a paper, of course; I am not ready for it. Perhaps three years from now, when the conference is held again. But I can see that it certainly is very worthwhile, more for the opportunity to meet prominent scholars than for the specific content of the lectures; these are worthwhile, to be sure, but they can, if one is interested in them, be retrieved from the journals in which they will ultimately be published, such as Vetus Testamentum.

While I am here in Strasbourg I am staying in a student residence near the university. Since I have trouble understanding some of the lectures given in German or French, I find myself dropping out of meetings and taking time to inspect the famous and picturesque city of Strasbourg (Ger. Strassburg), which is the most prominent of the Alsatian cities.

A meeting of world scholars in Strasbourg

Strasbourg was French up to the Franco-Prussian War, then German until the end of World War I, after which it became French again. To test where the true ethnic affinities were, I tried speaking some French to tradespeople, but often found that to be understood, I had to switch over to German, which I handled better. I visited the great Gothic cathedral with its uncouth single square tower, the romanistic church where John Calvin pastored French refugees before he returned to Geneva, and the walls and city-gates that surrounded the city. On one house next to the perimetric canal, I espied a not-yet effaced slogan, "À bas Hitler," meaning "Down with Hitler." The members of the conference also took an excursion to the ancient Convent of St. Odile in the Vosges mountains, as well as to the vineyards in the southern valley, where I was introduced to the wonders of Alsatian wine.

While the conference was still meeting, Dr. and Mrs. Muilenburg treated me to a real French supper in one of the very good restaurants. We took this occasion to compare notes on the precise nature of the research that I would be carrying out in Leiden. On another occasion he and I met with Piet de Boer, who agreed to guide my research in Muilenburg's absence. I also had the opportunity to become acquainted with two of de Boer's doctrinal students, Jaap (Jacob) Hoftijzer and Tom Sprey.

Hoftijzer shows himself to be a very meticulous scholar. His published works are very solid. He is rewriting a philological lexicon on ancient Semitic texts. Sprey is also a good scholar, but his wife's perpetual struggle with a bad back keeps him from engaging in research as intensively as Hoftijzer.

To get to Strasbourg, I had travelled by train from s'Hertogenbosch through the southern Netherlands, Belgium, Luxembourg, and the northern reaches of the Alsatian region of France. I simply reversed this itinerary on the way back, arriving back at s'Hertogenbosch after dark had fallen. Then I faced the dilemma of how to travel through the North Brabant countryside in order to arrive at the relatively inconspicuous place of Almkerk, where my wife, children, and mother-in-law were waiting for me. I experimented by taking a bus to a place called Heusden, which was at least in the right direction and turned out to be, in fact, close to Almkerk. In order to obtain further directions, I found it necessary to talk my imperfect Dutch in a bar where the locals were speaking a distinctive dialect not altogether intelligible to me. They were not, however, critical of my accent but instead appreciated the fact that I, an obvious foreigner -- and an American especially -- was endeavoring to use their language. They remembered the Americans very favorably in that town for their push to drive out the Germans who had been occupying their lands for four long years. They helped me get a local taxi to complete the end of my trip. From Heusden we crossed rivers and lowlands, all in the pitch darkness. I reached my destination exhausted, but was gratified to find that all was well with my dear ones. They had been treated like celebrities and would have been glad to have stayed longer, but the following day we travelled on to Noordwijk in order to participate in the Fulbright orientation.

Orientation in Noordwijk aan Zee. This was a resort town on the North Sea coast, just above Katwijk, where our apartment would be. Both towns lie on the high dune that separates the sea from lower ground inland. Windmills and modern diesel pumps force the water from the canals and ditches into the sea at this and other strategic locations. This pumping has to occur, to be sure, at low tide.

The entire Fulbright group for the year 1956-57 had been brought to Noordwijk with their dependants by Dr. Johanna van Dullemen, administrator of the entire Netherlands program, to spend two weeks in a well-designed and well-administered orientation program. This consisted of lectures by notable persons and field trips to interesting and important sites. We were quartered in Hotel den Hollander, a three-star hotel lying on the "Boulevard," a promenade avenue along the fringe of the sea. The seawaters were calm during our stay, inviting us to bathe and swim in them if we should wish to do so, though few of us found time for it. Even the children were kept busy playing and learning about things they would be experiencing as they attended schools in this strange new land.

A major concern of this program is to make the Fulbrighters conversant in essential Dutch, hence they receive daily language lessons by professional teachers. I am, to be sure, beyond this and accordingly am excused. However, I find something useful to do with my time. Discovering that nothing along the same lines has been designed for the children, I offer to tutor them myself. In the absence of specially prepared curriculum materials, I use the cartoon strips in the daily newspaper, which help these children connect Dutch words with what they see. Children have a natural attraction to pictorial materials, and especially to animated action. I take them through the scenes as drawn by the cartoonist and try to help them understand the essential structure of the language in this way. Our own Judy and Garry especially enjoy this, Judy of course more than Garry, since he is only six and is about to enter first grade.

We receive very nice meals in the dining room. The children are generally in charge of a governess. They receive their own meals in a separate dining room. Garry enjoys being honored on his sixth birthday, September 10, which is celebrated by all the children with noise-makers, funny hats, and a wonderful cake with candles.

We made special effort to become acquainted during this preparatory program with the two other Christian Reformed families who were present. They were both to be connected with the Free (Calvinist) University in Amsterdam. One was Henry Zylstra, an English professor at Calvin College. The other was David Holwereda, just out of Calvin Seminary. These two gentlemen were doing their academic work under the auspices of the CRC's sister church in Holland known as the Gereformeerde Kerk. That was the approved way of lecturing or studying in Holland.

Already -- by doing my work at a public institution within a noteworthy modernist mileau -- I am placing myself under grave suspicion in the CRC. Why am I doing it this way? Very simply, to retain my freedom and my integrity, which will be very difficult to do if I attempt to hide behind the mask of orthodoxy.

One evening Betty and I are informed that we have received guests at this hotel. They are waiting for us in the hotel lobby. These visitors turn out to be two of Betty's cousins from Leiderdorp, a bedroom community outside the city of Leiden, where the university is. Though they are dressed up, they have cycled the entire distance in order to call on us. They are acting on information from Ma Schouten, who is spending this period with one of her sisters. The names of these visitors are Gerrit and Riet van Houwelingen. He is a principal of a Christian middle school in Leiderdorp and shows himself to be a gentleman of some learning. How marvelous, we think, to be welcomed to the Netherlands in such a remarkable way and with such conspicuous yet humble effort on their part. Gerrit and Riet turn out, however, to be just two out of the sixty-plus first cousins, aunts and uncles of Betty, many of whom we are destined to meet during this Fulbright year.

Dr. Johanna van Dullemen proves to be a fine administrator. I continually find her helpful. One thing that is indispensable for opening up new contacts is to know the persons who are directly responsible, hence she brings to our classes prominent persons in government, the arts, the professions, the church, and the school system. She makes it a certainty that the Fulbrighters shall receive maximum value for the time and effort spent here. I feel myself to be very fortunate indeed to have this magnificent opportunity for self-betterment.

Life in a Dutch fishing town. After Noordwijk aan Zee came Katwijk aan Zee. In mid-September the five of us, Betty, Grandma, Judy, Garry and I, settled into the tiny apartment that had been located for us, and immediately we set to work to make it as homey as possible. We were located on the Boulevard, a street running north and south along the beach, as in Noordwijk. Every day we were able to look out our front window to observe people on the sand and in the surf. We saw school children coming after school to dig holes and construct castles. Trawlers would be dredging for shrimp and mussels a few hundred feet from the shore. Men riding stout horses would be doing the same, venturing out into the water to their horses' necks. Far out large ships and small could be seen sailing north or south. When we first arrived the sea was calm and the air was warm, but gradually the season changed and storms began to come. What a marvelous display that was! It was a mighty pageant that the storm put on, churning up the waters and creating whitecaps as far as the eye could see! A special delight was to walk along the beach at sunset after a storm, watching the gorgeous colors of the sunset play on the rough waters charging towards the shore.

The Fulbright program director had obtained our apartment for us, and she could not have done better. Our rent was only 145 Florins (better known as Guilders). The landlord, Mr. Parlevliet, could offer this low rent because it was off-season. During the summer tourists -- usually Germans -- would have been paying 900 Florins for the identical accommodations, and Mr. Parlevliet would have been glad to have them -- much as he resented what the German army had done to the Katwijkers from 1940 to 1945, blowing up their buildings to make bunkers and in the end reducing them to eating tulip bulbs.

The entire length of the Boulevard was crowded with apartment buildings similar to ours and rising to the third or fourth storey. All of these particular buildings had been newly reconstructed with money administered by the Dutch government and derived from American loans or grants. The Parlevliets had lost their property along with the others and had been forced to find makeshift quarters somewhere else, but they were now in their glory. They made sure to rebuild better than before. The Parlevliet's were gratified to rent now to Americans -- Americans of Dutch descent, which was even better -- and especially to be able to rent to a real, bona-fide Domine!

Katwijk was more than a resort town. As long as anyone could remember, its inhabitants had been engaged in the herring enterprise. Week by week, their small, round-bottomed ships would venture far out into the North Sea above Scotland, not returning until their holds were full. In the old time the herring boats had a shallow draft and an unusually broad beam to enable them to rise up on the surf onto the beach, from where the fish could then be unloaded for processing and distribution. These ships had unsightly sideboard keels that could be let down on either beam to increase stability when it was needed, but they were awkward and unsightly and reduced the speed. An inner harbor could be reached through a chain of canals. In this inner harbor there were wharves for unloading and buildings for processing fish and storing nets. This area was known as Katwijk Binnen ("Inner Cat Town"), in distinction from Katwijk aan Zee ("Cat Town on the Seashore"), where most of the people lived.

Standing next to the old white church on the strand was the granite statue of a fisher-woman and her daughter, waiting vainly for their men to return from the sea following a storm. It had been dedicated by Queen Wilhelmina to honor the long list of fathers and brothers who had lost their lives in storms at sea. It also gave expression to a solidarity in suffering shared by the community and, indeed, the nation, while epitomizing the spirit and the tragedy of a fisherman's hazardous existence. I especially valued that because my maternal grandfather and namesake, Simon Tamminga, had also been such a fisherman, though he came from Friesland, the northeastern part of the Netherlands.

Most of the native Katwijkers dressed in sombre black and lived as their ancestors had done. One would see children and adults in wooden shoes. The people were extremely pious as well as stolidly conservative. Many adults whom we encountered recognized us as foreigners and tried to ignore us, but we were able to develop a warm relationship with certain persons such as our landlord and his wife, as well as with the friendly grocer from whom we bought our victuals.

Churches in Katwijk. So far as we could tell, there were only two churches of any size within the town, the old white one on the strand, which belonged to the original Hervormd ("Reformed") congregation, and a large ugly brick church in late Victorian style near the city center, also Hervormd but of a later generation and more up to date. We tried out both, but felt unwelcome in each of them, hence we ended up as regular worshippers at the much less commodious edifice of the Gereformeerde church instead.

Dutch "Hervormd" and "Gereformeerd" mean the same, but they designate separate denominations. The first appellation is authentic old Dutch in which the prefix "her" means "again," as does the equivalent Latin prefix, *re-*. "Hervormd" was chosen by the Protestants, and specifically the Calvinists, who were successful in the Eighty-Years War with Spain. During the nineteenth century, secessionist groups chose the Latin prefix to take its place and then added the more traditional Dutch past-participial prefix "ge" at the beginning to make an artificial hybrid meaning the same thing.

This is our very first Sunday in Katwijk. We have noticed the striking old church on the strand, the old fishermen's church, and we have decided that we would like to have the experience of worshipping there. Having taken note of the hour set for morning worship, we five (Betty and I, Grandma, and our two children) show up in our Sunday best about twenty minutes early. We choose a pew on the right side, about two-thirds of the way from the front. Hardly anybody is in the church. We sit quietly, gazing about to take note of the arrangements and the decor. Heavy beams support the roof. There are no decorations of any sort. A large open Bible is propped on a stand upon the communion table, symbolizing the message, "God's word is here." There is a high raised pulpit on the left side of the chancel and an array of organ pipes across the front.

Worshippers clothed all in black begin to enter, but none of them come to sit near us. Suddenly our repose is shattered by the voice of a middle-aged man whom we identify as the koster, or custodian. "You are not allowed to sit there," he says in Dutch sotto voce. *"That pew belongs to one of our regular church families. You will have to sit over there on the left, close to the pulpit." We are totally embarrassed and rise out of our places to remove ourselves elsewhere. Instead of proceeding to the left front, as directed, we march out through the front door and depart. We are offended at such crudeness and insensitivity toward strangers. "If we are not good enough to sit in that pew, we are not good enough to remain in their church. Perhaps we will find another church in this town that follows the gospel!" So much for the old white fishermen's church! They may be good at catching herring, but they know nothing about fishing for men.*

The following Sunday we are standing before the closed wooden doors of the other Hervormd church, the large Victorian one in the city center. There are a few other latecomers. Realizing that the morning service is about to begin, we are bewildered by a seeming indifference towards late comers. Suddenly one of the doors swings open a few inches and a man's head appears. This talking head demands to know, "Wil je binnen komen (Do you want to come in)?" As if we would be standing here if we did not want to come in! Anyway, we say yes and are allowed to come through the door and follow our usher down the main aisle, then along the front of the chancel to seats directly underneath the raised pulpit. Over a thousand disapproving eyes stare as we pass. We feel chagrined that we are being put on display as unwelcome strangers. We do remain this time for the service, and we do enjoy the sermon. After the service is over and we follow the congregation out of the door, however, no church member smiles or makes a friendly gesture. We who were made a spectacle as we entered are ignored as we depart. This congregation's unaccepting attitude destroys any spiritual blessing we might have received from worshipping with them. This situation offends not only my personal feelings, but also my professional standards as a minister who has always taught and believed that the first duty of all who call themselves Christians is to receive strangers into their midst.

More or less by default, then, we went on the third Sunday and on all our remaining Sundays in Katwijk to the Gereformeerde church.

It did not look much like a church. It was entered through a courtyard and consisted of a single large square room with pews for two or three hundred. At the front there was a raised dais, with the communion table in the center holding not only a Bible but a pewter flask and plate for Communion. A novelty for Holland was a large white vase filled with large white chrysanthemums, placed alongside, rather than upon, the communion table. It was a rarity to see flowers in a Dutch church at that time, in spite of the fact that the Dutch love flowers and often bring bouquets home with them from the market. No doubt this congregation felt that the whiteness of vase and flowers was in keeping with the intended purity of their worship.

We enjoy the worship services here and are more or less recognized as belonging. Fortunately, no one asks me to preach a sermon. Although I do speak Dutch, that would be only for an informal setting. I would soon be stuck if I had to preach or pray in public, activities that require a mastery of set phrases and patterns appropriate to dominees, but beyond my awareness or ability.

It seemed ironical to us that the Gereformeerde Kerk, coming out of the Secession movement of the 1800's which led to the formation in America of both the RCA and the CRC, was the most liberal of the three -- not so much in doctrine as in morals and liturgy. This differ-difference was more sociological than theological. Beyond that, the Gereformeerden showed effects of historical circumstanstances that had not affected the Hervormd congregations. The latter had not been affected by the liberalism of the 1800's. Theologically, these two Hervormd congregations stood squarely on the old Canons of Dordt. The Gereformeerde church, on the contrary, reflected a more sophisticated theological development, sharing not only the tradition of purging in the *Afscheiding* ("Breaking away") but the more culturally relevant stance of Abraham Kuyper and the *Doleantie* ("Grieving"). We felt at home there. Mr. Parlevliet, our landlord, was an elder in this church and used his influence to make sure that everyone was fully aware of the presence of a *Dominee* from America, with his family.

Our living quarters. Now I wish to describe our little home on the third (Dutch: second)[7] floor of Meneer Parlevliet's apartment building. It was indubitably inadequate for five persons -- but we made it do, as the Dutch themselves would. The stairway was very narrow and steep -- so steep in fact that Betty damaged her knee climbing up it and eventually required treatment at the medical clinic in Leiden.[9] One would arrive in a hallway with doors leading to our small living room, to our even smaller kitchenette, to our toilet cum shower, and to three separate bedrooms -- one for Betty, Garry and me, one for Grandma, and one for Judy. Grandma got a tiny chamber looking out over the sea, which I appropriated by day as a place to type my dissertation. Judy had to share her miniscule bedroom with Garry during the day as a playroom, where the two often constructed legos atop my stacked-up Marine foot-lockers covered by one of my Marine blankets. At night Garry had a single bed next to our double bed, all in the one somewhat larger bedroom. But that was not all that this cold room contained; it was also the place for an orange crate doing service as an icebox since there was no refrigerator. We were expected to bring our perishables three storeys down into the kelder (cellar), but this arrangement was preferable to that. The kitchenette had only a pair of gas burners to cook on and used water heated by a *geyser*, or gas wall heater. Betty and Ma had to work side by side in this small space, and accordingly were forced to keep meals simple. The living room, finally, contained a dining table with four straight chairs, two arm chairs, and a coal stove which provided all of our heat, as a consequence of which I was ever busy coaxing the best out of it and then damping it down at night so that it would burn again in the morning. I soon saw thewisdom of paying more for the best Limburg coal, which produced coals that seemed to keep on glowing indefinitely.

We ate simple meals, which satisfied our eager appetites resulting from a great deal of walking. Our evening meals would invariably consist of boiled potatoes, meat and gravy, a cooked vegetable, sometimes a salad, and either canned fruit or pudding for desert. We all especially loved the Dutch pudding, or "vla" as it was called, which could be bought in bottles from the milkman, vanilla or chocolate -- or better still, both at once! Whenever we had company we would buy little tortes from the bakery. There was nothing

---

[8] The Netherlanders call the ground floor the "parterre" (French "upon the ground") and what we call the second floor, the first floor, etc.

[9] Our visit to the medical clinic did little to inspire confidence in Dutch medicine. A half dozen students gathered round as the professor spoke, and then they took turns feeling Betty's leg. Somehow they got it right: Betty needed a lift in her shoe!

resembling "fast food" or any other kind of snack with the two exceptions of raw herrings dipped in chopped onions and *patates frites*, a wonderful kind of fries that would be eaten from a paper pouch containing a special Dutch mayonaisse that we all relished.

I was often away at the University, but when I was home during the day I would especially enjoy reading while sitting near the large front window, listening to the surf pounding the shore and watching the people, young and old, who were active outside our window. We could almost tell the time of day by observing a small group of retired fishermen, clad all in black, who were sitting on a certain bench just opposite our window, every day but Sunday. The virtually complete lack of motor vehicles enhanced the charm of this bucolic scene.

On several occasions visiting relatives would ask to be allowed to spend the night in one of the children's beds, thinking nothing of the crowding. The same would be the rule when we visited relatives far from Katwijk. Betty and I would usually get a double bed of sorts, but the children rested on make-do quilts and pillows. At one home we occupied beds in an unfinished attic. Toilet facilities were sometimes out of doors, hence we became familiar with the old-fashioned "pō," (from French "pot").

Making do in the local schools. Judy was in the fifth grade and enjoyed every moment at the nearby Christian school. She acquired two very special female friends from her class. One was the daughter of the principal and the other was the child of two deaf parents, for whom this girl was constantly doing all manner of chores.

Garry was in the first grade but did not do well. There were no proper facilities for his class, which met in a room belonging to the Gereformeerde church. Looking in one day, I observed that Garry had to sit on a straight adult-sized chair, with his feet dangling. He was not learning much beyond the alphabet, hence we sent for first-grade reading books from his old school in Passaic and made the effort to familiarize him with what the normative first-grade curriculum required.

Visiting relatives. This heading could mean "relatives who visit" or "the act of paying a visit to relatives." The first is as appropriate as the second. Often our daily routine was disrupted by visitors: aunts, uncles and cousins of both sexes, arriving from north and south, from east or west. There were moments when all the chairs were occupied and many persons present were sitting or squatting on the floor. Betty and Grandma would be kept busy in the tiny kitchenette making fresh batches of coffee and tea.

On the other hand, we were invited on various occasions to visit several days at a time in one or another home of a relative. Always this would require considerable preparation and much physical effort since we had no car and would have to rely on buses or trains, carrying all our luggage with us. Our favorite visiting places were the "pension" of a female cousin, Mien, and her friend Cor in Bloemendaal, near Haarlem; also the "woonwagen" or trailer home of cousin Arie near Steenwijk, which lies east of the Ijsselmeer, (formerly "Zuyder Zee"); also the house on the dike in Almkerk, where we stayed with our baker-uncle and his family; also the small houses of Uncle Kees in Breda and of Uncle Dirk the schoolmaster in a tiny village south of Rotterdam called Zuidland. Most of all we enjoyed the old brick house of Uncle Dick Verkerke in the southern city of Bergen op Zoom (an old garrison town), where we especially enjoyed the company of cousins Dick and Riet Verkerke and of Tante Marie Schouten, who had travelled with us on the *Zuiderkruis*.

This opportunity to be received on many occasions by loving and enthusiastic relatives must be credited with vastly expanding the cultural and educational impact of our Fulbright year abroad. Everywhere we were busy hearing and speaking -- as well as we could -- the Dutch language, thus removing many of the barriers to communication and understanding that often prevent tourists and other visitors from gaining the maximum benefit from the experience of living in a foreign land. Thus we felt well justified in choosing these very special experiences as our next step along the pathway to a higher professional status and a broader area of service.

Since Katwijk was some distance from any railway, relatives who came to visit always came by private car or by bus. This minor level of inconvenience only added to the joy and conviviality that inevitably ensued. Our only regret was that visitors could not stay overnight with us, as they were accustomed to do with their own relatives. They could plainly see that we were already jammed together to the maximum in our tiny apartment.

Dick and Deanie are engaged. They have arrived together on Dick's motorcycle. They do make a very cute couple all dressed up in leathern coats and helmets. They have come all the way -- fifty miles or more -- from Almkerk, crossing the Maas by ferry as we had done and competing with automobile and truck traffic on the busy highways in order to come here. We enjoy their company to the limit, and at the end of the visit send them off on their speedy machine. We do wish we could put them up. Maybe some day we will be in a position to show them a broader welcome.

My work at the University of Leiden

At the moment I am doing what I do five days each week, standing in a crowd of mainly women and children waiting for the tram to take them home to Katwijk after a day of shopping in Leiden. They are very loud as they jabber away to one another in their outlandish Katwijker dialect. Because I am a man and obviously a foreigner, they mostly ignore me. Not completely, however. I am feeling a strange sensation on my left foot and look down to discover its cause. The little boy belonging to the woman next to me is relieving himself on my shoe! I have observed that Dutch kids -- especially Katwijk kids -- think nothing of doing this in public. They are like dogs in this respect, peeing wherever they wish and in front of everybody. I am a bit surprised that this particular boy is doing it with evident approval of his mother. Not knowing exactly how to complain in Dutch, I just pull my foot away and let him go at it. But this is not the end of my being mistaken for a fire plug. As the tram arrives, it stops just where I am standing, so I step forward and prepare to climb in. This does not quite please the mother whose kid has been abusing my foot. She crowds up behind me and attempts to elbow me out of her way. I understand this to mean, "Ladies first," but, having no reason to consider this crude woman a real lady, I remain steadfast. When she persists in her assault, I turn halfway to her and say in my best Dutch, "Als 'tu b'lieft, mevrouw (If you please, ma'am!)." She is shocked and surprised. All she can think to say is "Ontstrande ding (rude thing)!"

Our home in Katwijk aan Zee was conveniently located with respect to Leiden. Many times daily an electric tram shuttled back and forth over the fifteen or so miles separating the two. Once I arrived at the eastern end of the tram line, which lay just opposite the railway station and the bus depot, I had a three-quarters of a mile walk, crossing over several canals, to arrive at the University library on the Rapenburg. The library was directly opposite the "Nunnenhof (nuns' court)," which had been taken over in the sixteenth century as the university center. The main administrative offices were there. Other buildings belonging to the university were scattered about in the near vicinity in such a way that a stranger might scarcely suspect that he was in the heart of a great and famous educational establishment. From time to time I would visit some of these buildings to attend lectures in which I was interested; for instance classes in Arabic and Ugaritic -- a modern and a very ancient Semitic language, respectively -- each of which was taught by a renowned expert.

Although my special field of Old Testament was taught as a branch of theology, I deliberately avoided all the current classes in theology in order to spend more time on my doctoral research. Each morning I would climb up a flight of stairs from the entry foyer of the university library and find my assigned place in a large reading room designated for "Oriental Studies" -- "oriental" meaning in this instance "Near Eastern" and having nothing to do with the remote cultures of Asia such as China and Japan. Once the attendant in my reading room understood the nature of my research, he very willingly brought numerous volumes of technical studies for me to peruse. I became especially well acquainted with a young doctor whom I had met at Strasbourg and whose oral examination in defense of his dissertation I was invited to attend. This was Jacob (Jaap) Hoftijzer, who had written on "The Promises to the Patriarchs" and was revising a large dictionary of ancient Semitic cognates (C. F. Jean-Jacob Hoftijzer, *Dictionnaire des inscriptions sémitiques de l'ouest*, Leiden: E. J. Brill, 1965).

Because I usually worked both mornings and afternoons in this study room, it was necessary for me either to take a sack lunch from home or to walk a few yards along the Rapenburg to what was called the Mensa (Latin for "table"). This was a place where students could buy sandwiches, soup, etc. There was no regular dining hall as such.

I enjoyed the sandwiches and soup, which I found tasty as well as cheap. I was somewhat astounded at the fact that limonade (pronounced "lee-mo-na-duh"), meaning a bottled fruit drink, was more expensive than good Heineken lager. Accordingly, I became a great afficianado of Heineken's. I have found no other better.

Something rather shocking has just happened in the student Mensa. A brash American guy, a typical loud-mouthed student from Brooklyn, NY, has just arrived in Leiden and intends to study Arabic. He is very irritating to listen to: rough, harsh and blunt. I have no idea how he might have learned to talk that way, but he certainly epitomizes the "ugly American," and I am embarrassed for him in the presence of my Dutch collegues. He has asked me to show him where he can get lunch, so I take him to the Mensa. I buy my own lunch from the attendant, using the best and most polite Dutch I can muster. This Brooklyn guy knows no Dutch at all, which might be excusable of a newly arrived, but he audaciously chooses to speak

German to the attendant, who happens to be carrying about in his memory some bitter experiences with the Wehrmacht and Gestapo. That would be a risk and an offense in itself, but he speaks his German precisely with the bullying cant of an S.S. officer. I see the attendant's face go pale as he reaches for his meat cleaver. Menacing this brazen fellow with it, he curses him in good round Dutch and tells him to leave before he puts it to use on his skull.

Most American visitors had no sense of the deep resentment that lingered in the hearts of the Dutch people, who were brutally trampled on for five years by the German occupying forces. Leiden had been at the very center of resistance. Both students and professors had been so bold in denouncing the Germans that the university was shut down completely until the end of the War.

To this ugly American I say, "You fool, you are a perfect idiot for talking that way to a Dutch citizen who has gone through the War. You sound like a Nazi stormtrooper -- you, a Polish-American Jew, of all people!"

It was important to my project that I should gather a complete bibliography of Dutch Old Testament study for the period, 1860-1914, hence I was regularly asking to have dozens of heavy volumes toted to my desk. Inevitably, the head librarian came to see the wisdom of allowing me stack privileges, the right to go anywhere in the building to check whether I actually had a need for a particular volume -- something that would be automatically granted in an American college or university, but an undefined threat to the European sense of order. As my list of consulted works expanded into the thousands, I on one occasion found myself the object of derision, coming, I was shocked to see, from a German candidate in Old Testament. "That is work for clerks," was his comment. He could not understand the relevance of studying the history of a critical discipline.

It is a good thing that James Muilenburg is supporting my research in every way and is confident that I will bring it to a solid scientific conclusion!

On occasion my research project took me outside Leiden. I paid a visit to the National Library in The Hague, Utrecht's university library, a library of medieval and renaissance Judaism in Amsterdam, and others. I also interviewed several leading Dutch Old Testament scholars, including Th. C. Vriezen at Den Bilt and Nicolaas Ridderbos at the Free University in Amsterdam. Towards the conclusion of winter I set myself to full-time writing.

Grandma's tiny bedroom will serve as my study since it is the only place where I may have sufficient privacy to become creative. I have my portable typewriter, brought from America, with me. It stands on a small table alongside Grandma's bed. I study my notes, then type for a few pages, then pause to smoke a cigarette. True, I am not a cigarette smoker, but this is just right in the present circumstances. As I puff sensuously, I gaze through the window. The quiet motions of the water soothe me while stimulating my thoughts. The words flow out in a smooth and steady rhythm.

Getting around in Holland. Moving about in the Netherlands was never easy in those days. Since the great express highways of later decades had not yet been built, Dutch drivers were confined to the old, narrow and congested roads. Only three of our particular relatives were ever able to offer us motor transportation. One of them was Betty's cousin, Arie van Houwelingen in his Citroen when he took us across the Afsluitdijk ("Cut-off dike") and through Friesland to his place south of Steenwijk. Another was Dick van der Wiel, who did not have a car of his own but borrowed one from the garage where he was working in order to supply us with transport from his home in Almkerk to Betty's uncle's house in Bergen op Zoom. Finally there was Dick Verkerke, who took us on a trip to Belgium and the Rhineland in the spring. Apart from these generous and much appreciated free rides, we depended on buses and the very efficient and convenient Dutch trains. One time we found ourselves on a ferry boat crossing the broad Maas River, transferring from one bus to another.

Always it was I who did the lugging of heavy suitcases. Who else? But on one occasion it was worse because Garry had injured his heel while riding behind me on a borrowed bicycle. He could not walk, and the result was that when moving from a train to a bus at the railway station in The Hague, I had to carry him on my shoulders while struggling with two heavy suitcases, one in each hand. Fortunately I was in good physical shape, which resulted basically from my daily walks back and forth from the tram station in Leiden to the university library.

We realize that we are dressed differently than the Dutch people. We do not intend to show off, and are just wearing what we are accustomed to wear at home. Betty happens to be wearing a beautiful, long, rose-colored coat with a white fur collar. My suit is rather sombre, but I am wearing a necktie that is much too bright for European tastes. The children, too, have pretty outfits on. We are sitting in second-class seats on a train from Haarlem to Bergen op Zoom, a distance of about 75 miles. Just behind us in the railway car are a group of ordinary Dutch travelers who are talking to one another about how odd we look ("raar" is the word they use).[10] Betty and I get mischievous smiles on our faces as we listen to what they are saying about us. At the right moment I lean back and say in perfectly adequate Dutch, "Yes, good people, maybe we seem queerly dressed to you, but we understand what you are saying. We believe in keeping our opinions about you to ourselves." Eyes pop open in amazement and soon all faces are turned away in embarrassment. "Too bad," I think, "I was hoping that they would take it as a joke and smile back at me, but it looks as if we have turned them off by our candor."

Thanksgiving Day in Leiden

The five of us are enjoying a Thanksgiving Day dinner in the most elegant restaurant in Leiden, along with all the other Fulbright participants and Dr. van Dullemen. It is Thanksgiving Day, 1956. Though it is not a Dutch holiday, Dr. van Dullemen knows the importance of Thanksgiving Day for Americans and capitalizes on the fact that we are in a peculiarly strategic location for observing it because right here in Leiden is where the Mayflower company resided for a few years prior to their voyage to New England. A bronze plaque commemorating the Pilgrim presence in Holland is fixed to the rear wall of the Pieterskerk, where they held their own services in the years prior to 1620. A beguinhof (orphanage and war-widows' residence) where they were actually sheltered stands nearby.

---

[10] Crazy or nutty

Before entering the restaurant for dinner we gathered in the Pieterskerk to hold a commemorative Thanksgiving Day service, with me as liturgist. I stood in my Sunday suit, high above the congregation in the *preekstoel* (pulpit), expounding the meaning of Thanksgiving Day. I thought it wise to speak only briefly, realizing that the hearers would be impatient and uncomfortable in this unaccustomed place. It was hard to be heard in the vast empty space without electronic amplification. Besides, the Dutch churches are dead cold in late fall and winter because they are not heated. One sees little wooden charcoal burners piled up in a corner for the use of the worshippers, if they choose to use them. The parishioners may put glowing coals in them and place their feet on them to keep them a little bit warm -- the original hotfoot!

Our dinner is finished except for the dessert. The waiters produce a confection and, as we receive our portions, we are astonished to see that it resembles good old American pumpkin pie. But can it be? To be sure, pumpkin pie is a delicacy that is entirely unfamiliar to the Dutch people. Something is wrong with our pie, however. The pastry is pretty much as we would bake it, slightly more firm and less flaky. But we see also that the layer of pumpkin filling is only a quarter of an inch thick. What is happening? What is this all about? I am sitting next to Dr. van Dullemen, so I lean over and ask. Her face lights up and she chuckles, "Yes, this is the second half of last year's dessert. One of our previous Fulbrighters wanted to help us in our annual celebrating of Thanksgiving, so he shipped me a quantity of American-made pumpkin pie filling, sufficient to feed an entire contingent of guests. I turned this over to the chef of the restaurant last year with a recipe for making American pumpkin pie, but he thought that just a thin layer of filling would be sufficient and so saved half of the consignment for this year. Now we are getting the second half!"

Eating Dutch pancakes. One weekend during the fall of 1956 Betty and I were lavishly entertained by the Holland-America Club of Hengelo, a city located in the far-eastern border region of the Netherlands, just opposite German Westphalia. This area is referred to as the *Achterhoek* ("far corner") of the Netherlands. While the kids stayed home in Katwijk with Grandma we took the train to Hengelo. We spent overnight in the lovely home of one of our Dutch hosts. Other Fulbrighters were invited as well, each individual or couple going to a different home. We were told that most of the members of this club had lived or studied in the States at one time.

They impressed us with their strong concern that we should admire Holland in the same degree to which they admired the United States.

We were taken sight-seeing in the surrounding area and found it very scenic and unique. We were intrigued with a baroque moated castle, still kept up as it had appeared in former centuries; also a late Gothic Roman Catholic church with remarkable original statuary. Best of all was a pancake house where contests were held to see who could eat the most pancakes. We were invited to try some of these pancakes as a farewell treat.

We are shown a painted tablet recording past champions. Several stalwarts have eaten over a hundred at a sitting, but they were all beaten by one remarkable fellow, who ate 130! We are told that his life was as short as his girth was wide. "Golly, Betty," I say in mock enthusiasm, "if the pancakes are that delicious, we will probably want to eat a large number of them ourselves!" We are invited to sit down on benches and the freshly baked pancakes are placed on the table before us. We are encouraged to enjoy as many as we wish, but no one in our group aspires to beat the champion. Betty looks at me inquiringly, as if to ask, "Do we really have to eat these?" I am wondering the same thing, but I say, "Honey, just take one at first. You'll probably find it wonderful." There is syrup to pour over the cakes, but they need no butter because they are already greasy. Betty takes one and I take two, cutting the cakes into squares with a knife and fork before stuffing them into our mouths. They taste pretty good, I must confess, but neither of us likes anything that appears so uncooked as these do. Betty is unable to finish her one cake. To be polite, I eat my two and then take one more, washing them all down with plenty of coffee. Some of our Fulbrighters seem to be doing better than this, but ere long each of them is finished. Our Holland-America Club hosts and hostesses keep on for a while, but no one is able to get beyond ten. We really wonder about the fellow who claims to have eaten 130. It is certainly not strange that he had a short life!

Lecturing to Dutch high-school teachers. I was gratified that Dr. van Dullemen was willing to take advantage of my professional status as an ordained minister. She was able to arrange to have me preach at the American Church in The Hague, where the audience were kind and appreciative even though I received the impression that they were expecting more of a mainline-church sort of preacher. Soon afterward I received a wonderfully warm welcome when I delivered a lecture on "Religion in America" to a half hundred or so secondary-school teachers gathered for a retreat at an old castle in a very scenic locale. This was located in the scenic Veluwe region south of Amersfoort and north of Arnhem. I was picked up at the nearest railway station and driven to the castle while the conference was engaged in other business. I was introduced and began my lecture, all in English, which the audience seemed to understand very well. I kept in mind, however, that they were not accustomed to the American accent -- I should say, Mid-American accent -- and accordingly I tried to articulate my words as clearly as possible. Though I did not have any specialized knowledge about my subject, I had found a good book in the university library that was useful. Following the lecture there were many questions which led to further discussion, followed by a delicious meal and warm fellowship.

When the questions begin to come in -- in English, of course -- I decide to switch over to Dutch. This is a strategic move that puts the audience at ease with me. I seem to amaze them, and even myself, at my fluency; maybe the good wine helps! Several persons come right out and declare their delight with my ability to communicate effectively in their own language. They are especially intrigued with the fact that I am of third-generation Dutch heritage and have now returned, as it were, to my roots. When all the questions have been answered, I receive a warm round of applause. Certainly this experience will make me more confident of the linguistic skills I have been able to acquire.

Officiating at the funeral of Henry Zylstra

Betty and I arrived at the main Amsterdam train station about an hour ago and have made our way to a chapel belonging to the Free

University where Dr. Henry Zylstra had been lecturing on English literature as Fulbright professor. I have mentioned that we met him at the Noordwijk orientation. His wife Mildred has requested that I officiate at his funeral since she identifies me as a Christian Reformed minister. This will be an onerous task for me, not only because of the tragic circumstances of Henry's death, but also for the strange surroundings and the difficulty of knowing what the Dutch guests will be expecting of me on such an occasion. Of course, I have more sense than to try conducting the funeral liturgy in the Dutch language, hence I shall simply proceed in English, which they all understand. It so happens that there is no specifically Christian Reformed liturgy for a funeral, but I have both a Presbyterian and an Episcopalian Book of Worship with me from home. I like the Episcopalian order better, but these Amsterdam Calvinists will probably prefer the Presbyterian.*

Henry Zylstra was an extremely popular professor at Calvin College. He was a founding member of the newly launched *Reformed Journal*, along with George and Henry Stob, Harry Boer, and Lester De Koster. Here in Amsterdam he and his wife were fortunate in being able to rent an absent professor's house located in a modern residential district some distance from the heart of the city. One Sunday in late winter, as they were making their way home and stood together on the street corner waiting for a bus, Henry suddenly collapsed and died. This came as a complete shock because Henry had seemed healthy and strong. Mildred was thrown into a panic trying to summon help, and experienced great difficulty making arrangements for the funeral and the return to America. She was fortunate in having the ready and expert assistance of Dr. van Dullemen, who arranged to have Henry's body flown home for burial in Grand Rapids. His body was not allowed to be transported on the airline unless it was embalmed. This in itself would have been no problem to us Americans, but the Dutch are not accustomed to embalming their dead, instead delivering them as soon as possible to the grave, ordinarily on the next following day.

There are not many undertakers in Holland who do embalming, but the one Mildred has called has favored her by doing the embalming on her husband and then placing his body in a casket.

This now stands open before us as we proceed with the funeral service. I can hardly take my eyes off the gruesome sight before me. Now I am able to appreciate more positively the cosmetic arts that are routinely practised upon the dead by American morticians. True enough, some of them go much too far and paint the corpse to resemble a movie star. That doesn't have to be done! But this Dutch undertaker has attempted nothing whatever of the sort. He has not relaxed the facial muscles, nor has he arranged the hands and arms in a peaceful pose. Henry lies before us just as he must have looked at the moment of his seizure: gasping, contorted, grimacing in anguish! The mourners from the Free University faculty reveal the same sense of shock in their own features, and I have to wonder how I must look to them. If I am showing in my face and demeanor anything of the horror and dismay that I am feeling, I wonder how grim I must look to them. But I will only be copying them. In such circumstances my plaintive words of hope and promise seem hollow and void.

As I later learned, poor Mildred Zylstra had to live the rest of her life with the direct effects of this tragedy. Not only was she deprived of a husband; she was deprived of a livelihood. Although the Calvin College faculty certainly must have spoken kind and encouraging words to her, they could do little to help make up for her financial loss since there was no pension system at the time. The most that they could do for Mildred was to give her a job in the college library.

Discovering skeletons in my closet. My mother had maintained contact with a great aunt of hers over the years. This lady lived in the city of Amsterdam and her family name was Alkema-Beintema. (That is how the Dutch write a married or widowed woman's family names. Her maiden name was Beintema, the same as that of my maternal grandmother. Alkema was the name of her deceased husband.) Mother informed her that I was going to study in Holland under the Fulbright progam, and when our prospective address became available, she informed her of that as well. The result was that welcoming flowers were on our dining room table when we first arrived in Katwijk. Alkema-Beintema came in person to pay us a call soon afterward, accompanied by an adult son. We treated them with such hospitality as we were capable of under the circumstances. Her

298   The 1950's: Discovering skeletons in my closet

response to this was that we would now surely have to come to visit her in Amsterdam, but we were unable to find time for this until the spring of 1957. We were very reluctant to take this second step in our relationship because we had misgivings about her intentions.

We did well to be cautious about her. She belonged to a religious group known as the *Zwarte kousen*, "black stockings" -- the nickname of a denomination of ultra-Calvinists who had much blame for others and considered themselves to be the true elect. In the spring of 1957 Betty and I did go to see her, and the visit was a revelation of where things actually stood. We were warmly welcomed when we arrived at her tiny house alongside one of Amsterdam's canals, where she lived with a maiden daughter of middle years. We enjoyed the excellent supper she prepared for us. When it was time for us to get started on our way back to Katwijk, Alkema-Beintema turned to me with a solemn face and asked, "Are you really a minister? You do not dress like one. Can I really trust you? I have something I want you to have." I reassured her about the first and expressed modest hope regarding the second. Then she handed over a manila envelope containing things she had written pertaining to some of my mother's ancestors from "way back when." As she relinquished these things to my grasp she looked sternly into my eyes and said, "I must trust you to do the right thing with the information that is in this envelope. Up until now, I have never been able to find anyone to give this to."

Betty and I do not immediately look inside this packet. We are first taken by Alkema-Beintema's son, an Amsterdam policeman, to see the Rooze buurt (Rosey borough), an area on one of the central canals with show-windows in which prostitutes are sitting, like mannequins in the windows of department stores. This gentleman seems quite proud of this unique phenomenon. After showing us this, he takes us to the train depot. It is next morning before we have a good chance to read what is inside, and we are all shocked -- Ma Schouten included.

With Ma's help the handwriting is legible. My misgivings rise as I read the half-dozen sheets and I begin to perceive Alkema-Beintema's true motive in pressing this material upon me. She is playing the role of condemning the two unfortunate persons whose fate she describes. I make out that she first writes about a lady who might be Grandpa Tamminga's mother or grandmother, a pitiable hunchback whose life was very hard for her. One day she was missing. The searchers discovered her in the rainbarrel, drowned. Obviously she was seriously depressed and driven to suicide by an irresistible urge that no one could understand, least of all herself. As Alkema-Beintema writes about her, she is holding her up to public scorn: wicked people like this hunchback should not be allowed to escape misery through self-destruction! They must instead be the objects of perpetual ignominy.

The second person described in the packet is someone on the Beintema side. In fact it is someone my mother knew very well, her Uncle John who had the dairy in West Sayville. Alkema-Beintema wants to make sure that I understand why this person emigrated to America. He had to! She tells of the circumstances that made him leave the Netherlands. He had to work very hard and with little reward on his father's dairy farm in Friesland. Apparently he was not the eldest son. The law in that part of the country was that only the eldest son stood to inherit his father's property. This law was written to guarantee that farms would pass intact from generation to generation. Nothing would go to the younger siblings, one of which was apparently my great uncle John. In despair for his future he tried to conceal from his father a newborn calf. He secretly raised it for himself but somehow got caught and was haled before a magistrate. There was no doubt concerning his guilt. Alkema-Beintema does not say whether he admitted his guilt and pleaded for mercy. The sentence that was laid upon him offered a choice: the penitentiary or emigration to America.

Alkema-Beintema was very emphatic in her condemnation of this man. Perhaps she thought there should have been no choice at all because it turned out that he actually profited from choosing emigration. Although this, too, happened many decades ago, she was continuing to hold him up to unremitting scorn.

As much as I deplore the pathologically condemnatory motivation of this old-fashioned woman, I am grateful to have this little bit of light on my ancestry, for whatever it may be worth. We who have received part of our genome from the Tamminga's and Beintema's certainly know what it is to be susceptible to chronic depression, but we also seem to have an instinct for justice and the determination to improve one's lot.

This entire branch of Dutch relatives turned out to be like grapes gone sour. We offended them greatly when we refused to invite the entire tribe for a great holiday on the beach at Katwijk, which was what they were counting on. Our tiny apartment was certainly not adequate for a crowd. Oh yes, they might think it was, but it would be we, not they, who would be imposed upon. Besides, I was frightfully busy writing the final portions of my doctoral dissertation when all this happened. When they would write to ask to be allowed to come for an afternoon, I would always say "later." Then, when we eventually did invite them, they were too angry to come. We received a bitter letter from one of the daughters denouncing us as conceited Americans. We were told straight out that the members of their family would henceforth have nothing to do with us. Somehow we did not consider this a grave loss.

All in all, this was an educational experience for us. We learned something of the carping littleness that goes with close interaction in Dutch family life -- some of which has crossed the Atlantic and has become all too typical of immigrant life in America.

Working with the "Kuenen gezelschap"

I have been freezing ever since we started reading the Dead Sea scrolls over an hour ago. I am hoping for a break soon so I can get up and walk around a bit and go to the bathroom. Piet de Boer, our leader, is hosting us at home in his upstairs study, but he doesn't have much heat up here for a cold winter evening. I believe the temperature must be in the fifties (our fifties, that is: Fahrenheit). My legs are numb and it is hard for me to keep from shaking. I would never make a good monk!

This cold is distracting me from doing my best at translating. I feel that it is important for me to show what I can do. The material is in fact familiar because I have been reading the Manual of Discipline with Muilenburg, and, as I have mentioned, I have made my own complete and original translation of the scroll known as *"The War of the Sons of Light Against the Sons of Darkness,"* which everyone at Union had thought was so good that they requested a copy of it.

Professor Pieter Arie Hendrik de Boer was the successor of Bernardus Dirks Eerdmans, who in turn had been the successor of W. H. Kosters, who followed the famous Abraham Kuenen, the great scholar who is credited, along with Graf and Wellhausen, with the so-called New Documentary Theory of Pentateuchal origins. Thus Leiden -- right where I was at that time! -- had been the very den of the tiger -- or one of them! It was very significant to me that de Boer's relationship with the orthodox Reformed community out of which he had come was strained and even hostile, a situation that precisely fitted Eerdmans, his own teacher, and now Jaap Hoftijzer, his own student and eventual successor in the Old Testament chair at Leiden. De Boer was in fact a deeply devout man who had been denounced by his own kinfolk, but who considered it a pressing religious as well as scientific duty to oppose biblicism and supernaturalism in the church wherever they were found. Thus de Boer measured himself very much by the model of Eerdmans, and eventually by that of Kuenen himself. I understood very well that he and his students were curious concerning what was to happen with another conservative scholar, now coming into their midst. Would I lay the finger of judgment upon them and all that they stood for? I made sure that, relatively conservative as I was, they would find nothing to complain of in my scholarly method or in my attitude to my fellow scholars.

I never took a course with de Boer or attended his academic lectures, yet I became his friend and admirer and learned some important lessons from him to apply to my own career. One thing I learned was to exercise absolute integrity in the handling of Holy Writ, even if this meant repudiating the role of church dogma as a determining element in the exegetical process. Besides rejecting didactic orthodoxy, de Boer repudiated the marcionizing reductionism that had been so popular among liberal scholars like Harnack, effectually reducing the Old Testament to the status of prologue to the New Testament while attributing to it no unique spiritual value, so far as Christians are concerned. One thing in particular that I learned from de Boer, and that has helped me a lot in the development of my own theology, was his research on "the son of God" appellation as it is applied to Jesus Christ by the New Testament. The early disciples most certainly would have taken this expression in a Hebraic sense to mean "one filled with God, one like God, one acting as God." It was the hellenizing church in the post-apostolic age that interpreted this term in an ontological sense, and orthodox church tradition has long since formalized this in its creeds.

Not caring to be popular, Piet de Boer was courageous and unflinching in his defense of what he thought right and true. Many people who came to know him did not realize it, but he had been a leading figure in the Dutch underground against the Germans. When they closed down the university, he lost his job. When he returned to his professor's chair at the end of the War, and ever since, he continued to resist German influence in Dutch and Allied politics, to the point of heading a strong public protest against the appointment of the first German general as head of NATO.

Another brave action of his concerned the influential German periodical, *Zeitschrift für die alttestamentliche Wissenschaft*, which had been abused as a propaganda tool of the Nazis during the War. To counter its influence de Boer organized the IOSOT, or International Organization for the Study of the Old Testament, and helped establish its organs, *Vetus Testamentum*, for international scholarship and *Oudtestamentische Studien* for Dutch scholars. In his latter years he staunchly resisted the attempt of Israeli scholars to monopolize these enterprises.

This was the man who agreed to be my counselor in the research I was doing during my Fulbright year. I realized that he could be counted upon to be as rigorous as James Muilenburg himself in keeping me both competent and honest. There was a bond between him and me similar to that between Muilenburg and me. We all three came out of rigidly conservative Reformed families.

Precisely because de Boer demanded so high a standard for himself in the face of orthodox opposition, he would not tolerate any vacillation in my methodology. I was anxious to demonstrate to him my competence and my independence from church dogma. Nevertheless I was far from allowing myself to be "brain-washed," even by him. I was determined to remain in complete control of my own theological and scholarly development.

It was in fact another scholar at the seminar who offered a model of what I would call ideological liberalism: William Holladay. Bill was not participating in the Fulbright program but had come to Leiden at his own expense. Upon graduating from Pacific School of Religion he had come directly to Holland. Dissatisfied with what he had learned about the Old Testament at PSR, he had been unhappy as well with Old Testament studies as they were conducted at Utrecht, where he had first arrived. Although he had not studied Hebrew at PSR, he learned it quite quickly and compehensively from Jaap Hoftijzer. After obtaining a doctoral degree at Leiden he went on to become a rather distinguished Old Testament scholar.

The other young scholars in attendance at the seminar were Jaap Hoftijzer, Tom Sprey -- whom I had met at Strasburg -- and Wim Boers, who was later associated with the Leiden Peshitta project.

My discomfort is relieved upon the appearance of Mevrouw de Boer, a very sweet and intelligent woman, coming with hot coffee and biscuits. When we return to our reading, I am given my turn to lead for a while, and I do very well. This activity has nothing to do directly with my dissertation research, but it is important for me in that it gives me close contact with some of Holland's present and future leading Old Testament scholars.

A baby with a "waterhead"

I have asked Tom Sprey and Professor de Boer to look over the first specimin of my draft, the part which sketches the religious and intellectual history of the Netherlands during the middle part of the nineteenth century, when Abraham Kuenen taught at Leiden. It is a critique of this scholar's work on the Pentatech in particular that is to be the cornerstone of my dissertation, so I need to provide a background for the period in which he worked. This will be especially important for English readers.

De Boer's response is critical in a positive way and I am able to benefit from his suggestions. I can, however, do little with Tom's appraisal because he has somehow received the impression that the introductory chapter is intended as a major segment. But that is not what it is! It is only a general introduction. Sprey writes, "De kind heeft een waterhoofd, Simon. Zijn hoofd is veels te groot voor zo'n kleine lichaam (The baby has a waterhead, Simon. His head is much too large for a very small body)." Duly thanking each critic, I use this as a warning to make sure that this baby's body shall indeed grow large enough to fit its head.

Visiting scenes of World War II. In May of 1957, just a few weeks before our return to America, Betty and I got a chance to visit parts of Belgium and Germany -- in particular, those that were the scenes of Germany's final defeat. The itinerary was not of my own choosing. Dick Verkerke, Betty's cousin on the Schouten side, had an Opel which he invited us to share with him for a three-day circuit of historic battle sites. He expected that I, as a veteran of World War II, would have a vital interest in these places, but so did we all.

Dick was in his thirties and had himself been in the War -- that is, during Holland's rapid collapse in the spring of 1940, when he was captured and briefly held as a prisoner, then released and forced to walk home from the battlefield where the Dutch army had briefly withstood the juggernauts of the *Wehrmacht*.

At the last moment, Dick's sister Mien (Wilhelmina) joined us, to make a *gezellig*[11] party of four. Dick proved to be a wonderful tour guide. I thought he should have become a travel agent rather than a banana wholesaler. He was fluent in English, French and German, as well as in Dutch, and found good occasion to use them all on this trip. From Bergen op Zoom, which is an old garrison town from the time of the Eighty Years War and its aftermath, we drove southeast to Dinant, a Belgian fortress on the Meuse (Maas), and from there we entered the Ardennes region, making our way to one the most famous battlefields of the War, Bastogne. That is where a small force of Americans held fast during the Battle of the Bulge. An American tank still stands in the main village square. A placard has Gen. McAuliff's one-word response which so puzzled the Germans demanding his surrender: "Nuts!"

We continued on into beautiful Luxemburg (the country and the city, both attractive and picturesque) and spent our first night in Treves (Trier), an old Roman border town with standing ruins. The next day we made our way eastward down the serpentine Mosel to its confluence with the Rhine at Coblenz. We then took our way northward along the right bank of the Rhine to Cologne, where we lodged for the second night. The third day took us to Monschau with

---

[11] An almost untranslatable word meaning "comfy, congenial, delightful"

its *Fachwerk* houses, then through the Ardennes forest back to the Meuse and onward to Margraten cemetery on the southern edge of Holland, where thousands of American soldiers are buried, and finally back to Bergen op Zoom.

We had been in some of the most strategic places of recent military history. A sight that I shall never forget was that of vast areas of rubble and ruin in Coblenz and Cologne, both of which had been laid waste through intense and repeated Allied bombing raids and during the final Allied push into Germany. We also got acquainted with the wonderful Riesling wines from the Mosel and the Rhine; we could have fought a battle just for them!

These impressive sites would serve as our introduction to Germany, where our family was destined to spend a sabbatical leave in the schoolyear, 1965-66.

My big chance: an appointment at Drew Theological School. Betty, Ma Schouten, Judy, Garry, and I travelled on the *S.S. Statendam* for our trip home. We were returning in early June without any prospect of my employment. I would not be able to return to Northside CRC in Passaic because after almost a year of vacancy, the latest minister they called had accepted and would soon be on hand. My candidacy had not been advertised in *The Banner* because during our final months in Katwijk I had been focusing instead on entering the teaching profession. But I had not heard of any teaching offer. Upon our arrival in New York harbor, I was prevented from immediately contacting Dr. Muilenburg because of an accident on the pier.

I cannot walk with my body straight and erect on account of the injury to my lower back which I sustained on the Holland American dock in Hoboken last week. We have a tremendous amount of baggage, including two great trunks, because all four of us, and Ma Schouten too, have been in Holland since early last fall. Naturally, it fell on me to manage this baggage and get it all through U. S. Customs. It would have been an easy job if the stevedores had brought it all together in one place on the dock, but what has happened -- wouldn't you know it? -- is that they put half of it under the letter D and half of it under V. The tickets read "de Vries," but the Dutch more or less ignore the prefix "de" and alphabetize according to the stem-word, in this case "Vries."

That is what had unfortunately happened, and it was up to me to remedy the situation. So I dragged all the trunks and suitcases that had been placed under V many yards to D. I was almost finished when I felt a numbness in my lower back and could not straighten up. I almost went into a panic, but help soon came. We put in a phone call to Dr. George Stob, and he agreed to put Betty and me up until I should recover well enough to go on to Michigan. My brother-in-law came with a wheelchair and took me to his waiting car. He drove Betty and me to Stob's parsonage while he, Minnie, Ma Schouten, Judy and Garry accepted the hospitality of other old Passaic friends, the Peter Terpstra's.

George and Joan Stob once again proved to be true friends in a pinch. For the first few days I didn't try to get around much. George said that what I had was muscle fatigue, which would gradually get better. He took me to a chiropractor, who x-rayed my spine and put my body in some twists, but that did not solve the problem.

Now, four days after arriving in America, I am walking bent and leaning to one side. I need to see Dr. Muilenburg so urgently that I insist on going into New York to visit him in his office. Although my apparent lameness is of concern to him, he seems tremendously glad to see me. A few words pass between us, and then he blurts out, "Simon, where have you been? Barnie Anderson at Drew has been trying to contact you at the address in Holland that you gave me, but without success. Are you going to be able to go out to Madison, NJ if they still want to interview you?" My answer is naturally "yes," and he makes the call. Anderson is delighted to hear that I am at hand and invites Betty and me to have dinner with the faculty that very evening. It seems that their veteran professor of Old Testament, John Patterson, has retired and that the dean's attempts to attract prominent scholars like Herbert May and Jim Ross have been fruitless. Before we take our leave, I am offered the job of replacing Patterson and we are given assurances about the theological school's intention to meet our family's housing needs. A vacant house on campus will be available for us, and we will be allowed to have our dog Prince with us as well.

Betty and I make our way back to the Stob residence with this wonderful good news. They are delighted as well as surprised. And what about my back? Well, I am still limping three days later when a friend of George's, an M.D. from Cadillac, MI, stops by for a visit.

When I hear that he specializes in back injuries, I ask him if he can help me, and sure enough, he puts me through a few twists and pulls and pronounces me cured. And so I am!

Dr. Muilenburg was delighted that I had been invited to join the Drew faculty. Before I gave my decision to Dean Anderson, Muilenburg communicated to me the following excellent counsel:

> I think that you would do well to find another denominational loyalty....I cannot see that you would gain anything by remaining with your own church. Too much water has gone under the bridge during the past few years. I hope that you will both feel that you are now on the main stream of Christian faith, the stream which has its deep sources in Scripture and in Jesus Christ and in His Church, and the rivulets and sloughs are gone....At Drew you would be allowed freedom, you would be considered an equal with other colleagues, and whatever position you take theologically would be respected. You do not need to be told that you must be yourself, think your own thoughts, and teach what you believe to be the true meaning of any Scriptural passage. You have the instincts of a scholar, and you will not be traitor to them, I feel sure. You have seen enough of Dean Anderson and Bill Farmer to realize that they are at heart close kin of yours. (Letter dated June 25, 1957)

Disillusionment with Drew. I soon communicated my acceptance to Dean Anderson and prepared to move to the Drew campus. What he had promised was all very gratifying to us, but our enthusiasm was deflated by the way we were treated after we actually moved to Drew in early July. Much of what had been promised was withdrawn in one way or another. Dean Anderson had promised us a house on campus; instead we were forced to live in a three-room student apartment, which caused unfortunate consequences, such as the fact that Betty's mother could not be with us, but had to remain with Minnie and Paul. Also, the dean had promised that we would be able to have our dog on campus; instead, he made us get rid of him simply because students were not allowed to have pets and we were living in student housing. Does that make good logic? No matter: the dean was not going to back us up.

Who is this lady whom I see walking towards our student residence? Can it be Joyce Anderson? Yes, it is, and what does she want? We welcome her into our small apartment and after a few pleasantries she abruptly announces, "Dean Anderson [her husband!] has decided that you cannot keep your dog here because the students living in this building are complaining and want to know why they may not have pets." We don't say much. We are too stunned at the realization that Barnie is so scared to be the bearer of bad tidings that he has actually sent his wife to do his dirty work. What a revelation!

What is so bad about this situation is that our children hated to leave Princey behind when we went for the year to Holland, but knew that a kind couple would keep him and be nice to him, and that we could get him back from them. That first; but even worse is the fact that I must now bring Prince to this couple again -- and what if they won't take him back from us?

This was difficult for us because we loved our dog and had just recently retrieved him from the lovely young church couple who had been keeping him for us all this time.

When I go back to them to ask if they will take him back and may even be his permanent owners this time, they understandably refuse and say, "After having Prince for a whole year, it was awfully hard on our kids to part with him. Now that we have handed him over, we just cannot think of taking him back and going through the same thing again." So Prince will end up in a tavern near our former church on Myrtle Ave., and it is there that he will spend the rest of his days, keeping the bartender company.

Lest the impression be given that we were overly sensitive about how we were being treated, let it be said that this was how things proved generally to be at Drew, for other faculty members as well as for us. For instance, Larry Toombs, my colleague in Old Testament, had been forced to live away from his family for a whole year while working at a dig in Palestine, for the simple reason that Anderson was nursing Drew's image as a promoter of biblical archaeology. On the other side of the picture is the fact that pushy young fellows like Bob Bull were allowed to have more than their fair share of influence and attention.

I soon found good reason to believe that Barney Anderson had come to look upon me as a reproach upon his own inadequacies as a recruiter. I could tell that every time he looked at me, he was wishing that another were there in the place of me. To confuse matters even more, whenever he met Betty he acted as if he did not know who she was.

The dean asks Betty to provide the refreshments at the next following faculty meeting, with Mrs. Will Herberg to assist her. Because this grande dame refuses to help, Betty has to do all the work alone. After the faculty members have consumed Betty's goodies, the dean arises and says, "I wish to thank you, Mrs. Herberg, for preparing these delicious refreshments!" Mrs. Herberg comes out of the kitchen to acknowledge this overture while Betty remains behind in the kitchen unrecognized, stunned at the dean's Freudian blunder.

We were being given the impression that we did not really count for much at Drew. We swallowed our hurt and humiliation, resolving to launch out into a career of teaching with this distinguished faculty in spite of these discouraging circumstances.

We make the decision to leave Drew

The present impasse turns out to be directly connected with the rather strange circumstances under which we arrived at Drew last summer. I was a fill-in, let's face it. What Anderson desires more than my academic nurturing is to have another shot at hiring one of the big-name Old Testament scholars whom he had tried to recruit the previous summer.

My mentor at Union Theological School, Dr. James Muilenburg, had advised me to make it perfectly clear to anyone thinking of hiring me that I would be unable to accept a one-year appointment under any circumstances because I was fully deserving of a tenure-track appointment, and that was what I told the faculty on our interview during June of the preceding year. In spite of all his sweet words, Dean Bernhard W. Anderson, himself one of Muilenburg's pupils from Pacific School of Religion, pulled the "bait and switch" trick on me to serve the illusions of grandeur that he held for Drew. He had been seeking only well-known and established scholars for his seminary as a way of promoting his ambition of making this school into a second Yale, and I was a make-do.

The 1950's: We make the decision to leave Drew

A severe shock was in store for me. In a letter to James Muilenburg I confided to him what was happening:

> I am getting along well with my teaching, but have been discouraged by Dean Anderson, acting for the Faculty Committee, from having high expectations for my coming year at Drew. The question of my reappointment and promotion has come up, partly as the result of my expected receipt of the doctorate in May....They offer to reappoint me as Instructor on a one-year basis, with no increase in salary and with an ambiguous offer to obtain more adequate housing for my family. The reason they give for their decision is that they have not been able to get a very good idea of my potential effectiveness....Digging into their reason, I got Dean Anderson to state that their fears were chiefly on two points. First, they have no assurance that my theological commitment has been acclimatized to the Drew atmosphere, and second, they assert that I have failed to enter into faculty discussions on theological and practical issues in such a way as to indicate my full willingness and ability to make a worthwhile contribution....Now, I feel that any misgivings that Drew may have about me are as much their own fault as mine, and I am wondering whether to think of continuing here under any conditions....I am ready to admit that I am by nature somewhat reticent. To this has been added all the obstacles and inhibitions which have necessarily attended my somewhat painful transition....Nevertheless, my wife and I have earnestly endeavored to develop a social and professional basis for being wholeheartedly accepted....Much of the fault lies with the faculty of Drew, Dean Anderson and...Lawrence Toombs not excepted. There have been only two or three on the whole faculty who have shown a personal interest in us....They have all been outwardly friendly. They have professed to be very democratic and open-minded. But there has really been precious little attempt on their part to draw us into a close understanding....As to their doubts concerning my theological commitment, I must say that...I still have questions and misgivings. I don't know whether I can ever be completely happy at Drew. Still, I try to enter fully into a constructive discussion, and am prepared to meet them more than half-way....In view of their continuing standoffishness and their lack of enthusiasm for me, I earnestly believe that it would be the best thing for me to drop out of the picture here. (My letter dated March 26, 1958)

Since I had also communicated the above sentiments to Dean Anderson, I cherished the hope that I could still gain favor in his eyes by becoming less reticent and defensive. With emerging spring, Betty and I actually started to search for a satisfactory house for our family within the Madison area. We succeeded in finding a house nearby that would be sufficient for our needs, and by inquiry we discovered that a G.I. Mortgage might make it possible for us to purchase it, although the government had announced that this was to be the final year for this program. We saw that it would be necessary to decide within the present school-year whether to apply. To make this move I needed to have some assurance of what was on Dean Anderson's agenda, so I called upon him one day in late spring to tell him of our plans and dreams.

Barney does not seem at all glad to hear of my initiative in this matter. On the contrary, he says, "Simon, maybe it would be best if you started looking for a teaching job somewhere else." I do not know what I am hearing. I am thinking, "Yes, I shall take another year of Instructor status if I must, but don't send me away! What have I done or not done to deserve this?" I try to pry out of Anderson why he is now urging me not to stay at Drew under any circumstances. "Is there some complaint about my teaching? What is it?" He will not answer, because he cannot. No, that's wrong: he cannot answer because he will not.

How ironic! Here I have been struggling to decide whether I really want to stay at a place like Drew, and the dean at Drew is now telling me that maybe I should not be planning to stay here, but should go somewhere else.

This left me utterly dumbfounded, but I very soon learned precisely what Dean Anderson had in mind. He was putting me down and shaking me off so that he would have an excuse to renew the pursuit of his previous candidates! All this talk of theological confusion and professional remoteness was a sham. He had to have some excuse to go hunting again.

Within a day Anderson was on a plane to Oberlin to recruit Herbert May for a second time. When May refused, he went up to Smith College to recruit Jim Ross again. When Ross declined, Anderson gave up and came home. He was now too ashamed to see me face to face or even talk to me over the phone. Instead he sent me an impersonal letter announcing that I had been reappointed as Instructor in Old Testament for a second year, with a huge $100 per year raise! What about my doctorate, didn't it count? I had been promised a promotion as soon as I should receive my degree, and that was to be this spring! But I had already experienced Barney Anderson's inability to remember his promises. It did not matter, because I was now in no mood to stay on and take more of this insensitive manipulation.

In a letter to Dr. Muilenburg dated March 26, 1958 I tell him what has happened. His advice to me is to put my name in at the Union placement office for recommendation to a teaching job elsewhere. I do not decide immediately which steps to take, but I do write a letter to Anderson that has little in it beyond, "Thank you, but no thank you." I have seen through Anderson and know full well that he is not a person I can rely on to consider my interests and promote my career.

I defend my dissertation and receive my doctoral degree. Just going to seminary after college and the War had transcended all my youthful dreams and aspirations. Choosing to go on to graduate school was something I had never expected to be doing. I had no idea of what earning a graduate degree in theology would be like. When God moved George Stob to urge my going to graduate school, and more particularly when Harold Dekker recommended that I consider going to Union in preference to Princeton, I found myself in a situation that was similar to that of my three years in the Marine Corps. I was called, I was driven onward, I was acting beyond what I believed to be my native capabilities. I certainly felt like a knight -- a knight in service to his lord -- called, obedient, willing.

Choosing to go specifically to Union Theological Seminary, a school that I had never even heard of previously, was such an egregious seizing of opportunities that I feel certain that I was being led from above. And then to land in the care of a professor who knew where I was coming from because he himself had been there -- this goes beyond coincidence! James Muilenburg was the very scholar who could teach me his potent methodology, a biblical theologian who could turn the Word into something lively and throbbing, the pastor who sensed my deep and protracted deprivation. I worked like a slave for him because I knew that my every word and thought would be respected, weighed, corrected, and then nurtured!

The Union Th.D. program was the hardest to get into and the hardest to complete, and therefore I had to do it -- not something close to it, or something resembling it, but the real thing!

Theoretically the Th.D. and the Ph.D. were equivalent in prestige, but in fact the Ph.D. has often been preferred by candidates for its marketability and has therefore all but driven the Th.D. from the field. At a time when teaching jobs began to be at a premium -- and that means ever since about 1965 -- college and university administrators in the United States began to encounter difficulties in assessing the Th.D. as a requirement for appointment. Accordingly, they have given the jobs to Ph.D. candidates and passed over the Th.D.'s -- a fact of which the authorities at Union certainly became aware, and for which they attempted to make belated atonement by urging their Th.D. people to request a piece of paper from the Registrar's office stating that they were now Ph.D.'s instead. It seemed shameful to me that one should have to apologize or make amends for doing superior work, for that is what the Union Th.D. program surely was in its day!

When I first arrived at Union in the summer of 1949, one special Th.D. entrance requirement was to take two one-hour oral examinations, one on a leading philosopher and the other on a leading theologian, as chosen by the candidate. I think I may have been able to pass these by choosing Plato as my philosopher and Calvin as my theologian. I was at the time in the midst of a one-year seminar on Calvin under the direction of Professor J. T. McNeill; that would take care of the theologian. Also, I had belonged three years in the Plato Club at Calvin College and had actually read some of Plato's works in Greek; that ought to take care of the philosopher. But by the time (1953) that I returned to Union to resume my graduate studies, this requirement had been dropped, so I did not have to do it after all. That took down its prestige a bit, no doubt. All the same, the point is that this had never been a requirement for Union's Ph.D. candidates. The Th.D. was designed to be more difficult and therefore more prestigious, and that was the degree that I was determined to earn for myself.

A second thing to consider is that the entrance requirement for candidates for the Union Th.D. was to first complete their B.D. (now M.Div.) degree in addition to an A.B., whereas the Union-Columbia Ph.D. candidates were allowed to go directly from their college A.B. program into their doctoral program -- all depending, to be sure, on their proficiency and scholastic achievement.

The situation became a bit confused, but not unmanageably so, by the fact that I had spent my first year at Union, back in '49-'50, working for an S.T.M. degree, which ordinarily would not have been credited towards the doctorate, but because it was a Union degree it was counted as my first year in the doctoral program. I had to work as efficiently as possible in order to pull this all off, and it certainly would have been a cheaper, easier and quicker path for arriving at my high academic goal had I remained in Passaic another year or two and finished my work right there in New York. But again, I chose the hardest way -- the more demanding and at the same time the more adventuresome. I uprooted my family, found cramped lodgings and a strange *via operandi* in a foreign land! Maybe not entirely strange, but certainly different. Perhaps I was not being fair to my two children, yet neither of them complained, for it was their adventure as well as my own. I could not have achieved this without the assistance of the Fulbright program, bless them! Nor could I have carried it off if my wife Betty had been reluctant to support the effort. God's gracious gift to me has been a cooperating and enthusiastic family and friends who have been true friends, everywhere and always and in every circumstance of life!

When the time came for my decision, I knew positively that I should go to the Netherlands, and specifically to Leiden, if I were to turn out a worthwhile and original study of Abraham Kuenen and his times. I knew that I needed to study the biblical criticism of Kuenen and his colleagues if I was to achieve any kind of clarity concerning the legitimacy of the historical-critical method of studying the Bible and the Old Testament. That now had priority. It had to be faced, and it had to be faced then!

Now all that is past, accomplished. I have written my doctoral dissertation of almost five hundred pages and am ready to defend it in an oral examination.

Graduate schools are always grateful when a degree candidate is able to carry his thesis through to completion within a circumscribed period of time. My being on the spot in Leiden, where documents difficult to find elsewhere were ready at hand, and my temporary release from the ordinary duties of the ministry, enabled me to complete a draft of my doctoral dissertation during May of 1957, prior to my return from the Netherlands. However, the circumstance of my being out of the United States made it impossible for me to turn it over to the dissertation committee until the second week of June, 1957, which made it too late to be considered for the granting of the Th.D. degree until the following spring. I should have known that. It might have enabled me to work with less haste and certainly with less strain.

I did not hear from Muilenburg again until after the New Year, 1958. To my surprise, he informed me that I must rewrite a section in which -- as he said -- I had failed to offer a sufficiency of supporting details. This was in the chapter on B. D. Eerdmans. When I presented the original draft, I had felt that I had done well enough on that section, but I was not at all dismayed at Muilenburg's request. If details were what he wanted, details were what I would give him! And I did. I still possessed thick unused files on Eerdmans. Setting to work with a will, within a month I offered him a document possessing 85 more pages than the original.

The oral examination on my dissertation is held on February 26, 1958. At the time designated I enter the examination room at Union Theological Seminary and find that all the members of my examination committee are in the room. Appropriately, three faculty members in Old Testament are present: James Muilenburg, Samuel Terrien, and a new man, George Landes. Additional members are Johannes Beker, a New Testament scholar, who has been asked to read my dissertation because he comes from Holland and did his doctorate there, and Cyril Richardson, who is in Church History and is a member of the committee because my dissertation deals with a significant aspect of church history -- specifically, the development of biblical exegesis in Holland in its influence on theology and preaching.

It so happens that one other person is present in the room, a photographer who hops about taking shots for a forthcoming brochure for Union. The photographer soon excuses himself and Professor Muilenburg calls the session to order. This is the big moment I have been preparing for! Muilenburg asks me to state the rationale behind my dissertation, as well as the methodology I have employed in carrying it out. I do so with great animation. I want to make these scholars feel as excited about my accomplishment as I have been, and am now. When I am finished I offer to enlarge on any point that may have aroused their curiosity or concern. Each committee member takes a turn at asking some such question, and I reply as cogently and succinctly as possible. All present -- including myself -- are smiling and relaxed throughout the process, and when

the time comes to vote, there is no dissent. Dr. Muilenburg concludes by remarking that my dissertation is one that the seminary can be very proud to have sponsored. "It is only once in a great while," he says, "that a study of such breadth and depth is presented. You have done a real service to theology in general, and to biblical interpretation in particular, both in Holland and in the world at large, by demonshating so convincingly how the two came together at the time and under the circumstances that you have analyzed."

I was granted the Th.D. degree at the annual commencement in June. It was a grand occasion. The ceremonies were held in Riverside Church, with John Foster Dulles as the main speaker.

I find myself sitting with my fellow degree candidates during the impressive graduation service. When it is time for the ten doctoral candidates to be presented, Professor Samuel Terrien, functioning as Secretary of the Faculty, comes forward. My name is called and I move forward to the chancel of the mighty Riverside Church to shake President Bennett's hand and to have Professor Terrien place the hood over my shoulders. What an exalted feeling I have when it became my turn to be thus honored! I have now arrived at the pinnacle of academic achievement.

I know that it is a great and good thing that I have been able to accomplish during all these toilsome years since graduating from Calvin Seminary. This is very similar to the day when I shook the hand of the Assistant Secretary of the Navy and received my commission from the Commandant of the Marine Corps Schools -- only this is far greater and far higher! Fifteen years of toil and struggle separate the occasion of my commissioning and the day of completing my doctoral program at Union. That day certified my potential; but its significance faded once the War was ended and I could resume my true pathwuay to an even higher service. This day certifies more than my potential; it certiJies my proper place in the world of scholarly learning and teaching! It also provides the high level of self-understanding that comes only through stern self-discipline, a long struggle, and a triumphant achieving. Thank God, I now know who I am! I am ready at last, reaćy to be really me, ready to be God's more proficient servant in a very special form of Christian service! I am proud that I have done the whole academic bit at the highest possible level of achievement. Whatever may happen to me, and wherever I may go, I shall never regret that I have exerted myself to such an extent and have even excelled among my peers.

My provisional return to the Christian Reformed pastorate. Too bad that I had not already received my degree when I first came to Drew! Then I would have been immediately placed on a tenure track and not become raw meat for the jackals. As it turned out, my name and academic degree, "Th. D.," would soon be adorning the bulletin board at a church in Holland, MI.

Betty and I had been completely disillusioned with the political pettiness that seemed to go with seminary teaching and felt a desparate need for some security and acceptance. The Union placement office did not have at the moment any openings that would be suitable. As James Muilenburg wrote:

> Perhaps the tsansition from ministry in the Christian Reformed Church to teaching in such an institution as Drew was too sudden and violent. But the fit·st year is always difficult; I shall never forget the hard time I had getting started. What to do next is rather a difficult question, and I don't think you ought to be too precipitate about deciding. I doubt whether you would be happy in returning to your former situation, i.e. in the ministry of the Christian Reformed Church. On the other hand, there have been no openings in the field, so far as I am aware, i.e. openings which would meet your interests and qualifications....Just at present I know of no prospects....I think we must face the realities of your position: you are equipped I think to serve admirably and effectively in some institutions; in others you would doubtless confront conditions not unlike those at Drew. (From his letter dated March 31, 1958)

These were the main reasons why I made a temporary turn in another direction and accepted a call to become pastor of the Fourteenth Street CRC in Holland, MI. At the time I received this call, there was the possibility as well of my being called to the First Reformed Church in Grand Haven, MI, but this did not result in my receiving a call from that church.

I am on a trio in First Reformed in Grand Haven but do not receive the call because, as I later find out, one of the Fourteenth Street elders goes to the church when I preach there and informs some of the people that I have also received a call from them and am very likely to accept it, so that there would be little sense in them calling me too. This is a little mean, but it surely does show some healthy intensity of desire on the part of the folks at Fourteenth Street.

Somehow the issue of transferring my ordination from the CRC to the RCA did not come up in this context. Probably what happened is that Paul and Minnie, who were RCA members, informed the First Reformed Church people that I might be very much interested in becoming their pastor. True, this was a possibility as far as I was concerned, but I had never thought of it until then. After all, I had been baptized and made confession of faith in an RCA church. I was in fact destined soon to become a minister in the RCA, rejoining the church of my boyhood years. This was to come about in fewer than four years, as I will tell later, upon my acceptance of teaching assignments at Hope College and Western Theological Seminary.

A major factor in my acceptance of the Fourteenth Street call in the spring of 1958 was the influence of Professor Clarence De Graaf, a prominent Hope College professor of English, as well as vice chairman of the Fourteenth St. consistory, who persuaded me that their church needed my kind of progressive leadership, and that I could expect to have a major influence in the college community. He also felt that by pastoring in Holland, I would be likely to catch the eye of the authorities at Western Theological Seminary. James Muilenburg shared the view that this would be a wise move for me in the present circumstances:

> I cannot help but feel that you are being led. I emphasize that we must be cautious in saying such a thing because our human blindness and concern may blind us. Yet there are so many factors in the situation that I am inclined to urge you to consider this possible opening at the Christian Reformed Church in Holland very seriously....First of all there is the situation within the church and within the denomination. I believe you may be called to make a distinctive contribution in the life of the community and in the Church at large. You have an irenic disposition; you know the theology and temper of your church from the inside and at the same time you have been exposed to the methods and results of modern biblical criticism....In the second place, I believe all that De Graff has to say about the possibilities for the next few years within the Reformed Church and in Western Seminary are of considerable importance. The administrative officers as well as the members of the faculty would have the opportunity of coming to know you and of seeing you function in a large and important church. If I may say so, I believe that your training at Union and Leiden would stand you in good stead among many of the more thoughtful members of the community....Hope College and Western Seminary have been making great strides in recent years, and I can easily envisage you taking a place in their plans as they

come to see and know you. (Letter from Muilenburg dated May 16, 1968)

Much of this rationale proved out in the ensuing three or four years, but neither De Graaf nor Muilenburg could possibly have guessed how badly I was about to be treated in the CRC.

A camping trip to Michigan by way of California. Once it had been decided that we were leaving Drew for sure and moving to Michigan, we also decided to take time out and make a vacation of it, while touching base once again with my close kin in California: Hank and his family, Ruth and her family, and Mom and Dad. One thing that had to be done was arranging for a moving van to convey our furniture and books to our new destination. Most of our furniture was still stored in the parsonage attic in Passaic, and it was high time to retrieve it because the new pastor needed the space. Another thing that needed doing was to purchase an umbrella tent, sleeping bags for four, and a minimum of camping gear. We intended to camp all along the way to Michigan and California, and then on the way back, partly for the adventure but also because we could not afford anything more stylish or comfortable.

Judy and Garry grieve when they have to give back Princey. Now they are forced to say farewell also to a few new friends they have made. They are both especially fond of David Hines, a missionary family's son, who has been their only companion here on the Drew campus, and Judy's marvelous fifth-grade teacher at Greenwood School, Miss Marie Burke.[12]

In 1949, while travelling to Shanks Village, we had driven through Ontario and upstate New York, but this time we drove straight north through New York state in the direction of the St. Lawrence River at the Thousand Islands. Our first experience of using our tent and camping gear came in a remote forested region of

---

[12] David was killed by a truck while riding his bicycle in the vicinity of the mission school in India in which he was boarding. His parents were Methodist missionaries on leave at Drew while we were there. Miss Burke was one of those rare gifts to the teaching profession, who was able to recognize and encourage the special talents of our daughter. Judy kept up a correspondence with her for many years.

320   The 1950's: A trip to Michigan by way of California

central New York state. On a second night we camped on the St. Lawrence in Ontario after crossing over the Thousand Islands Bridge. We had a new car now -- new to us, that is. We had bought a used Ford sedan of recent vintage and still in reasonably good shape from a dealer in Madison, NJ. It brought us safely to the end of the first stage of our trip, the home of Paul and Minnie Luytjes in Spring Lake, MI.

"Now listen, children," I admonish. "Here are paddle pops for each of you to enjoy. We are not going to stay here to eat them because it is hot and crowded and dusty, so you just eat them while I drive. But mind you, be careful not to spill any ice cream on the upholstery of our new car. I'll be very angry if you mess it up!" I am not paying attention to what is going on in the rear seat as I return to cruising speed on the highway in the direction of Toronto. "I have warned the kids, and I will trust them."

The weather is really hot. We have no air-conditioning, but we are keeping the windows closed right here because so much dust is flying around. Garry starts to cry. I prepare to stop the car. He cannot lick his ice-cream fast enough to keep it from dripping on the floor and upholstery, so he has opened his window part way and has put his hand with the paddle pop outside, with the result that the wind has blown the melted ice cream back into the car and all over his face and hands. And of course the upholstery is a mess. At the earliest opportunity, we find water to clean off car and boy. It was not immediately apparent whether Garry was crying because he messed up the car or because most of his ice cream is gone. In matter of fact, he is crying because he is afraid of being punished. When I comfort him with the assurance that I will not punish him, he stops crying. I wish I could find another place along the highway where I could buy him another treat, but there is none.

We stayed overnight with Paul and Minnie and then drove to Holland to help with the unloading of our books and furniture. After that, we were on our way west again. We arrived in Denver, my home town, and were put up by Aunt Rick, the second wife of Uncle Sid, who was now deceased. Aunt Rick invited the Tamminga cousins in Denver to visit with us. We had a lot to talk about, this being our first visit to the city of my birth -- not counting the time I was there without my family while attending a meeting of Classis --

since 1945, when World War II ended and we all came home from our wars. Quite a few of my cousins had been living in or near Denver at that time, but they were almost all gone now -- dead or moved away.

The Rocky Mountains were fun. We drove straight west over the mountains to Grand Junction, where we added another marvelous sight to our collection. I had never seen the Colorado National Monument (few people have, even Coloradoans) lying in the extreme west of the state. I had heard that they are wonderful, and they are. We took our time to drive on up on tortuous, scary roads in order to witness these remarkable sandstone formations. When I would drive too fast or come too close to the edge of the road, a chorus of fright and imploration would assail my ears: "Daddy, Daddy, don't drive so close to the edge! It's a long way down to where we would end up if we went over the precipice." This made me remember how scared I had been in my own boyhood at being close to the edge like that. My dad would sometimes drive on narrow mountain roads that were little more than gravel tracks. Once I was so terrified at being close to the edge that I clasped my hands over my eyes and scarcely dared breathe.

"Daddy," asks Garry, "What is a red rock? You keep talking about them, but I don't know what they are. What are you talking about?" "Garry, a red rock is a rock that is red, that's all there is too it. Like that big one over there. Oh sure, they are not the kind of red that your crayon makes in your coloring book. It's the color of that pretty rock, like the color of an Indian's face.

This trip was unremarkable, except in the heavy exertions that were required in setting up our tent and taking it down again. We all tried to puff up our air mattresses but no one except I succeeded. I helped Betty cook dinner as well as breakfast on our Coleman stove. The children wanted to help but were tired from the driving and inclined to run off even when they were needed. So they had to be scolded. The strain began to tell on me and I would become cross and impatient. Judy and Garry do not remember this as a happy trip for them. The lesson we learned is that one should not try to camp and also drive long distances on the same trip. It is just too wearing. Mt. Rushmore in the Black Hills was the only camping site where we took our time to enjoy the sights and relax.

322   The 1950's: My father berates me for deviation

My father berates me for deviation from strict orthodoxy, I. One of our major purposes in making this family trip to California in the summer of 1958 was to touch bases once again with my parents. Our most recent trip had been in 1953, just before I went to Synod and before moving to New Jersey. True, Dad and Mom had come out our way for a nice visit while we were in Passaic, but it was time now for us to call on them.

My parents were now in their early sixties. Back in '53 we had found our parents in Modesto, a small town in the northern reaches of the San Joaquin Valley. Dad had gone into fruit ranching and he loved it, but Mom could not endure the loneliness of farm life. They were about to terminate this rather tentative way of life and make a more permanent home in the Bellflower-Artesia area, where they were to spend their declining years. Mother was to live until 1976, Dad until 1990.

When we made our way to see them this time, they had moved southward to Fresno, lying in the central part of the valley. Summers are very hot and dry in the San Joaquin Valley.

I am not at all happy to be visiting my parents in Fresno because I am uncertain about what they -- especially Dad -- are going to say about recent developments in my career as a minister and in some of my theological convictions. At least they ought to be gratified that I have now given up my position at Drew and have accepted a call to still another Christian Reformed church!

I have often encountered difficulty in trying to explain to my parents how my thinking has been changing over the years. Most of the time it has seemed futile to even try. They just do not have enough education to understand what the issues are. I have written them faithfully, week by week, and have sent them copies of some articles I have published. Mom doesn't really know or care much about this; she always goes back to saying, "John dear, remember, you must always be humble." Dad is much more perceptive and at the same time much more likely to be admonishing me to remain on what he considers to be the straight and narrow. He still cherishes that wonderful summer of 1942 when he had me to himself in Redcliff and Pando. We had enjoyed long talks and our souls and minds had company together. Dad greatly admired me as I was then. He desperately wanted to keep me like that always. But isn't that the familiar temptation of all doting parents, to keep their children inno-

cent and pure? Dad realized that I had to grow intellectually but was afraid that I would stray from the path of being his shining white knight! Yes, that is it! He wanted me always as his shining white knight.

To tell the truth, my own mind is not at peace after what has happened at Drew. I thought I was set, and now I am not. My future seems blighted just when I am coming into my own. I don't really want to go back to a Christian Reformed type of piety. Here I am, a doctor of theology, no less, and from the most prestigious seminary in the whole world, but what difference will that make to the kind of ministry in which I will now be engaged? I seem to be going backward instead of forward. This is intolerable to me after I have worked so hard and stretched my mind so far. It is almost like 1950 again, when I gave up studying at Union and became a Christian Reformed minister in a dinky little town in Iowa. I wondered whether I would ever make my way out of that trap, and now I seem to have gotten myself into another!

Fresno: what a place for me to be visiting my parents! This was the very same town where a mean and ugly cop accosted our family back in 1935 when we wanted to eat our sandwiches in his park. To be sure, Dad and Mom were not living in the town, but some miles away, on still another ranch. I shall never forget how bleak and lonely their house appeared as we approached it. Maybe it was my dark mood that made it seem that way. As always, Mom was warm and cordial, but Dad acted as if he wished that we had not come. He was brittle and tense, and had hardly a kind word to say. For Betty's and the children's sake he tried to be polite, but it seemed to me that he had been waiting for this chance to dress me down. And for what? For even suggesting that to minister in another setting might be God's way for me! The irony lies in the fact that that is precisely how he once kept his own integrity and principles, remaining loyal to the First Reformed Church in Denver in spite of his father's tail-dragging back into the First Christian Reformed Church in Denver. That had been hard on Grandpa's ego; he was looking for support from all his sons and daughters and just assumed that Dad would do what he had done. But Dad's attitude had been, "First Reformed Church took me in when our family honor was at stake, and I am not going to desert it now, just because my parents want me to be back in their crowd!"

Now it was topsy-turvey; I was playing my dad's former role. I won't try to reproduce the tense conversation we had, except to repeat his final warning: "John, this may be your last chance to prove true to your calling. You had better get down on your knees and do a lot of praying. The Christian Reformed Church is where you belong. That is the way God has been leading you through all these years. I don't want to hear any more of your doubts and misgivings about our beloved church!"

My mother is crying as she waves her farewell. Dad is standing there on the porch, sullen and angry. I haven't tried to answer his tirade and am just trying to keep from crying myself. I have gone into what I call "my whiteout," when things seem a blur and all the color is washed out.

Slowly the Ford rolls out the driveway and enters the road. We find the highway that follows north. Although Betty and the children are in some kind of shock as well, they soon recover and find things to distract them. Thank Goodness! How awful that we have travelled thousands of miles for this! What a shame that my children had to see their grandfather railing at me, a man of principle and conviction!

It is hours and days before I am able to leave Dad and his wrath behind me and think of something else. But my poor Mom! I pity her that she has to live with Dad when he is like this.

Our life and work in Holland, Michigan

There is a lot of furniture to be transferred from where the movers put it to where it belongs. Judy, Garry and Grandma will each have a separate bedroom in this new parsonage, and there is a large master bedroom for Betty and me. One thing this house does not have is an office for the pastor, me. My office will be some rods west, across Central Avenue, at the far end of the brand new church building located on the southwest corner of 14th Street and Central Avenue.

It didn't hit me while I was busy around the parsonage because I had much to do in helping get everything straightened out!

We haven't seen most of our belongings for two years. The first year we were in the Netherlands and last year we were in the student apartment at Drew, where we had very little space for our own furni-

ture. It just had to stay in Willard Van Antwerpen's parsonage.

It was two days after we arrived in Holland, back from our California trip, that it hit me!

Sufficient order has been established in the parsonage to allow me to get away and check on my books and other belongings that have been deposited in my office at the church. I turn the key and walk in. Here I am in a fresh-smelling new office; I will be the very first pastor to occupy it. My books have not been placed on the shelves. That will be my task, and they are still in their stacked-up packing boxes. Here is my old desk -- my familiar old $17.61 walnut desk from way back on Alexander Street in 1947! My 47-cent wooden swivel chair is here as well.

At length I ran out of trivialities and diversions and focused my attention on the reality of my being right here and not somewhere else. Turning my upper body while standing still, I looked from one corner of the office to the other and asked myself, "What am I doing here? I don't belong here! I'll never be able to live up to this congregation's expectations of what a solid Christian Reformed minister ought to be, and while vainly trying I shall certainly lose the focus and concentration on my career that I have painstakingly been building up during the last several years."

Who really am I? If I don't belong here, where do I belong?

In spite of these misgivings about being in the wrong place and pretending to be what I could no longer be, I made the resolve to perform to the best of my ability all the ministerial duties that I had contracted for in accepting the call to this church. I resolved to give the church one hundred percent, nothing less. With characteristic energy and dedication, I conducted every service of worship in good order and with imagination. Reaching down into my "barrel" for the third time, I resurrected many a good sermon, never simply repeating it but reshaping and even redesigning it. With many it was not possible to improve on the exegesis, but with almost all there was an opportunity to design a new application. It made a large difference that I was active in pastoral calling and counselling because knowing the needs of individual parishioners lent credence and a sense of urgency to my homiletical applications.

At least in my time, sermonizing occupied a large portion of the typical Christian Reformed pastor's time and energy. There were two Sunday sermons each week and special sermons for weddings and funerals; also sermons for special church days such as Thanksgiving Day, Christmas, Old Year's Eve, New Year's Day, the annual Day of Prayer, Good Friday, and Ascension Day. The barrel helped -- in fact it was indispensable. No one can be creative as often as this rigorous schedule demands.

For the first time I was wearing a ministerial robe in the pulpit. Previously I had worn a plain black business suit -- wool, of course, summer as well as winter -- but I wished to display by donning the so-called Geneva robe that I felt myself to belong in the mainstream of Protestant ministry. The local RCA ministers were wearing them and gradually the CRC clergy were taking them up as well. True, there was minor opposition coming from the ultra-conservative camp, but when church members observed that wearing the gown at least fostered an element of dignity in the minister's liturgical leadership, and when they were informed that this had been the garb of John Calvin, they readily gave it their acceptance.

As in my previous parishes, there were catechism classes to teach and interest groups to lead, each competing for the minister's time. There never was any question about whether the minister should teach catechism; that was always his duty. But the rest were based on a discrete choice on his part. Not being able or willing to do all, I chose to lead the young people's society and the Mr. and Mrs. Club because Betty and I felt the strongest affinity with the age-groups represented by these organizations. Betty met also with the senior Ladies Aid, and she encouraged her mother, who could now spend a large part of her year with us, to meet with this group as well. Also, Ma joined an informal group of widows who sought out cordial times in one another's company.

New adjustments for our children. The only members of our family whose social life suffered were Judy and Garry, who found few close friends to whom they could attach themselves. They did have their classmates at their respective Christian schools, but found that they were very "cliquey" and simply froze out newcomers. I knew that Judy could probably take care of her own social needs, but I was worried about Garry. Hence I encouraged him to join the Webelos and later the Cub Scouts and Boy Scouts. I also sent him during the summer to a sport clinic at one of the local public schools, but Garry did not do well and soon asked to be excused from it. There were also the satellite organizations, Calvinist Cadet Corps for boys and the Calvinettes for girls, but I discouraged my children from joining them for the simple reason that I did not think they needed more indoctrination than what they were already getting.

Betty hangs up the telephone and returns to the Sunday dinner table with a troubled look on her face. "Garry," she says, "that was your Sunday School teacher, who called to report that you walked out of her class before it was finished and went home. Did you think that you had a right to do that without her permission? If you have been disobedient and disrespectful towards your teacher, you will have to be punished."

Tears well up in Garry's eyes as he answers, "Aw Mom, she said to our whole class that if they were bored and wouldn't listen to her, they could just stand up and go home. Honest, that is what she told us. I was surprised, of course. I was bored, we all were. The others were afraid to leave, but I trusted what she said and I left." I know that Garry is telling the truth and I will not think of punishing him, but now I have an angry Sunday School teacher to deal with.

I get the teacher on the phone and ask her to clarify what has happened. It was pretty much as Garry says: she did give the class permission to leave, but she did not expect them to actually do it. Apparently it was just a ploy to get them to behave better and pay attention to what she was saying. I reply, "I certainly am not going to punish Garry for being honest with his own feelings and for trusting that you meant what you said. I am going to ask Garry to tell you that he is sorry that the class's behavior was so bad that it caused you to say anything so extreme. He may be expected to be sorry about that; I am too. But if there is any apologizing to be done,

I think that it is you who should apologize, not your class. I do hope that you will all get along better in the future."

While I am saying this, a vivid memory floods my mind. I see Corp. Young trying to bribe me. I see Sergeant Luther trying to make up with me. I recognize another instance in which an "illegal order" may have been issued.

Standing between the past and the future. Holland, MI is a unique town first of all because it celebrates its Dutch heritage as a tourist attraction.[2] In the years when we were there, both Judy and Garry wore Dutch costumes in the Tulip Time parade fashioned by their mother and grandmother. They also wore *klompen*, or wooden shoes. Garry joined the street scrubbers while Judy joined the baton twirlers.

Another way in which Holland was remarkable was in the large number of churches it had, most of which were RCA or CRC, with a smaller number in churches of other denominations as well. Latino farm workers were beginning to settle in Holland, but there were no blacks. Culturally, the town was dominated by the presence of Hope College, an institution of the RCA. There were parallel schools at the primary and secondary levels: public, Catholic and Christian, i.e., Protestant. Apart from the fact that almost all the RCA students went to the public schools and were taught by RCA teachers, there was very little difference between the kind of instruction and student activities going on in each. The two denominations -- kept separate through inertia -- were very similar in doctrine and in practice.

I found that I was well respected in Holland and that Clarence De Graaf was right after all. The college students did come to my services. The circle of CRC ministers, moreover, made a place of welcome for Betty and me, both socially and professionally. The couple occupying the Maple Ave. CRC were John A. De Kruyter and his wife, the former Angie Beukema, but we never became friends.[3] Our former landlord, Harry Vander Ark, and his wife represented the rather new Holland Heights CRC, but we never became close friends with them, either. There was, to my regret, precious little liaison on

---

[2] Pella and Orange City, IA, do it too, but they are simply following Holland's example.
[3] See "What I learned while off the road in a rainstorm" in "The Nineteen Forties."

the ecumenical level, but once monthly the CRC ministers and their wives would hold inspirational gatherings at which topics of general interest were discussed. When I discovered that they were less conservative than I had anticipated, I agreed to read a paper to them on the topic, "Recovering a Historical Revelation," in which I urged an approach to Scripture that takes the human element seriously and that distinguishes between biblical inerrancy and biblical infallability. My heart was warmed at the generally approving response to this presentation, but there were ultra-conservatives in the group who would soon make mischief over it.

Perhaps this isn't such a bad place for me. I may be able to exert theological leadership after all, in spite of my misgivings.

Canoeing in Algonquin Park. Eugene Osterhaven had been Professor of Systematic Theology at Western Theological Seminary for many years when I first came to know him. Ever since his youth he had been an ardent fisherman and canoeist, and he regularly took small groups of seminarians to far-off spots that were good for canoeing. He had come looking for me on the basis of Clarence De Graaf's recommendation and had sounded me out regarding the possibility of my becoming professionally involved at Western. When our conversation turned to canoeing, I asked whether Garry and I might go along on one of his trips. It happened that he was presently preparing to take his son and three Eagle Scouts on a trip to Algonquin Provincial Park north of Toronto; and yes, I would be very welcome to come along and bring Garry with me. Here would be my very first opportunity to realize the dream I once shared with Arvin Roos of exploring the great Canadian wilderness!

Thus it was that in late August of 1958, when Garry was almost eight years old, we were sitting in Gene's station wagon, driving on through the night to a destination more than 400 miles east of Holland. Gene brought all the food and equipment, much of it from supplies he kept ready for spontaneous trips like this one. He and I took turns driving, with Garry asleep between us most of the time. The four Scouts were in the seats behind. In tow was a trailer loaded with three aluminum canoes. As we arrived at the Headquarters Camp at the southwestern corner of magnificent Algonquin Park, we took note of the fall colors that were just then beginning to burst out among the pines and spruces. I had never before been in such a beautiful, unspoiled place as this. We had come at an ideal time; there were no mosquitos and few summer tourists.

As it turned out, we met only two human beings during a four-day swing through a chain of lakes towards the north. These were rugged-looking young fellows laden with a huge lake trout they had caught, their baggage, and their canoe, making their way back from a remote wilderness lake whose identity they intended to keep as a secret for theirselves. When these fellows had to portage, one would carry the fish and the baggage, while the other carried the canoe. Our jaws dropped to see this. It took two of us to carry one canoe between us.

We too caught plenty of fish, but no lake trout, mainly because we lacked a strong steel line needed for catching lake trout, which feed on the deep bottoms of lakes. We paddled from lake to lake, portaging on trails between them and often doing a lot of wading. With the fish that we caught and the supplies that we were carrying, we had plenty to eat.

Garry carried his own small pack. On one occasion he stumbled on a root and toppled head over heels. I had to pick him up and carry his pack for him for a while. Garry was very enthusiastic to be part of this adventure, and eagerly did his full share of paddling.

Each night we would hear wolves howling. It sounded as if they were very close, but we had been told that their howling could be heard scores of miles away. It did not matter because it made us tremble just to hear their plaintive wailing, however near or far they actually were. Bears were there too. Though we did not see them, we saw their signs. Gene took the wise precaution of hoisting our provisions high up in a tree, where the bears could not reach them. As we would sit each evening around the campfire, a wide variety of theological concerns would be aired. We did in truth feel very close to our Creator in this gorgeous unspoiled paradise.

Driving some miles farther into the park, we left our vehicle and trailer and paddled across a lake. We then made a long difficult climb from the far shore to reach a remote lake that was reported to be full of trout, pike and walleyes. They were there all right, and it did not take us very long to catch our limit. We found more than fish. Just as we were preparing to retrace our route back to the car, we spotted two gaunt young men appearing from the mouth of a creek that fed into this particular lake. They told us that they had been three months in remote wilderness in the interior of the park, portaging from one creek to another in order to make an on-the-spot government survey of beaver and other small fur-bearing animals. At the same time they had been looking for signs of poaching. Now they were at the end of a rugged, demanding summer job, haggard and heavily bearded, eager to return to their college.

My dear old pal Arvin: these two rugged looking guys could be you and I at the end of our fantasy trip from lake to lake across Canada, as we planned it together in the study hall of Littleton High School so many years ago. Now I have experience enough to know how difficult such a trip would have been! It would have been fun all right, but it would also have been heavy and dangerous work. I am glad that we never made that trip; I'm not up to it, and I doubt that you are either. These two young fellows have made their trip with a clear aim and purpose. They speak only of how hard it was -- anything but pleasure. To listen to them, anyone would have to be an imbecile to do what they have done just for the fun of it! But good Lord, what a beautiful place this is!

The unstable situation in the Christian Reformed Church at the close of the decade. A half-year after coming to Fourteenth Street CRC in Holland, I had the following to report to the man who had become my spiritual father, Dr. James Muilenburg:

> You will be interested to know of a controversy that is developing in the Christian Reformed Church over biblical inspiration, and of my small part in it. A few of the seminarians at Calvin have been so brave as to question the doctrine of absolute inerrancy and thereby have provoked a violent reaction from conservative quarters. I really do mean violent. The Banner is full of denunciations of "creeping Modernism" and of passionate defences of verbal inerrancy. This will come up to the Synod in June, when perhaps not only the students in question but the president and one professor who have defended them will be hurt. I do not care to meddle much in this affair, but upon the request of our local ministers' meeting...I have read them a short paper arguing for what I called "Recovering a Historical Revelation." You can surmise the content from the title. The reaction in the meeting was quite favorable, which shows that many of our ministers do feel uneasy about verbal inerrancy and want to be more truly biblical. The paper is presently circulating among some of the informed lay-leaders, including a couple of Hope professors and some of my own consistory members. I do not care to take part in polemics, but I am determined to speak for the truth as I see it. I may have something to say in the seminary controversy this summer since I am an alternate delegate from the Holland Classis to the Synod. Besides, beginning in June I will be a Trustee of Calvin from our Classis and may become involved in many interesting developments....
>
> I really wonder where I could be of greatest influence. The Christian Reformed Church really seems to have little desire for my qualifications. Other men -- safe men -- are being chosen for seminary and college positions. I can be useful preaching the Gospel in this community and can have some influence in wider areas...yet I think that religion in America in general might need and appreciate the biblical emphasis that I would surely bring in my work if I were to be in an academic position outside this denomination. (My letter to Muilenburg, April 13, 1959)

This was Muilenburg's response:

> What interested me most in your letter was the account of the controversy in the Christian Reformed Church; this sounds very promising. Sooner or later the leaders of the denomination, especially the theological teachers, will have to face up to what is going on in the world of responsible

theological thought and biblical study. I can well understand the furor raised by the questioning of the doctrine of the inerrancy of Scripture, i.e. verbal inerrancy. It was gratifying to read that you wrote the article on "Recovering a Historical Revelation"; that was superbly conceived because this is pretty much the heart of the matter. If I may say so, I do not think it is you who are the heretic, but rather those who seek to impose a rational consistency upon a faith which defies it. This is not to take God's revelation in history seriously but to make a stereotype of it. I hope that your native reticence and kindness will not prevent you from asserting yourself further. The issue is neither personal nor speculative; rather, it concerns the nature of our faith, and I mean faith in the living sense of the word, faith in the immediate situation in which God meets us and met the men of the Bible. (Muilenburg's letter dated April 30, 1959)

During my three years as pastor in Holland, MI, I kept receiving word from Dr. Muilenburg and the Union Placment Office regarding various teaching opportunities, but the time and the place had not yet come together. All the same, these inquiries did serve to remind me that the larger world of professional scholarship had already claimed me, that it was not a question of "whether," but of "when." Furthermore, I was finding rewarding outlets for my scholarly skills, such as an invitation to compose a lengthy list of articles for Professor Samuel Terrien to be included in the forthcoming *Interpreters Dictionary of the Bible,* of which he was Old Testament editor. Two of these articles have been regarded by many as definitive and have been widely appreciated for their quality and relevance: "Sin, Sinners," and "Old Testament Chronology."

I had an inkling that I would soon be moving on again, but hardly did I imagine that my next move would be as socially and psychologically disruptive as it actually turned out to be. I envisioned the future moment of my inevitable farewell from the CRC and its ministry as one of respectful, if not affectionate, leave-taking, with good will and brotherly love on all sides, but it was not to be. As it turned out, I did succeed in retaining for myself the prerogative of choosing when and how it was to take place, but the enforcers of right doctrine had the satisfaction of being able to aim a swift kick at me as I passed out the door!

My manifesto. This is what I presented to the ministers' meeting and later published in the *Reformed Journal* (April 1961). I wanted to stimulate discussion on this topic because the Synod had appointed a study committee to work out an official position on the inspiration and authority of Scripture, and this was the propitious time for persons like myself to submit their views. I was quite certain that I would soon find a teaching position outside the CRC, but I would not want to leave definitively without making a clear statement of where I stood and where I desired the church to go.

Recovering a Historical Revelaion

I

Christianity has inherited a historical view of revelation. We Christians believe that the divine revelation found in the Bible has been mediated historically, that is, through the life and experience of a particular historical people, Israel, and that it culminates in that most unique historical appearance, Jesus Christ. God made use of all of Israel's ordinary human experiences, of all their cultural and historical involvements, even of their sin, error, and suffering, in order to teach them lessons of eternal validity and convey to them (and through them) a revelation of His will for mankind. We realize that the writers of Scripture were finite men of flesh and blood, very much akin to their listeners and readers. The Mediator Himself was, according to the flesh, very much a Jew, a true son of Hebrew culture, speaking to His countrymen as one of their own, though He was far more than merely one of their own.

This is to say that in His marvelous way, the infinite, eternal God gave His saving truth through finite, historical processes. We are familiar with anthropomorphisms, the descriptions of the ineffable God in human terms, so common in the Bible. In a sense the entire Bible is one great anthropomorphism, in which the eternal and transcendent God approaches His creatures in a temporal and immanent framework, speak- to them in language they can understand, that is, in their own terminology and according to their own limited conceptions. It is this that makes the exegesis of Scripture necessary.

II

We can more fully appreciate this genuinely historical revelation when we look at the wooden theory the Mohammedans believe in. They say that at one given moment in time, at a particular place, an angel dictated the Quran to their Prophet, word for word. That is, their sacred Book came full-blown from heaven; it was a direct penetration or irruption into the finite world by an utterly transcendent message from the Almighty.

Islam has no Mediator; Islam has no historical revelation, it is a religion of sheer transcendence.

We discover a tendency toward this same conception of revelation in some of the intertestamental literature, as in the *Assumption of Moses*, where the Torah is said to have been prepared in perfection in heaven before being given to Moses -- who was thus not its author but only its guardian. This is in effect also the way in which Joseph Smith said he received the Book of Mormon: an angel showed him where it lay buried; all he had to do was read it with the supernatural glasses the angel provided.

Christian believers of simplistic mind are tempted to adopt a view of revelation greatly akin to this concept. They acknowledge in theory that there were human authors involved in the process, but in effect this matters little. John and Luke, and the other writers who penned the words, are of little practical importance; the only one who really counts is the Primary Author, God. This view has great attraction for the simplistic mind: if it were left to it to decide what kind of sacred Book it would prefer, it would choose one that came directly from heaven, one that is simply and clearly the Book of God, like the Quran.

Reformed theologians have understood, of course, that this concept is an utter distortion. We have to take the Bible for what it really is -- the embodiment of a *historical* revelation -- not for what we might prefer it to be. Reformed thought has therefore rejected the mechanical theory of inspiration and has set forth the doctrine of organic inspiration. By this it is meant that the Primary Author of Scripture made full use of all the historical, psychological, and literary conditions in which each of the Biblical writers were involved, in order to make known in a progressive way (leading to Christ) His eternal truth.

The trouble is that some have failed to do real justice to this doctrine of organic inspiration. Thus, very often when the human and cultural aspect of Scripture has been elaborated, conservatives have cried in alarm, thinking that the divine authority of Scripture was being challenged. The rise of rationalistic criticism has, of course, rightly put conservative Christianity on its guard in this crucial matter. Modernism, and the humanistic thinking associated with it, has denied the supernatural aspect of biblical revelation, making the Bible a purely human book. But in their effort to defend the supernatural, conservatives have often allowed themselves to be driven into the opposite error of doing injustice to the finite, human, historical aspect of revelation, in contradiction to their theory and in contradiction to what the Bible plainly shows itself to be.

Christian thought has been involved here in a perplexing dilemma, a dilemma inherent in the very concept of revelation, namely, that of the Infinite God revealing Himself to finite man in understandable (that is, necessarily finite) forms. We may be sure, however, that God intended it this way. Believers are challenged to embrace this dilemma in sheer and simple faith, without striving to resolve it rationalistically.

All who are of rationalistic, simplistic, or authoritarian inclination swing inevitably to one extreme or the other. It is not only the Humanist and the Modernist who do this: the humanistic rationalist sees nothing but man, history, culture; the fundamentalist rationalist, on the other hand, thinks he sees only God -- or cares to see only God. Now, without debating which error is the worse, for both are bad, we observe that both have fallen into the trap of oversimplifying what needs to be left by all means in dialectical tension. Oversimplification is bound to minimize either God's role or man's because it fails to understand how these two can appear together in the same reality. Indeed, how can the Bible be both completely divine and completely human at the same time? This is a stunning paraclox. We do not need to expect that feeble man will ever fully comprehend this; we are only to believe it. The question is, will we accept God's revelation for what it really is? Will we accept this paradox, or will we attempt to destroy it?

Let us remember that the Bible also requires us to believe the tremendous paradox that Jesus Christ was both fully divine and fully human, that is, truly infinite and truly finite, at the same time. It also teaches that God is absolutely sovereign in every human act, for which our wills are yet freely and fully responsible.

Far from detracting from the glory of divine transcendence, the human dimension only increases it. The more clearly we see the real humanity of the Mediator, the more we may stand in awe of His divinity. The more we accept full moral responsibility, the more we marvel at the wisdom of divine sovereignty. And the more we appreciate the real historicalness of Scripture, the more we may rejoice in its validity as supernatural revelation. I do not know whether we could really respect a Bible that came as the Quran is said to have come. For superstitious minds such a Bible might have great appeal. But to worship truly God's infinite wisdom and power, we need to respect the great mystery of a genuinely historical revelation.

III

Many people seem unable to distinguish between scriptural infallibility and scriptural inerrancy. The two are not the same. A recognition of the real meaning of historical revelation cuts the ground from under those who insist -- often with great emotion -- that an infallible Bible must be inerrant. If the Bible really has been mediated through finite, fallible men, should we not expect shortcomings and misunderstandings, both in the form and in the material of their recording of that revelation?

This question comes quite apart from two others that have to be asked: whether the Bible really does teach that it is inerrant in its human aspect, as some say; and whether there actually are, or are not, real mistakes. Both of these questions have to be asked honestly, and with humble acquiescence to what painstaking, unbiased exegesis (not eisegesis -- reading our preconceptions into the Bible) tells us. The church may not avoid its responsibility to investigate these problems carefully. The dignity of God's Word demands it.

But for the present let us consider only the first question. Should we not expect errors, shortcomings, mistakes -- call them what you will -- as a mark of the human mediation of God's revelation? If devoted scholarship should inform us that there really are mistakes or irreconcilable discrepancies, is there anything in our acknowledgement of historical revelation that would prevent us from accepting their verdict? What does it mean to be human? The human mind never possesses absolute truth on any subject. It is bound to err in some degree. As long as we men are finite, whatever we do or say will be characterized by failure to understand fully. No man possesses omniscience, not even when serving as a vehicle of God's revelation. To err is nothing but a condition of our finitude. Finite man can never possess perfect or absolute knowledge. As such, there is no moral culpability in being prone to error; although the blindness of error is intensified by sin, in itself it is only an intellectual, not an ethical, shortcoming.

Our trouble comes from failing to keep clear in our minds that miscalculation may be ascribed only to the human aspect of Scripture. This does not in any way impugn Scripture's validity as infallible divine revelation; we are simply holding fast to the paradox of the infinite speaking through the finite. If we respect this paradox in all of its implications, we shall not have to take recourse to the desperate theory that in the act of inspiration the Holy Spirit suspends ordinary psychological processes in the minds of the human authors of Scripture in order to keep them from any error whatever.

Those who do take recourse to the theory just mentioned ought to realize what they are doing: they are transferring to the human process in revelation the divine (exclusively divine) quality of infallibility. This is in effect to make men as God, to make them infallible. Inconsistently, many who reject the docetic Christology that transfers the qualities of Christ's divine nature to his human nature, thus utterly confuse the infallibility of Scripture in its divine aspect with its fallibility according to its human aspect. If the Bible really taught this about itself, we would have no alternative but to accept it; but there is plenty of indication that this is not what the Bible teaches.

It is wrong to demand of the Bible more than what God intends it for. It is the supreme and absolute authority on religious truth; its revelation of God and of His plan of salvation is infallibly true. This revelation of infallible truth comes to mankind through a historical, culturally conditioned process that shows in many ways the marks of human finitude. Of course, God possesses true and absolute knowledge of all matters, historical and scientifc as well as cosmological and religious; but it was His good pleasure not to convey such historical and scientific knowledge to us in the Bible, but His revelation about Himself. This is the real Treasure. If a recognition of the implications of a historical revelation means that we have this Treasure in an earthen vessel, let us be assured that the Treasure is not contaminated by the humble quality of its container.

Why then do some wrest the Scriptures and resort to all kinds of special pleading and wishful thinking in a vain attempt to transfer the divine attribute of infallibility to the human, finite aspect of the enscripturation of God's revelation? Those who resort to endless harmonizations and forced interpretations may think that they are honoring the Bible and defending it, but what they are in fact doing is subjecting it to dishonor and needless attack. Let all defenders of the truth make certain that they dig their trenches in the right places, lest the real citadel fall helpless before the enemy.

IV

If we want the Bible to be for us a truly living book, we must learn to take seriously its historical, culturally conditioned, humanly mediated character. It was indeed written by men of like passions with us; yet the Almighty in His unique wisdom revealed His saving truth through them.

Our belief in the infallibility of Scripture remains unshaken. As the Scottish divine James Orr once wrote, "The most searching inquiry still leaves us with a Scripture, supernaturally inspired to be an infallible guide *in the great matters for which it was given* -- the knowledge of the will of God for [our] salvation in Christ Jesus, instruction in the way of holiness, and the hope of eternal life, which God, who cannot lie, promised before times eternal.'" (*Revelation and Inspiration* [New York, 1910], p. 217; italics mine)

6
THE NINETEEN SIXTIES AND BEYOND --
When I Become God's Man by Being "My Own Man"

It was a hard decision when I was called upon to leave the Christian Reformed Church and its professional ministry, but it had to come because I had grown beyond it. When it did come, I was certain that God wanted me to step on through this institutional and ideological curtain that had been sheltering me and into something ahead that remained at the moment dark and undefined. After some false starts I did succeed in finding a place of highest service, a professorate in a brand new seminary of the Methodist Church. Reassuring things happened during the first two decades of my teaching ministry at this school which made me quite certain that God had chosen this place for me, and me for this place. What I did not fully realize as I entered the profession of theological teaching at this school was that my institutional duties would become a base for my parallel career of wide-ranging scholarly research and writing, hopefully defining my most lasting contribution toward the furtherance of Christ's kingdom here on earth. As I worked and taught at this school, I came to be known nationally and internationally as an authoritative exegetical interpreter of the Old Testament Scripture. I produced seven large scholarly books and almost two hundred scholarly articles in the fields of Old Testament exegesis and theology while at this post. My colleagues have assured me that much of what I have produced promises to remain important long after my death.

What then about the "shining white knight" image of long ago? Was this still me? Before I attempt to answer this, I wish to point out that I have long since jettisoned my parents' image of me as a staunch and faithful warrior for their narrow brand of Christianity. Following the experience of having served in a real shooting war, I became quite impatient with any doctrinaire and militant concept of the Christian ministry. The only shining-white-knight metaphor that could still have any relevance for me would be one that repudiated militancy and coercion in matters of doctrine or pious behavior. It is, on the contrary, the qualities of honor, obedience and integrity which this metaphor suggests that continue to have attraction for me.

The prospect of an appointment at New Brunswick Theological Seminary. In 1960 I began a new year and a new decade inspired and assured by these words from Professor Muilenburg:

I suspect we see eye to eye pretty well on the issues, but if we did not, it would not matter. I know your integrity, ability, and Christian concern. These qualities are not always associated in one person. So take heart, Simon. The day is with you, I feel sure; the truth is that the life of our faith is involved; arid orthodoxy is not true to the Scriptures to which it so avidly appeals. (Muilenburg's letter dated January 5, 1960)

In the same letter he made mention of an opening at the older RCA seminary in New Brunswick, NJ:

> There is an opening in the Old Testament field in Australia, but I suppose you and your wife would not be interested in going on so long a trek. I do not doubt that there will be other openings. Hugh McLain died recently of heart-failure. You know he was at New Brunswick. I am keeping you in mind although Vernon Kooy would be happy to move from his New Testament chair. He doesn't think the Board would approve of the shift, however. So I am hoping that we may have an opportunity to recommend you.

Shortly afterward, I wrote Professor Muilenburg expressing interest in the New Brunswick possibility and giving him further details about the growing controversy over Scripture in the Christian Reformed denomination. I took this occasion as well to share with him how I thought I had developed theologically since first becoming his pupil ten years previously:

> As I think how different my theological outlook is today from what it was ten years ago, I am amazed. I can sincerely say that you have had more influence in bringing this about than anyone else I know of. I read, for instance, some of my first sermons, and realize that they sound entirely like the statements of the Chr. Ref. rigorists whom I now oppose. You must have been discouraged by my lack of responsiveness during my first year at Union. Yet you paid me a compliment then that started me thinking and gave me something to live up to. Do you remember what you said? "Simon, I really am convinced that you want to be honest." To my puzzled and fearful mind those words provided an anchor of self-esteem and of hopeful purpose, even while they somewhat surprised me, since I had never thought of myself as cherishing anything else than complete honesty. I understood what you meant, however, and your words have ever since been a reminder and stimulus. I humbly hope that I may continue to merit this praise. (My letter dated January 16, 1960)

Within a month or so Muilenburg had some particulars concerning the New Brunswick position:

Welcoming Dutch relatives as immigrants 343

I do want to let you know...about the situation at New Brunswick. You are still very much in the running; indeed your name is under serious consideration....They are looking for a man with scholarship and faith, one who is devoted to learning and dedicated to the Kingdom of God, one who exemplifies, so far as possible, the qualities they discerned in Dr. Mac Lean, who was respected and loved by students and faculty....I feel that this is the post for you, that it would give you the liberation you inwardly desire, and that your gifts would come to their best expression there....We shall adopt a policy of watching and waiting. I am sure you are not writing to them unless they make the first move. Psychologically that would be unwise. The overture must come from them. Let those who know you speak in your behalf. (Letter dated February 13, 1960)

There was, however, another strong candidate, Virgil Rogers, who was at the time teaching at Princeton Seminary. Doubtless the New Brunswick people held discussions with him, and he eventually got the position. I shall have more to tell about this in what is to follow.

Welcoming Dutch relatives as immigrants. Pa and Ma Schouten had been very generous towards their Dutch relatives at the end of World War II, when it was again possible to send packets of food and clothing. In their letters, some of them mentioned the possibility of their emigrating to America, as Pa and Ma had done in the aftermath of World War I. Two young families of their relatives did emigrate to Canada, which at the time was more liberal than the United States in their admission regulations. Another young family, that of Kees and Rea van Houwelingen, were sponsored by Paul and Minnie for settlement in the Grand Haven area, where they have lived and prospered ever since their arrival. It so happened that while we were living in Passaic this couple with three young children arrived by ship in Hoboken, NJ, from whence we transported them to our parsonage for a temporary stay. When it was time for them to journey on to Michigan we brought them and their luggage to Grand Central Station in New York City. They have proven to be warm and faithful friends of ours ever since.

That had come to pass in the winter of 1955-56, just a few months before it was time for our own departure to the Netherlands under the Fulbright program. A few years later, during the winter of 1960-61, a different set of cousins emigrated, coming to Holland, MI with their baby. This was at our invitation and under the sponsorship of the 14th St. consistory. We had to work it this way because as a minister I did not possess any real estate which could be identified as security for sponsoring them. Always we had lived in a parsonage owned by a church, and this situation was not to change until we should acquire our first house upon entering into theological teaching in 1962.

The persons being welcomed were Betty's cousin, Dick van der Wiel, son of Uncle Piet, the baker of Almkerk, with his wife Deanie. They stayed in our parsonage in Holland, MI some weeks, until the Building Committee succeeded in locating and furnishing a rental house for them. This Dick and Deanie are the couple who travelled so far on a motorcycle to visit us in Katwijk aan Zee. Ever since their arrival in America we have been especially close to them. Dick has distinguished himself as supervisor at the Grand Rapids city garage.

A peremptory interview with the Calvin Seminary faculty. I informed Professor Muilenburg by letter of an important meeting I was about to attend:

> The Calvin board meets Feb. 3-6, and I must attend. I am keenly interested in the forthcoming faculty recommendation for Wyngaarden's successor. I know that my name is being mentioned, but do not think I have any chance, due to political circumstances within the church. (Letter to James Muilenburg dated January 16, 1960)

My former professor of Old Testament, Dr. Martin Wyngaarden, was about to retire and the faculty had been conducting the usual search for a successor. Some time ago, upon being contacted by John Kromminga, I gave him permission to request my dossier from Union, but I did not ask to be considered a candidate. Having heard nothing further from him, I correctly assumed that he and/or the faculty had passed me by in favor of another candidate. The faculty had in fact presented for nomination a single name, that of a man who was about to finish a year of graduate study at the Free University in Amsterdam.

From the information supplied to the Board of Trustees, it appeared that the candidate had no graduate degree and also had no intent of working for anything beyond the "doctorandus"[1] status that was to be awarded at the end of the current year of study. At least one member of the Board, Rev. Tyman Hofman, considered this to be very strange in light of the fact that I, who was a member of this Board, had fully completed work on the doctorate in Old Testament, had received the Th.D. degree, and had a year of experience teaching it at the seminary level. He asked me in the Board meeting whether I had been interviewed by the seminary Faculty, and when I answered

---

[1] Makeshift Latin meaning "one in progress towards the doctorate"

No, he made a motion that the Faculty be requested, while the Board was in session, to gather for the purpose of interviewing me, and that the Board defer action on the Faculty's nomination until this had transpired.

That is how it came about that I found myself in the faculty room at Calvin Seminary face to face with the assembled professors, a few yards distant from where the Board was meeting. Only one of the faculty members was a survivor from my days as a student, Martin Wyngaarden himself. In the big blowup of 1952, he had survived the guillotine even though he was the only faculty member at that time who had actually done something reprehensible and actionable. In his office as Registrar, he had been caught altering student grades after the professors had submitted them, yet he had been allowed to stay on unchastised, while Stob, Boer, Hendriksen, and Rutgers had been discharged.

I enter the room where the seminary faculty are waiting. I shake hands with each professor and then take the chair to which I am invited. The seminary president, Dr. John Kromminga, speaks a few words of welcome. Before moving to the interview, he asks whether I have anything to say, and I reply as follows: "Yes, I do, President Kromminga. If it is proper for me to do so now, I wish to apologize for the inconvenience that any of you may have experienced in being summoned to this interview by the Board of Trustees. As a member of the Board I certainly had no wish or expectation that it would ask me to submit to an interview, but courtesy requires me to go through with it, now that the Board has asked me to do so. Nevertheless, I wish you to know that I neither expect nor desire that you should place my name in nomination for a position in Old Testament at Calvin Seminary. I hope that your response to the Board will be that you cannot nominate me because I have no wish that you should do so. But of course, while I am here, I shall try to answer any questions you may have."

The interview began with some rather general questions from two of my personal friends on the Faculty who had been my former teachers. These were questions primarily aimed at bringing out the details of my professional preparation beyond what I had acquired at Calvin Seminary. I did not disguise the fact that I stood high in the esteem of James Muilenburg and other Union faculty who were acquainted with me, and that I was presently active in seeking a teaching position at one of the schools to which I was being recommended. In other words, I rather bluntly communicated the fact that they needed not to bother nominating me because I was anticipating more attractive possibilities elsewhere.

Because he is such a devious and duplicitous man himself, Wyngaarden cannot restrain from suspecting me of deviousness and duplicity. But what can he find in my record to attack? You would be surprised! "Dr. De Vries," he queries, "what would you say about the following statement," and he proceeds to read something with which I am vaguely familiar. I hardly know how to reply because I know nothing of the background of the statement, or where it came from. I offer some sort of non-committal response. "Dr. De Vries," he continues, "You made that statement yourself in such-and-such an article in The Banner *of such-and-such a date. It clearly exemplifies the naturalistic error concerning the origin of religion." I immediately discern the intent of the game he is playing and seek to disarm him by saying, "If that were true, Professor Wyngaarden, how do you suppose that it slipped by the critical scrutiny of the* Banner *editors, all good Christian Reformed theologians?"*

Wyngaarden attempts his gambit with one more "quote" before I put a stop to it. "Professor Wyngaarden," I say, "I observe that you have been keeping score on me and are determined to find errors where there are none." Turning to the president, I say, "I came here for a frank exchange of opinions and expected to be respected for the well-considered views that I have developed in my professional career up to the present. If you are going to allow this to degenerate into an inquisition, I must ask to be excused from further questioning. I respectfully request that your response to the Board of Trustees be that, since I am not at all interested in a teaching position at Calvin Seminary, it would not be in order for you to nominate me."

I cooled my heels in a corridor while the faculty deliberated its answer and conveyed it to the Board. After the Board heard it, I was summoned to take my usual place.

The chairman asks me to stand and then reads to me the recommendation of the Faculty: "Dr. De Vries, the Faculty reports that it is not able to recommend you because it finds that your views on Scripture are in conflict with the Belgic Confession, one of the doctrinal standards of our church." He asks me if I have any comment, and I say, "Yes, Mr. Chairman, I do. I am surprised and even astonished because during the interview this issue never came up. We did not discuss the Belgic Confession or how my views might agree or disagree with it. As far as I am concerned, the faculty cannot nominate me because I am not interested in the position. That is the reason I gave you before I was asked by you to confer with the faculty, and that is the reason I gave to the Faculty. That is the reason, and the only reason, I give to you now." I continue: *"I have tried to show my respect both for you and for the Faculty by consenting to an interview. Now I call on you to show the same respect for me. Inasmuch as the question of my adherence or non-adherence to the doctrinal confessions never came up in our discussion, I hold the Faculty in error in making this the basis of their negative recommendation. I request that their report and the minutes of this entire matter be removed from your record and be sealed from public distribution. I will submit this reply in writing and request that it be sealed along with your minutes of this entire matter."*

The chairman so ordered and the matter was ended so far as the Minutes of the Calvin Board of Trustees were concerned. He found it advisable, however, to admonish the curators to complete confidentiality for the simple reason that I had not requested this interview. I returned home from the meeting mentally exhausted and psychologically battered.

"Of course," I say to myself, *"they are wrong about the Belgic Confession. It does say that everything stated in Scripture is true and must be believed, but I think this should be interpreted as applying to matters of doctrine and not to historical details or trivialities.[2] That is how I think Guido de Brès intended it, though he might wish to change the wording if he were alive today. But the whole rotten affair stinks. I did not ask for this, and why would they not honor my frank statement that I am not interested in a job at Calvin Seminary? When a man is taking polite leave of them, do they have to kick him in his behind as he is going out the door?"*

The nominee was hired, and he proved to be the man to stand guard at the portals, keeping Christian Reformed biblical studies where they had been in the nineteenth century. He is still, to this day,

---

[2]"We receive all these books, and these only, as holy and canonical, for the regulating, founding, and establishing of our faith. And we believe without any doubt all things contained in them -- not so much because the church receives and approves them as such but because the Holy Spirit testifies in our hearts that they are from God, and also because they prove themselves to be from God." *Belgic Confession*, Art. 5

a *doctorandus*, and proud of it! He has been the driving force behind an all-too-popular new translation of the Bible, which sows confusion and prejudice in many corners of contemporary Christendom.

Enigmatic treatment by the New Brunswick president and board of trustees Betty and I would not have had any resentment over Virgil Rogers's appointment, were it not for the shoddy fashion in which we were treated once we showed up, at New Brunswick's invitation, to be interviewed and to deliver a trial lecture. This was on April 26th, 1960.

The very fact that Betty was invited to come along at additional expense to the seminary was reasonably interpreted by us as an indication that I was at the top of their list. We were met by President Justin Vander Kolk at the Newark airport and were entertained in his home with a lavish faculty reception. Talk about a warm welcome! The faculty wives were especially amiable towards Betty and tried to impress upon us both how much they would welcome us and how well we would enjoy living with them in New Brunswick. They even took Betty for a ride and showed her suitable places for us to live.

Things almost mysteriously changed once I had delivered my necessarily rather dull lecture on "The Seat of Sin According to the Bible," and after I had been interviewed by the Board of Trustees. Later Vander Kolk mentioned to Muilenburg that they had been put off by the seriousness of my presentation. They had been hoping for something more jocular and lighthearted. But why hadn't they told me that entertainment was what they were expecting? I could have told jokes, if that was what they wanted!

I have a different assessment of what was going on. The chairman of the Board, a domineering and obviously influential man, was persistent throughout the interview with the Board in his attack on my Christian Reformed associations, even after I explained that I had been brought up RCA, and he would hardly listen to my explanations of how much I was at loggerheads with the CRC leaders. Nevertheless, I did not lose heart at his negativism because of the faculty's enthusiastically expressed wishes to have me as their new professor of Old Testament.

Betty and I remained alone with Mrs. Vander Kolk while waiting for her husband to return with the Board's decision. She became increasingly nervous and fidgety about the long delay. He finally entered with a blank -- almost stunned -- look on his face and hardly said a word as we ate our supper together. When the meal was finished, I said that we should be on our way and needed to be taken to the train station in order to catch our plane for Michigan. I said this to test out Vander Kolk's intentions. He had met us at the airport when we came; would he take us there now, on our return? He opted to just take us to the train.

While taking us to the station, he said nothing one way or the other. We knew the word must be unfavorable, but he would not say so. I felt like an accused man standing before the bar, being hauled off to jail while waiting in vain for the judge to pronounce his verdict. We did not receive the result until long after returning home, and then it was (1) through Muilenburg's letter, deploring what had happened, and (2) through confronting Vander Kolk in person at the Hope commencement in June, when I demanded a final word from him -- as if I didn't know! He and his wife were at their daughter's commencement and he was apparently not in the mood for anything unpleasant. He had nothing to say except that the seminary would continue to consider me as a prime candidate in the event that the faculty should be expanded. I could get nothing more out of him. It is still inexcusable that he had no feeling for the inconvenience Betty and I had experienced in taking a round trip out east while I was so very busy at my parish.

The only hypothesis for explaining Vander Kolk's very strange behavior that has any real cogency is that his Board of Trustees handled him roughly on this or other issues, and he felt too chagrined to try explaining to Betty and me what had happened. Perhaps he had gone out on a limb either in wishing to appoint me or in the way he allowed his faculty to behave towards us. All the same, the president is not to be excused for failing to give us the Board's answer in a direct and confidential manner. It was bad enough to go home empty-handed, but he added to the pain of it by behaving as if he had no obligation to tell us why this had to be.

On top of the experience of my rough treatment by the Calvin board and seminary faculty, this baffling treatment from a school that should have been ideally suited to my talents simply drove me into deeper uncertainty about where I stood and what my future would be. The ironic thing is that within the span of two short years I had received shoddy treatment at two venerable New Jersey seminaries, Drew and New Brunswick. Fortunately Dr. Muilenburg did not withdraw his support. Shortly before I confronted Vander Kolk at Hope College, he had written as follows:

> We are not going to be daunted by this. Other openings are bound to arise, and while New Brunswick did seem ideal to both of us, there are other institutions in the country where I think you would find yourself at

ease. One can't change his ways very easily or act differently from what he really is. You are more reflective, more reserved, and less demonstrative than most people; you are not inclined to wear your heart on your sleeve, to be resilient or hail-fellow-well-met, or humorous. You are serious, conscientious, devoted to high ideals of academic integrity and honesty. All this is admirable to my way of thinking, but I do wish you might loosen up a little more, engage in lively discussion, speak out, etc. I say all this because I am so much interested in you and your future, and our relationship is such, as I hope, that you will not take offence at plain speaking. I am not saying that you should imitate others, that would be foolhardy. But it is well sometimes to compare oneself with others who seem to be moving ahead and to ask oneself whether he might possibly learn from them....One has to learn the accent and patois of his generation if he is to communicate himself effectively to it. Well, enough of this. I am standing with you and will, of course, give you such support as I am able (Muilenburg's letter dated May 15, 1960)

Apparently my character was still admirable in the eyes of an admirable man such as James Muilenburg. It was my personality that could perhaps stand some improvement![3]

Tattlers on the Calvin board receive a tick on their fingers. Most of the Calvin curators obeyed the chairman's admonition not to divulge the matter of my interview with the seminary faculty, but two from Classis Alberta took it upon themselves to publicize it in their newsletter, thus spreading the alarm, as they thought, against incipient heresy. Though my name was kept out of print, my classis was mentioned. I was not aware of this development for some weeks, but eventually heard rumors and innuendoes, and realized that something was amiss.

On the docket at the next following meeting of the Board of Trustees was the matter of censure against the tattlers. A committee was appointed to recommend what discipline was to be applied. There was, however, much public sympathy for the erring brethren, so that it was no surprise that the committee should return with the recommendation that the matter go no further than admonishing these brethren not to do it again.

---

[3] By this time I was well on my way towards the clinical depression that was eventually to ensnare me. It was a good thing for me that a man like Muilenburg could still express faith in me and cherish high hopes for my future, for the worst was still to come!

"We must be careful," they say, "not to damage the reputation of these brethren by making too much of what they have done." After the curators vote to accept this advice and welcome the erring brethren back into the meeting, I rise slowly to my feet, request to be recognized, and ask, "Should not the Board also be concerned about my reputation? Why is it all right for these men to slander me and disobey the Board, and not get censured for it? Does the Board want to go on public record as applying two different standards?" No person present attempts to answer this question for me.

A Reformation Day sermon that backfired. My family had always voted Republican -- except during the Depression, that is. Being Republican was like religion to them, but as the Depression deepened my Dad and Mother had switched to Franklin D. Roosevelt for president. However, they wouldn't stick with him when he ran for a third, and then a fourth term. Though they were grateful enough to the Democrats for getting the country out of the economic doldrums, they did not think that it was "according to Hoyle" to go beyond the precedent of two terms and no more, set by no one less than George Washington himself.

I could not vote while still in college because I was too young. Not too young to fight, but too young to vote! In 1940 I joined a bunch of Calvin students at a rally for Wendell Willkie in Campau Square and even got to shake hands with him. But of course he did not make it against Roosevelt, and I was very, very grateful that we still had Roosevelt as president when World War II broke out!

In the fall of 1944 I was old enough to vote and did so by absentee ballot, as a great number of servicemen did, and of course it would have seemed like treason to have voted against our great Commander-in-Chief. Alas, he did not serve very long in his fourth term, and we got Harry Truman, who was widely despised at the time. I must credit myself, though, in supporting him when he cashiered the pompous Douglas McArthur. I had occasionally seen something of this kind of courage during the War: standing up to a popular and powerful officer who got out of line.

In 1952 I changed my presidential vote to Eisenhower -- more because he was a victor in war than for any other reason. To tell the truth, I became rather lukewarm about Eisenhower because he was not doing well in some of the areas that I was beginning to prize on the basis of the Christian values I was acquiring at Union Theological Seminary; and so, when Eisenhower took Richard Nixon in 1956 as his vice-presidential running mate, I switched to the Democratic ticket, and I have remained a loyal -- though sometimes very critical

-- Democrat ever since. That went for Betty too.

Like a lot of people, I greatly admired John F. Kennedy. We were living in Holland, MI, in the fall of 1960, when this man ran against Nixon for president. During his campaign, Betty and I spoke freely with each other and in the presence of our children. We had decided that we must look beyond Kennedy's Catholicism and vote for him on the basis of his democratic principles, many of which were ours as well. It will be remembered that prominent preachers such as Norman Vincent Peale were at the time making a big fuss about Kennedy's Catholicism. They claimed that no faithful Catholic could be loyal to the Pope and to our American Constitution at the same time.

People in the city of Holland, MI seemed to be about 99% Republican. Unavoidably, Garry and Judy were chided and ridiculed in Christian school when they came wearing Kennedy buttons. All the other students were of course for Nixon. We were not terribly distressed about what our children were experiencing, but I was thinking that, as a preacher, I might have the duty of trying to at least get my parishioners to consider the issue of whether Christians should be denouncing a candidate purely on the basis of his denominational affiliation. In order to make my point as emphatic as possible, I decided to preach on this issue, and I chose Reformation Day Sunday on which to do it. I deliberately picked this day because it was when all the other Protestant ministers would be chastizing the Catholics. Quite a daring thing for me to do! The people would be expecting from me the standard anti-Catholic tirade, and here I would be using Reformation Sunday as the occasion to say good things about the Catholics. Unavoidably I would be blamed for electioneering both for a Democrat and for a Catholic. How would I have the gall?

"My dear fellow Christians and fellow Protestants," I begin, "sometimes the best way to celebrate a great occasion is to take stock of ourselves to see if we are living up to what we profess. Such an occasion is Reformation Day because it reminds us that our forefathers did not leave the church of Rome out of scorn and hatred, but out of loyalty to the gospel. The gospel makes some stern demands, and one of them is to love our enemies as ourselves, as Jesus said. Yes, in resisting the errors of the Church of Rome we Protestants have not made enemies of fellow Christians who happen to belong to the Roman Catholic Church. They are still our brethren -- yes, erring brethren -- in Christ. What we should be doing is promoting ways in which we may work with them, even while we try

A Reformation Day sermon that backfired

to persuade them to leave what we believe to be their errors.

"Fortunately, Catholicism in America and in some other countries has recently been making some positive accommodations to Christian truth as we Protestants see it. In America they have done a great deal in working for democratic principles -- democratic, that is, with a small 'd.' Yes, many Catholics also adhere to the program of the Democratic party, but though some might oppose their political ideology, at the same time one should thank God for moving American Catholics towards the same democratic principles that we cherish.

"On Election Day I want you to vote for your candidates according to your own convictions. I would not try to persuade you one way or the other. But what I am urging upon you is that you resist the effort to blacken the man who happens to be the Democratic candidate for president, mainly -- or solely -- on the claim that his Catholicism makes him unfit to serve as our next president. If you have thought of Mr. Kennedy or any other Catholic candidate as unfit for high office in our democracy only because of his religion, just remember Jesus' command to "love your enemies." If the Catholics have sometimes been our enemies, the Holy Spirit may just now be at work to make them better friends of Protestants and better citizens of our republic."

I felt very good after having given this sermon, but the feeling did not last long. Many church members seemed to appreciate my sermon and shook my hand warmly. I knew that there would be trouble when I greeted a rather self-important looking stranger -- a first-time visitor from Grand Rapids. His eyes were livid and his body trembled as he asked how I would dare speak like this before a Christian Reformed congregation, and on Reformation Sunday at that! I did not try to answer him except to say that I hoped he would come to think otherwise. But he must have spread his words of denunciation far and wide because I began getting phone calls mainly from strangers who felt the urge to express their outrage. To tell the truth, I had not anticipated how fierce such callers could become in their denunciations. It became so bad during the following two weeks that both Betty and I lived in dread of picking up the telephone. Most callers would refuse to give us their names. Others would say who they were, but it made little difference because we did not know them, either way. I only realized that I had stirred up a hornet's nest!

I heard subsequently that Lester De Koster, future editor of *The Banner* and erstwhile Democrat, had given a lecture in a similar vein somewhere in the Chicago area, with much the same effect. The difference between him and me was that he could live it down because he was a layman, while I was ordained and therefore could be deposed from office and kicked out of my salaried position if my enemies could only find my Achilles Heel and have a way to strike me down.

In retrospect, I am proud that I have done this. It is not that I care much about promoting the interests of a political party that most of the Christian Reformed reject. The issue was my right to originality and independence of thought in carrying out my pastoral duties. Am I to subordinate what I believe in to the dominant ideology in the CRC? That is the issue. As history will show, the powers that be in the CRC always aim to crush original ideas as well as creative persons. This is vicious! This is demonic! No church body can thrive as long as it is dominated by those who systematically suppress anything and anyone who threatens to challenge their supremacy.

James Muilenburg promotes me as Union's hot prospect. In 1960 the name of James Muilenburg was one to conjure with. On both sides of the Atlantic, and on the rim of the Pacific as well, he was regarded as America's most brilliant and influential biblical scholar. He was particularly appreciated by the Germans, who counted him as one of their own. He had had a remarkably variegated career, having held professorial or administrative positions at prestigious schools in Nebraska and New England before taking his first seminary teaching post at Pacific School of Religion prior to his appointment at Union Theological Seminary in New York in 1945. He remained at Union until 1963. After a guest-lectureship at Western Seminary, he joined the faculty of San Francisco Theological Seminary in San Anselmo, there to remain until retiring to Pilgrim's Place in Claremont, CA in the early 1970's.

That Muilenburg was a prolific scholar was well known to those, like myself, who were benefitting from what he had written as well as from what he was teaching in the classroom, and a mistaken impression can be gotten by judging his productivity mainly from the list of published volumes with himself as sole author, such as *The Way of Israel*, published by Harper in 1961. The fact is that he poured his main energies first, into guiding the work of his bachelors', masters' and doctors' theses, and second, into a great abundance of articles and published sermons.[4]

Once while working in the Union library I made a list of the doctoral dissertations which James Muilenburg wholly or partially supervised, with or without participation of the graduate department of Religion at Columbia, and there were 27 of them -- 27 within the span of Muilenburg's eighteen years at Union.[5] Besides, there was a large collection of masters' theses, like my own on "The Concept of the Fear of God in the Old Testament." Supervising all this placed a heavy demand on Muilenburg's time. He knew how to be severe, and fairly frequently he would show an erring pupil the door. But for those who were ready to become scholars like himself, he was a constant source of correction and inspiration. Every one of us said, "I want to be like James Muilenburg!" To undergraduate students he was an incalculable influence, as one will see in the widely-read tribute by the novelist, Frederick Buechner.[6] As Buechner and numerous B.D. students at Union experienced, Muilenburg made religion not only reasonable but urgent!

During the decade of the 1960's this man was my constant guide and counsellor. He had taken a special interest in me ever since I first entered his classroom back in 1949-50, and he continued now to keep his hand on my shoulder. As he himself confessed, he saw much of himself in me; i.e., a strong interest in the same questions of Bible and theology that occupied him, and the same struggle that he had experienced growing up in Iowa, going to college at Hope, avoiding seminary and going instead to Yale. In some places in his letters he alluded to these struggles, using them as an encouragement to me.

---

[4]See the bibliography of R. Lansing Hicks in T. F. Best, *Hearing and Speaking the Word. Selections from the Works of James Muilenburg* (Chico: Scholars Press, 1984), pp. 435ff.

[5]E. R. Achtemeier, Ph.D., 1958; W. Brueggemann, Th.D., 1961; A. E. Combs. Ph.D., 1963; B. T. Dahlberg, Ph.D., 1963; E. R. Dalglish, Ph.D., 1955; S. J. De Vries, Th.D., 1958; F. Dumermuth, Th.D., 1956; E. M. Good, Ph.D., 1958; N. K. Gottwald, Ph.D., 1953; W. J. Harrelson, Th.D., 1953; E. J. Hamlin, Th.D., 1961; R. L. Hicks, Th.D., 1954; F. Holmgren, Th.D., 1963; T. M. Horner, Ph.D., 1955; J. J. Jackson, Th.D., 1962; R. F. Johnson, Th.D., 1953; K. Kinoshita, Th.D., 1963; V. H. Kooy, Th.D., 1953; J. K. Kuntz, Th.D., 1963; T. M. Mauch, Th.D., 1958; M. L. Newman, Th.D., 1960; C. P. Price, Th.D., 1962; J. F. Ross, Th.D., 1955; S. Szikszai, Th.D., 1954; P. L. Trible, Ph.D., 1963; J. M. Ward, Ph.D., 1958; H. M. Yaker, Ph.D., 1956. When I later showed this list to Dr. Muilenburg, he said there were more, and I am sure that there were, but the purpose of making this list is simply to illustrate how widely diffused Muilenburg's tutorship actually was.

[6]"James Muilenburg as Man and Scholar," from *Now and Then*, New York: Harper, 1983, pp. 15-19

The 1960's: James Muilenburg promotes me

I am not going to claim that I had any special hold on James Muilenburg. There are those among his former students who wish to bask in the reflected glory of having been at some time associated with him. They would like to assume that the great prophet's mantle has fallen expressly on their own sholders. The truth is that we all had a piece of him, but in the unwearied readiness that he always showed to me, I was given the feeling that, in God's providence, he was there especially to help and inspire me.

The years between 1960 and 1962 were the crisis years of my career because this was when Muilenburg was most active as my advocate. Judging merely by the number and length of the numerous letters he sent me during this relatively short period, I was, and still am, given the impression that my career and welfare were his major preoccupation and concern. He was constantly active in searching for the most suitable place for me. I on my part was continually turning to him for understanding and advice. He seemed to know everybody worthwhile knowing in our profession. He was not willing to recommend me to just anybody, but would wait for the right sort of position. This was to be either a seminary or -- even better -- a university with a graduate school of religion and theology. Not just a college nor the humanities department at a university. In other words, he recognized that I had a mission, a destination, a special calling; and he worked diligently to help me meet it. I have already shown how he advised me about first coming to Drew and then leaving it to take a church in Holland, MI; also his role in getting me an interview for a position at New Brunswick Seminary. From others of his and my own letters, I am able to illustrate further how he guided me in the aftermath, up until I became safely positioned at Methesco:

> Dear Simon: Your letter reached me yesterday. I wanted to write before, but I thought it better to wait until you had received definite word from New Brunswick. I knew that there was nothing more I could do in your behalf. It is indeed hard to take, and I can feel some of the disappointment and pain. It is natural that you should raise many questions about your future, and perhaps you are tempted to be more discouraged than you ought to be....You have excellent qualifications, of that there is no doubt; yet one always has to meet the brute fact of competition. I certainly am not despairing, and I hope you will not be....Now Simon, take courage. Do not allow this discouragement to daunt you and lay you low. There are times when we have to wait, like watchmen for the morning. After all there are many, many things that would be much, much worse, and you can thank God that from these you

have been delivered. We shall find something yet! (Muilenburg's letter dated June 8, 1960)

Muilenburg advised me against an opening at a Presbyterian seminary in Brisbane, Australia, thinking as I did that to move my family so far away, with no assurance that the relationship there would be mutually pleasing and fruitful, would be more risky than my situation would warrant.

During this interval I was also asking his advice on two new ventures on my part. One question I had was about submitting to the Society of Biblical Literature's Monograph Series a revision of my doctoral dissertation in the form of two separate monographs, one on Abraham Kuenen and another on B. D. Eerdmans. He wished me all the best in this first venture. The other was about the possibility of committing myself to another study year abroad, preferably in the Near East. His feeling on this was that it would be foolish for me at this juncture to uproot my family and put myself effectively out of competition for jobs that might turn up. This is how he wrote me:

> One has to wait until openings turn up....I am not going to recommend you for positions which I know would not suit your case or your particular gifts and proclivities....Some time I hope you and your wife may be able to go to Palestine...but now isn't the time. The job should come first....I refuse to be discouraged, and I hope you will not be. Let us see what the coming weeks and months turn up. (Letter dated September 11, 1960)

I had to report to him soon after receiving this advise that the editor of the monograph series had turned my manuscript down. Exploring with Muilenburg alternative possibilities for getting it published, I commented on his suggestion that I should cultivate the attention of Prof. Lester J. Kuyper, head of the Old Testament department at Western Theological Seminary:

> I can report that I have been able to enter into a very intimate relationship with Lester Kuyper, and seem to be held in high regard by several members of the Westerm Seminary faculty, including the new young president, Harold Englund, so much so that Kuyper has revealed to me the fact that they are thinking of expanding the biblical department by adding me to their faculty. This, however, appears to be merely in the thinking stage....If it comes, it may not be for several years, since they already have one man in OT, one in NT, and two in English Bible, with

an enrollment of less than 100. Of course, this possibility is interesting to think about, as is also the possibility (mentioned to me by Justin Vander Kolk) that I will be considered at New Brunswick if more appointments are made there. (My letter to Muilenburg, November 12, 1960)

In the same letter I discussed misgivings I had about the lingering presence of fundamentalism at Western Seminary and urged Muilenburg to feel free about recommending me to less conservative schools:

I want to say once again...that you must not be overly cautious in considering the suitability of openings that may arise. I am no more the person I was ten or five years ago, nor even the person I was at Drew....I now feel perfectly confident that I could work creatively in many environments other than the most conservative....I am determined that I will succeed wherever I go when I leave here, that I will not disappoint the confidence that you have in me....In any case, I feel that this should be my last year in the Christian Reformed Church. I simply do not belong here anymore; there is no future for me in this denomination.

Western Seminary decided that there was no possibility of hiring me at the present moment, although there too I would remain a top candidate for a future opening. Meanwhile I was informed that I was on the short list at Perkins School of Theology (another Methodist seminary!) and was being considered as well by Huron Theological Seminary in Ontario, Canada. Perkins ended up hiring someone else, and I declined to be chosen by Huron because it represented high-church Anglicanism, to which I would have great difficulty adapting myself.

At this juncture I was feeling keenly the growing hostility against me within the Christian Reformed Church. My wife and children were feeling these pressures as well. There were no valid arguments for staying where I was and many strong arguments for moving on. This is what I wrote to Muilenburg in this situation:

I wish to avoid giving you the impression that I am unduly impatient, and yet it is important that you understand how greatly my attitude and circumstances have changed since I came to Holland three years ago. Then I was ready to face with some eagerness the opportunity of again doing pastoral work, because I was not yet thoroughly certain whether teaching or preaching was my real calling; and to face with some optimism the challenge of returning to the jurisdiction of the Christian Reformed Church because I allowed myself to retain the hope that I might soon see (and perhaps even be instrumental in) a real improvement in its theological position. Besides, there was the opportunity of cultivating contacts at Hope College and Western Seminary. Moreover, I was strongly influenced by my family's needs for greater stability and security.

At the end of these three years, none of these considerations bind me any longer: my family is now prepared to make any reasonable adjustment involved in accepting a position in teaching; the contacts I have established at Hope and Western hold promise for future years, but can scarcely be improved by my staying any longer; my denominational connections are proving more a burden and threat than a source of satisfying involvement....I see that I have far outgrown the church....I find myself increasingly isolated, ostracized from strategic positions....The seminary board...has passed me by again to appoint an untrained but flashy fellow whose best assurance of success is the vehemence of his polemic against all forms of critical theology. To see this convinces me more than ever that I have no future in this church....

I am convinced that I am not only in the wrong church, but in the wrong work. I see my pastoral work becoming more and more a drag upon my theological and scholarly development. I find myself losing contact with scholars and issues....I receive no encouragement, no stimulus, no incentive. A scholarly pastor may be permitted, but is seldom encouraged. (My letter to Muilenburg dated March 27, 1961)

Dr. Muilenburg had me so much in his mind that he wrote me within a month to repeat his promise to lead me through the crisis I was experiencing.[7] I was a bit amazed at how dry the well seemed to have become. I began to wonder whether I had poisoned the well by being so difficult to place. "Is it possible that Muilenburg finds it so hard to get a good position for me because I have been turned down at so many places?"

A week later he wrote again, this time to advise me against being enticed to join the faculty of Religion at Western Michigan University.[8] Dr. Cornelius Loew, a vigorous man who was a Union graduate and a former tutor-assistant of Paul Tillich, had not only invited me to Kalamazoo, but actually showed up one Sunday evening in Fourteenth Street church with two of his colleagues to hear my sermon. After the service he not only expressed strong interest in hiring me, but explained that the reason why he was not going to do so was the face-to-face consultation he had had with

[7] Muilenburg's letter of April 21, 1961
[8] Muilenburg's letter of April 27, 1961

Muilenburg, who told him not to hire me because my place was in a seminary somewhere. "He wasn't Yahweh," Loew explained to me, "but I couldn't go against his wishes so strongly expressed." I warmly thanked Dr. Loew for the honor of being considered.

The Christian Reformed Synod demonstrates zeal for dogmatic purity and scorn for its Church Order. Following the Board of Trustees debacle, my position became increasingly intolerable. The church was in a furor. Sides were drawn up between the *Torch and Trumpet* crowd and those who followed the line of the *Reformed Journal*. As I predicted, the members of the Board of Trustees had not kept the report of my interview with the seminary Faculty confidential, as they had been sternly instructed, and those who spread the alarm against me had not been censored for their disobedience. Nothing whatever had been done to deal with their breach of order and trust, hence they knew that anything they might wish to do to me in the name of CRC orthodoxy would remain unchecked.

Ever since that moment three years previously when I first entered my empty study and suddenly realized, "What am I doing here," I had resolved to establish some meaning in my unexpected and unprincipled return to the CRC by seeking the right opportunity to have my say about the issue of biblical inerrancy, which was dear to them but no longer tenable for me, since I am one who has made his own diligent and unbiased study of the Bible in my doctoral dissertation. My article, "Recovering a Historical Revelation," had been intended as my final testimony. I had been circulating it in certain circles since I first came to Fourteenth Street church in 1958, so when I became reasonably certain that I would begin teaching Hebrew at Western and Bible at Hope in the coming fall semester of 1961, I asked Henry Stob to print it in the *Reformed Journal,* so that all my friends, as well as my enemies, should know where I now stood, and had stood for the eleven years since I was ordained. I had not intended to stir up dust so long as I was still under CRC discipline, but I made a miscalculation in supposing that no one would have an opportunity to take action against me before I would have resigned my clergy status in the CRC. I was nothing but astonished at the suddenness and virulousness of the reaction.

My article attacked the idolatry of biblicism as espoused by the CRC, arguing instead for a doctrine of scriptural infallibility that does not deny the humanness of the biblical writers or the adventitiousness of the process by which human words have become the Word of God. Although Stob advised against printing this article on the grounds that it would be certain to bring my ministerial status in jeopardy, deep down in my curious heart, I wanted to find out just how far the church would actually pursue someone who had crossed the official line. I did sincerely wish to keep my own congregation out of any controversy, but when I presented this article for publication I was confident that they would not be involved because I was planning to leave the CRC within a few months. But it was not to be that way. I also wished to spare my parents' feelings, but that did not happen, either.

Maybe I haven't been realistic in my expectation of being able to avoid unwanted side effects, but if my bold move to have my last say has to be ugly, too bad! I want this manifesto to stand officially uncondemned and unsuppressed as I move on to a wider destiny. I do this so that others may be able to say, perhaps many years from now, "Look, this is what Simon De Vries has said, and it has not been ruled out as heresy!" If the CRC cannot tolerate what I say, it condemns itself. One day, some in the church will admit that I have been right, that the Bible really does show this about itself. I dedicate my statement to those persons.

Some will claim that I am testing the limits of tolerance. In a sense that is true. I acknowledge it as another of the experiments of which I am so fond, testing how far an institution with authority will actually go in punishing those who point out its errors. I need to know this, as least in principle, before I take my leave.

The right of Holy Scripture to be judged by what it actually claims for itself and shows itself to be has to have priority over any arbitrary and ill-conceived doctrine that this denomination -- or any denomination -- seeks to impose upon it. The idolatry of claiming that the Bible is something other than what it shows itself to be is the worst idolatry of all, and I refuse to submit to it. I wish to help others escape from it as well.

I had found myself the target of hostility and suspicion ever since my peremptory interview with the Seminary faculty in the spring of 1960. This had begun long before the publication of my article and had now been fanned into a furious flame. The heresy-hunters were roused to determined action during the eight or so weeks between the publication of my article and the meeting of Synod in early June. Two who had once been members with me of the seminary choir, but who were now "movers and shakers" -- one a tattler from Classis Alberta -- came to visit me in my office in order to voice their objections, my defense being an appeal to specific texts of Scripture that undermine the doctrine of biblical inerrancy; but Scripture by itself, i.e., the Bible without the prop of church dogma, could not convince these brethren. As they departed, I felt sure that they could be counted on to stir up strong opposition against me.

Soon after this interview I received an official letter from the Bluffton-Muskegon consistory with a list of questions they requested me to answer. My own forthright reply did not lead to further discussion, but was immediately put to use by them as the basis of a direct appeal to the coming Synod, which was to meet during the first week of June. I thought that this move was bound to run into a parliamentary roadblock, and that they would be instructed to approach first my own consistory. That was what our Church Order explicitly required.

I tell Betty that I think it might be wise for me to put my head in the door at Synod to find out what it is doing with the complaint that the Bluffton Church has sent them concerning my Reformed Journal *article. I haven't felt worried about reaction to it because, if they do have a charge to bring against me, they are obligated to follow the Church Order and come first to my Consistory here in Holland. That is surely what the Synod will tell them to do: first go to the Consistory, then go to the Classis; then you may come to the Synod, if that is still necessary. That is what the Christian Reformed Church Order requires. In a month or two I am out of here, and after that the Synod cannot touch me. Since I have already taken an appointment to teach next year at Western Seminary and Hope College, I shall promptly resign from Fourteenth Street church and from the Christian Reformed denomination, moving my ministerial credentials to Classis Holland of the RCA (Reformed Church in America).*

I am presently sitting in the old Calvin College chapel where Synod regularly holds its meetings. The topic which they are at the moment discussing has nothing whatever to do with the Bluffton appeal. During the afternoon coffee break, I join a small group of like-minded persons who are present as delegates or observers, who inform me that Synod probably won't debate the Bluffton matter, but has nevertheless appointed a special committee to advise it what to do. This turns on my warning-signal because Synod will now feel obliged to do something direct and immediate. The gentlemen at my table feel the same way. To my objection that this violates the Church Order, some reply that the Synod, if sufficiently aroused, as it appears to be, will inevitably find a way around it.

As we discuss these matters I notice that the President of Synod has walked over to our table and is looking directly at me. I certainly know him; he is well-known as the editor of the Dutch-language periodical, De Wachter. *He is also the pastor of a prominent church in the Chicago area. He is in fact the very man who first brought me to Calvin twenty years ago, William Haverkamp![9] He addresses me as follows: "So, it is you who is stirring up all this trouble! Is this the bright-faced lad I brought to Calvin twenty or so years ago? You were once such an ardent and clear-thinking young man. What has happened to you? Why are you spreading this filth? How dare you come to my Synod and pollute it with your presence?"*

I can hardly believe what I am hearing. Such raging, such hostility! Such a complete lack of fairness and judiciousness on the part of the one who has been elected to guide Synod in its search for the truth! This is worse than my interview with President Volbeda twelve years ago when I was graduating; this is more judgmental and vicious. The blood has drained from my face. I feel stunned. I feel like someone who has been raped!

One of our group, my former professor and my colleague in Passaic, George Stob, who himself has been shamefully injured by the Christian Reformed Synod, stands up and sternly says, "How dare you attack a fellow minister in this way? Consider your office, man. It is your duty to uphold fairness, order and justice, not to go around attacking individuals in this outrageous way!"

Averting the inquisition the synod intends for me. The Synod of 1961 decided to appoint an *ad hoc* committee of three "to consult with me in the presence of my consistory and report back to Synod the following year." The synodical brethren knew they were on shaky ground by encouraging the heresy hunters as they did, so they did what confused assemblies always do -- appoint a committee. And in customary political style, they asked for one member who would presumably be for me, another who would be against me, and one neutral -- though in fact in any fair judiciary or investigative organ, all the members should have been neutral![10] To make sure that this fish did not slip off their hook, when the nominating committee made their report just before Synod adjourned, they removed the purport-

---

[9] See "I arrive at my apparent destiny" in "The Nineteen Thirties."

[10] As a matter of fact, the (first) *contra* committeeman they appointed was a popular preacher by the name of Leonard Greenway, who had previously been expressing vehement opposition to my views in public -- by no means a fair or judicious man!

364   The 1960's +: Averting my inquisition

edly most sympathetic member from the nomination and substituted an ardent *Torch and Trumpet* man in his place, thus creating a committee consisting of one "neutral" member plus two of my most implacable critics![11] It appeared that no delegate seemed to expressed misgivings about the Synod's violating of Church-Order procedures along with the accepted rules of fairness and decency.[12]

Apparently, this Synod felt no compunction about persecuting one of their loyal own -- who, as they should have known -- was driven entirely by a devotion to the sacred word of God in Scripture as great as, or greater than, any they could claim for themselves. Most of my own Consistory members and many church leaders who understood what was going on were exasperated at all this undemocratic and unchristian behavior on the part of hyper-orthodox zealots in and out of Synod. It was a scandal -- not for me, because I was blameless of moral fault in this matter -- but for those who claimed to be orthodox and righteous, yet violated every rule of order and decency in order to get at me. They accomplished nothing more than they would have done without all this furor: my departure from the CRC ministry. That was going to happen anyway. They tried to push me, but it wasn't their push that drove me out; I left at my own volition, and at my own time and place. Good military tactics, as commended by the famous Marshall Clausewitz, requires the rule that I was following: "Never retreat except from strength." I was retreating from strength, not from weakness. From truth, not from falsehood. From loyalty to God's Word, not from disloyalty. In this case I believe the CRC to have been in opposition to God's Word and certainly to the rule of Christ, "Brethren, love one another!" If the committee as appointed had actually shown up at my consistory door, they would have been met -- I am assured -- by a roomful of my staunch defenders! The door would have been slammed in their face.

The thing that grieved me most in this entire affair was the gross ingratitude and complete lack of Christian love that was revealed. I certainly deserved better. I had nurtured three of the denomination's most hurting and needful congregations with loving care and selfless devotion. I had come back to the CRC, not once but twice, after extended leaves of absence -- first in 1946, after my three years

---

[11] My *"et tu, Brute"* was for a man from whom I had regularly bought my car insurance while in Passaic. It was he who made the motion to stack the membership of this committee against me! Apparently personal obligations counted for very little to such zealots.

[12] I am told that my case eventually bore some fruit in a later synod's adoption of a Judicial Code, which came too late to benefit me.

of military service, then again in 1958, after my Fulbright year and my teaching year at Drew -- laboring for the growth and well-being of the church in disregard of serious misgivings. Maybe I did not know better when I hurried out of my Marine uniform in order to enter Calvin Seminary; still, I did it out of loyalty and out of love. Then for eleven years -- the prime years of my life -- I performed onerous and inconspicuous work, not picking what might have been easier, more flattering, or more financially rewarding.

When I left Drew for very good and conscientious reasons, I *did in fact* have other places to go. Though Dr. Muilenburg wanted to keep me for a seminary post, he did mention that Bryn Mawr needed someone immediately, and that others might open up soon. As it turned out, Methesco was worth waiting for, but my point is that I could have -- and probably should have -- left the CRC years before, but I did not, and it was not out of timidity, or stupidity, or lack of imagination and ambition.

More than anyone, it was James Muilenburg who knew and understood how strong my loyalty had been to the CRC. It was because I could respond to the challenge of providing leadership that I came back to the denomination by way of Fourteenth St. Holland, repressing for the moment my serious worry that the move might hinder my career. The fact of the matter is that it did hinder my career -- not destroy, but hinder. I was at the time perhaps a strong enough candidate to do this, but it could have turned out to have been a professional disaster for me. I did not know that this would happen, but I certainly feared it. If I or anyone better than me would do something like that in the contemporary dog-eat-dog academic market, it would almost certainly be the end of his or her hopes altogether. It was risky even at that time, perhaps more risky than I thought. It worked out to my advantage because *then and there* I was good enough, and because Muilenburg had influence *then and there*, and certainly because God was still providing and leading!

I did not want any of this nasty business to happen. It is now all but certain that I will be teaching next year at Hope and Western, and I have already advised my consistory that I expect to announce my resignation in order to move into a teaching ministry. Hope and Western may prove to be temporary help-outs because I keep hearing from Dr. Muilenburg that he is remaining very active in finding me a more appropriate position elsewhere. So I'm going -- no question about it! Nevertheless the CRC has hired its hangmen to wound me before I can make a gracious withdrawal. They want to punish and disgrace me, if they can.

It is truly hard to believe that the denomination whose donkey-work I have been doing for more than a decade can now show so little gratitude and appreciation that they are falling all over themselves for a chance to strike me down before I can move on to ministry elsewhere. But alas, so it seems to be!

My father berates me for deviation from strict orthodoxy, II. I decided that this was the time to do some sharing with my dad and mother. When I got Dad on the phone I tried to bring him up to date on what had been happening. I wanted him to understand the issues and perhaps obtain his approval of what I was now planning to do. That was still important to me -- Dad's approval and understanding! Mother's too, of course. However, I should have known that it would be impossible for them to understand or sympathize!

As I speak to him on the phone, Dad cannot listen impassively. He is as he was at his home in Fresno. He and Mom have moved farther south to Bellflower, where they will probably remain to the end of their days. Unfortunately for me, that area is a seedbed of Christian Reformed know-nothing intolerance, from where Dad has already been getting some negative innuendoes about me, and he is angry! "How can you do this to me?" is his attitude. It is not to his credit that he is more worried about having to endure his fellow-parishioners' scorn than about supporting me, his son, in the eschatological struggle in which I find myself. Neither comfort nor encouragement is to be gained from him!

It is hard for me to hear this from my own father, and as I listen to him rant I grow faint within and enter another of my familiar whiteouts. I hear his voice, but it seems far away. Everything around and within the room in which I am sitting loses its color and turns pale. I am paralyzed into immobility. It is hard to find words to answer because I am stunned at receiving this ill-treatment from my own father.

I had neither wished nor intended that my career moves, and especially this ridiculous furor over my Reformed Journal *article, would in any way result in my parents' unhappiness. Now that it is that way, I can do little to win them to my side.*

The henchmen certainly know how to hurt someone falling from grace! I am just glad that their precious committee won't get to exercise the guillotine on me after all! I was loyal enough to go through all this, but where now is their loyalty to me in return for my devotion and sacrifice?

I move my camp to Hope and Western. James Muilenburg wrote me again towards the end of June, 1961, when the fat was already in the fire about my article on "Recovering a Historical Revelation." I had in fact received new feelers about teaching part-time at Western Seminary. Very shortly I was destined to join the faculty at Hope College with a special assignment to teach Hebrew at Western. The Muilenburg's were at the moment away from Union and therefore not current with these developments. This is what Dr. Muilenburg wrote while unaware of what was happening:

> I still have hopes for Western Seminary and possibly Hope College, though I am confident that your strength lies with the former rather than the latter. I did write the president of Western a very strong letter in your behalf. But Western Seminary has its conservatives too, I suspect. What I mean is those who have a fear of anyone coming from Union. (Letter from James Muilenburg dated June 26, 1961)

When he heard what action I had taken, Muilenburg was overjoyed with the good news. He felt that I was very wise in leaving the Fourteenth Street Church and in resigning from the CRC in order to accept employment at Hope College and Western Seminary. This is what he wrote me by way of congratulation and advice:

> Of course I am delighted that the appointment has come to you; this is the best news for a long time, and you have my hearty congratulations. I now hope that the time will not be long before you receive a full-time appointment at the Seminary. I have always felt that your effectiveness would be given greatest opportunity there. I am sure, too, that you will find the environment congenial to you. Kuyper and the others will make excellent colleagues. I am wondering whether you may not feel inclined sooner or later to transfer your membership to the Reformed Church; this would free you from the harrassments of tensions in your own denomination. (Letter dated August 13, 1961)

After I had been some months in my new work of teaching, Muilenburg had the following to say about my prospect of being accepted by the ultra-conservatives at Hope College and Western Seminary:

> I was tremendously interested to read all that you had to say about your work at Hope College and Western Seminary. Your schedule seems to me to be impossibly heavy; I don't see how you can do it all. The work at Hope and Western would be enough to occupy all a

man's time. What troubles me, however, is the old problem of what some of the people there consider theological orthodoxy. I fear I should not be able to cope with it. On the one hand, I am still convinced...that you belong in a seminary; you have heard me say this often enough. On the other hand, I do not see how you can ever rest content under the constant harrassing of the self-appointed "defenders of the faith." The naked truth is that they are the ones who are basically heretical, for they do not know what historical revelation really means and what its consequences are so far as our methodology of study is concerned. To reduce the divine revelation to logical consistency is to superimpose upon it a rationalism of the crassest sort....We who seek to take history and historical revelation seriously are closer to the Bible than the Fundamentalists. (Letter from Muilenburg dated December 20, 1961)

Our Waukazoo Woods intermezzo. The schoolyear 1961-62 deserved to be regarded as the most unique and disconnected year of our lives so far. The past was no longer haunting or threatening us, yet the future remained entirely beyond discernment. I was officially out of the Christian Reformed ministry, so that there was no longer anyone who was after my hide, anyone to bring me to task, anyone to threaten my livelihood and my professional standing.

I resigned from the Fourteenth Street church as of August 31, 1961, but at the congregation's request I continued performing the duties of pastor and preacher right up to the end of September. This arrangement created a month in which I was doubly burdened with Fourteenth St. duties and full teaching assignments at Hope and Western.

I do not know how I held up under it, particularly since the work of moving out of the parsonage was entirely up to me and two faithful helpers. These helpers were Betty's cousin, Dick van der Wiel, and Tom Lindsay, a parishioner. The moving of our furniture and books was accomplished in Tom's "Seven Up" truck. Of other former parishioners who helped us at this difficult transition, we were especially indebted to the kindness of Mr. and Mrs. Albert Buursma, curators of the Gold Estate on Lake Macatawa, who arranged for us to rent a grand house in Waukazoo woods belonging to the wealthy Gold family. It was large, commodious, and well kept. It had an expansive yard and was bordered by a forest of great beech trees. It was also close to Lake Macatawa, though not right on it. We could swim off the pier that belonged to the estate. This house had plenty of living space for the five of us (including Betty's mother), and we all loved it. We rented it for $100 per month and might have purchased it for $10,000, had we stayed in the area.

I am now RCA -- Reformed Church in America -- the denomination in which I was baptized and made confession of my faith. This is Betty's church as well, in the sense that she was RCA when we first met and until we were married -- though, to be sure, *not the church in which she was baptized and grew up.*[13] Professionally speaking, I am now more or less back to where I was three or four years ago, when I taught at Drew. I am engaged full time in higher education once more, teaching Beginning Hebrew at *Western Theological Seminary and Old Testament and New Testament introductory courses at Hope College.* My faculty status is that *of Assistant Professor of Religion and Bible at Hope.* We have transferred our church membership to the Third Reformed Church in Holland, were we are deriving tremendous blessing from the freer though faithful spiritual atmosphere.

I like the professors best at Hope, but the students best at the seminary. Naturally, Hebrew is the subject I like the most, even though I have to deal with a class of 38 students because Hebrew is required for ordination. (So also in the CRC and in Presbyterian denominations.) I do not like the Old Testament Introduction and New Testament Introduction courses I am assigned to teach at Hope because the classes are grossly overcrowded, with 50 students in each,[14] because the students are immature and difficult to engage intellectually, and because I am obliged to work from Bernhard W. Anderson's highly popular but very dull introduction, Understanding the Old Testament, *on which he is making a mint. For New Testament I am obliged to teach from Key and Young's parallel volume,* Understanding the New Testament, *definitely inferior to Anderson. Also, I have to contend with the serious irritation of being assigned to share an office at the college with an excessively raucous and gabby professor of psychology, Earl Hall. If it were not for the fact that I have an alternative office at the seminary, I would never get any work done.*

I wish that I could say that everything was lovely since we began to take up this new mode of existence, but there were some things that rubbed salt in the old wounds. For instance, we made a serious mistake in keeping Garry in the Christian School system for another year, while taking Judy out of it. She flourished in her new setting, but not he. First, he had to adjust to being in a brand new school, Rose Park Christian School. A move like this is hard enough for any

---

[13] The Berean (Reformed) Church in Muskegon, pastored by Harry Bultema (see in "The 1950's," "The untimely death of Gerrit Schouten")

[14] My student load in my one year at Hope was 300.

sixth-grader. Add to this the fact that his new teacher turned out to be an old Calvin acquaintance of mine (a fellow member of the Mission Society!) who now hated my guts and descended to taking it out on my child. One day, when Garry wore his Boy Scout uniform to school he was, with her approval, derided and condemned. It was supposed to be: Calvinist Cadet Corps![15] What this teacher may not have known was that her attitude towards Garry was carried out in the play-yard by intolerant bullies. Once he was forced to allow a long board to be placed across his chest, with two boys teeter-tottering on each end. I didn't especially blame the boys so much as I blamed the system that allowed and even encouraged anything so outrageous to happen. Above all I blamed myself -- or Betty and me together -- for failing to appreciate realistically that "no man can serve two masters." Garry deserves our apology! We were trying to please everybody at the same time, but it turned out that there were some who would take our courteous accommodation to community mores as a sign of weakness and lack of Christian conviction.

To some extent our distress over our son's misfortunes was offset by our daughter's achievements. She enjoyed her new life at the West Ottawa High School, and for the first time since we arrived back in Michigan she felt free to express her true self in creative ways. As in sixth grade in Madison, NJ, where she was already singing in public, she made much of her gift for singing here, taking a starring role in high school performances such as "Annie, get your gun!"

Feelers from two Methodist seminaries. We survived an autumn of strenuous labors and then a winter of super-heavy snowfalls; 131 inches fell in Waukazoo woods! One day in late February I received a letter from a new Methodist seminary, St. Paul's School of Theology in Kansas City, MO, inviting me to fly out there for an interview in connection with a professorate in Biblical Studies.

If I do accept this opening in Missouri, my future will prove to be as unconnected with my Waukazoo intermezzo as my life in Waukazoo has been in relation to my previous life in the Fourteenth St. parsonage. This juxtaposition of events creates certain anxieties, but we remain confident that God will surely go before us and show us where we must go.

---

[15] Shades of Pine Street kindergarten and Miss Cutler! Why is it that unmarried women are so likely to become tyrants in the schoolroom? Are they perhaps old maids because they are already tyrants, or does the opportunity of domineering a classroom full of defenseless children turn them into tyrants?

I made the trip to Kansas City and came home with an offer from the St. Paul School of Theology. The salary they offered was pretty good: certainly a lot more than at Hope or Western. I promised them an answer within a week, intending to say yes. There was only one detail that I did not like very well, that I would have to teach New Testament as well as Old Testament courses. I was to have the title of Professor of Biblical Studies. Be that as it may, just a few days after I returned, I was called out of class to receive a long distance phone-call, and it was from another Methodist seminary (my third!), the new one in Delaware, OH, familiarly known as "Methesco." St. Paul and this one, whose actual name was the Methodist Theological School in Ohio, were the two new theological schools recently authorized by the General Conference, the others being Boston, Drew, Wesley, Duke, Emory, Gammon, Garrett, Perkins, Iliff, and Claremont. This phone call was from the Dean of Methesco, Dr. Van Bogard Dunn, and he wanted to know whether I would be interested in exploring the possibility of accepting a position in Old Testament at his school. Receiving from me an enthusiastic yes, he asked me to meet him at the Grand Rapids airport next evening and discuss this over dinner.

I immediately communicated these developments to James Muilenburg, my true spiritual father, and he quickly replied as follows:

> Your letter...was not unexpected. I had had a long talk with Dean Dunn of the Ohio Methodist Seminary, and later in the week a letter arrived from Dean Holter of the Kansas City Seminary. I know both seminaries, but not in any thorough way. All that I have heard is favorable, though I had one report...that the Ohio institution was in a better financial position than the other....Both institutions are respected here at Union, and the prospects for their future...seem very bright indeed....I was favorably impressed by Dean Dunn. He seemed to me to be a very wise administrator. He was personally attractive, but rather balanced and reserved in a good way. He was much impressed by my reference to you and took the copy of your doctoral dissertation with him for examination. He said when he left that he intended to get into touch with you.
>
> The more I hear from you about the situation in Michigan both in the Christian Reformed and the Reformed churches, the more I am convinced that you would do well to sever your ties as soon as opportunity offers....As to which of the institutions you should go I cannot give you any certain advice. I suspect both institutions have their advantages....I am attracted to the Ohio institution I must say, despite my first paragraph, but this is probably due to the fact that I have talked face to face with

Dean Dunn and I know something of his dreams and ambitions for the institution. I was much impressed by what he had to say. They want scholarship, competence, and strength. (Letter from James Muilenburg dated March 6, 1962)

Dean Dunn visits Grand Rapids in a snowstorm
Holland is about twenty-five miles from the Grand Rapids airport, so it should not be much of a drive to pick up Dr. Van Bogard Dunn and then go on to the hotel where he will be staying. I invited him to be our house guest here in Waukazoo woods, but he replied that it would be better for him to just plan on staying overnight in the very comfortable Pantlind Hotel, and to have dinner with Betty and me there.

The sky to the east is very dark, and as we approach Grand Rapids we run into a blinding snowstorm. Very carefully we make our way to the airport, where we inquire whether Dr. Dunn's plane from Columbus will make it in. "Yes, it is delayed, but it is on its way." So we wait a while, wondering what first, the weather, and then Dean Dunn, will produce.

For most of an hour there is no break in the snowstorm. We become anxious and a little restless. After another half-hour delay, the plane touches down and approaches the terminal. As the passengers unload, Betty and I look closely for a gentleman who might be Dr. Dunn. I do not have a photograph of him, but fortunately he does have one of me, the one that has been attached to my dossier from Union, and with this to guide him he discovers us. He is happy to see us, happier than normally because he is so glad to be down on the ground in one piece. "Whew, that was the scariest plane ride I have ever had," he says. "I have been on a lot of planes, but this ride was the wildest. We just kept circling and circling as we gradually descended, and at one point we seemed to stand perpendicular to the ground, almost hanging vertically. At last we could glimpse the terminal and before long we landed safely. I'll never forget this ride!"

Dr. Van Bogard Dunn was professor of New Testament at Methesco as well as Dean. Before coming to Ohio he had taught at Duke Divinity School, where he had earned his Ph.D. degree, but at the time of his appointment to Methesco he was a pastor in west Tennessee. It was actually because he was in a church and not in an academic position that Bishop Hazen G. Werner and the Board of Trustees had picked him to be dean of the new seminary in Ohio. The Bishop was known for his heavy-handed administrative policies, and he was determined to have a dean -- as he thought -- who would be subservient to his wishes. Dunn seemed a good prospect because he had been under connectional authority while serving as a pastor in the west Tennessee area. The theological school had been in operation for just two years, but had already received so many students that it was necessary to expand the faculty beyond the original six or seven. The next two appointments, he explained, were to be in Pastoral Care and Old Testament. The school had received dozens of dossiers for both positions, and among those for the Old Testament position I stood out as the one they should appoint, partly for my strong academic performance but also because I had put in significant service as a working pastor. "That's what we really want," Dr. Dunn emphasized, "theologians and teachers who know by actual participation the demands the parish makes on the pastor."

So maybe my putting in nine years in the parish ministry was, after all, of some importance in terms of my eventual career as professor in a theological seminary. I always thought so, in spite of the fact that most of my teaching colleagues at Methesco never seemed to think that it mattered one way or another.

Dr. Dunn (or "Bogie," as he preferred to be called) told us that the faculty were so struck by my dossier that he immediately flew out to New York to have an interview with Professor James Muilenburg. "I have never read such a laudatory letter as what I found in your dossier from Union, and Muilenburg confirmed every word of it when I came to his office. You can't believe, Simon, what he told me about your character, your integrity, your skill as a biblical scholar, your commitment to the church and the pastoral ministry! You are definitely my man, if you are willing. But if you are seriously interested, it will be necessary for the two of you to reverse what I am doing and fly out to Ohio to be interviewed by the faculty, the sooner the better."

We conversed at some length over an excellent dinner served in the restaurant belonging to the Pantlind Hotel. When we were pretty well talked out, we thanked Bogie for coming to Grand Rapids at such apparent hazard and predicted that it would all be worthwhile in the outcome, if God should so lead us. We assured him that we would immediately make arrangements for the trip to Ohio. Leaving him there in the hotel lobby, we took our leave and drove over the snow-covered highway to our home.

Now, all of a sudden, I have two calls, two appointments! It should not be too difficult to decide which of the two I should accept.

374   The 1960's +: I find my niche at Methesco

I find my niche at the Methodist Theological School in Ohio. A few days after our interview with Dean Dunn, Betty and I made a trip to Delaware, OH, the home of the new seminary. There was a related Methodist institution in this city of 20,000 known as Ohio Wesleyan Universiy, which was a well-regarded liberal-arts college founded in 1842. The city of Delaware was only a few decades older than that, having been established in the year 1808. Being so near the geographical center of Ohio, it had been at one time a serious candidate for becoming the state capital, though the choice went to Columbus. Betty and I first met the faculty and the president, Dr. John W. Dickhaut, answering all their questions, then were taken around the city to see what was there. In the hands of some enthusiastic faculty wives, Betty got a preliminary look at some possible choices for a house to buy. The two of us were entertained at the commodious Tudor-style mansion of Bogie and Gerry Dunn.

One question that had been raised while I was being interviewed by the faculty that I thought odd was whether, when I left Drew, this had been at my own volition. My antennae were up and I understood immediately what was behind this question. Someone wanted to know whether I had been kicked out. I resolutely replied that I had in fact been reappointed, which was true enough, and that I had Dean Anderson's letter in my file in case anyone should desire to see it. Because this question was raised by Jeffrey Hopper, our junior Professor of Theology, it seemed rather obvious that it must have come from someone familiar with the scene at Drew, where Stanley Hopper, Jeff's father, was Dean of the graduate school.[16]

Apart from mild flurries of this kind, the message came through clear and strong that the Methesco faculty and administration were so taken with me that they were entirely clear and convinced. It would be, then, a question whether Betty and I were also clear and convinced. Nevertheless, before we left for the airport to return home, I was able to give Dean Dunn the assurance that I would immediately decide between St. Paul and Methesco, and give him our answer without delay.

Within a few days I phone Bogie to give him our affirmative answer to his offer. The seminary will pay our moving expenses. We are all excited and happy about it -- although Judy has a hard time accepting that she can no longer be close to her newly found

---

[16]The question reflected the concern of my colleague in Old Testament.

boyfriend, Peter Kammeraad, from Holland, MI. We can do little more than promise her that we will take trips back to Holland now and then, and we encourage her to invite Peter to visit her in Delaware as often as possible.

Methesco was the third Methodist seminary to offer me a job, the other two being Drew and St. Paul's.[17] What was it about me that the Methodists like? Drew was old and prestigious, but had not been a happy place for complex people like me. St. Paul and Methesco had been equally enthusiastic, but it was not very reassuring that the two invitations were from brand new institutions. I would rather have been invited to teach in a better-established school with a strong graduate program.

"But perhaps Methesco will develop me," I say to myself. "Anyway, this will be a fresh start for all of us, and we will have a dean with a strong background in theology, as well as experience in preaching and pastoral work. He has done very well so far in enlisting scholars with a strong theological commitment to join the faculty."

Faculty persons on the Methesco faculty when I joined it or who joined it at the same time I did were: *New Testament:* Van Bogard Dunn, Moody Smith, Fred Gealy; *Old Testament:* Everett Tilson; *Church History:* Clyde Manschreck; *Systematic Theology:* David C. Shipley, Jeffrey Hopper; *Preaching:* Van Bogard Dunn, Edward Meyer; *Church Administration:* Harold Williams; *Pastoral Care:* Arthur Foster; *Christian Education:* Robert Browning; *Theological Bibliography:* John McTaggart, Edward Hunter.

---

[17] At the time I was also on the final list at Perkins Theological School at S.M.U.

A place of beauty and comfort to call our home. I count no fewer than six trips, five of them roundtrips, that were needed to bring us and all our possessions to this new job and new home:

(1) In early March, Betty and I flew to Ohio for an interview with the faculty and administration, with the vice-chairman of the Board, Dr. John Mount, present. We were entertained in the home of Dean Dunn and his wife Geraldine. Before we returned home, I received an offer of the position.
(2) A few weeks later, I flew to Columbus for interviews with the Committee on Education of the Board of Trustees and the Board Chairman, Bishop Hazen Werner, in his office in downtown Columbus. Following dinner at the Columbus home of the seminary president, Dr. John Dickhaut, I flew directly home to Michigan.
(3) In late May, while I was being interviewed by the entire Board, Betty and Paul made a provisional inspection of the house we were soon to purchase at 35 Darlington Road in Delaware. The same evening we had a visit with the owners and received their final offer. While on the way home the ensuing night, Betty and I decided to purchase this house if the owners were willing to accept our final offer, which they were.
(4) Early in June, Betty, I and Garry drove to Delaware to check out our new house and determine what needed to be done to it. Two items that would be immediately discarded would be grey drapes covering two entire living-room walls and a flimsy rug sprawling over the upstairs hallway.
(5) In late July, Betty and I drove to Delaware to finalize our business with the owners and perform provisional cleaning and remodelling. We labored during a very hot week to wallpaper the kitchen and repaint all the cabinets.
(6) A sixth trip was needed for moving all our belongings to our new home at the end of summer. The seminary paid for the van, which was crammed with the acquisitions of a dozen or more years. Our car could carry little more than Betty, me, Judy, Garry, Grandma, and Peppy, our toy fox terrier -- very soon to find his end while chasing an unidentified Delaware female.

Obtaining a family home was left entirely to individual faculty members; there was no special provision to assist them financially in this except in paying the moving bill, but our faculty colleagues did show themselves more than ready in helping us shop for a house and move into it. One particular house on a two-block street in north-central Delaware, a striking Dutch colonial in a row of three, caught

Betty's eye, but unfortunately it was not for sale.

On our visit in late May, after viewing five or six houses the realtor had to show us, we began to fear that our search might prove entirely fruitless, when Dean Dunn telephoned us that someone had seen a notice in the Ohio Wesleyan newsletter of a "For sale by owner" offer for the very house that Betty had admired so very much when we came down here in early March. The owner turned out to be an OWU religion professor who had just accepted an appointment to Hartford Seminary, Dr. John Priest.

I have been occupied all afternoon getting final approval of my appointment from the Board of Trustees, meeting at the same time as Commencement. While I am thus occupied, Paul and Betty have been busy looking over the Dutch colonial home that the Dean has told us about. We then discuss their findings over the dinner table at Bun's Restaurant in Delaware.[18] Betty is fairly excited about the house, but of coure she sees a lot of work because it is tired and shabby. Paul doesn't like it very much and strongly advises us to go for one of the new split-level houses across the street from Hayes High School. But Betty is thinking of the need to accommodate her mother. We will definitely be needing four separate bedrooms, and the split-levels have no more than three. We have an appointment to see the Priest house after we finish here, and are looking forward to meeting both Professor Priest and his wife Gloria.

This house was the middle one of three Dutch colonials in a row -- all built at about the same time and by the same builder, who was himself the first occupant of the house to the north. Our lot was about 60 feet wide and 200 feet deep. A single-stall garage stood behind the house at the north side of our lot.

The house had been manufactured and marketed by Sears Roebuck Co. back in 1924 and constructed a year later. Sears had a plant in Illinois where all the individual parts, each of which was separately numbered, were manufactured. This house appeared as "The Amsterdam" in their catalogue. It was an "Honorbuilt" model, meaning that all materials were of the finest available. It had such features as 12′ floor beams, oak flooring throughout, French doors, an

---

[18] Bun's had been in existence since the middle of the last century. It was a true city institution where old friends came to fellowship with one another. It was so special that it was allowed to suspend a sign saying "Bun's Restaurant" over the street.

378   The 1960's +: A place of beauty and comfort

excellent brick fireplace, a hot-water gas heating system, and similar amenities throughout.

We visited Professor John Priest and his wife Gloria at their house that same evening and reached a tentative purchase price, which, with a G.I. Mortgage, we figured might be somewhat within our ability to pay. The Priests initially asked $23,000, but we got them to come down to $20,000 during our visit with them, and to reduce this by another $200 when I telephoned them from Michigan the following day. The need to sell quickly to allow them to begin searching for a new home in Connecticut was certainly an inducement in their decision to lower their price so drasticallty. Leaving out an agent as middle-man in this instance saved them and/or us several thousands of dollars.

We were able to remain living in this comfortable house during the entire thirty years in which we resided in Delaware, OH, and then sold it for $142,000, bringing in approximately seven times the amount we had paid for it in 1962. This was not all profit -- far from it! Our selling price would reflect all the repairs and improvements done by us and expenditures paid by us, all needed in order to bring it up to its potential utility and beauty.

At last a living wage. There were three matters of special concern to our family as we made our move to Methesco and Delaware: (1) an adequate financial package; (2) access to higher education for our teenagers, Judy and Garry; and (3) a good house to live in that we could afford.

The house I have already described. The salary I was being offered was $8,800 for the first year, with the expectation of modest annual increments. This was more than a thousand dollars per year higher than I had been receiving at 14th St. Church and later at Hope

College. At Methesco I was hired on as "Associate Professor" and was put on a tenure track, with the expectation of becoming full Professor within five years. All of this was modest enough in view of my previous experience and ranking at institutions I had served, as well as my demonstrated capabilities as a potential teacher and creative scholar. In light of the fact that I had been Assistant Professor at Hope College, it seemed right that I should now become Associate Professor and that I be given tenure within the relatively short period of two years. In order to give my colleagues opportunity to scrutinize me at some length, however, it was deemed best that I not receive a promotion to Professor until I had been at the rank of Associate Professor for five years. As a matter of record, I was given tenure in 1964 -- two years later -- but did not become full Professor until 1968, six years later rather than five.

I saw no reason to make an issue of this because it reflected school policy and did not imply any hesitations regarding my fitness to serve at this institution. This arrangement was the result of trying to balance what I might deserve objectively over against my relative position with relation to other Methesco faculty, who were almost all young, talented, just-getting-started scholars like myself.

Until 1968 my annual salary increases were miniscule, but after that date I received several large salary boosts until I was being paid at the highest allowable level within my grade. Nevertheless, there was and always would be a gap between my salary and that of my Old Testament colleague, even when we were both full Professors. It was impossible for me ever to catch up with him because he had come to Methesco as full Professor and had been at Methesco two years longer than I had been.

A good policy that had been put in effect at the school's inception was our pension scheme under TIAA-CREF,[19] in which an additional 10% of one's salary was paid by the school into the retirement fund, along with 5% from one's salary. This seemed generous, but was in fact lower than the plan at OWU, where the faculty paid 5% and the Board 13%. Anyway, when I retired from full employment twenty-five years later, this had built up to a quarter million dollars, which was converted into a generous annuity guaranteeing monthly payments throughout my life and that of Betty.

There was also an insurance policy to cover total disability and participation in the Blue Cross-Blue Shield health scheme. Both Betty and I had occasion to make use of the hospitalization policy,

---

[19] Teachers Insurance and Annuity Association, College Retirement Equities Fund

but -- we are grateful to be able to add -- not the disability policy. As I shall tell, there came a time when I became disabled to a certain extent, but not so severely as to keep me from functioning in my profession.

A perquisite of my job that we were able to make very good use of was an arrangement whereby Methesco and OWU would provide full tuition to faculty family members of these sister institutions at each other's school. Theoretically, family members of the OWU faculty had the same opportunity as Methesco faculty family members, but hardly made use of it -- an exception being Bette Meyer, the wife of OWU's Vice-President of administration. When it became apparent that almost all the benefit devolved upon our faculty, the OWU professors voted to cancel it -- but fortunately not before both our Judy and our Garry had managed to graduate from OWU. It was in this way that my erstwhile plaint to Dr. Ed Vanden Berg of 14h Street CRC was answered. I had asked, "Ed, how am I ever going to be able to afford college tuition for my children if I can get no more than a $200 annual increase in my salary?"

God was paying attention and is taking care of our need.

Favorable omens

It is summer, 1962. I am moving my books into my new office in Werner Hall at the Methodist Theological School in Ohio. The nickname "Methesco" was proposed by Professor David Shipley when he joined the faculty; it is an acronym for Me(thodist) The(ological) Sc(hool in) O(hio).[20] *This time I do not have to ask, "What am I doing here," because this is the right place for me, I know it.*

Following my first class in the fall semester, I walk smiling into Dean Dunn's office and say, "Bogie, I find it quite wonderful to be engaged in teaching at this school. I feel sure that my relationship with you and the faculty is going to be nothing like those that I left behind in Drew. I am gratified by the fine Christian spirit that I am encountering here!"

After having been at Methesco a year, I wrote James Muilenburg to tell him how I felt about Methesco. Everything seemed to justify the enthusiasm that I had expressed to Dean Dunn:

---

[20] Current usage is "MTSO."

You will be glad to know that I constantly find my work entirely satisfying, though always demanding. My previous waverings and doubtings are gone. I have successfully adapted to the work, the position, and the environment. My conservative background, while continuing to serve me in good stead by adding a dimension of depth to my understanding, no longer is capable of holding me back, so that I now find myself entirely within the mainstream of theological discussion and biblical research. I am always learning from others, but discover that I can at the same time contribute something significant of my own. (Letter to Muilenburg dated October 13, 1963.

Two years after my appointment at Methesco, I wrote an even more enthusiastic assessment of the influence I was having in my teaching at this school:

More and more I observe that our faculty and students are taking the Bible with greater seriousness. Thus the faculty is scheduling soon a colloquium on the hermeneutics of the Old Testament, which I am to chair. The students are eagerly participating in courses on exegesis and biblical theology. Enrollment in the biblical languages has shown marked improvement....Particularly encouraging has been the response to our summer clinic for preaching, in which I have been in charge of lecturing on exegetical methods. My colleague and I were able to make a real impression on the men who participated in this clinic by showing them in a practical way how sound exegetical methodology can make a vital difference in communicating the word of God. (Letter to Muilenburg dated October 21, 1964)

Was this heaven? It was, it truly was -- but only for a moment. To tell the truth, four sinister factors were already at work to disturb my paradise: (1) the paranoid narcissism of my Old Testament colleague, (2) the eventual ending of the dynasty that was to come about with the retirement of President John Dickhaut and Dean Van Bogard Dunn; (3) the havoc that was to come with creeping egalitarianism and the politics of color and gender; and (4) my own private hell, clinical depression, which was already incipient and would eventually grow to monster proportions.

Participating in the program of Ohio's new Methodist seminary. If any section of United States Methodism deserved to have its own theological school, it was Ohio, for that state had more Methodists than any other region, the next following being North Carolina. There were more Methodists in Ohio than any other kind of Christians --

382   The 1960's +: The program of Ohio's seminary

Catholics included. That resulted from the fact that it was Methodism that had been the most successful in peopling the new American frontier north of the Ohio River and south of the Great Lakes. Even today one can go from village to village and town to town anywhere in Ohio and find that, if there is only one church, it is Methodist.

Back in the 1950's, when the development of a new theological school within the state of Ohio received the approval of the General Conference,[21] there were influential people in the Methodist Church, inside and outside Ohio, who had been making an effort to gain approval for organizing the projected new theological school on the same campus, and in organic connection with, the Oberlin Graduate School of Religion -- or, failing that, to combine it with Bexley Hall, the theological adjunct (Episcopal) of Kenyon College -- as a single vigorous new center of ministerial training within the state of Ohio. In either case, the main motivation would be to bolster prestigious, long-standing institutions in need of being rescued financially. But part of the rationale was to provide the new Methodist seminary-to-be with intellectual vigor and professional integrity at its very inception. It certainly would need that if it was to compete with Duke, Emory, Boston,[22] and the like. Although the new faculty would have welcomed an opportunity to assure ready-made academic respectability as well as significant ecumenical connections, most Ohio Methodists were not concerned with bolstering outside institutions. Instead they insisted upon a theological school that would be primarily responsive to the needs of their own constituency, and that implied that it should be located in a place that would be convenient to Methodists throughout the state. The choice seemed truly blessed from God when Ohio Wesleyan University donated an attractive expanse of land near the old city of Delaware for a seminary campus.

There was widespread concern at the time to prevent this new school from becoming a preacher factory under the tight control of the resident bishop, known to be ruthless in creating structures for

---

[21] At the same Conference St. Paul's was approved for Kansas City.
[22] Ohio had been one of Boston's prime recruiting grounds.

extending his episcopal power and control. In this light we may understand that much of the initial agenda for faculty discussions at the school, as well as for consultations between the Faculty and the Board of Trustees, came to be focused on the crucial question of who would have the authority to appoint the professors. There had to be absolute integrity in this process if the taint of bias and the suspicion of croneyism were to be avoided. It so happened that Van Bogard Dunn turned out not to be the complaisant dean that the bishop counted upon and anticipated. The bishop and the board has said "All right" to Bogie at the time of his appointment when he insisted upon uncontested authority to initiate all recommendations for faculty appointments -- but apparently he had not been taken seriously enough, for in the year prior to my own appointment a professor of Homiletics (preaching) was to be appointed and the bishop was eager to promote his own candidate, but Dean Dunn was having none of it. Instead he nominated his own candidate and thereby initiated a struggle into which the new faculty eventually had to intervene on the dean's side. One of the very first faculty meetings I attended after my arrival in Delaware was one in which the faculty voted to communicate its misgivings about this unprincipled politicking to the American Association of Theological Schools, which was just at the point of deciding whether to approve our school for full accreditation, whereupon the board and the bishop were forced to give in, and the principle of integrity in faculty appointments was vindicated.

I have always been grateful to have been a witness to and participant in this event because it provided me with a clear understanding concerning who was boss over the academic program at Methesco -- boss over the faculty and boss over the curriculum. That in turn made me all the more enthusiastic about the design for the curriculum that the dean was proposing, and in which the traditional divisions between specialties or disciplines were clearly embraced: Bible, Old and New Testaments; Systematic Theology; Historical Theology; Practical Theology in all its branches. The decision to adopt a nomenclature in which the element, "theology" or "theological," was an element encouraged the various specialties of the curriculum, like my own, to be in intimate consultation with one other. No one was to practise his specialty in isolation. For example, Systematics had to be answerable to exegesis and biblical theology; Church History had to be concerned mainly with the religion and theology of the church, rather than with persons or administrations or events. In addition, the main point of urgency about providing a good library was the recognized need to enable facile access to a wide range of bibliographical source materials appropriate to our common theological task, and for the needs of professors as well as of students.

Not only did we have this common goal in our teaching; we cultivated it in special colloquies and faculty retreats. Several of our faculty members were advocating at the time the existentialism of Heidegger and Bultmann, while others were more attached to the Biblical Theology movement that was popular at the time. I was aware of the weaknesses of those two movements and saw to it that the sort of scholars and theologians who had influenced me should come to lecture for us, including James Muilenburg, Samuel Terrien and James Smart of Union Theological Seminary and Brevard Childs of Yale.

Alongside John and Charles Wesley, the big man in American Methodism at the time was Walter Rauschenbush, an early proponent of the Social Gospel. Our faculty members were all committed to the civil rights movement. Dean Dunn along with certain others of my colleagues became activists as well as eloquent propagandists for this movement. In June of 1965 Bogie and I, with four hand-picked students, spent a week in Jackson, MS, lodging in the homes of prominent black leaders and canvassing black neighborhoods for first-hand experience with what was going on in that key community. This was just one year after three young men, one of whom was black, had been murdered at New Philadelphia.

The Delaware community was, in general, antagonistic to our activism and outspokenness, viewing us as radicals and pariahs. On the other hand, some professors appeared to me to be showing off how "liberal" they were and I refused to be swayed by them. Whatever part I allowed myself to play would have to come out of my biblical commitment, and I readily found all the support I would need from the Bible, and especially the Old Testament -- a truly people-centered book.

It was clearly stated at the time of my appointment that the seminary would do all that was needed to ensure that I should have time enough to carry out the focused research that I had already shown myself capable of. I was to have my fair share of teaching assignments but was to be spared from major administrative responsibilities. The school could agree to this because of the unusually strong recommendation of Professor Muilenburg. Eventually I came to regret that I had been singled out in this way, for to those who preferred that I be kept out of key committee assignments, it gave an excuse to discriminate. It also encouraged the twisted thinking of my Old Testament colleague, who arranged to keep as many students as possible out of my classes so that he could have them, flattering me with the suggestion that I should be teaching specialized subjects rather than spending time with beginners.

When I took up research and writing in earnest, I encountered a problem for which nobody at our school had a solution. There were no funds for research assistance or for the typing of manuscripts, and as a result I had to do everything for myself. That is when I envied scholars at institutions where there were these facilities. I could have had secretaries and student assistants had I stayed at Drew. On the other hand, this was better than Hope College, where I did not even have an office to myself and where the library was entirely inadequate for research. It was more like Western Seminary except in that I had far greater freedom. Methesco's library was more or less equivalent to what I would have had at Western.

I was able to content myself under these restrictions with the expectation that sooner rather than later I might be moving on to something better -- but nothing better came. *This was it for the duration!* A seller's market had changed to a buyer's market, and never changed back again. The deficiencies due to the War had been remedied and there were more candidates than positions to be filled. Also, the older one got, the less chance one could expect to have for moving on elsewhere because financially pressed institutions (and aren't they always financially pressed?) are not likely to hire people with rank and tenure, like myself, since they would be forced to pay more salary. It became more and more difficult to get jobs in higher education, no matter how good one was. The only exception would be if you became very, very famous. I became well known nationally and internationally, but certainly not famous.

Methesco tried to establish high standards for its faculty, and this led it to offer regular sabbatical leaves. These were supposed to be used for increasing one's skills, and that is how I used them. I was on leave at Tübingen University in Germany during the year 1965-66, at the Institute for Advanced Theological Study in Jerusalem during the spring of 1973, at King's College in London during the fall of 1978, and at other times close to home but working hard. My excursions in foreign places not only provided research opportunities, but the chance to become known and get to know other scholars. Furthermore, I attended numerous conferences, seminars, research projects, and examinations at places near and far, always increasing my learning while sharing my own ideas concerning theological education and my specialty, Old Testament exegesis and theology.

I often preached either during the seminary chapel hours or on Sundays in various churches. I loved doing this and I was generally well appreciated. This was especially the case at the First Presbyterian Church of Delaware, where our family were members for most of our period in Delaware. My sermons were always different in style and content from those preached by many other professors at our school, which tended to be without a firm anchoring in Scripture. I followed the method of preparation that I advocated for my students and tried to show that I had listened for the very special message of the text. My motto was then, and still is, "The word of God is living and active, sharper than any two-edged sword, discerning the thoughts and intents of the hearts."[23]

At the time of my appointment I had discussed the matter of my ordination with Dean Dunn and Bishop Werner, and neither of these dignitaries had been especially desirous of having me transfer to the Methodists. In fact, Bogie was seeking to build an ecumenical faculty -- even while the school's focus would remain on Methodism. Therefore I let my ministerial credentials remain temporarily in the RCA, transferring from Classis Holland to Classis Lake Erie.

I might have done well to transfer my ministerial credentials to the United Methodist Church. Since central Ohio had hardly any Reformed churches, I decided instead to become a Presbyterian. I had as a matter of fact little contact with my ministerial colleagues in the RCA and generally had to travel at least a hundred miles to be able to attend its classis meetings. This consideration lead me to apply to the Columbus Presbytery of the Presbyterian Church (USA) in 1965, and I have remained a minister in good standing in that denomination ever since. I made a strong effort to become involved in the affairs of the Columbus Presbytery and also went out regularly to conduct worship services in Presbyterian as well as Methodist churches without pastors. In 1986 I was a delegate to the General Assembly of the Presbyterian Church (USA) meeting in Minneapolis. I am presently listed among a small number of "Associates at Large." I will not give up my ordination for any reason. It is especially precious because I have put so much effort into receiving it and have such a positive ideology concerning it. I now find myself far from the portals of the CRC in which I was first ordained, but I am and always will remain a minister of the church of Jesus Christ, with the world as my parish.

---

[23] Heb 4:12

The work of training future ministers in Old Testament interpretation. Under the semester calendar, I would have the entire class of entering students every other year. In this introductory course I offered them an entrée into the entire range of Old Testament books, including the Apocrypha, dealing also with the history of the ancient Israelites and their religion. In other courses I explained to them their responsibilities in preaching from the Old Testament and showed them in detail how to carry them out. I also taught them to recognize the relevance of Old Testament theology for the church and the modern world. Optional for them was the study of Hebrew, but I tried to convince them to take it as an elective, and one time succeeded far beyond my expectation. This happened in fact the second time I taught the full-semester introductory course; forty-three of my beginning students showed up the following semester in my course in Beginning Hebrew -- an astounding number in light of the fact that ministerial candidates in the Methodist Church are not required to learn Hebrew or Greek, and generally opt out of doing so.

I very much loved teaching Hebrew. I had taught it both semesters during the year I was at Western Seminary, and I learned from this experience that beginning students need a balance of theory and practice in order to read the kind of Hebrew they would find in the Bible. The main thing was to enable them to enter into the Hebrew mode of thinking. There were simplified reading texts to practice on first, then portions of the Hebrew Bible itself. The best students usually went on to study Hebrew exegesis in advanced courses, with special attention to handling the critical apparatus accompanying the standard critical text. Language courses that I taught in addition to Hebrew were Biblical Aramaic, Septuagintal Greek, and New Testament Greek.

I also greatly enjoyed teaching exegesis courses designed for students without Hebrew. As much as I might have preferred them having Hebrew as a tool, I could not leave them totally unprepared.[24] Accordingly I taught them in all my English-language exegesis courses to use what language knowledge they did have to the best possible effect, reading the English translation intelligently, with responsiveness and imagination.

At the time, the Revised Standard Version (RSV) was popular. In addition to the fact that it translates a superior Hebrew text, it helps the untutored reader by supplying alternative readings and by scan-

---

[24] Pastors who have learned Hebrew in seminary often find themselves too much in a hurry to use it effectively in preaching. This is a touchy issue in seminaries where Hebrew and Greek are required since the majority of students do not go on to acquire

ning the poetry. One advantage of the King James Version was that it placed everything that was not literally supported by the Hebrew original in italics. If anything, this implied that the italicized words should not become the basis of a sermon -- a rule that was sometimes disregarded, with ludicrous effects.

Because my Old Testament colleague would not share the most popular books, which were Genesis, Job, Psalms, Isaiah, and Jeremiah, I was obliged to become inventive. I offered a course on "Pentateuchal Traditions" in the place of just Genesis, courses on Ezekiel and the Minor Prophets in the place of Isaiah and Jeremiah, courses on "The Wisdom Literature" and "the Postexilic Literature" in the place of just Psalms and Job. Other favorite exegesis courses of mine were "Israel's Historiographic Literature" and "Deuteronomy and the Prophetic Movement"; also "The Historical Geography of the Holy Land," designed for students preparing to visit the land of the Bible, and "The Achievements of Biblical Religion."[25] In addition, I was inventive regarding teaching methodology, preparing a special worksheet as a guide to students in my non-Hebrew exegesis courses. After choosing a "text," they were to complete a sequence of steps for gathering information, and at the end they were to prepare a brief outline of a sermon they might preach upon it. I received great satisfaction in observing my students grow in self-confidence in dealing with Scripture by following these directions.

Although this kind of instruction is essential for aspiring ministers, it is equally comprehensible to educated and spiritually minded laypersons. I would begin my course by saying, "You all take the Bible seriously and agree that it lies at the core of Christian piety. Preaching from the Bible is a basic part of Christian ministry. For those of you who are serving student parishes the need to know how to do this is especially urgent. Without instruction, you are likely to be troubled and confused about how to carry out this responsibility, so let me try to instruct you. That is what this worksheet is for." I would then continue with the following:

"Please do not use your not knowing Hebrew as an excuse for giving up or copping out. Good commentaries will tell you most of what you need to know concerning the meaning of words and Hebrew style, and please do not disregard this information simply because

---

sufficient expertise to become fully effective.
[25] My book with the same title was the textbook for this course.

the Old Testament comes out of a foreign culture and from a very ancient time. It will turn out to be relevant in spite of these peculiarities.

"The first thing you need to do is select your text, which may be one suitable for the liturgical season if chosen from a Lectionary. Otherwise you may choose it with a particular pastoral situation in mind. This will be tentative -- and you may decide to discard a text and take another. While you are making your final choice, be sure to note the mood of the passage, whether it is joyful or sorrowful; also its apparent purpose, whether it censures, admonishes, or comforts; also whether it is didactic, narrating, or worshipping. Does your text have a question? Does it give an answer? Does it agree or disagree with other Old Testament passages, and is it traditional or innovative? Are you aware whether it has been used as a messianic passage in the New Testament or as a prooftext for Christian dogma -- and do you think this special choice has been justified?

"Other things to think about before you go to work are whether the various Bibles that you have access to disagree with one another, and if so you should decide whether the differences are simply due to the English style of the translation. It is also important to note whether the passage is in prose or in poetry. Bibles published before the beginning of the twentieth century generally did not scan poetry, and that includes the King James Version; hence you should be following a translation such as the Revised Standard Version. The difference between prose and poetry is the one most important literary fact that you need to take note of. You need to be aware of Hebrew poetry not only because its lyricism is an important exegetical fact, but also because of the prevalence of synonymity as a common element in Hebrew poetry.

"Now you should get out all your resource books. A minister needs good and helpful books on his shelf to tell him what he does not already know, just like a doctor or lawyer. They do not have everything in their heads, nor can you. Be sure to purchase the very best commentaries and other helps available, and then use them intelligently. The scholars who wrote them may be considered as experts, but remember that they are not infallible, that they often disagree with one another on details, and that you need to use your own eyes and apply common sense.

"Before you work on the text as such, it is important to gather information about its background and setting. If your text mentions historical, geographical, archaeological, cultural, or religious details, be sure to use your commentaries to find out what you need to know. Remember that the truth God has given in the Bible is historical, culturally determined, and people-centered.

"Next study the text itself, first the linguistic details, with special attention to the meaning and bearing of crucial words and phrases. Theological ideas and especially traditional concepts that connect this text with others like it will be important. Look for literary and thematic parallels. Try to find out is your text has played an important role in the development of a traditional concept, ideal, or historical figure.

"Now you come to the most important question of all: analyzing the formal structure of the text. This is almost always overlooked, but you must do it because the form and structure are the indispensible clues to the intention and meaning. You must try to find out three things in particular: (1) the boundaries and shape of the literary unit you are working with, (2) evidences of alteration or expansion into a new structure, and (3) the individual intentions both of the original composer and of a disciple-redactor responsible for the expansion, if there was one. There is a whole new discipline that has devised the rules for this called 'form criticism.' Although a knowledge of Hebrew certainly helps in carrying this out, you can do part of it yourself on the basis of the English translation.

"Try to find clear boundaries between your text and its context, then study the internal structure, looking for points of transition, stress and climax. It will be at the climax that the main idea of the passage comes to focus, and it is there that the text addresses us as a word of God rather than in embellishments and incidental elements. Don't ever preach on an embellishment. It is there only as a purely literary feature and has no independent ideational value.

"Another important thing that form criticism aims to accomplish is identifying the genre of the passage and its formal setting. 'Genre' is a French word that we are stuck with because there seems to be no suitable English equivalent. The Germans have 'Gattung,' meaning 'a slot or category into which something fits.' The new commentaries, Old and New Testament, are now paying attention to this because it is the clue you need to the text's intention and therefore its meaning. If your text is prophecy, what genre of prophetic discourse does it display? If the text is narrating, ask which genre of narrative it belongs to, rather than taking it naively as a literal reporting of *actual events. Is it an historical account or chronicle that you are dealing with, or is it an annalistic report? -- then you must assume that it as based on actual facts, depending on the accuracy of the source. Is it an anecdote, a legend, a saga, or even a myth? Incidentally, the Bible lacks any true myth similar to the Flood or Creation myths from Babylonia, but it does contain what I call rebaptized elements of myth, particularly in the fall story in Genesis.*

"Whatever the genre is, identifying it is crucial to how you are going to preach on your text. Once you have done this, you are ready to make an essential comparison, that between the text within the ancient faith community and the text in address to the modern or existential situation of yourself and your social group. That is an enormous gap; but yes, it can be bridged if both ends are firmly anchored. The precise point at which you should anchor the first element is where the original intentionality comes to expression. Who is speaking? Who are the addresses? What does the speaker intend, and what do the hearers wish to hear, or need to hear? What is to be the effect of making this connection -- is it for rebuke or is it for reassurance? You may feel confident that if it is saying something unpleasant or unwelcome to the original addressees, yet remains central to the biblical message in general, divine transcendance is emerging to warn or rebuke the hardhearted and unregarding, while comforting the suffering and the despairing.

"This is very different from what most churchgoers are likely to hear from their preacher. He will either be mouthing moral platitudes or comforting those who are already comfortable. He may be wise, he may be popular, but he is not a spokesman of the divine word if he only tells people what they wish to hear, standing in the way of a transcendent word trying to break through! What he should be is an enabler -- one who helps needy souls to receive God's message.

"You should try to determine where this passage shares common ground in human aspirations and expectations, and then where it surprises, rebukes, or transcends popular ideals and aspirations. Find out what is new here: what in particular does God want us to do or believe? What the text demands of the ancient faith community is likely to be what it demand of your own very modern congregation.

"You are ready to write your sermon when you do one more thing: make it authentically pertinent to your people -- and remember to include yourself. That is where your training in the rest of the seminary curriculum must guide you. Systematic theology helps us formulate the teaching that is based on the Bible and is shaped in the

experience of the church. Church history tells us how believers have exercized their calling in the past and how the church came to be as it is today. Each of the various disciplines within Practical Theology helps you pattern the ancient word to modern needs. Besides, there is your own experience: share it and compare it! Then your bridge will be well anchored on the opposite shore. The bridge reaches from where the ancient people of God stood to where you and your people are today. This is the way to make the Bible come alive!

Edward Meyer, our Professor of Homiletics, joined me in alternate years in putting my worksheet to use in our team-taught course, "Preaching Texts from the Old Testament." The feature that was added for this joint course was the sermon that would be built upon it. At the beginning of the course, each student was to prepare his own best sermon from an assigned text. This would be critiqued and then the worksheet would be assigned. After this was critiqued, the altered, final version of the sermon would follow. Usually the second sermon would be significantly different from the first, and understanding precisely how this came about would secure firmly in the student's mind the vital role of competent exegesis as an antecedent to preaching. Ron Figgins, one of our most confident and articulate students, made the comment at the end of the term, "This course is the cream of the curriculum!"

Robert Tannehill, our New Testament professor, joined me and Ed Meyer in publishing a series of articles based on this methodology for our school journal with the title, "Preparation for Biblical Preaching." These appeared from 1967 to 1972 in the *Journal of the Methodist Theological School in Ohio.* Fourteen texts from the Methodist Lectionary were treated in sequence, seven from the Old Testament and seven from the New Testament. Professor Meyer would write an opening section called "The Preacher Approaches his Text"; Tannehill or I would then respond to -- or better, react to -- this in a new section, "The Preacher Studies his Text"; Meyer would react to this in a concluding section, "The Preacher Develops his Text." This was a very effective way of walking student preachers -- as well as experienced pastors -- through the daunting task of preaching responsibly and respondingly from the Bible. I was and am very proud of this effort, and take satisfaction in knowing that it has blessed many.

This method went against the biblicistic delusion that the historical and literary settings of individual Bible texts are of little consequence. It also went against the practice of using Bible texts as prooftexts for doctrines. These errors block out and nullify the procedures I have advocated and are themselves nullified by them.

The biblical text demands to be heard on its own terms!

My changing relationship to James Muilenburg in the late sixties and early seventies. As I have stated, the year 1965 was a landmark in the shift from a seller's market to a buyer's market with regard to finding jobs for Ph.D.'s. I too experienced it to some degree, and probably was not active enough in trying to adjust for it. It had been my observation that a superior person receiving a doctoral degree from Harvard, Yale, Princeton, Duke, Chicago or Union Theological Seminary/Columbia could count on being well employed following graduation.

That is the way it was with me. Once I got my Th.D. from Union I could be fairly well assured of getting a good teaching job -- in my case, depending on whether I actually wanted it, the main question being, "Did I really want it?" I first of all had to make up my mind whether it would be pulpit or lecturn for me, and it took me some pains to decide this. I then had to find out for quite sure whether I wanted a teaching job in the CRC or not. More and more clearly it became evident that I could not be the biblical scholar I wanted to be and remain even a pastor in the CRC, let alone a seminary professor. But then it was a question whether I could adjust to teaching in a school of more liberal orientation. Drew really wanted me but didn't know it. New Brunswick wanted me but had to hire Virgil Rogers first. Hope wanted me badly, but didn't try very hard to keep me when they had me, and Western Seminary just wasn't ready to offer me a position I could not refuse. Finally I was hirable and I got two offers at the same time. I went to Methesco rather than St. Paul's, and maybe the choice was wrong. Anyhow, it seemed right enough in the early years; but to tell the truth, I never doubted that if Methesco did not suit me, I could soon find another job more fitted to my desire. I especially hoped to have a chance to teach in a graduate school of theology, for I was quite confident, and am confident still, that I had (and have) solid capabilities as a teacher of doctoral students.

There are two reasons why such an opportunity never came to me: (1) just when I got restless, the job market shifted to buyer's; and (2) after 1963, when Muilenburg retired from Union and went off to San Anselmo, he no longer had his fingers in the beehive. News of jobs here and there would come to him, but as a rule it was his colleagues and successors at Union who were involved in promoting the interests of the Union doctors. Many who had relied on Muilenburg's superb judgment in the past continued to consult him, but the power he had enjoyed was gone. I found myself inquiring about job possibilities in the late sixties, but what I mainly consulted him about was my publishing projects and scholarship applications. In the seventies, when Dr. Muilenburg had moved to Claremont to retire, he could do little more of this kind of service to his former students because of the increasing debilitation that was wrought by Parkinson's.

Following 1969 there was another important factor: the restructuring of the Society of Biblical Literature, inside and out. New leaders took the important jobs, such as President and Editor, out of the hands of the veterans. Whole new empires of patronage were erected. I was not part of this restructuring, and without the gigantic figure of James Muilenburg to stand behind me, I became gradually isolated and may even have been viewed by some as somewhat eccentric -- doing my own thing, and I think doing it well, but having little connection with the new mainstream of popular activity.

To some extent, much the same thing was happening with regard to my political position on the Methesco faculty. I was pretty much allowed to work at what I wished, but was given little help and encouragement, particularly by my Old Testament colleague, who never in the 30 years I was at Methesco said one appreciative word to me for what I achieved -- not for my several books, and not even for the one that had been inscribed for him, *Prophet Against Prophet*, which was published in 1978.

I dedicated my first book, *Bible and Theology in The Netherlands*, to James Muilenburg in the following words: "To him among my teachers who has taught me best to know and love the Scriptures." He was profuse in his praise of this book and of all the others that he lived to see.

I continued until the end of his life to share my thoughts and aspirations with Professor Muilenburg. I would tell him everything about my professional life. One thing I complained to him about was a low level of concern at Methesco for the serious scientific study of Hebrew and Old Testament criticism. My colleague did not help counteract this general deterioration; instead he used the Old Testament almost entirely for civil rights sloganeering. This is how I wrote to Muilenburg about how I was dealing with this situation:

I am discovering some potentialities within myself, and developing much interaction, doing original research in the area of Pentateuchal tradition criticism....My present position provides many satisfactions, as well as many valuable kinds of stimulation to excellence...but as I grow increasingly devoted to original research I become more vexed by our limitations...as well as by the heavy emphasis upon the "practical" concerns of the ministry. My feeling toward this latter is ambivalent....I am very much concerned about teaching for practical consumption, yet there is a real danger in our situation that research may be forced to give way to the urgent needs of the day." (My letter of October 30, 1966)

I also wrote to him about my recognition that Methesco was developing in a direction contrary to my gifts and interests:

I have been grateful for the opportunity to teach here in Delaware. The reasons I have previously explained, so they need not be rehearsed to you here. One of these reasons was the relief of getting free from the shackles of an oppressive orthodoxy. I have flourished in a climate of free theological discussion; I have not only survived in it but have learned to contribute creatively to it from my own essentially unaltered central commitment. Now, however, this school is starting to settle down upon a particular theological "line," and to commit itself increasingly to uncontrolled experimentism and shallow activism. Bogard Dunn, our dean, has always seemed a sensible man, but he now appears unable to control the increasingly dominant group who are leading the school in this direction. Methodistic subjectivism and activism are proving more and more irresistible in the development of this institution, in spite of some of our grandiose hopes to the contrary. So I think it inevitable that it will soon become nothing but another second- or third-rate trade school, incapable of gaining high academic standing. This is all the more tragic in view of the opportunity that has arisen in the closing-down of Oberlin and (soon) of Bexley Hall; with the right leadership we might have moved ahead to fulfill the role of significant theological leadership in this state. We do, of course, have some very good people teaching with us, but these will leave, I have no doubt. Already the "solid" people on our faculty are finding themselves effectively neutralized or isolated, i.e., put out of positions where their influence can count in holding back this trend to mediocrity and theological frivolity. (My letter of April 24, 1967)

Muilenburg could offer me little else than praise and admiration, and he did this generously, while deploring the situation I described:

> Your literary output is remarkable, and it is as good in quality as it is in quantity, which is considerable. You are to be congratulated, and I do so with pride. I have pondered long upon the matter you raise concerning your professional future for several reasons: in the first place, I am always interested in your own career and am concerned that you should be in a climate that is conducive to the scholary pursuit; and in the second place, the situation you describe is by no means unique in theological education today, and it causes me no little disquiet. I fear I belong to another age, not only in time but in way of thinking and living. I often say that I can make nothing of it....It is clear that you find yourself in much the same situation as I find myself, and precisely for that reason I fear that I cannot be of much help. The only ray of light is the new interest in religion in colleges and especially universities. Ironical as it may seem, I think you might find a university post congenial to your scholarly proclivities, but I would not know how to go about establishing the right contacts. (Letter from James Muilenburg, May 8, 1967)

Muilenburg was of course delighted to receive my book, *Bible and Theology in The Netherlands*, which was ready in the spring of 1968, and in which he was able to take a special interest on account of his own Netherlands heritage. He flattered me with language such as the following: "You are one of the most productive of all the students who have taken their doctor's degrees under me and your articles are all stamped with competence. I am always gratified by your wide-ranging interest and by the diversity of subjects with which you deal."[26]

Eventually Dr. Muilenburg found himself promoting my interests in the possibility of an appointment at one of the schools belonging to the Graduate Theological Union in the Bay area, as well as in encouraging my involvement in the form-criticism project headed by Professor Rolf Knierim of Claremont:

> It was a delight to see you in Berkeley....I wish very much that we might get you here on the Pacific coast, especially in the Graduate Theological Union, which would profit much from your presence. I cannot go into this in writing for certain reasons, but I want you to know that I am deeply interested in the future of your scholarly career. It was gratifying to see you in the group that met at the Claspers. As you are perhaps aware, many of the men who were there are associated with the form-critical project headed by Rolf Knierim and Gene Tucker. Together with

---

[26] Letter from Muilenburg dated May 16, 1968

several other scholars (most of them German) I am serving as counsellor to the group.

I appreciate more than I can well say your generous words, Simon. I can only reply in all honesty that the greatest reward a teacher can have is his students, and this applies to you a fortiori. I am proud of your achievements; indeed, there are few of my students who have been more productive than you. (Letter from Muilenburg dated January 27, 1969)

Dr. Muilenburg did not make it to the 1969 meeting of the Society of Biblical Literature, which was held in Toronto. I sent him a lengthy letter on Nov. 11, 1969 informing him of the events that had effectively restructured this society and the teaching of religion in North America. I thought it especially important to tell him of an address by Claude Welch in which he informed biblical scholars that they would henceforth have a very minimal role to play in the professional study of religion -- a prognostication that has been especially fulfilled in the activities of the sister society, the American Academy of Religion, in which the Bible presently plays almost no role whatever.

One may be sure that, were Muilenburg still a young man, he would have found an effective way of becoming involved in these new structures and programs. To my letter, he replied at length with regard to my own professional position:

As to your own particular locus in the SBL, I think you have already received some recognition. I was much pleased to have you with the form-critical group at Dr. Clasper's home last year. You did indeed deserve that distinction, but the fact is that you were invited by persons who know what they are doing. I hope very much that you can continue as a regular member, and I gather from what you say that this is a possibility....Your reviews in periodicals call attention to your presence in the scholarly community as well as to your competence. One avenue of considerable importance...is by way of Union Seminary where your dossier speaks eloquently of the high estimate in which you are held by your teachers and others. We shall have to reconcile ourselves to the fact that Harvard is pretty much in the saddle these days; to many administrators the name is magic. Moreover, it does have a first-rate faculty in biblical and Near Eastern studies. There is a large number of graduate students there now, and they are of high quality, I understand....Yet, having said this, let me add that even Harvard has found it difficult to place its men. I have been told more than once that some college presidents prefer to have men who have received the kind of training you had at Union and Columbia. That is, they are not content with having as members of their faculty persons whose work has been almost exclusively linguistic and archaeological. (Letter from James Muilenburg dated December 1, 1969)

Once he moved to Pilgrim Place, Muilenburg's letters began to fall off. He was not privileged to enjoy his retirement because of the onset of a debilitating disease. He was unable to keep working at what was to be his *magnum opus*, a definitive commentary on the book of Jeremiah. At first he complained only of loss of memory and mental acuity, but ere long it was diagnosed as Parkinson's disease. He passed away in the spring of 1974.

A devil in my paradise. As I have mentioned, my first decade at Methesco was wonderful, but the two following decades were of mixed quality. During the seventies I became progressively sicker, and it took the entire decade of the eighties, and more, for me to recover.

On the road to recovery I tried with the aid of my therapist to review the events of my stressful life in order to identify the factor or factors that had contributed towards making me sick. For a long time this was a confusing task, but I am now quite certain what it was. To start, there was my genetic heritage. My dear mother was hospitalized four times with severe unipolar depression, so how could I have expected to escape it? I am not fooled by the name, "nervous breakdown," nor am I persuaded by my father's unwavering assurance that it all began with the 1918 flu epidemic. In the light of what I have learned, clinical depression is certainly what my mother had. She had it, her sister had it, several of her brothers had it, my elder brother has had it. Who knows about Mom's parents and more remote ancestors such as the poor hunchback great grandmother in the rainbarrel?

Even with a bad gene, however, one may escape severe illness if there is no crisis to precipitate it. I am certain now that the precipitating cause was not Dad's censure, much as it hurt to be the recipient of it. Why couldn't Dad understand? I loved him and wanted to be loved by him. I wanted him to approve of my hard choices and praise my integrity. But his refusal and inadequacy were not what brought on my crisis. I could handle Dad's anger and disapproval. I could handle them because I knew why Dad was so censorious and why he could not comprehend the nature of the transformation that had occurred in my thinking. Bright as he was, he had been poorly schooled. He knew very little about alternative ways of doing Christian theology, and he had all the intolerance of a cornered animal. By understanding why he acted as he did, I was able to rise above his anger. A further gratification was the realization that my independence and my integrity were exactly his own most prominent virtues. He had taught them to me and I was only being like him!

Early on, I could be surprised when Christian people did outrageous things to me. I was surprised when my grandmother and her super-pious neighbors censured my fisticuffs in protection of my fiancée from insult, acting because honor counted more than a goody-boy image. I was surprised and angry when the CRC home-missions committee refused to consider my very reasonable request for a summer assignment more convenient to myself and my young family. I was both angry and surprised at President Volbeda's willingness to sacrifice his own dignity and his complete lack of respect for me.

Eventually I could hardly be surprised anymore, but it could still hurt. I was grieved but not surprised to find so little regard in my own denomination for my high achievement of obtaining a Union doctorate and securing a teaching job in a reputable seminary. I could hardly believe -- though I was not surprised by -- my seminary faculty's craven falsification of the outcome of an interview I had not requested. I was not surprised that the matter of my article on "Recovering a Historical Revelation" should elicit opposition -- but certainly at the Synod's unseemly haste and disregard of their own rules in a ludicrous effort to mow me down. I deplored all these insults and injuries when they were given, and I deplore them still.

I could go on. I was grieved but not surprised at being lied to at Drew. I was grieved at the unfeeling blundering of the New Brunswick president. Things like this should not happen among Christians. But it was not these things that brought on my depression. They only toughened me and actually helped clarify my thinking. They left scars and callouses rather than unhealing wounds.

I was all in all a pretty tough hombre, and no weakling. There was only one way to crush my spirit completely, and that was to prevent me from fulfilling my quest for self-understanding and fulfilment. What a grand disillusion it was to find my place of refuge to be a place of discomfort and frustration! Here was the seminary post I had been waiting for, the school where I expected to find my every gift affirmed and my long course of training justified.

My self-esteem collapsed when I recognized that I was being systematically denied the opportunity to bring my "gifts and graces" to full employment in the teaching program of Methesco because of the infantile envy of a paranoid colleague, in deference to whom my other colleagues were willing to yield because of his reputation as a "hero" of the civil-rights movement. I, on the other hand, was treated as though I had nothing special to offer our students. My military service and my eleven years of pastoral ministry apparently counted for nothing.

When this discrimination was tolerated by those who had the power and responsibility to stop it, I realized that I had been brought to Methesco only to serve as a kind of ornament to adorn the new school's image. *Imagine, a new professor who is already a creative and published scholar!* But the more I actually came to live up to this praise and the more competent I proved myself to be, the more worried my colleague in Old Testament became about preserving his popularity with faculty and students. Thus I found myself in a no-win situation, and I could do little about it. Because I was so good -- not because I was so poor -- he didn't want the students to have me as their teacher.

I too desired to be popular with faculty and students and I was -- to the extent I was allowed to be. How badly I needed to be loved and accepted! But my colleague could not respect my needs or honor my merits. He only thought of how lovely it was for him to be able to dominate the faculty and be adored by the student body and the alumni.

* * *

ALLOW ME TO EXPLAIN precisely how this came about. During the first years, our school was on the semester calendar. All the entering students -- Juniors as they were called -- were required to spend their first semester in Old Testament Introduction and their second semester in New Testament Introduction. My colleague and I alternated, year by year, with this assignment. The result was that we had commensurate access to the student body and thus equal opportunity to influence their choice of further courses. After a few years, however, the faculty made three decisions that gave my colleague an opportunity to put me into a position in which I would rarely become the teacher of incoming students. The first decision was to go onto a three-quarter system in order to make it possible for Ohio State students to enroll for our courses, and *vice versa*, but few students from Ohio State actually enrolled in our courses while few of our students took courses at Ohio State. The second decision was to enter into a joint program with two other seminaries in the Columbus area, the Pontifical College Josephinum and Trinity Lutheran Seminary. *Ecumenism -- how marvelous it is!* The third and most fateful decision was to allow the second part of the required introductory course in Old Testament to be taken either at Josephinum or Trinity. My colleague saw this as an opportunity to persuade almost every entering Junior to go directly from his own first-quarter course (he of course always insisted on being first) to a follow-up course at either of these schools, bypassing me. Since most were attracted to this arrangment, they took advantage of it. I had sound grounds for opposing it, especially because there would be no written tests or examinations, and protested to the faculty that it was poor educational policy to allow it. I ended up having only a few Methesco students in my second-quarter course, and eventually only a very few hardy survivors in my elective courses that were designed to follow the two introductory courses in Old Testament.

As one would understand, I resented and deplored this. One remedy that I tried was persuading the faculty not to allow the second course to be offered off campus. They refused. The other remedy that I tried was to confront my colleague, the dean, and the faculty with a plan of my own for a schedule of courses that would remove the inequity and give me the equal access that I deserved. I wrote this up and sent it to my colleague, but he disdained to respond. I then sent it to the dean, but he didn't want to get involved. That did it! I had no recourse. There was no way out. I had no option but to back down.

For a whole year I was in a blind fog of fury. I could no longer speak to my colleague or to the dean. Eventually I discerned that this anger was consuming me and I decided to try the tactic of overwhelming my colleague with goodwill. I dedicated a book to him -- which he ignored. My wife and I went to dinner with him and his wife on a weekly schedule. Nothing helped relieve me of the deep sense of inferiority that resulted from this demeaning, futile effort. That is why I descended the slippery path into my private hell!

When I was taken to the mental health center of Riverside Methodist Hospital in Columbus on a Saturday in late February, 1981, I had all the classic symptoms of major clinical depression, but didn't know it. I did not know what depression was even when I had it. How astounding that I, an experienced pastor and teacher, did not recognize what I had! But even that is not as astonishing as the fact that my family doctor could neither recognize it nor treat it. Time and again I complained of my symptoms, but he just urged me to ride my bike and take some valium. If I had only known what was really wrong with me, I might have been able to do something to avoid a great deal of suffering and psychological hurt, both to others and to myself.

I had had this a long time before it reached a crisis. On my sabbatical in 1973 I accomplished nothing. Becoming a victim of physical abuse in 1977 and going to trial against my assailant in 1979 turned out to be extremely destructive of my mental stability. Although I was able to hold class to the very last, during the years 1978 to 1981 I wrote virtually nothing. I could no longer pray and hated God![27]

I was confused, I had no energy to face even minor problems, I had a poor appetite and low self-esteem, I was inclined to break out in anger at any moment. My most alarming symptom was my self-destructiveness. I thought constantly of taking my life, even while my mind remained keen enough to remind me that if I did this, I could not afford to botch it and leave my wife with a permanent invalid on her hands.

With a rush I was swept into madness. It came on slyly and suddenly. During December of 1980, while on a short study leave at Claremont Graduate School, I had been restless and confused, again accomplishing nothing. The day after flying home to Ohio, I kept an appointment with my ear specialist. After he checked me out, he informed me that I had rather severe hearing loss, especially for upper-frequency sounds essential to understanding speech. "Perhaps you received severe damage years ago, and only now are noticing its effect." From all the firing while in the Marines, I would suppose! But then he asked the same question he must have asked of innumerable patients with symptoms like mine, "And do you have any ringing in your ears?" "You don't? That's odd. Almost everyone with upper-frequency hearing loss has tinnitis."

"Do I have any ringing in my ears -- what he calls tinnitis?" No, none at all. I drive home to Delaware and inform Betty of this strange and disturbing question. She does not know what to make of it. "Anyway, it is lucky you don't have any," she remarks, and I suppose she is right, I'm just lucky. "But I certainly don't feel lucky." Very tired, I go to bed and to sleep, but awaken with a start in the middle of the night from a horrifying noise in my ears. The prophecy has given rise to its fulfilment. I do have tinnitis! Hurrying back next day to my doctor, I report this alarming condition and in desperation appeal for a remedy. When I am informed that I very

---

[27] On the other hand, from the very first day of my hospitalization I saw myself as brought from the dead and knew I would get better. That is when I personally and dramatically experienced what it is to be "born again!"

likely will have to cope with this ringing permanently, I am filled with shock and horror. The doctor doesn't seem to take it very seriously and I cannot understand why. He does not seem to understand what is happening inside my brain. He has in fact actually produced this ringing by inquiring whether I had it, but has no awareness of what it is doing to me!

What was actually happening was that a very deep and severe depression had seized me and, among other horrors, was aggravating the effect of an otherwise unpleasant but manageable trauma to my auditory organ. The more noise in my head, the more I worried. The more I worried, the louder the noise became. Now I was exploring in earnest for a way of putting an end to my suffering.

I awaken in the night with the cry, "O God, why are you making me suffer like this? My head is throbbing and ready to burst!"

Jeff Hopper was on the phone. "Simon," he said, "I have some very sad news. Ron Williams just died of heart failure." I could not say anything but "thanks for calling!" I was paralyzed. A cannonball had just been shot through my stomach. I couldn't go to the funeral for fear that I would break down completely. Ron was only forty years old.

"John dear, you must always remember to be humble!" "Yes, Mom. Is this humble enough?"

At last I could no longer sleep. I became so weak and confused that one morning I collapsed in a main corridor at the seminary. After another terrible night, during which the dean and our professor of pastoral care tried to help Betty decide what should be done, she and our president brought me to Riverside Hospital.

* * *

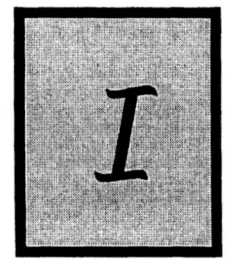

I have been left all alone in a dark and frightening place. A "man" seizes hold of me and wrestles with me all night, until the breaking of the day. When the "man" perceives that he cannot prevail against me, he touches the hollow of my thigh and puts it out of joint. I won't let go of him, so he begs, "Let me go, for the day is breaking." But I reply, "I will not let you go, unless you bless me." To this he says, "I won't change your name; maybe it's Simon and maybe it's John, but either way, you have striven with God and with men, and have prevailed." When I say, "Tell me please what your name is," he replies, "Why is it that you ask my name -- don't you already know?" With this reply he departs, leaving his blessing upon me. I call this "My Peniel," for I too have seen God face to face, and yet my life is preserved." As the sun rises upon me I pass Peniel, limping because of my thigh.

7
A Commission Fulfilled

THE BATTERED OLD WARRIOR is now more wizened and grizzled, but he has survived and is doing well. There are new rips and dents in his armor, and he has wounds and bruises that he will feel until he dies. He now knows that even in Elysium, there are pitfalls set to bring one down and enemies posing as friends. But he continues to hold his head high. The glory of hard-won victories cannot be taken from him.

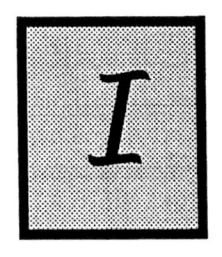

I reach the true goal of my quest: being scientifically as well as theologically honest about Holy Scripture. My colleagues at Methesco continued to call me their "grand master" and were proud when young scholars being interviewed for teaching positions would brighten with recognition when they heard that I was teaching there. "Oh yes, I certainly do recognize the name of Simon De Vries. He is known all over as a fine scholar. It would be a privilege to be able to teach with him!" At Methesco I was no longer in peril because of my theological beliefs since the freedom claimed by all others guaranteed my own. I had been rescued from dogmatic orthodoxy and was safe from ever again being scorned as a heretic on the issue of biblical inerrancy. What I was nevertheless unprepared for -- in spite of my cautionary experience at Drew -- was the politicking that seemed to go on perpetually wherever Methodist scholars and clerics were gathered to do the Lord's business. I had no comprehension of it and no preparation against it. If I had only been exempted from my poor mother's bad gene, I might have coped with these problems in some effective way, learning to defend against them if not to master them. Instead, they lurked as unseen roots to trip my unwary feet and throw me to the ground.

To be sure, I do not intend to blame Methodists alone for this. The Presbyterians and adherents of all denominations -- clergy and lay -- are often obsessed with power. Even the Christian Reformed leaders with whom I had to deal had a passion for controlling other believers in their fellowship, doing this in the enforcement of what they considered right doctrine as well as in their enforcement of what they considered to be pious living. The obsession with *institutional power* is the perpetual bugaboo of all free-thinking, self-directed (or divinely directed) spirits in their midst.

As I have said, it grieved me deeply to lose my rightful and appropriate access to the students at Methesco. For a while I enjoyed this access, but it was purloined from me. Someone was jealous of my talents and popularity. Someone did not want the Methesco students to take my courses -- not because I was an inferior teacher, but because I was superior. Someone knew how to corrupt the decision-making processes so as to assure him power and popularity among the students and alumni, leaving me with scraps. It was more important to the school to accommodate this narcissistic and ambitious man than to assure that my gifts and talents should be equally accessible to all who came to study at our school.

In the final analysis, however, it has to be taken into account that what I was striving for was not popularity among our students and alumni, not even power in the academic community, but what I had claimed as my goal and guideline ever since I first knew James Muilenburg at Union back in 1949-50: the power and the opportunity to be truly "honest." The touchstone of my career has been that word *honest*. "Simon, I now realize that you intend to be entirely honest," he said, setting the course of my entire career as a minister, teacher and scholar.

I realize that, since being "honest" as Muilenburg meant it became the goal that first set me on a true course, I should not now grumble if certain other professional rewards have eluded me. I also realize that Muilenurg was not raising a question about my personal integrity: fairness, openness, judiciousness, commitment to duty, and the like. *He was raising the question of my willingness to be honest about the Bible!*

I had just written a paper for him in one of his courses in Old Testament exegesis, and he liked what he saw. He had been very much concerned about my intentions since I first showed up in his course. Would I behave like the typical fundamentalistic biblicist that one might expect from Calvin Seminary? Would I contrive a way of sidestepping the evidence of the biblical text assigned to me? No, he was gratified to find that I possessed the rudiments of *professional honesty*. He saw no tendency to propogandize, manage, sidestep, or put "spin" on the biblical text. He recognized that I was willing to take it straight -- even when I might do so with fear and trembling. That is what he meant when he said I was "honest." I knew it; and ever since I first accepted this as the hallmark of my ministry and my scholarship, that is what I have intended to strive for and be worthy of.

Always to be honest when I am handling the precious Word of God. Honest to the plain meaning and intent of a competently studied and scientifically analyzed Holy Scripture.

My work on the Bible during my Calvin Seminary days -- before I had come to Union -- had left me both confused and suspicious. I left at the end of three years with the feeling that I had been cheated in ways I did not thoroughly understand. I tried to rationalize this, preferring to believe that my professors had simply been incompetent, rather than conclude that they were practicing a deliberate policy of blinding and bewildering their students when scriptural issues arose. My disappointment was a source of frustration to me, for I had grown up from childhood loving the Holy Scriptures and devoutly desiring to understand them better. I had learned Greek and I had learned Hebrew, but I had not learned nearly enough about the Old Testament or the New Testament written in those languages. I felt anxiety deep in my gut about the prospect of trying to share what I had learned about biblical interpretation with future parishioners because I realized that what I had been taught could not be right. What would be more wrong in my ministry than that? I had been left in the lurch with regard to the solemn yet glorious task of sharing the Bible with others! I had been told wrong and would not know how to tell others what was right.

This explains why I reacted as I did to Professor Muilenburg's word to me on the occasion I refer to. A door had been opened in my mind and heart, and could not be shut again. I would be *honest to the Bible,* no matter what!

Honest to God means honest to God's word in Scripture!

During the closing years of my pastoral ministry I came to be viewed with alarm and suspicion by many in the CRC simply because they could not appreciate that I had received a genuine conversion experience on this issue. I was now under a stronger call from God than ever. Now my openness to God was to be judged by my openness to the scientific study of Scripture. I felt a strong sense of duty and knew that I had to obey.

All right -- so I will have to give up trying to be a pastor in the denomination in which I have been ordained. I will kiss goodbye to any prospect of teaching at Calvin College or Calvin Seminary. There will be dear ones and friends who will not understand and will be grieved -- my dear parents in particular. Their esteem and confidence I may have to leave behind.

But the intent to be open and honest was not enough. I needed to learn how to use that honesty and that openness in an effective and professional way, and to apply this to the critical study of the Bible. That is where the help of my teachers at Union became crucial to me. James Muilenburg and Samuel Terrien in particular proved to be superlative teachers and enthusiastic advocates of the Bible's message, historically understood. They and others were able to communicate their enthusiasm to me and furnish me with the know-how I needed. There was surely divine leading in this, but this demanded my own response to that leading If I had not seized the opportunity that presented itself to go to Union Seminary in the summer of 1949, I would never have met these superb teachers. I was convinced then, and I am convinced still, that God had moved me to go to that school and at that time so that I might fall under the influence and guidance of talented and dedicated men who had been where I then found myself. I did respond, bringing with me the native capacities that God had bestowed upon me. My teachers at Union skilfully and effectively nurtured them in order to make of me a thoroughly competent scholar in the sacred task of handling the holy word of God in Scripture. Let me add that if I had never become a professor and even if I had never left the Christian Reformed ministry, my entire outlook would have remained permanently shaped by what these teachers taught me.

In the course of the events previously narrated, I eventually became a member of a theological school faculty in which I was given broad opportunities to do the imaginative exploring that became the hallmark of my Old Testament scholarship. The results may be seen in a lengthy list of scholarly articles and books bearing my name. Some of these writings were developed out of lecture courses offered the students at Methesco, for there was an intimate interrelationship between my lectures and my scholarly investigations. Methesco students were able to carry helpful insights derived from me into the parish ministry. But I went beyond the restrictions of parish practicability wherever new light from Scripture led the way. Often one new discovery would lead to other delightful new findings, opening up new vistas as in undiscovered passages in an underground cavern.

Some will say that I have been too scholarly -- more scholarly than one needs to be as a pastor and preacher, but I deny this. No matter how arcane some of my researches may have seemed, the person who I was as I did my research and writing was in a fundamental way the same devout student I had previously been, the same enthusiastic minister of the divine Word, the same eager teacher of budding ministers.

My mature self-understanding. Now in my latter years, I define myself essentially as a Netherlands humanist in the style of Thomas à Kempis and Desiderius Erasmus, rooted and nurtured in American Protestant culture. Like Thomas I find the core of vital religion in a close walk with God, and like Erasmus I enthusiastically embrace my tradition while subjecting it to rigorous rational scrutiny. Like them, I am uneasy with every form of scholasticism, ancient, medieval, or modern. I might wish to be able to say that I am also like Martin Luther and John Calvin, but while I take many things from these reformers, I do not look to them for models of how biblical religion ought to be lived out in contemporary religious experience. The most essential thing I have taken from Calvin is his insistence that the Old Testament is equally part of God's Word with the New Testament. He was right about that, but he stumbled in subjecting everything Hebraic under the rubric of Christology. I maintain that the essence of biblical religion is already full-formed in the Old Testament. Judaism and Christianity have each their peculiar tradition of interpreting this, but for me it is fully rich and satisfying all in itself. What the New Testament has added is its model of a God-man in an eschatological age, and for me that is pedagogically and liturgically meaningful, but does not constitute the essence of biblical piety.

What the acceptance of the Old Testament on an equal footing has done for people of my Reformed and Protestant heritage is keeping the Old Testament open and viable as a potent though often neglected source for contemporary spirituality. Would that the leaders of the denomination I served so long would actually allow the Old Testament to become open and viable for them, not in lip service but in actuality, if only to save themselves from complete capitulation to

Fundamentalism, which appears to be the only alternative! A grim prospect confronting us at the commencement of a new century and millenium is that know-nothing Fundamentalism is sweeping all that is broad and deep in religion from the scene.

I continue to feel a strong attraction to the religion of my childhood, but am thankful that I have progressed beyond it. For instance, the old Dutch Calvinists went rather far -- but essentially they were on the right track -- in sticking to the Psalms for their singing. In their deepest spirituality they used these as a means of associating themselves with David, if not with Moses, gladly speaking to God and praising him in the words of the psalms of Israel. The monks in their cloisters, chanting these same psalms, also knew this spirituality. This practice has died out many decades past among most Dutch immigrants in America and is fading away in the Netherlands as well, but as I view the widespread degradation of church music across the spectrum of contemporary Protestantism, I experience a longing for some of its profound spirituality.

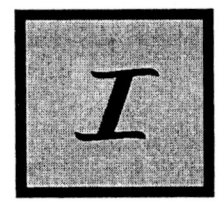

In concluding my pilgrim's account, I appropriate laden words from the Psalms that describe me and my pilgrimage. Every word, every phrase, seems to be speaking directly of me while epitomizing my life before God.

> **One thing have I asked of Yahweh, that will I seek after,**
> **that I might dwell in the house of Yahweh all the days of my life,**
> **to behold the beauty of Yahweh and inquire in his temple.**
> ....
> **Teach me thy way, O Yahweh, and lead me on a level path because of my enemies.**
> **Give me not up to the will of my adversaries,**
> **for false witnesses have risen against me and they breathe out violence.**
>
> **Hear a just cause, O Yahweh, attend to my cry,**
> **give ear to my prayer coming from lips free of deceit!**
> **From thee let my vindication come, let my eyes see the right!**

If thou triest my heart, if thou visitest me by night,
if thou testest me, thou wilt find no wickedness in me,
my mouth does not transgress.

With regard to the works of men, by the word of thy lips
I have avoided the ways of the violent.
My steps have held fast to thy paths, my feet have not
slipped.

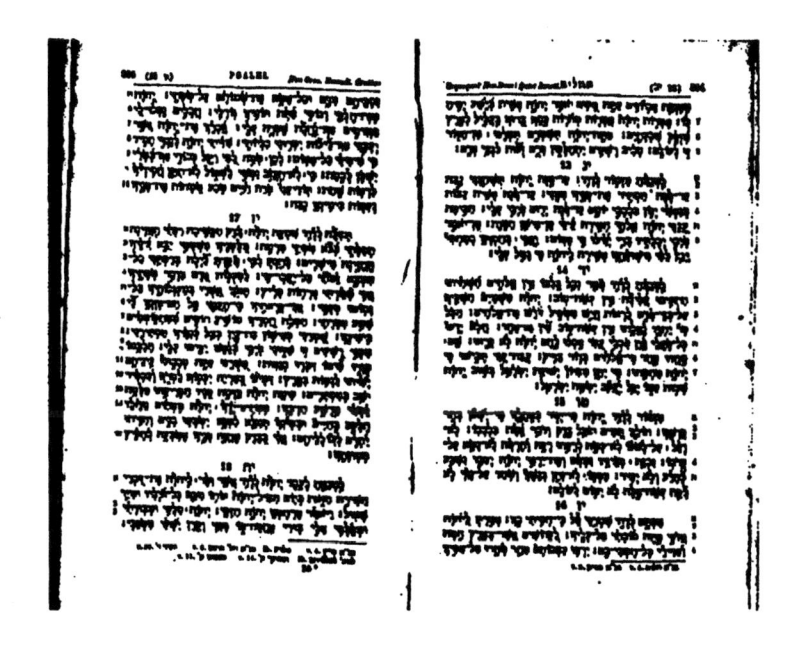

I call upon thee, for thou wilt answer me, O God;
Incline thine ear to me, hear my words.
Wondrously show thy steadfast love.

O Savior of those who seek refuge
from their adversaries at thy right hand,
Keep me as the apple of the eye,
hide me in the shadow of thy wings.

I shall behold thy face in righteousness;
   When I awake, I shall be satisfied with beholding thy form.
. . . .
I believe that I shall see the goodness of Yahweh in the land of the living![1]

---

[1]Rearranged from Psa 17:1-7, 14-15, 27:4, 11-13

APPENDIX
Some fruits of my biblical interpretation
1. Studies in exegesis, criticism and methology
1. "The Hexateuchal Criticism of Abraham Kuenen," *Journal of Biblical Literature*, 82 (1963) 31-57; **2.** *Bible and Theology in The Netherlands. Dutch Old Testament Criticism under Modernist and Conservative Auspices, 1850 to World War I*, Wageninen: Veenman, 1968; second edition with new Preface, New York: Peter Lang, 1989; **3.** "A Review of Recent Research in the Tradition History of the Pentateuch," *Society of Biblical Literature 1987 Seminar Papers*, pp. 459-502; **4.** "Kuenen's Pentateuchal Research in Comparison with Recent Pentateuchal Studies in North America," P. B. Dirksen and A. van der Kooij, eds., *Abraham Kuenen (1928-1891). His Major Contribution to the Study of the Old Testament (etc.)* [Oudtestamentische Studien 29, Leiden: Brill, 1993], pp. 128-47

Only those having diligence and discretion in asking appropriate questions of the biblical text -- and at the same time the humility to wait patiently for an unfolding of the Scripture's own answers -- can rightly discern what the biblical text means. The fact is that God's self revelation in the Bible comes in bits and pieces -- never totally or massively. Just as fragments of evidence for God's "general" revelation lie everywhere in nature, evidences for his special revelation in Scripture lie near at hand throughout this ancient book, but the right methods must be used for unlocking these bits of evidence just as much as in natural science. My methods might seem less attractive than the popular procedure of "dumbing" the text down to the lowest common denominator -- one size for all -- but to do less renders one insensitive to God's voice in Scripture.

While unfolding the layers of tradition history and the stages of literary development underlying the canonical text, I have worked along the lines of the researcher in the natural sciences, searching for clues and establishing hypotheses on the way to a better understanding of how the biblical text came to be as it is. What I do is scientific, but there is art, feeling, even reverence in it. In my hands the text of sacred Scripture is not treated as something cold or uninvolving. On the contrary, biblical criticism and exegesis include a warm involvement in the search as well as a passion for the outcome. That is because the object of this search -- the Bible -- is itself warm and passionate!

World-respected scholars such as Muilenburg and Terrien have taught me this. Unfortunately this methodology is no longer as securely dominant as it was when I was striving to come to terms with it as the answer to the fundamentalism of my early years. A deconstructuralism has emerged in recent years that pretends to be more advanced than the scientific criticism I have been taught, yet this is suspect for the fact that it occupies much the same ground as the naive fundamentalism of the past in its claim that nothing matters except the final form of the text. Nothing else matters, it claims, because we cannot actually know enough about the prehistory of the text to gain any certainty about it. This destroys the main achievement of my entire life -- understanding and responding to the *historical revelation* that has produced the Bible. If we give up believing that the Bible is a historical book, we will give up believing that it is revelation. I have advocated this concept at great peril to myself and will not allow it to be cashiered or jettisoned. If we have no sense of how the Bible came into its present form, it stands open to the most fanciful interpretations and becomes vulnerable to serious misuse.

It is normal for young scholars to continue writing and doing research on the particular passage(s) or special problem(s) treated in their dissertation, thus becoming experts of a sort in the narrow field of their concentration. But my topic did not lend itself to further scrutiny of that kind. It was comprehensive and complete in itself. I was nevertheless determined to publish the results of my dissertation in a form accessible to non-specialists because it offered a model of how biblical criticism ought to be done. My 1963 article on Abraham Kuenen's Hexateuchal criticism (1) made a strong impression and has been recognized as a classic statement in the history of the discipline. Here I had my earliest opportunity to publicize some of the otherwise inaccessible information from my doctoral dissertation that was of special interest for biblical scholars. Morton S. Enslin, editor of the *Journal of Biblical Exegesis,* commented that he regarded it as a model of what such an article should be: thorough, fair, significant.

While in Tübingen, Germany, on my first sabbatical from Methesco, I prepared a more complete account of Kuenen and his times in my first published book, *Bible and Theology in The Netherlands* (2), having arranged both for an English and an American publisher to share presenting it to the reading public. This was to some extent a rewrite of my dissertation, but with drastic modifications in the service of readability. At the end of the book I was in a position to summarize the numerous individual ways in which the theological developments I had studied led to an improved state of scholarship within the biblical field. One major development that I predicted has in fact taken place -- the general acceptance of a reverent biblical criticism among scholars of the Dutch Calvinist revival and in the Dutch Catholic Church.

In my participation in a Seminar on the Pentateuch under the auspices of the Society of Biblical Literature, I prepared an exhaustive survey of scholarly writing on Pentateuch narrative texts and forms to serve as a basis for the work of the seminar (3). Upon the centennial of Kuenen's death a memorial volume was published in Leiden containing my comparison of Kuenen's methodology with that of two contemporary North American scholars, George Coats and John Van Seters (4). Although my concern for good methodology goes far beyond the issues opened in my dissertation, these writings have done an important service in putting Dutch Old

Testament criticism in its proper place of importance within the framework of world scholarship.

2. Studies on individual passages, linguistic questions, and literary phenomena
1. "Remembrance in Ezekiel. A Study of an Old Testament Theme," *Interpretation*, 16 (1962), 58-64; **2.** "Consecutive Constructions in the 1Q Sectarian Scrolls," T. Naamani et. al., eds., *Doron. Hebraic Studies* [Festschrift for A. I. Katsch], New York: National Association of Professors of Hebrew, 1965, pp. 75-87; **3.** "Note Concerning the Fear of God in the Qumran Scrolls," *Revue de Qumran*, 18 (1965), 233-37; **4.** "The Syntax of Tenses and Interpretation in the Hodayoth," *Revue de Qumran*, 19 (1965), pp. 375-414; **5.** "The Acrostic of Nahum in the Jerusalem Liturgy," *Vetus Testmentum*, 16 (1966), 476-81; **6.** "The Origin of the Murmuring Tradition," *Journal of Biblical Literature*, 87 (1968), 51-58; **7.** "The Book of Nahum," "The Book of Habakkuk," "The Book of Zephaniah," C. M. Laymon, ed., *Interpreters One-Volume Commentary on the Bible* (New York-Nashville: Abingdon, 1971), pp. 491-500; **8.** "David's Victory over the Philistine as Saga and as Legend," *Journal of Biblical Literature*, 92 (1973), 23-36; **9.** "The Development of the Deuteronomic Promulgation Formula," *Biblica*, 55 (1973), 301-16; **10.** "The Time Word maḥar as a Key to Tradition Development," *Zeitschrift für die Alttestamentliche Wissenschaft*, 87 (1975), 65-80; **11.** "Temporal Terms as Structural Elements in the Holy-War Tradition," *Vetus Testamentum*, 25 (1975), 80-105; **12.** "Deuteronomy: Exemplar of a Non-Sacerdotal Appropriation of Sacred History," J. I. Cook, ed., *Grace Upon Grace, Essays in Honor of Lester J. Kuyper* [Grand Rapids: Eerdmans, 1975], pp. 90-105; **13.** *Yesterday, Today and Tomorrow. Time and History in the Old Testament*, Grand Rapids: Eerdmans, and London: SPCK, 1975; **14.** *Prophet Against Prophet. The Role of the Micaiah Narrative (1 Kings 22) in the Development of Early Prophetic Tradition*, Grand Rapids: Eerdmans, 1978; **15.** "Observations on Quantitative and Qualitative Time in Wisdom and Apocalyptic," J. G. Gammie et al., eds., *Israelite Wisdom: Theological and Literary Essays in Honor of Samuel Terrien* [Missoula: Scholars, 1978], pp. 263-76; **16.** "Time in the Bible," *The Times of Celebration* [Edinburgh-New York: Concilium, 1981], pp. 1-13;" **17.** "The Vision on the Mount: Moses, Elijah and Jesus," *Proceedings of the Eastern Great Lakes Biblical Society*, 3 (1983), 1-25; **18.** *1 Kings* [Word Biblical Commentary 12], Waco: Word, 1985; **19.**"The Forms of Prophetic Address in Chronicles," *Hebrew Annual Review*, 10 (1986), 15-36; **20.** "The Land's Sabbath in 2 Chronicles 36:21," *Proceedings, Eastern Great Lakes and Midwest Biblical Societies*, 6 (1986), 96-103; **21.**"The Schema of Dynastic Endangerment in Chronicles," *Proceedings, Eastern Great Lakes and Midwest Biblical Societies*, 7 (1987), 59-77; **22.** *1 and 2 Chronicles* [The Forms of the Old Testament Literature, 11], Grand Rapids: Eerdmans, 1988; **23.** "Moses and David as Cult-Founders in Chronicles," *Journal of Biblical Literature*, 107 (1988), 619-39; **24.** "The Three Comparisons in 1 Kings xxii 4b and its Parallel and 2 Kings iii 7b," *Vetus Testamentum*, 39 (1989), 283-306; **25.** "Prophetic Tradition and Canonization," K. Hagen, ed., *The Quadrilog* [Tavard Festschrift, Collegeville MN, 1994], pp. 377-87; **26.** *From Old Revelation to New. A Tradition-historical*

and Redaction-critical Study of Temporal Transitions in Prophetic Prediction, Grand Rapids: Eerdmans, 1995; **27**. "Festival Ideology in Chronicles," H. T. C. Sun *et al.*, eds., *Problems in Biblical Theology. Essays in Honor of Rolf Knierim*, Grand Rapids: Eerdmans, 1997, pp. 104-24

My first published article in this area of study was on the theme of remembrance and non-remembrance in the book of Ezekiel: God remembers, God does not remember; Israel does not remember, Israel does remember (**1**). But before going directly into more original exegesis on Old Testament passages of this sort, I did the equivalent with some of the Qumran scrolls. James Muilenburg, who had done some early research of his own on these documents, had set me to preparing what turned out to be the first English translation of the War Scroll (1QM), but it was not published. Just prior to coming to Methesco I published a lengthy analysis (**4**; cf. **2**) of a syntactical phenomenon characteristic of Biblical Hebrew, the *wâw*-consecutive imperfect, which appears inconsistently in the Qumran scrolls and not at all in the Mishna. Having dealt with "the fear of God" in my S.T.M. thesis, I took note of its relative non-appearance in the scrolls (**3**). However, I did not continue in this line of research because, following the frenzy of the first few years, the small group of scholars who had been charged with editing the unpublished fragments lost enthusiasm for making new texts available, and this discouraged young scholars like me from continuing to work in this field.[2]

Not long after I arrived at Methesco, Abingdon Press, the Methodist publishing house, engaged me to help write *The Interpreter's One-Volume Commentary on the Bible*. I went to work (**7**) on three very *minor* Minor Prophets, Nahum, Habakkuk and Zephaniah.[3] This in turn stimulated a spinoff paper on the acrostic in Nahum 1, which I read before the 1965 International Organization for the Study of the Old Testament being held in Geneva (**5**). Although I was getting my name before the scholarly world with publications of this type, it was apparent that I was still looking for my own special area of concentration.

In 1968 I wrote an article that was a model of the kind of exegesis I was interested in doing. Its title was "The Origin of the Murmuring Tradition" (**6**). I argued here that the narrative of the rebellion of the Israelites in Numbers 13-14 came into existence as part of an effort on the part of the Yahwist writer to validate the tradition of a conquest of Canaan from the east rather than from the south.

At this time my teacher, James Muilenburg, took a new position at the Graduate Theological Union in the Bay area and while there encouraged me to become part of the form-critical project which Professor Rolf Knierim at Claremont and Gene Tucker at Emory were organizing, on which he had agreed to serve as honorary advisor. At the same time I began an original research project that drew some inspiration from the form-critical project, but which was essentially of my own

---

[2] This was the general effect on scholars wishing to do extensive analysis in this field. It was not until the 1990's that pressure from the scholarly community was sufficient to get all the remaining unedited Qumran material before the public.

[3] In monetary terms this was virtual slave-work because I had to do a complete criticial analysis of the biblical text for a manuscript of ten pages, resulting in an average rate of earning of two cents per hour.

conception. I made a complete analysis of "the day of Yahweh" motif, so common in the eschatological writings of the Old and New Testament,[4] which in turn involved me in a study of time and history in the Old Testament and the publication in 1975 of my second book, *Yesterday, Today and Tomorrow* **(13)**. The most compelling of my conclusions were, first, that the "day of Yahweh" stands for any day with eschatological significance rather than a single day at the end of time; second, a distinction between *quantitative time* -- that which is measured, counted, and employed for calendrical reckoning -- and *qualitative time*, that in which temporal existence is fraught with special meaning; and third, that God confronts equally active mankind in historical event, his prime mode of self-revelation. These three conclusions have influenced most of my subsequent writings.

For this book I performed individual exegesis on hundreds of Old Testament and apocryphal passage containing the expressions, "in that day (past and future)," "today," or "this day," and "this very day" distinguishing between the functions of these forms in transitions, characterizing identifications, and epitomes. I was able to relate each expression to the ideology of individual literary strands as well as to formal genres. With these tools in hand I was well on my way towards becoming somewhat of an authority on the forms and structures of Old Testament narrative. In an article on David's fight with Goliath I showed that the statement, "And Saul took him *that day* and would not let him return to his father's house," in 1 Sam 18:2 functions as a concluding epitome for an entire clan saga that explains why and how an obscure Bethlehemite shepherd boy was elevated to become a Benjaminite chieftain **(8)**. In a study of the "promulgation formula" in the book of Deuteronomy I explained that expressions like "which I speak in your hearing *this day* (5:1)" reflect a standing cultic festival for covenant renewal observed by pre-exilic Israel **(9**; cf. **12)**. In an article on the time word *maḥar*, "tomorrow," I explained that expressions like "consecrate them *today and tomorrow*...and be ready by *the third day*" in Ex 19:10-11 have both ritual and ideological significance **(10)**. I argued **(11)** for a structural place for time-expressions like *today* or *this day* throughout what are known as the holy-war narratives (cf. Deborah's command to Barak in Judg 4:14, "Up, for this is the day in which Yahweh has given into your hand!"). From an analysis of Micaiah's repartee in 1 Kgs 22:25, "You shall see *on that day* when you go into an inner chamber to hide yourself," I was able to detect the literary interweaving of two separate prophet narratives, and this led to the publishing of my third book, *Prophet Against Prophet* **(14)**, in which I undertook to explain the entire redactional

---

[4]While working on my doctoral program at Union I had written a paper for Paul Tillich on this topic. Gerhard von Rad, the leading theologian of the Old Testament, had been calling attention to the importance of this subject in his writings on Old Testament Theology, Deuteronomy, and the "holy war" in ancient Israel.

history of the Old Testament prophet-legend collection. In a Festschrift for my teacher, Samuel Terrien, I prepared an essay on the way in which both the wisdom literature and apocalyptic conceive the phenomenon of time (15). The Catholic journal series, *Concilium*, published my definitive article for this subject, "Time in the Bible," in six different languages (16). When called upon to deliver the presidential address to the Eastern Great Lakes Biblical Society in 1983, I used Ex 19:10-11 to explain "he was raised on the third day according to the Scriptures" in 1 Cor 15:4 -- pretty far afield perhaps, but the best explanation I have ever known concerning the meaning of Christ's "three days" (17), coming up with an explanation that surprises both New Testament and Old Testament scholars.

It took me several years to prepare my contribution for the *Word Biblical Commentary* series on the book of 1 Kings (18) because it is just in that portion of the Old Testament that the Lucianic text of the Greek Septuagint appears to offer the most authentic text, one that is preferable to the Masoretic Text of the Hebrew. Scholars adhering to "evangelical Protestantism"[5] had been enlisted to write for this series. It was, and remains, an excellent series, allowing the author to prepare a fresh translation with discussion of textual problems, then analyze the form and structure, next discuss the meaning of important words and phrases, and finally define the proclamatory intent. This pattern brings the student of the Bible along the same pathway that I had been teaching at Methesco. For my commentary on 1 Kings, my previous analysis (14) of the genres of "prophet legend"[6] proved to be especially useful. In my "three comparisons" study of 1989 I explained the complex textual history underlying the apparent doublets, "I am as you are, my people as your people, my horses as your horses," in 1 Kgs 22:4b and 2 Kgs 3:b, and thereby put to rest the claim that Jehoshaphat of Judah was a willing dupe of Ahab (24).

In my later years my scholarly efforts were directed almost exclusively to the writing of major books of this kind. In recognition of the special expertise I had acquired in the form criticism of narrative literature, I was asked to prepare the volume on 1-2 Chronicles for the series, *The Forms of the Old Testament Literature*. (22) It was not the goal of this series to duplicate the treatment of other commentaries, but to make an original and thorough analysis of the genre, structure, setting, intention, and goal of individual passages and of larger units within the book assigned. For me it was a challenging and fulfilling opportunity to work through this often-overlooked book -- the final one in the Hebrew Old Testament and one that undertakes to explain the destiny and calling of Israel at a time when most of

---

[5] The word "evangelical" was to imply adherence to the Protestant doctrine of salvation by faith rather than by works (Paul; Augustine; Luther).

[6] The stories of Elisha and Elijah are not strictly historical but were created like the Christian legends to exemplify the principles and virtues of an ideal prophet. The term is useful and necessary if precision is to be achieved.

its institutions were no more than a memory from the hoary past. A number of spinoff articles followed the publication of this book: on the meaning of "the land's sabbath" in 2 Chr 36:21, (20), on the endangerment of the Davidic dynasty throughout the period of the kings (21), on the artificiality of the prophetic speeches in Chronicles as a token of the book's propagandistic character (19), on the meaning of Hezekiah's passover in the second month (2 Chr 30:15) (17), and finally one on "Moses and David as Cult-Founders in Chronicles" that has received special acclaim for explaining the role of the Levites and the quasi-mythological image of David in this book (23).

What I consider to be my most creative and significant contribution to Old Testament exegesis was a book as detailed and complex as *Yesterday, Today and Tomorrow* (26; cf. 25). The title was a somewhat enigmatic *From Old Revelation to New*, but the subtitle told what it was about: the tradition history of prophetic time-expressions, with special attention to the redactional processes involved. Setting out where I had concluded my previous volume, I analyzed each occurrence of expressions for future time, including "on that day," when functioning as a transition from original prophecy to an expansion. This discussion illumined the entire development of Old Testament eschatology, from preclassical prophetism to the most fullblown form of apocalyptic -- a process in which intuitive apprehension of the revelatory significance of imminent historical event was exchanged for a contemplative and ideological blueprinting of a final age. The most important conclusion of this book was that the Bible's own conception of divine revelation is dynamic, not static: not only does Yahweh speak to historical event, but alters and extends it to make it exemplary for a more distant day.

In looking back on this varied and extensive array of critical studies, I make the modest and I think altogether justified claim that I have never been ideological or prejudicial in this kind of work. I am reassured from observing the developmental pattern of my scholarship that God has been leading me to bring before the world insights promising to enlighten future scholarship. I have not gone my own way in this, nor have I proceeded haphazardly. Rather, I have worked from early conclusions to new lines of questioning, ever curious to view widening vistas of meaning in holy Scripture. In short, I have allowed myself to be led by the light I have received. Although I have grown uncomfortable with the shining-knight image, I still view myself as cautiously venturesome, and through it all, responsive to God's leading. I have received a commission and have fulfilled it.

This is assuredly how God leads! He leads through our willingness to trust our better selves and to put what we have learned in service to the beautiful, the just, and the true -- to create in imitation of him, to judge as he does, and above all to save as he has saved.

3. Studies on Old Testament hermeneutics

1. "Basic Issues in Old Testament Hermeneutics," *Journal of the Methodist Theological School in Ohio*, 5/1 (1966), 1-19; **2.** "The Early Years of Barth and Bultmann," *Journal of the Methodist Theological School in Ohio*, 5/2 (1967), 22-29; **3.** *The Achievements of Biblical Religion. Prolegomenon to Old Testament Theology*, Washington: University Press of America, 1983; **4.** "Rapprochment with Rolf Knierim," *Reading the Old Testament for a New Millenium*, vol. I (Harrisburg: Trinity Press International, 2000), pp. 116-37

The discipline of exegesis, strictly considered, is concerned with the meaning of passages within their own social and historical contexts. This is the basis of an historical approach to Scripture and of any legitimate line of interpretation based upon it. Each of my previously mentioned compositions exemplifies what I consider correct exegetical methodology according to this definition. It includes the study of the theological assumptions and preunderstandings underlying biblical texts of various genres, as well as expressions or affirmations exhibiting elements of theological understanding. Not every passage inviting exegetical study makes theological affirmations or has significant theological implications. On the other hand, virtually every passage betrays its own theological assumptions.

When the exegete attempts to relate these competing voices to one another, he or she may find it difficult to resolve differences between them and make them sound as one. In fact, this is impossible as well as inappropriate. There are a variety of books claiming to offer "an Old Testament theology" or even "*the* Old Testament theology," but it is an illusion to think that everything affirmed in, or implied by, the great assortment of individual texts in the Old Testament can be made to fit into any harmonious scheme.

Thus far the most successful treatment of Old Testament theology has been Gerhard von Rad's, and that because he gave recognition to divergent voices within the Hebrew Bible and attempted to arrange his materials in an historical sequence rather than according to a logical scheme. Yet even he was somewhat at a loss to identify the central and controlling element in the Old Testament. It turns out not to be simply the principle of "history as revelation," as he claimed. Obviously the attempt to write an ideal theology of the Old Testament will continue, but no book of this kind will succeed that ignores or suppresses undesirable or ill-fitting elements.

This line of research may remain on a purely scholastic level or it may lead to a present-day application in a process called "biblical hermeneutics." This is needed especially as a preparatory step towards homiletics, but it is required as well in any effort to create a normative and systematic theology. The great folly of much Christian dogmatics in the past has been its employment of scriptural passages as proofs for a propositional statement of some kind. No passage, either Old Testament or New Testament, means or teaches anything with dogmatic significance except from within its own proper setting. Or to put it simply, dogmatics of any kind without historical exegesis is worthless!

In my exegesis courses at Methesco I always made my students aware of the hermeneutical task that remains once exegesis is completed. How could I, who had been pastor for a significant number of years, forget this responsibility? If anyone knows that theology as pure theory is worthless and that it must be applicable to life if it is to have true value, it is I.

My two review articles on the hermeneutical debate around Rudolf Bultmann's existentialist hermeneutic (1-2) were early attempts to clarify for Methesco readers the consequences of relativizing the Old Testament to the advantage of the New. The majority of Old Testament scholars that I cited insisted on the inseparability -- if not always the equal authority -- of each Testament. It is especially scholars from the Lutheran and the Catholic traditions who have tended to make the Old Testament subservient to the New.

This tendency to diminish the status of the Old Testament continues in the present day and must be resisted with vigor. I undertook to do that when I published my fourth book, *The Achievements of Biblical Religion* (3). I made the point in this book that biblical religion is not defined by the New Testament, but by the Old Testament. Almost everything that makes a difference theologically is already set forth with a measure of completeness in the Old Testament, and the New Testament is to be understood as a special manifestation and powerful corroboration of it.

Throughout my career at Methesco and ever since, I have continued to ponder the special claim of the Old Testament on Christian spirituality. Two things of special importance must be demonstrated in establishing the authority of the Old Testament for contemporary piety: first, a norm within the Old Testament writings themselves as to what is supremely authoritative; and second, a rule by which the Old Testament norm becomes authoritative for contemporary life. In systematic theology, but especially in homiletics, a bridge must be constructed on the firm foundation of these two standards.

Shining White Knight, A Spiritual Memoir
Order Form

Use this convenient order form to order additional of
Shining White Knight, A Spiritual Memoir

Please Print:

Name_____

Address_____

City_____ **State**_____

Zip_____

Phone(**)**_____

_____ copies of book @ $21.95 each $ _____
Postage and handling @ $2.00 per book $ _____
Add 6% for Michigan sales tax $ _____
Total amount enclosed $ _____

Make checks payable to Simon J. De Vries

Simon J. De Vries
2013 N Cross Creek Dr., SE
Grand Rapids, MI 49508

Phone : (616) 241-5610